School Organization:
Theory and Practice

School Organization: Theory and Practice

Selected Readings on
Grading
Nongrading
Multigrading
Self-Contained Classrooms
Departmentalization
Team Teaching
Homogeneous vs. Heterogeneous Grouping

Marian Pope Franklin
University of North Carolina
Greensboro

Rand McNally & Company, Chicago

RAND McNALLY EDUCATION SERIES

B. Othanel Smith, *Advisory Editor*

Preface

There are many ways to organize schools and classrooms. The selections in this book were written or assembled to give readers a concise view of vertical and horizontal school organization and some of the best readings for the elementary, the junior high, and the senior high schools. Each chapter contains selections which explore various organizational alternatives. The bibliographies lead to further sources of information. It is hoped that the material will help school staffs and students of education to understand school organization more fully. It is also hoped that this material will reveal possibilities and new directions that could, and perhaps should, be tried.

I wish to express gratitude to the authors and publishers who have graciously allowed use of their material. Also, I want to thank the Research Council of the University of North Carolina at Greensboro, and my colleagues at that institution, Kenneth E. Howe, William P. Colbert, and Anne M. Kreimeier, for their encouragement and support. To my husband, Gwyn, and my parents, Mr. and Mrs. John J. Pope, my gratitude and appreciation for their continued faith and encouragement in the preparation of this volume.

Marian Pope Franklin
University of North Carolina
Greensboro, North Carolina
January 20, 1967

Table of Contents

TABLE OF CONTENTS

SECTION I

Introduction

Chapter 1

Dimensions of School Organization

Vertical and Horizontal School Organization

Marian Pope Franklin

In organizing a school two basic questions must be answered: (1) What will be the vertical organization; (2) what will be the horizontal organization? The philosophy and values held by the school staff, the school board, and the citizens of the community will determine how these questions are answered. Naturally, their decisions will affect the education of the students.

VERTICAL ORGANIZATION

Vertical organization is the plan a school follows both in distributing its students and in advancing them through a program. Vertically, the organization is either graded, multigraded, nongraded, or some combination of these patterns.

In a graded school students of a given age are placed together and are assigned a teacher. In order to "pass" to the next grade every student must cover a certain body of material. Students who do not, or cannot, cover the material are often failed. This graded plan was devised in 1848 by Principal J. D. Philbrick of the Quincy Grammar School in Boston, Massachusetts. Graded textbooks, graded courses of study, and graded

Reprinted from *North Carolina Education Journal* 32:12, 34, 35, December 1965, where it appeared under the title "Vertical, Horizontal, or In All Directions?" by permission of the publisher and the author. Dr. Marian Pope Franklin is Professor in the School of Education at The University of North Carolina in Greensboro.

standards soon followed the graded organization. By 1860 the graded
school was well established and today it is the most widely used plan of
vertical school organization.

Increased knowledge of human growth and development, however,
with accompanying recognition of individual differences, has caused a
number of educators to question the graded school concept. Educational
research has further revealed that the practice of nonpromotion is wasteful.
Alternatives to the graded system are needed.

Multigrading was introduced as a modification of the graded plan.
Multigrade classes are composed of students of several ages, abilities, interests, and grades. Each student considers himself in a specific grade, but
he is a member of a class that also has one or more members from other
grades. For example, a primary class in a multigraded room has approximately an equal number of first, second, and third grade students. Grouping within the classroom cuts across the grade lines. A student may move
from one grade to another in subject matter within his room.

Nine-year-old Johnny, in an intermediate multigraded class, could
be working at grade four in reading, grade five in science, and grade six
in mathematics. He is able to study at that level which fits him, and he
advances at different speeds in various aspects of his learning. All the
while he experiences a reasonable amount of success in his endeavors.

The multigrade plan is based on the assumption that students are
better off when they are placed in a class on the basis of their differences
rather than on their likenesses with sub-grouping within the class. Multigrading operates within a framework of a graded system, and grade labels
are retained. The plan is comparable to the one-room school which preceded the graded school of 1848. It is one alternative to the graded system.
However, it must be recognized that multigrading has not had wide
acceptance.

Nongrading is another alternative to the graded system. In such an
arrangement students are assigned to classes on some criterion other than
chronological age. In the primary years, for example, reading achievement is often an initial basis for grouping and classifying students. Later,
as school personnel become more adept in diagnosing needs and arranging
nongraded groups to meet them, other methods of grouping are used. Nongraded students are allowed to progress at their own rate in both the
elementary and the secondary nongraded schools. Grade standards, grade
labels, and uniform requirements are eliminated. A student covers as much
as he can during the term. The next term he begins where he stopped before, thus his progress is continuous. The curriculum, the instruction, the
materials, the report card, and the activities—all change in a nongraded
school. A curriculum study is also mandatory. All teaching and adminis-

trative procedures are adjusted to individual needs in a truly nongraded plan. The teachers strive to give each individual what he needs rather than what he is supposed to need because he is assigned to a certain grade. The success of the plan depends on teacher diagnosis and prescription.

HORIZONTAL ORGANIZATION

In addition to deciding on the vertical plan, a staff must also decide on its horizontal plan. Again, philosophical considerations and values are very important, for they determine the horizontal arrangement. Students may be assigned to so-called homogeneous groups according to some criterion, such as ability, achievement, interest, emotional condition, or physical handicap; or they may be assigned to a group that is heterogeneous on some factor. Students are also assigned to one teacher or to several teachers. This decision, too, is a horizontal organizational decision. The usual arrangements are: (1) the self-contained classroom; (2) departmentalization; (3) team teaching; (4) some combination of these alternatives.

It is important to note here that nongraded, graded, and multigraded groups all have horizontal organization and that they may have several kinds operating at one time. For example, students may be assigned to self-contained or to departmentalized classrooms, to an individual teacher for each class or to a teaching team, or they may be placed in either homogeneous or heterogeneous groups. These are all horizontal organizational decisions.

WHICH WAY IS BEST?

What is the most effective way of grouping students? Is there a difference in organizing for elementary and secondary students? Should students be grouped on the basis of ability or achievement? Do students do better when grouped homogeneously or heterogeneously? Should the curriculum be taught in self-contained or departmental arrangements? Is heterogeneous grouping preferable to departmentalization? Should we have teacher generalists or teacher specialists? Are there values in grouping students according to need and special abilities? Is the nongraded plan better than the graded?

Despite the fact that questions such as these have been asked and investigated many times in the 1900's, they are still not adequately answered in the 1960's. Some of the research studies supply conflicting findings. Some are not comparable because they do not have common purposes, terminology, experimental conditions, scientific controls, or subjects. Others have poor research designs because the researchers have failed to control many of the variables. A few appear to favor the individual bias of the investigator. Therefore, although the questions have been researched many times and there are some tentative answers, it must be concluded that the effectiveness or ineffectiveness of the various vertical and horizontal school organizational arrangements has not yet been established. It must be further concluded that such systematic experimentation and research in the area of school organization is long overdue. Why are we waiting?

The Hawthorne Effect In Educational Research

Desmond L. Cook

What is the *Hawthorne effect?* When, where, and how did the concept originate? If one seeks answers to these questions in such references as Good's *Dictionary of Education,*[1] the dictionary of psychological terms by English,[2] most of the books on educational research methodology, or the several issues of the *Encyclopedia of Educational Research,* the listings and indexes will not help him. This failure to index the Hawthorne effect concept is rather significant, since the phenomenon is so frequently referred to in explaining either the apparent conclusive or nonconclusive results of educational researches.

Even though not indexed, the term does appear quite frequently in the literature on research methodology, and its general nature is commonly recognized by researchers. The implications for educational research have not, however, been fully explored. The intent of this paper is to answer three questions: 1) What is the Hawthorne effect? 2) What are its implications for educational research? 3) What methods have been advanced to control the effect in research procedures?

WHAT IS THE HAWTHORNE EFFECT?

So far as I know, the term as it is now generally used first appears in written form in the book *Research Methods in the Behavioral Sciences* by Festinger and Katz.[3] In a discussion of experiments conducted in field settings, French contrasts laboratory and field experimentation settings and points up the problem of generalizing from each type.[4] He indicates that the difference between the two types is not in the nature of the research that takes place but in whether the researcher is working with real or

Reprinted from *Phi Delta Kappan* 44:116–122, December 1962, by permission of the publisher and the author. Dr. Desmond L. Cook is an Associate Professor of Education in the Bureau of Educational Research and Service, Ohio State University, Columbus, Ohio.

[1] C. V. Good, *Dictionary of Education.* New York: McGraw-Hill, 1959.

[2] H. B. English, *A Comprehensive Dictionary of Psychological and Psychoanalytical Terms.* New York: Longmans, Green, 1958.

[3] L. Festinger and D. Katz, editors, *Research Methods in the Behavioral Sciences.* New York: Dryden Press, 1953.

[4] John R. P. French, Jr., "Experiments in Field Settings," in L. Festinger and D. Katz, editors, *Research Methods in the Behavorial Sciences.* New York: Dryden Press, 1953, Ch. 3, pp. 98–135.

artificial social phenomena. French believes that the laboratory setting is artificial if the subjects behave differently than if they were not in the laboratory. To him, a field experiment is usually not subject to artificiality. Consequently, the problem of generalizing to other real life situations is thus avoided. He goes on, however, to point out an important exception:

> That this is not always the case . . . is well illustrated in the famous Hawthorne experiments. From a methodological point of view, the most interesting finding is what we might call the "Hawthorne Effect."

Let us look at the original Hawthorne experiments for this "interesting finding." In 1924 the Massachusetts Institute of Technology initiated a series of tests under the sponsorship of the National Research Council and the Illuminating Engineering Society to ascertain the relationship between illumination and production in various factory situations. The report by C. E. Snow[5] contains the results of the several investigations. One of the participating firms was the Hawthorne plant of the Western Electric Company. The tests conducted there are of immediate concern because it is from them that the term *Hawthorne effect* was eventually derived.

Three separate series of illumination-production tests were conducted at the Hawthorne plant. Space does not permit a detailed report of each series, but because the sequence of the series is important it will be described. In the first series, the investigators manipulated the lighting in three different parts of the plant. A general observation was made that production levels under the different amounts of illumination were always *higher* at the end than at the start and did not fall off even with a decrease in illumination. As a result of this first series, certain necessary modifications in procedure became evident.

> The results of this first winter's test, covering the three departments described, brought out very forcibly the necessity of controlling or eliminating the various additional factors which affected production output in either the same or opposing direction to that which we could ascribe to illumination.[6]

The second and third series of tests have high relevance to the topic, not only because of their subsequent results but also because of the methodological procedures employed. One must first be cognizant of the era in which these studies were conducted. In the early Twenties, industrial psychologists were working under the conviction that the traditional approach to scientific investigation of manipulating a single variable was a means of fruitful investigation. Under this approach, illumination change

[5] C. E. Snow, "Research on Industrial Illumination," *Tech Engineering News,* 8:257–282.
[6] *Ibid.*

was to be the independent variable and production the dependent variable. To overcome the limitations of the first series, the investigators set up the two subsequent experimental series using the comparable groups technique. They tried to control as many sources of variation as possible, as witness their physically isolating experimental groups from each other, placing them in separate buildings or parts of the factory. What were the results of these two investigations?

> This test resulted in a very appreciable production increase in both groups and of almost identical magnitude. The difference in efficiency of the groups was so small as to be less than the probable error of the values. Consequently, we were again unable to determine what definite part of the improvement in performance should be ascribed to illumination.[7]

The results of the third experimental series were quite unexpected, since the investigators *decreased* illumination rather than increasing it as in other studies.

> As the level of illumination in the test group enclosure changed to a lower value, the efficiencies of both the test and control groups increased slowly and steadily.[8]

Snow goes on to report the findings observed in other experiments on illumination conducted in other factory situations in several geographical locations. Of all the experiments described in his paper, only the Hawthorne studies have gained any degree of prominence. The reason for this we shall see later. What was the general conclusion from the series of tests conducted under the National Research Council's auspices? Snow points out the significant factor in one of his summary statements:

> Any investigation attempting to evaluate definitely the effect of illumination or some such influence must take the greatest of pains to control or eliminate all factors but the one being studied. Many of them can be controlled or eliminated, but the one great stumbling block remaining is the problem of the psychology of the human individual.[9]

The results of the investigations were such that one could not help but feel as Blum does in his book, *Industrial Psychology and its Social Foundations:*

> In most such experimentation the sponsors would have thrown out the evidence and the "crackpots" responsible; it would have been considered a nightmare to be repressed and suppressed.[10]

[7] *Ibid.*
[8] *Ibid.,* p. 274.
[9] *Ibid.,* p. 282.
[10] M. L. Blum, *Industrial Psychology and Its Social Foundations* (2nd ed.). New York: Harper and Bros., 1957, Ch. 2, p. 25.

Why have the Hawthorne investigations become better known than any of the other illumination experiments? Even though the experimental methodology became more and more refined through the successive experiments, the simple answer became more elusive, as Snow concluded. Blum says:

> It was clear that a direct relationship between illumination and production was nonexistent and that the answer would have to be obtained by attacking a different aspect of the problem.[11]

The direction which the research then took is described by two of the Hawthorne researchers, Roethlisberger and Dickson:

> Although the results from these experiments on illumination fell short of the expectations of the company in the sense that they failed to answer the specific question of the relation between illumination and efficiency, nevertheless they provided a great stimulus for more research in the field of human relations.[12]

The Hawthorne researchers then undertook a series of investigations designed to develop ways of studying the introduction of variables into work situations. Consequently, rest periods, working hour changes, and wage incentives were introduced and observations made of the workers' reactions to such variables. These studies were similar to the illumination experiments in that unpredicted results accompanied the changes as noted by Pennock:

> From these tests have come startling results, startling because they were unexpected as well as because they were sometimes contrary to accepted opinion. In the first place, there was a gradual yet steady increase in production regardless, to a certain extent, of test conditions imposed. . . . Now this unexpected and continual upward trend in the productivity throughout the periods, even . . . when the girls were put on a full 48-hour week with no rest period or lunch, led us to seek some explanation or analysis.[13]

Three hypotheses were suggested as possible causes and each in turn was subsequently rejected. Pennock's summarization of the results of the investigation begins to develop for us a meaning of the term Hawthorne effect.

[11] *Ibid.*, p. 50.
[12] F. J. Roethlisberger and W. J. Dickson, *Management and the Worker*, Cambridge, Mass.: Harvard University Press, 1941, p. 18.
[13] G. A. Pennock, "Industrial Research at Hawthorne: An Experimental Investigation of Rest Periods, Working Conditions, and Other Influences," *The Personnel Journal*, 8:296–313, 1929, p. 304.

We have shown that fatigue is not a governing factor in the performance of the test group, and have partially evaluated the effect of increased incentive due to change in method of pay, which leaves us convinced that the rather remarkable results we have been able to obtain with this group are due mainly to changes in their mental attitude. This we consider a major accomplishment of our entire study.[14]

The impact of this finding was so marked that it led the Western Electric Company to begin a series of investigations designed to explore the nature of employee attitudes. These investigations were characterized by an employee interviewing program which had a "non-directive" flavor somewhat prior to the work of Carl Rogers. This latter group of studies was to become highly influential in the development of the area of industrial psychology now known as "human relations in industry." A complete account of the various investigations, including the illumination experiments at Hawthorne, is presented in the book, *Management and the Worker*, by Roethlisberger and Dickson.[15] A retrospective view of the investigation and subsequent implications for industry are presented in *Hawthorne Revisited*,[16] by Landesberger.

Two observations can now be made, one relating to the method, the other to definition. Methodologically, the procedure followed by the illumination investigators is not unlike that often observed in educational research. A change is introduced and promising results are secured. This promising lead is followed up by carefully controlled experimentation to study more precisely the effects of the change. The results are too often similar to those obtained in the illumination experiments. Regardless of what is done, we have difficulty in attributing observed changes in the dependent variable directly to the manipulated independent variable.

From the several studies presented, a working definition of the Hawthorne effect can now be developed. French provides a start by stating that the marked increases in production were related not to the manipulated changes but ". . . only to the special social position and social treatment they [the subjects] received."[17] The special social treatment was created in turn by the "artificial" aspects of the experiment.

From this beginning, we might extrapolate the following definition of the concept: *The Hawthorne effect is a phenomenon characterized by an awareness on the part of the subjects of special treatment created by artificial experimental conditions. This awareness becomes confounded with*

[14] *Ibid.*, p. 309.
[15] *Op. cit.*
[16] H. A. Landesberger, *Hawthorne Revisited*. Ithaca, New York: Cornell University Press, 1958.
[17] French, *op. cit.*, p. 101.

*the independent variable under study, with a subsequent facilitating effect
on the dependent variable, thus leading to ambiguous results.* To go much
beyond this general definition at present is risky, due primarily to the lack
of any real evidence derived from direct study of the effect as to its behavioral specifics or components. I trust, however, that it will provide a frame
of reference for the rest of the paper.

WHAT ARE IMPLICATIONS FOR EDUCATIONAL RESEARCH?

Accepting for the moment the definition of the Hawthorne effect as
presented, what implication does it have for research in education? One
answer to this question can be found in a statement by Paul Rosenbloom
in the recent symposium on educational research sponsored by Phi Delta
Kappa. In describing recent experimentation with the mathematics curriculum in the state of Minnesota, Rosenbloom writes:

> There is of course in educational experimentation a so-
> called Hawthorne effect. It is well known that in an experimental
> situation teachers and pupils are more highly motivated, so this
> makes a certain problem. You know, for example, that in edu-
> cational experimentation, no matter what the hypothesis is, the
> experimental classes do better than the control classes.[18]

Ruth Strang, writing on reading research in the *Educational Forum*
for January, 1962, echoes the comments made by Rosenbloom:

> There are always uncontrolled variables that may influence
> the results. Thus at the end of the experiment, the investigator
> cannot choose but be apologetic; he cannot say with certainty
> that a given result was obtained by virtue of a particular teach-
> ing method which he wanted to study. The apparent differences
> in the two sets of results might be attributed to differences in the
> personality or enthusiasm of the teacher, the learning rate of the
> children, or any of the other factors we have already mentioned.[19]

The Rosenbloom and Strang quotations reflect the usual way of relating the Hawthorne effect to educational research.

The Hawthorne effect can also be used to account for situations where
no differences are observed between the experimental and control groups
at the end of an experimental period. How can such a situation occur? It

[18] Paul C. Rosenbloom, "Large-Scale Experimentation with Mathematics Curriculum" in *Research Design and Analysis*, R. O. Collier and S. M. Elam, editors,
Second Annual Phi Delta Kappa Symposium on Educational Research, 1961, Ch. 1B,
p. 11.
[19] Ruth Strang, "Reactions to Research in Reading," *The Educational Forum*,
26:187–192, January, 1962, p. 187.

might occur when an experimenter approaches a classroom to measure student performance before conducting the experiment. The pretesting of not only the experimental but the control group can become a signal to the latter group that they are the subjects of an experiment. They might also be able to identify the experimenter's purpose. Consequently, the control group engages in activities leading to such improvement that the final result is that both groups perform equally well at the end of the experimental period.

The Hawthorne effect has plagued the research methodologist for a good many years. Brownell noted it approximately ten years ago in a critique of research appearing in the *Fiftieth Yearbook of the National Society for the Study of Education:*

> More than once, serious doubt has been cast on the evidence for an experimental program of instruction when attention has been called to seemingly innocuous but actually influential factors. For example, the very novelty of a new system of instruction may make it attractive to teachers and learners alike, thus giving it a special advantage, and perhaps only a temporary advantage over the rival, traditional system of instruction.[20]

He goes on to tell about an investigator who became increasingly irritated at the gains in reading shown under experimental versus control procedures over a short period of time. This investigator said that he would outdo all other investigators by demonstrating even greater gains in still a shorter period of time. The suggested technique was to administer a reading test in the most lackadaisical manner allowed by the test directions and then within a few hours test students with the second form of the test but administered under such conditions as subjects would be at highest possible pitch of zeal.

Retreating still further to the past to demonstrate the researcher's awareness of the problem, one finds reference to the effect appearing in McCall's *How to Experiment in Education*, written in 1923.

> Though evidence on this question is meager, there is some reason to believe that the mere process of experimenting with new methods or materials of instruction attracts such attention to the traits in question as to cause an unconscious concentration, both on the part of teacher and pupil upon progress of these traits. As a result, it is supposed that a large temporary effort is called for, thus causing a large but artificial growth, and

[20] W. A. Brownell, "A Critique of Research on Learning and Instruction in the School." *Fiftieth Yearbook of the National Society for the Study of Education,* Pt. 1, *Graduate Study in Education.* H. B. Henry, editor. Chicago: University of Chicago Press, 1951, Ch. 6, p. 60.

that this artificial effort will evaporate if the novel methods or materials were used term after term.[21]

McCall even suggested a way of determining if the effect were present in a given experimental situation:

> If each succeeding term shows a flagging of effort and an elimination or reduction of superiority, the existence of such ephemeral effort may be assumed.[22]

Interestingly enough, the Hawthorne studies showed no such reduction over time and thus novelty as a variable explaining results was rejected during the course of the investigations.

Even with McCall's early warning, many educators have persisted in using the comparable-groups method, with the correlated confounding of experimental variables by what is now called the Hawthorne effect. But the sophisticated research methodologist in education no longer jumps enthusiastically upon the bandwagon of new instructional methods like programed instruction, educational television, language laboratories, team teaching, and other new techniques of instruction. Further, he cannot help but wonder whether recent curriculum revisions, which often show large gains in student knowledge, may not be contaminated by a type of Hawthorne effect.

As an example, I would suggest the recent situation in Wisconsin where the McGuffey Readers were adopted as supplemental texts to the regular basal readers. A news release noted that the pupils in the first four grades were as much as two years ahead of their grade level in reading ability.[23] The principal is quoted as saying that the students in the first grade were able to spell at fourth grade level, according to nationally accepted tests. He then went on to credit the success of the reading program to a system of phonics as opposed to the whole word method. Has it occurred to the principal that the ruckus created by the McGuffey issue (which included the firing of a principal who objected to adoption of the McGuffey readers) may have caused teachers, students, and parents simply to concentrate more on the reading process than ever before?

WHAT ARE SOME SUGGESTED SOLUTIONS?

Recognizing that our research efforts are often contaminated or confounded by the Hawthorne effect, is there anything we can do about it?

[21] William A. McCall, *How to Experiment in Education*. New York: The Macmillan Co., 1923, p. 67.

[22] *Loc. cit.*

[23] "Kids with McGuffeys Way Ahead," *Columbus Dispatch*, Columbus, Ohio, June 13, 1962, p. 9A.

If we had a complete answer to the operation and hence control of the Hawthorne effect in educational research, there would of course be no need for this section of the paper. We must recognize, as Roethlisberger has in his book, *Management and Morale,* an inherent difficulty in social science research:

> . . . the working hypotheses of these specialists [social scientists], particularly on their applied side, must be far less clear, distinct, and well formulated than in the more highly developed and exact engineering sciences. There is no simple way of thinking about or putting together the complicated events involved, and there is equally no simple way of dealing with them.[24]

But complexity is no excuse for inaction. Steps should be taken if at all possible prior to the experimentation, so that an apology will not be needed at the end. Levitt, in discussing the possible influence of an experimental climate on research results in clinical psychology, stresses early attention to the problem:

> . . . the experimenter should not lose sight of the possibility of a climate when he is designing his investigation, and should take whatever prophylactic steps are logically necessary to prevent its occurrence. After the data have been obtained, one may be led to suspect the operation of an experimental climate, but there is very little that can be done about it *post hoc.*[25]

The principal problem involved in controlling the Hawthorne effect is the establishment of what is referred to in science as a "closed system." Such a system is one wherein no event outside of it influences events within it. The establishment of a closed system in educational experimentation becomes very difficult because the research activity must be done in psychological or socio-psychological environments, both of which are relative to the structure of the subjects. As B. O. Smith points out,

> . . . the psychological environment is what the subject conceives it to be, and what he conceives goes back to his personal structure and the dynamics of his situation.[26]

Thus an experimental situation may be one thing to one subject and a different thing to another subject.

[24] F. J. Roethlisberger, *Management and Morale.* Cambridge, Mass.: Harvard University Press, 1941, p. 145.
[25] E. E. Levitt, *Clinical Research Design and Analysis.* Springfield, Ill.: C. C. Thomas, 1961, p. 111.
[26] B. O. Smith, "Science of Education," in *Encyclopedia of Educational Research,* W. S. Monroe, editor. New York: The Macmillan Co., 1952, p. 1148.

Two general solutions have been presented. The first is to abandon, more or less, the conventional experimental-control group type of research design. This action was recommended by Brownell in 1951 and is re-emphasized by Strang in 1962 in the article on reading research previously cited. Brownell admitted that new advances in statistical analysis would facilitate the use of the comparable-group design but felt that its inherent limitation of failure to control all variables, plus the training needed to become sophisticated with the new statistical procedures, prohibited the widespread use of this design. As an alternative, he suggested a procedure originating largely in the field of developmental psychology. This procedure consists of continuous observation to detect changes in student behavior upon the introduction of certain events by the teacher. In short, it would be a carefully documented observation of the teaching-learning process as it was actually carried on in the classroom. Brownell recognized that many persons in education would not accept this as good research methodology, but he felt that it had many possibilities.

Such a technique was not overlooked in the Hawthorne studies. In fact, almost all of the investigations carried on after the illumination experiments were of this type. The investigators in effect abandoned the traditional single-variable approach within the comparable-groups technique and resorted to an observational procedure. The introduction of the observer, however, was not without cost. He became a "confidant" of the girls, who talked with him about their work and personal problems. It was this expression of feelings which confounded again the results of a set of planned studies and led ultimately to the interviewing program.

Strang suggests another procedure:

> . . . it would be more useful to adopt the single group comparison type of experiment that is employed in the physical sciences. Here all the factors in the given situation are carefully described. Then one factor is modified and the resultant total factor is recorded. In this way we would gain some insight into the ways in which learning is affected by various complex conditions, including the pupils' prior experiences.[27]

This procedure, plus the one offered by Brownell, is preferred over the comparable-groups approach by Strang because she feels the attempts to use comparable-group experimentation in educational research represents a premature attempt to be scientific. The result, in reading research, has been misleading conclusions having detrimental effects upon the teaching of reading, she thinks.

The second solution is to continue with comparable-group experimentation but to develop experimental designs which not only are in-

[27] Strang, *op. cit.*, p. 188.

ternally valid but are also externally valid. External validity here means that generalizations can be made from the experimental situation to non-experimental situations which the former is said to represent.

Campbell identifies seven categories of variables affecting the internal validity experimental design.[28] These are history, maturation, testing, instrument decay, regression, selection, and mortality. He then goes on to point out that the interaction of these variables and of the experimental arrangements affects the external validity or generalizability of experimental results. Not all of the interactions are equally strong in various experimental designs, but they must be recognized. In a chapter on experimental design prepared for the AERA *Handbook of Research on Teaching*, Campbell and Stanley[29] indicate that some of the categories identified above can be somewhat discounted in comparable-group designs, but others cannot. They particularly point out the importance of what they call *reactive arrangements*. These are characterized by the ". . . play-acting, out-guessing, up-for-inspection, I'm a guinea-pig, or whatever attitudes,"[30] which are generated when the student knows he is participating in an experiment and tend to interfere with the external validity of the design. To overcome this limitation, the authors suggest that the experimental treatments and accompanying instrumentation (i.e., testing) be included whenever and wherever possible as part of the regular classroom procedure, if the results are to be generalized to other classroom units. In short, they would attempt to disguise the fact that an experiment is being conducted.

Correlated with this latter suggestion is a recommendation that, to avoid the singling out of individuals to be assigned at random to treatment or control groups and thus arousing their suspicions, regular classroom units with their regular teachers be employed as the means of minimizing individual reactions to experimental situations. Campbell and Stanley feel that such arrangements can be effective, since the process of experimentation is hidden from the student. They recognize, however, that if the *treatments* are other than variations of usual classroom events occurring at regular times in the yearly program, and/or if the *observations* (tests, etc.) are not considered a part of regular examinations, then we are still faced with the basic problem of cueing students.

Berg, however, raises the question whether it is moral and ethical to subject human beings to experimentation without their being aware of the

[28] D. T. Campbell, "Factors Relevant to the Validity of Experiments in Social Settings," *Psychological Bulletin*. 54:297–312, 1957.

[29] D. T. Campbell and J. C. Stanley, "Experimental Designs for Research on Teaching," Mimeographed chapter draft for *Handbook of Research on Teaching*. N. L. Gage, editor, American Educational Research Association. (Published separately. Chicago: Rand McNally, 1963.)

[30] *Ibid.*, p. 42.

fact.[31] His position is that psychological experimentation, and hence much educational research, must be done with "volunteer" subjects. If this restriction is accepted, we are squarely on the horns of a dilemma. One cannot experiment unless he informs his subjects, but informing the subjects will invalidate experimental results.

Opposed to the Campbell and Stanley position are individuals who suggest that we not try to hide the fact that an experiment is in progress but try instead to give equal exposure to both the experimental and control groups, thus establishing a type of experimental control over the Hawthorne effect. The national Research Council takes this position:

> As much attention must be paid to students and teachers in all treatment groups as in those of particular interest to the experimenter. Equal excitement must be generated, and all groups must identify with their respective procedures.[32]

Rosenbloom noted that this procedure was employed to a certain degree in conducting the mathematics experiment in the schools of Minnesota already mentioned. The investigators tried to make it something of a mark of distinction for schools to be considered a part of the experimental program.

Travers concurs with the idea that both the experimental and control groups should feel equally singled out, but feels that this technique is inferior to the suggestion that the groups be unaware of the fact that they are participating in an experiment.[33] He makes reference to a technique which has been commonly recommended for controlling the Hawthorne effect, and that is the use of a *placebo* treatment. Studies involving placebo treatments are quite common in the field of medicine, where one group receives the drug to be tested while the other receives a placebo made to appear and taste the same as the drug. This methodology is illustrated in Crest toothpaste experiments, advertised on television. Rosenbloom recognized the possible use of a placebo treatment in his study:

> Now the ideal thing would be to have placebos, consisting of conventional texts in lithographed form and stamped "Experimental Edition." But so far we have not been able to make the necessary arrangements for that. The best we have been able to do this year in our ninth grade class was to send to all control classes a lithographed pamphlet put out by McGraw-Hill called *Modern Mathematics for High Schools*. We gave instructions to

[31] A. Berg, "The Use of Human Subjects in Psychological Research," *The American Psychologist*. 9:108–111, March, 1954.

[32] *Psychological Research in Education*. Washington, D. C.: National Research Council, Publication 643, National Academy of Sciences, 1958, p. 24.

[33] R. M. W. Travers, *An Introduction to Educational Research*. New York: The Macmillan Co., 1958.

the teachers of control classes to supplement the conventional text with this material, and to tell their classes that we are trying to find out whether a good conventional text, supplemented in this way, is better than the experimental text.[34]

In a discussion of the use of placebo treatments in psychotherapy, Rosenthal and Frank suggest some criteria to test the effectiveness of this procedure:

> To show that a specific form of treatment produces more than a non-specific placebo effect it must be shown that its effects are stronger, last longer, or are qualitatively different from those produced by the administration of placebo, or that it affects different types of patients.[35]

CONCLUSION

The Hawthorne effect is not only a complex problem but also an important one. While the problem has been generally recognized and various solutions have been suggested as noted, there has been little direct experimentation to determine its qualitative and quantitative contributions to the results in research. Now, however, the U.S. Office of Education has provided Ohio State University with funds to investigate this problem directly over the next three years.[36] We are naturally hoping that this endeavor will result in better understanding of the phenomenon and thus enable us to control or discount its effects in a particular research study.

A story related by Herzog seems relevant to our discussion.[37] She tells of the little old lady who did her courting in the Nineties and who liked to tell about her grandmother's efficient chaperoning. Grandmother would just move into the living room where the two young people were sitting on the sofa. She would say, "Now you two young people go right ahead and visit and don't pay any attention to me. Just act as if I weren't here." As Herzog points out, there was some difference of opinion in the family about whether Grandmother thought they were acting as if she weren't there, but there was no doubt in anyone's mind about whether they were really acting that way. It takes a wary eye to be sure the research project is not playing a role like Grandmother's.

[34] Rosenbloom, *op. cit.*, p. 11.

[35] David Rosenthal and Jerome Frank, "Psychotherapy and the Placebo Effect," *Psychological Bulletin*, 53:294–302, 1956, p. 297.

[36] Cooperative Research Project 1757, "The Impact of the Hawthorne Effect in Experimental Designs in Educational Research," Desmond L. Cook, Director.

[37] Elizabeth Herzog, *Some Guide Lines for Evaluative Research*, Childrens Bureau, Social Security Administration, 1959.

Vertical School Organization

Chapter 2

Graded School Organization

Graded vs. Nongraded School Systems

Bert A. Goldman

Use of the dichotomy graded-nongraded implies some basic inherent difference between programs classified under one or the other label. Therefore, one might ask, what basic difference exists? Logically, it would appear from the labels that one system involves some key characteristic, a graded organization, not found in the other; and, this is a correct assumption to be sure. However, Halliwell prefers to refer to this major difference as one of degree of organization. Further, he says that "most, if not all, differences are of degree not kind," and "in actual practice the differences between graded and nongraded patterns of school organization are not as great as many people believe." Goodlad supports this view of nongrading being an organizational system, and he feels that it can be employed in kindergarten through thirteen years of education. DiPasquale's scheme of "interclass grouping based on intellectual competence" in required academic subjects is a further extension of organizational change, and he feels such a change should involve curricular change as well. Halliwell acknowledges the fact that there has been considerable commotion regarding the need for curriculum change during the last ten years, and even though nongrading has made a strong case for itself, he feels that rate is the variable which is often manipulated while curriculum, method, and materials are infrequently changed.

How do the two systems cope with individual differences? The early article by Cowen cites the observation of Horace Mann and Henry Barnard

Written especially for this book. Dr. Bert A. Goldman is Associate Professor of Education, University of North Carolina, Greensboro.

that a wide range of either ability or age within a graded system does not facilitate efficient teaching. Cowen believes that the graded school pays little attention to individual differences. Goodlad, too, points out the failure of the graded school to account for the range of individual differences within each grade level. In contrast, he describes the nongraded school as a system which places emphasis upon individual differences. DiPasquale very strongly concurs with this notion. In fact he feels that the failure of the graded system to take cognizance of individual differences has created the need for special pupil personnel services such as remedial reading programs.

DiPasquale identifies several negative effects of the graded system. Particularly, he zeros in on the dropout problem. He attributes this problem in part to the single standard of achievement imposed by the graded system which, if not reached, necessitates the repeating of grades. He cites a variety of social difficulties that may be precipitated by repeating grades, and then he presents a series of rather dramatic figures to emphasize the waste accruing from failure. Cowen adds to the dropout issue by suggesting that a paradox exists in secondary education because the very graded system designed to provide an education for all twelve- to eighteen-year-old boys and girls actually prevents some from completing the program.

What is the age of the two systems? Cowen's brief, but detailed historical sketch of the development of the graded system sets its official origin in the United States at slightly less than one and a quarter centuries ago. Halliwell's very succinct description of the growth of the ungraded system sets its successful beginning less than one quarter of a century ago with its real strength emerging during the past ten years. Thus, the settings, approximately one hundred years apart, within which each system evolved were undoubtedly different. For example, Goodlad draws some penetrating comparisons between the present and the past centuries with regard to the overwhelming increase in the amount of knowledge available today and in this century's tremendously greater number of scientists. DiPasquale's statement that "the graded elementary school was conceived and developed before we had scientific findings on child growth and development" suggests the effect that a difference in the amount of knowledge may have on decisions concerning school organizations. Is it any wonder that that which was considered a feasible organizational system for schools over a century ago may not be compatible with the recognized needs of this century's educational institutions?

What does the published research say about the superiority of one system over the other? DiPasquale, *et al.*, observed the paucity of research. There are few valid studies as Goodlad revealed, and as Halliwell noted, conflicting findings exist. In fact, Halliwell's own research findings were not consistent throughout. Obviously, more and better research on this subject is essential to drawing valid conclusions.

The preceding discussion was intended to aid the reader in tying together the articles of this chapter so that he might better understand the general nature of the two systems.

How the Graded School System Developed

Philip A. Cowen

School conditions somewhat parallel the cycles of business. During prosperous times money is spent freely on education and little accounting is demanded. During hard times money is scarce and greater scrutiny is exercised over its use.

Since the World War [World War I] hard times have been more or less continuous. Consequently schools of all kinds, from kindergarten to university, have conserved their resources. A number of changes have been proposed and some of them are in effect. Since this period of criticism has not passed, however, it is necessary to make further educational changes. Many of these changes should have been made by educators without the impetus of external forces. They are needed to raise educational practices to the point of meeting the demands of a social democracy.

When studying present educational problems it might be profitable to consider other critical periods through which schools have passed. Some of these stand out as being particularly helpful because of their relationship to the present plan of school organization. One such period saw the beginning of the graded school about 1850. A discussion of this development may help to interpret the present critical period.

It is difficult to say exactly when the graded system began. It is true that the first graded school was started by John Philbrick in 1848 in Boston. It had a unified curriculum and twelve assistants. This school, however, was not a spontaneous outburst. It was one of a series of events that favored the system.

Paul Monroe says that "both English and American systems are but the result of natural evolution out of the given conditions." Martin expresses the idea in about the same way by stating that "industrial and social changes . . . rather than theories of educationists are responsible for the modern school system." These changes were "the decay of the academies, the decline and fall of the district system, evening schools, scientific and technical schools, parochial schools, supervision by specialists, the improvement of school architecture, compulsory attendance laws, truant laws and truant schools." These, he says, are all "due to the change

Reprinted, with permission, from *The Nation's Schools* 8:25–32, September 1931. Copyright 1931, The Modern Hospital Publishing Company, Inc., Chicago. All rights reserved. Philip A. Cowen was formerly Research Associate, Educational Research Division, New York State Education Department.

from rural to urban life, consequent upon modern mechanical inventions and their utilization under the factory system."

EARLY FACTORS INFLUENCING GRADING

These points taken together present a strong argument to show that circumstances rather than planning aided considerably in creating the graded system. In fact, "Foreshadowings of grading may be discovered early in history. The exclusion of the 'A-B-C-darians' from the Roxbury Latin School in 1668 was a formal recognition of the principle of division of labor in teaching. . . . "

Shearer points out three steps that resulted in the graded school. These are: (1) an increase in the number of pupils sufficient to permit several to recite together in a given subject; (2) compelling all pupils to follow the same course of study; (3) a further increase in the number of pupils so as to permit a division of labor between two or more teachers. These steps show clearly that schools were forced by circumstances to devise a scheme to accommodate the increasing number of pupils.

At first differentiation was made by schools rather than by classes. This is illustrated in Boston

> . . . where from 1635 on there was a free Latin grammar school open to boys only. Early in the eighteenth century separate "writing" and "reading" schools were added, and in 1789 a report of the Boston school committee shows that there were in addition to the Latin grammar school three writing schools and three reading schools maintained under the town auspices for both boys and girls. . . .

However, in rural areas the increase in school population was at first met merely by

> . . . the erection of additional ungraded district schools. When concentration became grave, instead of erecting ungraded schools, pupils were divided into two schools either on the basis of success or of age. As the advantages of further division became evident even a three part system was created with primary, intermediate, grammar or secondary schools. Sometimes each of the three parts was divided into three years with a teacher for each year. . . . But throughout there were in operation two controlling factors—the extension of school offerings upward and a tendency to concentrate the labor of teachers upon a narrower range of instruction.

During the year 1863 when population was increasing as well as congregating in centers and thereby creating new school problems, the gradation of schools was widely discussed. The existing institutions for taking care of the problems of education were enumerated and characterized by Doctor Harrison in a lecture in 1836. He said, "Schools for popular education may be divided into the following: first, infant; second, primary or general; third, classical; Sunday; normal."

Infant schools aimed to develop "social kindness, bodily vigor, and tender sensibilities." The primary schools were for general instruction in reading, writing and arithmetic. In the classical schools pupils studied Latin, Greek and higher mathematics. Normal schools trained young men to become schoolmasters.

The early plans of grade organization are significant for two reasons, first, because of their bearing upon the immediate development of grades, and second, because of their value in helping to solve present problems of organization. Of all the men who discussed the problems of school gradation in the early part of the nineteenth century Henry Barnard and Horace Mann stand out for their continuously vigorous efforts.

In 1838 Henry Barnard expressed his ideas on gradation in an address. He said, "the great principle to be regarded in classification . . . is equality of attainments, which will generally include those of the same age." This point of Barnard's is worth noting because, although he says that attainment should be "the general principle" he further states that "great disparity of age in the same class is unfavorable to . . . efficient teaching." We find part of our present educational difficulties in the wide chronologic age range, such as six, eight or ten years, which is common in a single grade.

The emphasis that Barnard placed upon age is shown by his description of the various school units. He said that "Primary schools as a general rule should be designed for children between the ages of three and eight years. . . . Secondary schools should receive scholars at the age of eight years . . . who will attend . . . until they are twelve years of age. . . ."

Such a plan of organization although advocated nearly a hundred years ago would be an improvement over our present one if it were to be adopted. It would permit pupils of similar social ages to remain together. Within each natural age group it would divide pupils into small groups to secure natural competition in learning. With this organization pupils of varied interests and abilities who are kept in school by compulsory attendance laws could more easily be given an educational opportunity to meet their individual needs.

GRADING AN EARLY PRACTICE IN EUROPE

A certain amount of influence was exerted by men who visited schools in Europe, particularly in Prussia, and returned to write enthusiastic accounts of the pupil classification found there. Horace Mann, Calvin

E. Stowe and others took part in this movement during the thirties and forties. Mann wrote: "In all places where the numbers are sufficiently large to allow it the children are divided according to age and attainments; and a single teacher has charge only of a single class or of as small a number of classes as is practicable."

In his annual reports as secretary of the board of education in Massachusetts Horace Mann repeatedly discussed gradation. In his first report, for 1839, he said, "The population of many towns is so situated as conveniently to allow a gradation of the schools." In his second report, Mann said he had noted with pleasure several places where his suggestions had been adopted.

Two years later Mann, again discussing pupil classification, spoke of the disadvantages of planning a lesson for the average pupils of a class. He said:

> . . . some members will acquire it, and have much time to spare; others, with the greatest diligence, will not be able to master it. Hence some will grow proud, thinking themselves wonderful geniuses; others will be disheartened, finding no effort sufficient to save them from an obvious inferiority. It is difficult, in such a case, to say which party is most injured. A vast amount of harm is inflicted by injudicious teachers in mismatching scholars.

MANN'S VIEWS ON GRADING

Thus Horace Mann found from experience with random groups the most common arguments advanced today against ability grouping. He stood in favor of grouping pupils according to age and attainments in spite of the disadvantages. In this respect he agreed with Henry Barnard's ideas.

This agreement between Mann and Barnard on the basis of classification is further shown by a statement of Mann's:

> Should it be founded on age or attainment or both? I reply, chiefly on attainment; but let some respect be paid to age. On this point I have somewhat modified my views in later years. I would not put a large boy of sixteen into a class with a little girl of six or eight, because he can read no better than she. His backwardness, it may be, is his misfortune and not his fault. His position would be mortifying to his self-esteem. It would make him uncomfortable, and he would not learn so much. . . . Let him go in with those who are his equals in years, even though they should be somewhat further removed from him in attainment.

Before discussing the graded schools that developed between 1850 and 1870 I shall enumerate several influences, in addition to those previously mentioned, which entered into the movement.

In 1837 the first office of superintendent of city schools was created in Buffalo. The assistance this office gave to the development of the graded system can hardly be overestimated. Superintendents provided the leadership and planning without which little could have been accomplished.

During much of the time that the graded school was developing, the district system caused dissatisfaction. In 1843 Buffalo attempted to alleviate the difficulties by dividing the population into larger districts, "varying from 1,000 to 1,500, so that each district will contain nearly three hundred children. In each a schoolhouse is erected containing two apartments, in one of which a female teacher is employed to superintend the instruction of the younger pupils and in the other a male teacher, at a fixed and competent salary, to give instruction in the higher branches." The superintendent reports that "the system has thus far succeeded beyond the most sanguine hope of its projectors and friends. . . ."

Lancastrian schools are credited with helping to bridge the gap between ungraded, private and charity schools and the full-fledged city system of grades. In these a large school was divided into sections and each section into drafts. A pupil remained in one section for all studies but could recite in different drafts. Ability in reading determined classification in the lower sections and arithmetic in the upper. Pupil teachers and monitors took charge of the sections and drafts, thereby enabling a teacher to have a large school. These schools made education possible for a large number of pupils at a greatly reduced cost per pupil. Thus the habit of attending school was developed and the necessity for graded schools increased.

In 1848 John Philbrick, as previously mentioned, opened the first graded school in this country, the New Quincy Grammar School, Boston. This new arrangement of having one teacher take charge of a room was found to allow grading of the pupils, and "to be less expensive and more efficient . . ." than ungraded schools.

> By the fifties the agitation for the adoption of graded schools was much in evidence in the reports of state education officers. In New York, Pennsylvania, Connecticut, Massachusetts, Ohio, Illinois and Michigan, to mention a few of the conspicuous examples . . . the highest state officers offered to improve all schools by means of grading. . . .
> In Indiana the first report of the state superintendent of public instruction sets forth in 1852 a matured plan of school gradation. . . .

A report of the school committee of New Bedford, Mass., in 1851 states that for eight years their school organization permitted pupils to pass from grade to grade solely upon chronologic age. The committee expressed great dissatisfaction with such a plan because it permitted pupils to become lazy and indolent and yet it promoted them. This statement from New Bedford illustrates an attempt to use the democratic scheme advocated by Henry Barnard. It was replaced later with the grade as an achievement level instead of an age group.

THE OSWEGO PLAN

In 1853 Edward A. Sheldon began to reorganize the schools of Oswego, N.Y. He discarded all of the old district boundaries and made three kinds of districts. First, twelve primary school districts for an equal number of pupils were created. Second, schools to accommodate pupils between the ages of eight and ten years were called junior schools. Third, two senior schools were established, one on each side of the river, for pupils between eleven and fifteen years of age.

The high school was then planned for four years. It completed a continuous course of thirteen years. The units may be designated as 3-3-3-4.

This plan agrees in principle with the earlier ideas of Henry Barnard. It appears to be democratic because the successive units are designed for increasing ages. A system of promotion by examination with a uniform standard for all pupils would spoil this plan by making it possible for only a few pupils to reach the upper grades. Those who could not meet such a promotion requirement would be forced to remain in classes with younger pupils. Such is our plan today.

It was mentioned that state officials advocated graded schools in the early fifties. In his second annual report, in 1855, W. H. Barney, commissioner of common schools in Ohio, said, "It is gratifying to state that within the last two years, graded or union schools have been established in nearly one hundred and fifty towns and villages of this state, and that most of them are now in vigorous and successful operation."

In 1856, on the occasion of inaugurating the common school system in Charleston, S.C., C. G. Memminger described the proposed schools which he claimed would relieve the current difficulties of poor teaching. He explained that a proper classification of pupils would give classes of forty "selected at precisely the same grade of attainments."

Attention must be called to the connotation attached to the phrase "grade of attainments" by Memminger. This shows clearly that grades were recognized then as levels of achievement. We still attach that meaning to "grades," although we abbreviate the terminology. It is also interesting to notice that, according to Mr. Memminger, forty pupils of "precisely the same grade of attainments" could be found. This indicates the fairly crude idea of individual abilities that existed in 1856. We do not claim to find even two such pupils today, because we recognize more individual traits and we know more about their variability.

Three important changes in school organization were started in Rochester, N.Y., in 1862. First, the classification of pupils according to sex was abolished and duplicate schools were thus eliminated. Second, old district lines and officers were abolished, making the city one school district. Third, the number of elementary grades was determined by the number of years that were required for completion of the "best common schools." In Rochester this period was thought to be nine years, hence there were nine grades. Each was divided into three terms and "precisely" so much subject matter was prescribed for each term.

During this discussion little mention has been made of the high school. This omission was made purposely so that several points could be considered together. In the early stages of our educational system it was not thought necessary for more than a few persons to attend college, hence private academies and public Latin grammar schools adequately met the needs for college preparation. But with a growing spirit of democracy there came the demand for an extension of public education upward. This need was felt because the people wanted a practical education beyond that offered in the elementary schools.

HOW THE HIGH SCHOOL DEVELOPED

A town meeting in Boston on January 15, 1821, passed a report that established an English high school. This was the first public high school established in the United States.

W. J. Gifford in discussing "The Historical Development of the New York State High School System" said:

> The term "high school" had come into use in New York at about the time of the founding of the English high school of Boston (1821) to designate monitorial schools of academic or partially academic rank. We found that these schools were favorably considered at one time as the means of a state system of secondary public or quasi public schools for the purposes of preparing teachers and of providing scientific training, but that they were rapidly absorbed into either the common school or academy systems, in most cases with a change of name.

High schools did not flourish immediately. In fact, "There seems little doubt that until well toward the middle of the nineteenth century, the academy was regarded as providing the solution of secondary education in the state (New York)."

A statement from the third annual report of Supt. W. H. Wells, Chicago, in 1856 shows the stage to which the high school had been developed there.

Wells said, "The first examination for admission to the high school was held on July 15, 1856. The whole number examined was 158. Of these, 114 were admitted and forty-four rejected." Thus, 28 per cent of the candidates were denied admission. High schools in 1856 were not the democratic schools of 1931. Today, by admitting all pupils who pass eighth grade examinations the high school has a vastly more varied range of abilities and interests to accommodate.

"It must be evident from what has already been said about the development of school gradation in the United States that at the outset there was no uniformity of practice in the sectioning of the total educational offerings of local school systems. One state differed from another in the matter of preferred division, while there existed even among the local communities of the same state considerable diversity of practice."

The accompanying table gives various illustrations of the status of school organization at the close of this critical period.

Typical School Organizations, 1860–67

Year	Place	School Organization
1860	Bangor, Me.	Suburban, primary, mixed, intermediate, grammar, select, high
1860	Concord, N.H.	Primary, intermediate, grammar, high
1860	Newark, N.J.	Primary, grammar, high, normal
1860	Wheeling, W.Va	Primary, grammar
1860	Wilmington, Del.	10 grades (8 similar to primary, secondary and intermediate and 2 similar to grammar)
1862	Rochester, N.Y.	Primary, intermediate, grammar, free academy
1865	Newport, R.I.	Ungraded, primary, intermediate, grammar, high
1865	New York City	Primary, grammar, free academy, normal
1865	Oswego, N.Y.	Primary, junior, senior, high
1866	Troy, N.Y.	Colored, primary, intermediate, grammar, high
1867	Baltimore	Primary, grammar, high, city college
1867	Cincinnati	District, intermediate
1867	Columbus, Ohio	Primary, secondary, intermediate, grammar, high
1867	Jersey City, N.J.	Primary, grammar, normal, colored
1867	Louisville, Ky.	Primary, intermediate, grammar, male and female high
1867	New Haven, Conn.	As many as 12 grades in the largest buildings
1867	New Orleans	Primary, grammar, high
1867	Providence, R.I.	Primary, intermediate, grammar, high with classical department
1867	St. Paul, Minn.	Alphabetical, lower primary, upper primary, intermediate, grammar, high
1867	San Francisco	Ungraded, primary, grammar, high, special
1867	Worcester, Mass.	Suburban, ungraded, subprimary, primary, intermediate primary, secondary, grammar schools of third, second and first grade, high, classical and English

The various amounts of time that are allotted to these units of school organization further show the lack of uniformity of practice. If we assume that a grade means a year the following are illustrations of the years that are allocated to units in several places: 8-2; 6-7-4; 3-3-3-3; 2-2-3; 3-3-3-4; 6-2; 2-2-2-3-4; 4-3-3; 2½-2½-4-3 and 4; ?-5-5-4; 3-2-3-4; 2-2-2-2-3.

It is difficult to discover any central tendency from such a variety of plans of organization. These samples represent the practice between 1860 and 1867.

WHAT IS WRONG TODAY

Our present dilemma is school organization in which we have democratic ideas but aristocratic practices make it necessary to emphasize, by repetition, the development of such an inconsistency.

The early plan of organization advocated by Henry Barnard was again set forth, although slightly modified, in his recommendations to Congress in 1868 and 1870 while he was commissioner of education. In 1870 he again specifically said that there should be primary schools (including the kindergarten) for pupils from "three to eight years of age," intermediate schools for pupils from "eight to fourteen years of age," and secondary schools "generally including all between the period of twelve and sixteen years of age." In addition Barnard proposed special and supplementary schools for pupils with special needs who could not be accommodated in the regular grades.

It is particularly significant that Barnard stuck to these democratic ideas during the time when grades developed as achievement levels, promotion came by examination and the idea grew that only a few pupils should reach the upper grades.

Today, however, we say democratically that secondary education is for all boys and girls between the ages of twelve and eighteen. But we have not modified our somewhat aristocratic school organization so that all may actually arrive there, nor have we developed differentiated curricula to accommodate their varied interests and abilities if they enter secondary schools.

A Comparison of Pupil Achievement in Graded and Nongraded Primary Classrooms

Joseph W. Halliwell

It was the purpose of this study to determine whether there would be a significant gain in the achievement of primary grade pupils after a variation of the nongraded primary unit was adopted.

More specifically, the investigation sought to compare the achievement of 146 primary pupils who had been taught for approximately one year under a nongraded program in reading and spelling with the achievement of 149 primary pupils who had been taught solely within the framework of the graded class structure.

BACKGROUND

The past decade will stand out for educators as a period of marked ferment in education. Although most of the ferment has taken place at the secondary school level, the elementary schools have also been affected greatly. While several noteworthy experimental programs featuring the teaching of foreign languages, the utilizing of an individualized reading program and the adopting of new approaches to the teaching of mathematics in the elementary schools have been undertaken, little attention has really been devoted to curriculum reform. The activity in elementary education has generally been concerned with organizational changes which were primarily designed to group children for learning in a more efficient manner.

Of the many organizational innovations in the elementary schools, the most publicized and fastest spreading is the nongraded school. Although variations of this type of plan which had been tried in the past did not withstand the test of time (2), the nongraded program reemerged in the early 1940's and has made a strong threat to replace the traditional graded classroom within the last decade (6).

The nongraded elementary school or the more common nongraded primary unit represents an endeavor to facilitate through organization a plan for the continuous growth of the child in the early school years. The advocates of the nongraded program feel that their approach is diametrical-

Reprinted from *The Journal of Experimental Education* 32:59–64, Fall 1963, by permission of the publisher and the author. Joseph W. Halliwell is with State University College, Cortland, New York.

ly opposed to the rigid structure of the graded self-contained classroom. They feel that the graded, self-contained classrooms inevitably lead to the application of Procrustean standards (7).

It is difficult to define the nongraded program because of the unusually large numbers of variations of the program. Essentially, this type of organizational framework permits the student to progress at his own rate in the academic areas. Frequently, the curriculum or courses of study are broken down into sequential levels, and the child works with a group of children at his level. Thus, a second grade student may be working with a first grade reading group and a third grade arithmetic group. Sometimes, the curriculum, methods and materials are changed when a nongraded program is started, but more often no modifications other than rate are made after the advent of a nongraded program.

The champions of the nongraded organizational pattern have certain convictions concerning the graded, self-contained classroom, namely, that teachers, for fear of encroaching on the domain of the teacher in the next higher grade, or for lack of time, hesitate to teach advanced work to fast learners; that teachers in their enthusiasm for preparing everyone for the next grade frequently push slow learners too rapidly for efficient learning and produce anxiety and frustration on the part of the pupils (and teachers); that teachers have to create so many groups in order to provide for individual differences that a great deal of seatwork activity is necessary to keep the groups busy, thus, precluding the opportunity for immediate feedback and permitting reenforcement of incorrect responses; that although teachers are not too reluctant to provide materials on lower grade levels for slow learners, the wide range of ability in the typical classroom would involve several below grade-level groups; that in actual practice teachers do not group pupils in subjects other than reading with notable frequency.

The proponents of the graded, self-contained classroom have been critical of many aspects of the nongraded program. They frequently assert that in this plan level standards have been substituted for grade standards (16), that provisions for integrated learning are reduced (5), and that ability grouping has been resurrected (18). Once the non-graded plan of organization has been classified as a form of ability grouping, all of the arguments, research and emotion directed against ability grouping in the past are employed again.

In actual practice the differences between graded and nongraded patterns of school organization are not as great as many people believe. Several perceptive educators have been extremely critical of the operation of many nongraded programs because they have felt that curricular change has been overlooked and that concentration has been devoted solely to organizational change (11, 17). Frazier has pointed out that all too frequently nongrading results in the modification of only one dimension, rate of learning (3). Although Goodlad concurs with Frazier's general appraisal, he does focus attention on the possibilities for curriculum revision within the framework of the nongraded organizational pattern (5). However, a perusal of the literature concerning the nongraded organizational pattern indicates that in actual practice the differences between the graded and nongraded patterns of school organization are primarily organizational and not curricular, and that little attention has been devoted to exploring the possibilities for curriculum revision within the scaffolding of the nongraded organizational pattern.

A second consideration concerning similarity in organizational pattern between graded and nongraded programs is frequently overlooked. An analysis of these two organizational patterns reveals that both approaches utilize ability grouping. The nongraded structure features interclass and intergrade ability grouping in a subject such as reading whereas the graded structure features intraclass ability grouping for reading work. In the nongraded program children may be doing classwork at a level several years above or below grade norms. In the graded program children may be doing classwork at a level several years below grade norms, but rarely are children permitted to work at a level several years above grade norms. Thus, this major difference, organization, is basically a difference in degree.

Another major difference between the two approaches is that in the nongraded program the pupil frequently has different teachers for reading, arithmetic and other subjects. It is, however, important to note that the graded, self-contained classroom is rarely self-contained. Many, if not most, self-contained classrooms have special teachers for music, art, physical education, speech, or remedial reading. There is also a trend toward special teachers in science and foreign languages. In many nongraded programs pupils remain with the same class for social studies, science, physical education, music, art and language arts with the exception of reading and spelling. Once again, this major difference is merely a difference in degree.

Most of the research and argument mustered to support either of these approaches to elementary school organization assume the type of exaggerated dualisms that Dewey inveighed against so vehemently. Most, if not all, of the differences between these two approaches are of degree and are not of kind. In general, the most salient characteristics distinguishing the nongraded program from the graded program are that, within the framework of the nongraded pattern, there is less reluctance to increase the ceiling or lower the floor of instruction to whatever extent necessary to provide for individual differences, and to increase the number of teachers the pupil encounters for instructional purposes during the school day.

The research relative to the superiority of one of these approaches over the other is rather limited. Most of the proponents of the self-contained classroom cite the insignificant differences found between pupils taught in "homogeneous" and "heterogeneous" classes as illustrative of the lack of efficacy of the nongraded program (18). These partisans fail to take cognizance of the fact that most of the studies on ability grouping involved ability groups that rigidly adhered to graded notions. The high ability groups were usually not exposed to any advanced work. In such a group "horizontal development" or "enrichment" was the goal rather than vertical development or acceleration. In actual practice the bright groups frequently marked time or did busy work. The slow ability group was frequently taught by teachers with a zeal to lift pupils up to grade level. Rarely did such teachers begin instructions more than a year or two below grade level. Anxiety and frustration were two of the more common outcomes of such classes.

Goodlad has surveyed the literature on the nongraded pattern of organization up to 1960 (4). His conclusions are that there have been few valid studies conducted in this area and that the few studies done favor nongraded over graded patterns of organization (6). He raises the question as to whether negative reports have been withheld. McNemar's caution as to the probability of false rejections of null hypotheses because of journal editors' tendency to reject manuscripts which do not contain statistically significant results must also not be overlooked in this regard (12).

A number of recent studies by Provus (14), Morgan and Stucker (13), Skapski (15), Ingram (9) and Hart (8) have found significant superiority for nongraded patterns over graded patterns of organization while Carbone (1) and Koontz (10) found significant superiority for the graded pattern of organization.

Provus studied the effects of nongrading in arithmetic on fourth, fifth and sixth grade students (14). Children were allowed to proceed through the arithmetic sequence at their own rate of progress. His study yielded data significantly favoring the nongraded approach. Provus found that the superior students profited most from nongrading. The attitude of children toward math in the nongraded plan was not significantly different from the attitude toward math in the graded plan, but the teachers preferred the nongraded approach.

Morgan and Stucker compared the reading achievement of matched groups of 180 fifth and 226 sixth grade pupils assigned to self-contained and ability-grouped reading classes (13). At the end of one year the fifth grade classes grouped for reading on the basis of ability were superior in reading achievement to the self-contained classes at the .01 level of confidence. At the sixth grade level the ability groups were superior to the self-contained groups at the .05 level of confidence. The investigators felt that the advantages of this type of ability grouping for the bright pupil were obvious but they hypothesized that the advantage to the slow pupil was that he was permitted to function in a non-threatening group of children experiencing similar problems, and that maximum feed-back was possible.

Skapski undertook an investigation to determine whether second and third grade pupils who were involved in a nongraded program in reading achieved better than did pupils in a graded program and whether in such a program achievement in reading was superior to achievement in other academic areas (15). She found that the pupils in the nongraded program were significantly superior in reading to a matched group of pupils in a graded program and that the reading achievement of the nongraded group was significantly superior to the arithmetic and spelling achievement.

Ingram investigated the effects of a nongraded primary cycle on the achievement of third grade pupils at the termination of the cycle (9). The investigator was quite explicit in pointing out that the nongraded program was an administrative device for organizing learning and that the curriculum and methodology were not altered. The nongraded pupils were compared with former pupils in the school who had been taught under the graded organizational pattern and with other contemporary pupils in the same city who were completing the primary grades in schools featuring the graded structure. The pupils in the nongraded program were superior in achievement to the former and contemporary pupils in graded classrooms in paragraph meaning, word meaning, spelling and language at the .01 level of confidence.

Hart compared the arithmetic achievement of 50 third grade pupils who had been taught arithmetic in a nongraded program with the arithmetic achievement of 50 third grade pupils who had been taught arithmetic in a graded program (8). The groups were matched on the basis of sex, age, IQ and socio-economic status. His findings indicated a significant superiority in arithmetic achievement for the nongraded pupils.

Carbone compared the achievement of 122 intermediate grade pupils who had been taught in a nongraded primary program with 122 intermediate grade pupils who had been taught in a graded primary program (1). The two groups were matched on the basis of sex and age, and the influence of mental ability was held constant by means of analysis of covariance. The pupils from the graded primary classrooms were found to be significantly superior in achievement in all areas, vocabulary, reading comprehension, language, work study skills and arithmetic to the pupils from the nongraded primary classrooms.

Koontz studied achievement as a function of grouping by comparing the achievement of fourth grade pupils enrolled in homogeneously and heterogeneously grouped classrooms (10). Strictly speaking, this is not a study of nongrading, but since the homogeneous groups were permitted to progress at their own rate, the study has been included in this review. Utilizing a level analysis of variance design the investigator found that the heterogeneously grouped pupils were significantly superior to the homogeneously grouped pupils in the areas of reading and arithmetic. The difference in language was not significant.

This brief review of the studies conducted in this area gives some indication of the conflicting evidence. Goodlad has maintained that the apparent conflict may not be real and that it is possible investigators have simply compared pupils in two differently labeled "graded schools" (6). Furthermore, Goodlad asserts that Carbone's study is valuable in that in not finding significant superiority for the nongraded group it has demonstrated "what organization by itself cannot possibly achieve." Unfortunately, Goodlad has oversimplified the situation and has misinterpreted the significance of Carbone's findings. If one accepts the hypothesis that Carbone's nongraded groups may not have differed from graded groups other than in organization, it becomes rather obvious that the significant superiority of the graded pupils cannot be attributed to the curriculum or instructional practices, but must be attributed solely to organization, the very point that Goodlad had felt he had refuted. This notion would seem to be corroborated by Ingram's study in which the nongraded groups were found to be significantly superior to the graded groups despite explicit statements to the effect that the only change was in organization.

This summary of the research indicates that the problem of assessing the value of nongraded programs is quite complex and that much more research will be needed before such programs can be evaluated with any degree of validity.

The present study was undertaken in an endeavor to shed some further light, if possible, on the area of nongrading. It is the purpose of the present study to determine whether a nongraded pattern of organization in reading and spelling in the primary grades results in improved academic achievement.

PROCEDURE

The general plan of the study was to compare the spring achievement test scores of first, second and third grade pupils in a school which had inaugurated a nongraded program the previous fall with the spring achievement test scores of the previous school year when the school was organized solely on the basis of the traditional graded structure. At the first grade level only reading was taught on a nongraded basis. At the second and third grade levels both reading and spelling were taught on a nongraded basis. Thus, some second graders left their homeroom and went to a first grade classroom for reading instruction while other second graders went to third grade classrooms for reading instruction.

In both school years, 1959–1960 and 1960–1961, achievement tests were administered to the first grade pupils in June. The word knowledge and reading comprehension sections of the California Achievement Tests were administered to every first grade pupil. At the second and third grade levels the Metropolitan Achievement Tests containing sections on word knowledge, word discrimination, reading, spelling, language, arithmetic computation and arithmetic problem solving were administered during the second week of April in both school years. Although nongrading was only employed in the subject matter areas of reading and spelling, it was considered important to test the pupils in all the subject matter areas enumerated because frequently when new techniques are employed in certain areas more time is devoted to these areas to the neglect of other areas. At the first grade level the only scores available for the graded group were the word knowledge and reading comprehension scores of the California Achievement Test, so for purposes of comparison two subtests in the California were the only tests administered to the nongraded groups. The Lorge-Thorndike Intelligence Test (Nonverbal Battery) was administered to every pupil in the study. The IQ scores derived from this test were used as the measure of mental ability.

Only those primary grade pupils who had been in the nongraded program since its inception in September of 1960 were included in the nongraded sample. Any pupils who entered school after September 1960 or left before the achievement testing period in April 1961 were not included in the study. The resulting nongraded sample comprised 46 first grade pupils, 50 second grade pupils and 50 third grade pupils. The graded sample included all of the first, second and third grade pupils who were in the graded program from September, 1959, to the achievement testing period in April, 1960. The resulting graded sample comprised 52 first grade pupils, 50 second grade pupils, and 47 third grade pupils.

When the nongraded program was inaugurated, no effort was made to modify the curriculum or methodology. The nongraded pattern of organization was considered an administrative device for facilitating organization—and nothing more. Although the organizational structure was modified, the teachers, the basal reading series and the methodology were to be the same. However, as the term progressed more and more requests came to the office for more and different materials. The number of supplementary text requests increased markedly as did the number of requests for reading games, phonics workbooks, "easier spellers" and "harder spellers." Furthermore, the teachers felt that their attitudes had changed. The teachers of the slower pupils felt that they had become more tolerant, were slowing down the rate at which new materials were presented and were presenting materials in more variegated ways. The teachers of the brighter pupils felt that in the past they had underestimated the extent of the brighter pupils' abilities. Thus, while the original intent of the program was solely to modify the organizational pattern of the school, the program evolved into something more than just an organizational change. It therefore became evident that if any significant change in achievement were to be found, it could not be attributed to organization alone.

The approach to the statistical analysis of the data in the study was to be contingent upon a preliminary finding concerning the mental ability of the pupils in the graded and nongraded groups. If there were no significant differences between the mean intelligence scores of the graded and nongraded groups, the achievement differences between the two groups were to be tested by the simple t test technique. If there were significant differences in intelligence between the two groups, the achievement differences were to be tested by analysis of covariance.

FINDINGS

In the preliminary investigation the graded pupils in the first, second and third grades attained mean IQ scores of 104.93, 106.02 and 104.68, respectively. The nongraded pupils in the first, second and third grades attained mean IQ scores of 105.58, 104.81 and 103.43, respectively. When the mean differences in IQ between the graded and nongraded pupils were analyzed for statistical significance, it was found that the differences did not approach significance at any of the grade levels. It was decided, therefore, to compare the achievement test scores of the two groups by means of the simple t test technique since the intelligence test scores were virtually constant.

The data relative to the achievement of the graded and nongraded groups at the first, second and third grade levels are presented in Table 1.

It is readily apparent from the data in Table 1 that the nongraded pupils in first grade obtained significantly higher achievement scores in word knowledge and reading comprehension on the California Achievement Test than did the graded pupils. Both of the differences were significant at the .01 level of confidence.

Analysis of the data at the second grade level indicates that, although the nongraded pupils attained higher achievement scores than the graded pupils in every subject area but word discrimination, only in the area of

TABLE 1

Achievement of 149 Graded and 146 Nongraded Pupils as Indicated by Mean Grade Equivalents on the California and Metropolitan Achievement Tests*

	Grade	Graded			Nongraded			t test	P
		N	Mean Achievement	Standard Deviation	N	Mean Achievement	Standard Deviation		
Word Knowledge	1	52	2.48	.74	46	3.57	.82	6.75	<.01
Reading Comprehension	1	52	2.08	.80	46	2.86	.84	4.59	<.01
Word Knowledge	2	50	3.11	1.01	50	3.31	1.05	.95	N.S.
Word Discrimination	2	50	3.20	1.20	50	3.11	1.24	.41	N.S.
Reading	2	50	3.10	1.00	50	3.39	1.13	.21	N.S.
Spelling	2	50	2.69	1.09	50	3.12	1.37	1.63	N.S.
Total Arithmetic	2	50	2.42	.85	50	2.82	.93	2.22	<.05
Word Knowledge	3	47	4.31	1.25	50	4.62	1.36	1.15	N.S.
Word Discrimination	3	47	3.96	1.52	50	4.37	1.59	1.29	N.S.
Reading	3	47	4.10	1.48	50	4.38	1.58	.90	N.S.
Spelling	3	47	4.13	1.31	50	5.12	1.49	3.54	<.01
Language	3	47	3.93	1.39	50	4.29	1.39	1.29	N.S.
Computation	3	47	3.64	.97	50	4.27	.66	3.71	<.01
Problem Solving	3	47	3.76	1.38	50	4.39	1.47	2.17	<.05

* California Achievement Test was used in first grade.
Metropolitan Achievement Test was used in second and third grade.

arithmetic was the difference significant. This difference favored the non-graded pupils at the .05 level of confidence.

The data yielded by Table 1 at the third grade level reveals that although the nongraded pupils attained higher mean achievement scores than did the graded pupils in every subject area tested, only three of these differences were statistically significant. The differences favoring the nongraded group in arithmetic computation and spelling were significant at the .01 level of confidence and the difference in arithmetic problem solving favored the nongraded group at the .05 level of confidence.

DISCUSSION

The findings at the first grade level reflected a clear-cut superiority for the nongraded pupils over the graded pupils in the two reading subtests. At the second and third grade levels five of the six mean subtest scores in reading favored the nongraded pupils but none of the differences were significant. At the second and third grade levels both mean scores in spelling favored the nongraded group, but only the third grade difference was statistically significant. At both the second and third grade levels the mean scores in arithmetic favored the nongraded group. At the second grade level the difference was significant at the .05 level of confidence and at the third grade level the difference in arithmetic computation was significant at the .01 level of confidence, while the difference in problem solving was significant at the .05 level of confidence. It is readily apparent that although the nongraded approach was only utilized in reading and spelling at the second and third grade levels, the gains in arithmetic were as great, if not greater, than those in reading and spelling.

A cursory examination of the findings in this study might cause one to question the efficacy of nongrading in reading and spelling at the second and third grade levels. However, discussions with the teachers in the experiment who had taught the students in both the graded and nongraded classes yielded information to the effect that the teachers spent a good deal less time teaching reading in the nongraded program, enabling them to devote more time to arithmetic, social studies and language arts instruction.

In interpreting the findings in the current study, two important considerations should not be overlooked. The first is that the nongraded program had only been in operation for eight months at the time of this investigation. The second is that although nongrading in this study had originally been inaugurated solely as an organizational change, concomitant changes in methods, materials and attitudes also occurred.

In the light of the findings of this investigation it would seem that a nongraded approach to the teaching of reading and spelling has proved quite effective and is worthy of further investigation.

REFERENCES

1. Carbone, R. F. "A Comparison of Graded and Non-graded Elementary Schools," *Elementary School Journal*, LXII (November 1961), pp. 82–8.

2. Dawson, M., Editor. "Point of View About School Organization," *National Elementary Principal*, XLI (December 1961), pp. 20–47.

3. Frazier, A. "Needed: A New Vocabulary for Individual Differences," *Elementary School Journal*, LXI (February 1961), pp. 260–68.

4. Goodlad, J. I. "Classroom Organization," *Encyclopedia of Educational Research*, (New York: Macmillan, 1960), pp. 221–26.

5. Goodlad, J. I. "Toward Improved School Organization," *National Elementary Principal*, XLI (December 1960), pp. 60–127.

6. Goodlad, J. I. "Individual Differences and Vertical Organization of the School," *Sixty-first Yearbook*, N.S.S.E. (Chicago: University of Chicago Press, 1962), pp. 209–38.

7. Goodlad, J. I., and Anderson, R. H. *The Non-graded Elementary School* (New York: Harcourt, Brace, 1959).

8. Hart, R. H. "The Nongraded Primary School and Arithmetic," *Arithmetic Teacher*, IX (March 1962), pp. 130–33.

9. Ingram, V. "Flint Evaluates Its Primary Cycle," *Elementary School Journal*, LXI (November 1960), pp. 76–80.

10. Koontz, W. F. "A Study of Achievement as a Function of Homogeneous Grouping," *Journal of Experimental Education*, XXX (December 1961), pp. 249–53.

11. Lobdell, L. O., and Van Ness, W. J. "Grouping and Enrichment," *Education*, LXXXII (March 1962), pp. 399–402.

12. McNemar, Q. "At Random: Sense and Nonsense," *American Psychologist*, XV (May 1960), pp. 295–300.

13. Morgan, E. F., and Stucker, G. R. "The Joplin Plan of Reading Vs. a Traditional Method," *Journal of Educational Psychology*, LI (April 1960), pp. 69–73.

14. Provus, M. M. "Ability Grouping in Arithmetic," *Elementary School Journal*, LX (April 1960), pp. 391–98.

15. Skapski, M. K. "Ungraded Primary Reading Program: An Objective Evaluation," *Elementary School Journal*, LXI (October 1960), pp. 41–45.

16. Stendler, C. B. "Grouping Practices," *National Elementary Principal*, XL (September 1960), pp. 147–65.

17. Wilhelms, F. T. "The Curriculum and Individual Differences," *Sixty-first Yearbook*, N.S.S.E. (Chicago: University of Chicago Press, 1962), pp. 209–38.

18. Wilhelms, F. T., and Westby-Gibson, D. "Grouping: Research Offers Leads," *Educational Leadership*, XVIII (April 1961), pp. 410–13.

Inadequacy of Graded Organization—What Then?

John I. Goodlad

Some Values and Realities To Guide Educational Practice

In examining educational practice, each of us looks through a screen of values which imposes pleasing or displeasing colors upon what we see. At the head of my list of criteria for judging the adequacy of school structure are three which I apply as questions. *First, does the structure encourage continuous progress for each child?* There should be no undue pauses, no damaging gaps and no meaningless duplications—just steady progress geared to the irregular development of the child himself. *Second, what alternatives exist for placing children who do not appear to be profiting as they should in their present educational environment?* Most schools provide only for repetition or skipping vertically, with little or no provision for horizontal replacement of the child. In other words, if the child does not "fit" where he now is, only some kind of extra-legal provision is available for his readjustment. *Third, does the structure encourage a reasonable balance of success and failure?* It is estimated that approximately twenty-five per cent of children in the grades experience from seventy to eighty per cent of the failure. This situation does not appear to provide a wholesome balance of success and failure.

Twentieth-century education at all levels must take into account at least two major kinds of realities. *First, knowledge is expanding at an explosive rate.* This fact has been stated many times and in many ways. Robert Oppenheimer has said that most of the knowledge worth learning today was not in the textbooks when today's adults were in school. Others have said that the knowledge accumulated since 1900 is equivalent to the total of all knowledge that had accumulated prior to the beginning of this century. A perhaps more dramatic statement is that ninety-five per cent of the scientists ever born are still living. *The second inescapable reality is that human beings are profoundly different from one another.* There are biochemical differences; that is, differences in under-the-skin composition. Several hundred such differences have now been identified and classified. There are physiological differences; for example, differences in energy

Reprinted from *Childhood Education*, February, 1963, Vol. 39, pp. 274–277, by permission of the Association for Childhood Education International, 3615 Wisconsin Avenue, N.W., Washington, D.C. 20016. John I. Goodlad is Professor of Education and Director, University Elementary School, University of California, Los Angeles.

patterns, causing children to be quite different in their readiness for the activities school provides. And there are academic individual differences. In the fourth grade only fifteen per cent of the children are at grade level—that is, range from 4.0 to 4.9 in all subjects—at the middle of the year. At the fourth grade there is a four-year spread in over-all average achievement; at the fifth grade, five years; at the sixth grade there is a six-year range; and so on. These individual differences simply cannot be accounted for within the conventional graded structure of school organization.

At least two major proposals now before us on the educational scene seem to support the values and the realities enunciated above. The first of these proposes a longitudinal curriculum organized around basic concepts, principles and methods of inquiry in the various fields of knowledge. The second, closely related and designed to account for such a curriculum, proposes elimination of the stratified, lock-step grade system and the substitution of a nongraded plan.

Inadequacy of Graded System

When the graded school was established as the pattern for American education in the middle of the nineteenth century, the prevailing view of individual differences was quite different from the picture drawn above. Children apparently were regarded as fundamentally alike, major differences lying in areas of determination, application, hard work, and so on. "If at first you don't succeed, try, try, try again" was the slogan. Such a perception leads to reward and punishment as the major stimulants to and perhaps differentiators of progress. At that time, too, with knowledge expanding at a much slower rate, it may have been possible to define something called an elementary education. Today, the packaging of a few bits of knowledge considered to be of most worth is impossible. However, it is important to remember that the view of individual differences and the rate of expansion of knowledge current in 1850 were not in any way antithetical to the graded structure that was rapidly emerging and crystallizing.

Once the graded structure was established, it became necessary to fit the child to the structure. Nonpromotion was a natural concomitant. If the child doesn't succeed you simply have him do over again what he failed to do in the first place. But we now have a substantial body of research indicating that nonpromoted children do not learn as well as do their promoted counterparts; nonpromoted children are less well-adjusted personally and socially than are youngsters of equal ability who are promoted; nonpromoted children, more than promoted children, dislike school and wish to discontinue their formal learning as soon as possible.

It is possible for creative teachers to "beat the graded system," so to speak. But in so doing they must run counter to prevailing practices, proposing and initiating adjustments that deviate markedly from existing practices. Often they become nuisances to administrators and other teachers who prefer that things remain as they are and have been. To remedy this situation I would legalize the deviation of creative teachers in order that what they do may become accepted as standard practice.

Nongrading

In the nongraded school, grade demarcations are swept away. Some schools eliminate grade designations at the outset. Others move toward this step slowly, perhaps first experimenting with multiple-age or multiple-grade groups and in various ways deliberately expanding provision for individual differences within a given class. One of the major goals is to eliminate the grade-mindedness often firmly established in the thinking of teachers.

Essentially, nongrading seeks to recognize and deliberately plan for the range of pupil realities actually present in a given class. This means accepting the fact that there are children working at levels below grade designation, varying widely from subject to subject. At the top end of the scale, it is necessary to provide activities that would be classified at several grades above usual pupil grade placement. In so doing there is no fear of encroaching on the work of the next grade; there is no need to stop because the work of the grade has been completed or because the teacher above expects children to be neither above nor below grade assignment.

It is absolutely essential that there be a thoroughgoing redistribution of materials. Instead of a single set of textbooks for a class, for example, there should be five copies of this, four copies of that, seven copies of something else. Materials should be selected in anticipation of the range of accomplishments now present and to be present within the group as learning progresses.

Above all, there is no attempt to account for several years of pupil progress through an arbitrary and necessarily incorrect grade classification. Energy is devoted to providing for the range of individual differences that exists. By a system of overlapping the accomplishments present in any one group with the accomplishments present in lower and higher groups, it is possible to provide several placement alternatives for any given child at any given time. Thus, in an elementary school with six classes encompassing the first three grades—two classes per grade—there would be a spread of accomplishment ranging from less than kindergarten to above the fifth grade, depending upon the field of study in question. In the conventional graded plan, this pair of classes would be approximately alike in the individual differences recognized and in the instructional arrangements provided. Classes would be viewed in an end-to-end relationship, the conclusion of the second leading directly to the beginning of the third, and so on.

In a nongraded plan one might arrange for a pair of classes, X_1 and X_2, with an anticipated spread of individual differences from kindergarten to the usual second grade. Y_1 and Y_2 would anticipate a spread of from at least the conventional first to the conventional third grade. Z_1 and Z_2 would provide for a spread of accomplishment ranging from the second to the fifth grade. Now, it may be seen that one pair of classes overlaps another pair of classes. In fact, each pair overlaps each of the other two pairs, thus providing several alternative placements for any child at any given time. (See Figure 1.)

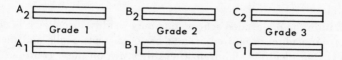

This chart illustrates several differences about the graded concept as contrasted with the nongraded concept. The graded school normally provides for a single year of expectations in each class. Thus each class at subsequent grade levels is in an end-to-end relationship. The child leaves off in A_1, for example, and moves directly to B_1 as though he had precisely finished the work of A_1. We know that this is not the way children are, and school organization should accompany reality rather than fiction. The first section of the chart shows a progression with each graded class picking up where the previous graded class left off.

The second part of the diagram shows two essential differences in nongraded structure. First, the spread of expectations for a single class encompasses more than one year. Thus X_1 begins well below the first grade (where many children are) and continues well beyond the conventional first grade for children who are capable of so progressing. However, the next class does not expect all children to come up to an equivalent standard; and so it begins a good deal back of where children left off the previous year but provides for a considerable extension beyond the year's work in order to take care of youngsters at different rates of progression. Thus each pair of classes overlaps each other pair of classes. You will note that the "Z" pair overlaps not only the "Y" pair but also the tip of the "X" pair. Such a gross overlap is not necessary, but it does indicate the variety of alternative placements possible for a child when the overlapping nongraded structure is used.

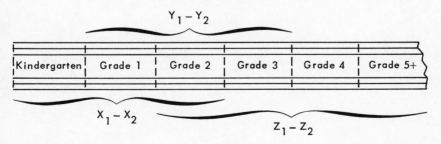

Figure 1

In the nongraded scheme there is continuous progress for each child; there are several alternatives for placing children who do not appear to be profiting from their present environment; and there is improved opportunity for a reasonable balance of success and failure because the classroom environment is designed to legalize several levels of accomplishments at any given time. Some children may be moved more quickly through the years of the primary unit. Some may take a year longer. In no case does a child skip; nor is he failed. Most children are a year or two "ahead" in some field or other; many are a year or two "behind" in something. The nongraded plan forces recognition of these realities. While it is indeed an organizational scheme, it is above all an expression of a philosophy of education.

Within the nongraded scheme one may readily visualize a longitudinal type of curriculum organized around basic concepts, skills and methods of inquiry. One identifies children where they are on these continua, making no effort to classify them according to an arbitrary, unrealistic grade standard. Children progress continuously along these continua with an appropriate balance of realistic success and failure. There is differentiated instruction for learners who obviously differ in ability to learn.

At present the nongraded scheme is most prevalent at the primary level. A few plans extend into the upper elementary grades. In an isolated community or two, consideration is now being given to the possibility of nongraded junior and senior high schools. There is no reason why the nongraded concept cannot be extended from kindergarten through the entire twelve- or thirteen-year structure of education. In fact, the very logic of nongrading leads to a continuous stream of elementary and secondary education. Logically, then, the nongraded plan leads to reduced discontinuity among elementary, junior high and secondary units of the school system as well as to elimination of the lock-step inherent in the traditional graded plan.

Dropouts and the Graded School

Vincent C. DiPasquale

The traditional graded school with its single standard and restrictive program for each grade and each subject is a Prussian import. Prior to the opening of Quincy Grammar School in Boston in 1848, there were no grade classifications and instruction was furnished on an individual basis.

The graded elementary school was conceived and developed before we had scientific findings on child growth and development, and before the strict enforcement of compulsory school attendance laws. Today it is a cumbersome anachronism.

And the graded school contributes to early school leaving as a consequence of its typical single standard of achievement. The standard is too high for some, too low for others. Those who can are often not challenged; those who can't are continually humiliated. Overageness, reading retardation, social promotions, and grade failure result.

The range in achievement and intelligence in the typical classroom is frequently too great for even a superior teacher to bridge. With a spread of six grades in achievement and sixty points in I.Q. in a seventh grade class, the standards, expectations, and instructional materials are often the same for all. The inevitable result is that some children are not reached. These conditions corrode personality and contribute to withdrawal or aggressive behavior, truancy, delinquency, and early school leaving.

The graded school predestines the slow to failure and frustration, the gifted to retardation and boredom. Its rigid molds are generally unadaptable to the individual child's growth pattern and capacity or to his own divergent abilities. In the graded school the most retarded are often the gifted. For example, it is not unusual for a fifth grader to be working at an instructional level of three or four years below his functional ability. Frequently, too, the only tools available to the teacher are the instructional materials of the grade he is teaching. Hence opportunities for vertical acceleration as well as horizontal enrichment are often missing.

The theory of survival of the fittest does not apply to early school leavers. On the contrary, studies seem to show that some dropouts who

Reprinted from *Phi Delta Kappan* 46:129–133, November 1964, by permission of the publisher and the author. Vincent C. DiPasquale is Director of the Campus School, Moorhead State College, Moorhead, Minnesota.

are fit are eliminated while others less fit receive a high school diploma.[1]

The graded school, anchored as it is to a prescribed curriculum and a fixed standard for each grade, begets the need for remedial reading, opportunity classes for the "misfits," and increased pupil personnel services in an attempt to help children "catch up" with their grade and "adjust" to school. It is often a futile attempt.

If each child were met where he is at each stage of his educational experience, grade repetition would disappear. The need for corrective reading programs and opportunity classes would evaporate, and demand for pupil personnel services to solve problems generated by grade failure would be removed.

Grade repetition and corrective programs are devices invented to make gradedness work. These devices are financially costly, always stigmatic, and quite often traumatic to child and parents alike.

Grade failure was conceived originally to give the child a second year to learn the essentials prerequisite to the next grade. However, it does not always work. Often the repeater does no better than he did the year before. Research indicates that he might have done as well, if not better, had he been permitted to go into the next grade.[2]

The psychological ill effects of grade failure are imprinted on the child's mind. His friends have left him behind. He has lost prestige. He is a year older in the same grade. Younger children are now in his class. Sometimes they know more and learn faster. He feels "dumb." He internalizes his difficulties daily, but there seems to be no escape. On the contrary, gaps in subject-matter learning are compounded by time. Graded expectations for him become increasingly harder to fulfill. The specter of failure hovers continuously, and the result is inevitable—on the surface he develops a crust of indifference or hostility, or a shell for withdrawal.

When a child repeats a grade, he begins to dislike school, if he does not already dislike it. When he fails twice, he doesn't want to go to school. When he fails three times, he is almost certain to be a dropout.

Human costs resulting from grade failure are largely conjectural. However, there seems to be some relationship between school frustration and rejection on the one hand and the incidence of mental illness and juvenile delinquency on the other.[3] Numerous investigations, for example, indicate that unsuccessful school experiences constitute "a complicating

[1] Beatrice Crump Lee, "School Dropouts," NEA Research Division Bulletin, April, 1963.
[2] Virgil E. Herrick, "Elementary Education Programs," Encyclopedia of Educational Research, Chester W. Harris, ed. New York: The Macmillan Company, 1960, p. 438.
[3] "Pupil Failure and Nonpromotion," NEA Research Division Bulletin, February, 1959.

if not precipitating factor in" juvenile delinquency.[4] Etymologically, the word delinquency means a state of being left behind. In the graded school, without question, children are left behind, with attendant evil consequences for their personality and behavior.

Financial costs of grade failure can be gauged fairly accurately. From numerous studies, we can estimate that in 1963–64 at least one million children were required to repeat a grade in order to "catch up." The average cost of educating each child for the same year was $455. The failure therefore cost the nation approximately 455 million dollars, or an amount greater by 155 million dollars than the cost of operating Chicago's public schools for the same year.

This sum spent on failure might have financed the following five-point program:

1. The establishment and support of 50,000 nursery school units.

2. The employment of 10,000 additional classroom teachers to help decrease class size.

3. The addition of 7,000 teacher aides in order to release teachers for exclusively professional services.

4. The addition of 4,000 specialists to increase medical, dental, psychological, and psychiatric services.

5. The establishment of free lunch programs for all children.

This program would constitute a major frontal attack on the dropout problem, which begins basically before the child starts school and is abetted by overcrowded classes, unrealistic graded expectations, and inadequate specialized services. Points 1 and 5 are suggested by the dire need of a large segment of our youth. Their plight stems from poverty and social disorganization in our adult population, from the distressed and blighted regions of Appalachia to the scarred and crime-infested neighborhoods in the inner city.

Another attack on the dropout problem should contemplate the elimination of gradedness and the implementation of a plan for continuous pupil progress.

At the very outset, it should be stressed that continuous pupil progress does not imply social promotion. Failure and promotion are the warp and woof of gradedness. These devices, as well as "skipping" grades, have no place in the nongraded school. Continuous progress can be defined as a carefully conceived plan of school organization which aims to provide a sequential curricular program differentiated in content so as to be compatible with the child's ability and synchronized with his unique timetable

[4] William Kvaraceus, "Delinquency," *Encyclopedia of Educational Research*, Chester W. Harris, ed. New York: The Macmillan Company, 1960, p. 368.

of growth and development. The characteristics of the nongraded school can be summarized briefly as follows:

1. The child is met where he is, not where he ought to be, at each stage of his educational experience. Progress is continuous.

2. The child has a school age, not a grade label. At the end of the scholastic year he is neither promoted nor retained. He simply advances to the next year, picking up his work in September where he left off in June. Continuity in the development of skills and concepts is assured. Gaps are not allowed to develop and multiply.

3. The child progresses at his own best pace. Children grow in spurts and plateaus; they do not grow in twelve graded segments. The structure and practices of the nongraded school attempt to be compatible with scientific findings in child growth and development.

4. The teacher at the end of the year is not confronted with decisions on failure and promotion, with all their negative implications. Unwholesome pressures and anxieties on the part of teachers and children are removed.

5. Marks reflect the progress the child makes at the instructional levels on which he is working in the several subject areas for which he is ready and capable. The child's marks are not related to a mythical and subjective standard for each grade—too high for some, too low for others—a practice of the graded school which is detrimental to mental health.[5]

6. Low or failing marks are not used as a motivational device. Their efficacy for this purpose, if we accept the findings of numerous studies, has long been seriously questioned. However, low or failing marks are sometimes used, though they are confined to accurate reporting of insufficient progress in terms of reasonable expectations based on the child's functional ability.[6]

7. Parent-teacher conferences supplement reporting and are indispensable in acquainting parents with children's strengths and weaknesses, explaining reasonable expectations for their child, enlightening them on the practices and philosophy of the nongraded school, and interpreting performances on objective tests.

8. Differentiated curricula and differentiated instructional materials

[5] Lester D. Crow and Alice Crow, *Mental Hygiene*. New York: The McGraw-Hill Book Company, Inc., 1951, p. 216, *et seq.*

[6] Functional ability may be defined as the known, demonstrable equipment of the individual applicable to learning at each stage of his total educational experience. It should be differentiated from potential ability, the zenith of which is, perhaps, seldom if ever attained. Existing tools cannot seem to measure it with complete accuracy. Functional ability, both quantitatively and qualitatively, would seem to be the manifest degree to which potential ability has responded to the stimuli and nature of the prevailing culture to which the individual is exposed.

compatible with the degree of intellectual maturity and sophistication of the student are the *sine qua non* of the nongraded school.

9. Criteria for classroom organization include objective test data, with emphasis on reading attainment plus teacher judgment. In cases of wide divergence, teacher judgment, in general, prevails. Obviously, teacher judgment is based on the child's day-to-day performance, which should be more valid than a child's performance on a single test. In some instances, where a child does not fit his classroom placement in a particular subject, he is scheduled to take this subject in another class.

10. A child's placement in September is not a sacrosanct decision, fixed for the entire academic year. A child can be moved from one classroom to another as growth, unusual progress, or new needs dictate. A child may at some time or other during the year fit better in another learning situation. Such changes follow case conferences on individual children with involvement and approval of teachers and administrators as well as parents.

11. Interclass as well as intraclass grouping is practiced in many nongraded schools. Reducing the spread in instructional levels permits the free play of competition as well as cooperation, generates interpersonal group dynamics, creates challenges which are attainable for individuals as well as the group, and permits the teacher to work with the whole class in many learning situations. The writer has not yet found a teacher who has disagreed with the proposition that a class with a larger enrollment working at about the same instructional level provides a more desirable classroom situation for efficient teaching and learning than a class with a smaller enrollment representing a spread of five or more grades in instruction. Classes are organized not on the basis of intelligence but on the basis of where children are in their developmental learning, with appropriate consideration, whenever feasible, of physiological and social maturation. Furthermore, in this type of classroom organization the child works competitively as well as cooperatively in the company of peers, in a situation which insures his status, self-respect, and success, at tasks which represent at once a challenge and an attainable goal. Classroom organization based on equal classroom enrollments and alphabetical arrangements is as outmoded as it is unscientific.

12. In the nongraded school the grade label is discarded because it is not an index of the child's school achievement any more than chronological age is an index of an individual's intelligence and maturity. Frequently, too, the grade label of a class prescribes and preordains the level of academic work which is to be done by all members of the group. Children who don't measure up to the expectations of the grade are doomed to failure, while those whose potential is greater are often cut short. The

ancient Procrustes bed continues implacably to operate in graded schools.

13. Some school systems have a nongraded organization in the primary unit only, whereas in some the philosophy has been extended to include grades four, five, and six. In still others, the required academic areas of the secondary schools are included. Elsbree and McNally seem to think that an elementary school which is half nongraded and half graded may suffer from a split personality. Some failures also accumulate at the end of the primary block of time, since some children will not master all the essentials prerequisite for promotion into the fourth grade.

14. Some children spend their first year in an intensive reading-readiness program. Yet at the end of the fourth year it is possible for some of these children to have attained a level of educational achievement in reading and in content areas much beyond the traditional standards of the fourth grade. In the conventional graded school such children would be required to repeat the first grade.

At this point the reader may infer that the writer advocates a system of deception and injustice in reporting student progress and a depression of standards in general. For example, it is true that Bill and John, both juniors in high school, the former taking basic communications (elementary grammar and writing), the latter taking a course in creative writing or English literature (college level), may receive the equivalent of an "A" and a "B" respectively. If courses are accurately labeled and described, however, there should be no resultant deception or confusion for student, parent, employer, or school official. Furthermore, different kinds of diplomas and certificates of high school attendance are awarded in many school systems.[7] This practice should be encouraged.

We must recognize that three or four years of English are basic secondary requirements and that current practice has a prescribed course of study for each year of English in grades nine through twelve inclusive. We must recognize, further, that among 300 freshmen in a given high school there can exist a spread in achievement equivalent to seven grades. Moreover, when, as generally happens, the 300 are compressed into a traditional program, those who cannot are hopelessly lost and those who are capable of higher performance are confined to mediocrity.

Therefore, what is advocated in required academic subjects is a system of interclass grouping based on intellectual competence. In the ninth grade instance just mentioned, there should be *at least* twelve sections of English. Each section should have its own appropriate program and all programs should be graduated in levels of difficulty and challenge from a fifth grade course of study in the language arts to a rigorous course in

[7] "High School Diplomas," NEA Research Division Bulletin, December, 1959.

literature and composition. The reader should not assume that this kind of organization fully removes the need for making additional provisions for small groups and some individuals within the class. The teacher, however, can spend the major part of a class period working with the whole class on common instructional activities, making provisions for group and individual needs whenever necessary. This kind of organization further suggests the advantage of group dynamics generated by individual involvement in competitive and cooperative effort.

In advocating interclass grouping we are navigating in deep water, but these waters are not uncharted. Our secondary system of electives has long been sensitive to different interests and to degrees of intellectual capability. Latin, advanced algebra, chemistry, the practical and the fine arts, all respond to the reality of divergent abilities and aptitudes. Therefore the principle of interclass grouping has long been practiced in secondary school organization. However, this principle has been virtually ignored in organizing classes in required academic areas such as English and social studies. In these and other areas it is equally important that a student's placement be sensitive to criteria of preparation, aptitude, and competence.

Interclass grouping can be illustrated also by citing related practices in athletics. The football coach organizes his athletes into various squads from scrubs to varsity. He may have as many as seven or eight teams, with his top eleven constituting the first string. Experience, desire, size, physical and mental agility, and capacity for individual as well as cooperative performance are used in grouping players. Among teammates as well as with opponents, competition throughout the season remains intense. A player can be shifted from one team to another. He moves up or down, depending on growth and development and the quality of performance as he vies daily with teammates for a position and with opponents for victory. A coach recognizes that the apogee of achievement is directly related to the degree of competition existing among comparable players.

To be sure, the organization of classes based on criteria of preparation and competence is hard and exacting for the administrator. It demands refinements in curriculum construction and class organization which respond continuously to the varying needs of youth. But we have the grave responsibility of increasing the holding power of our schools and in creating opportunities for all children to learn in a measure fully commensurate with intellectual endowment and aptitude. To achieve this, strong administrative leadership—imaginative, forthright, and courageous —should be exercised; leadership based on considerations of personal expediency should yield. Boards of education have a tremendous responsibility here, demanding complete abstention from administrative involvement and adherence to qualities of stability and faith and vision. Teachers, too, should be receptive to change; in fact, most are.

The nongraded elementary school has won considerable acceptance in the twenty-two years since its inception in Milwaukee in 1942.

Stuart E. Dean has reported that one-fifth of the urban centers of the country for the school year 1958–1959 were using some form of the nongraded primary plan and that 13 per cent of the urban places not using any form were contemplating its adoption.[8]

Although research on the advantages of the nongraded school is limited, the writer can confirm these empirical observations based on seventeen years of administrative experience:

1. The nongraded plan contributes to a decline in truancy and the number of dropouts.

2. There is a marked improvement in teacher morale and student achievement.

3. There is perceptible improvement in student behavior. Emotional health and ego development are enhanced.

4. The incidence of vandalism and break-ins is markedly reduced.

5. Parents observe that children "like to go to school," and readily come to accept the concepts and practices of the nongraded school.[9]

6. Standards of achievement are raised, since the child works in each subject area at a level compatible with his functional ability.

In summary, the writer proposes the abandonment of gradedness with its corollary, the single standard of achievement for each grade and each academic subject *required* for graduation. The proposition is predicated on the premise that "gradedness" is incompatible with scientific findings on child growth and development as well as the demands of mass education, condemning many to failure and the very able to boredom and mediocrity. The substitution of nongradedness in the elementary schools and in the required academic areas of the junior-senior high school with marks based on individual progress in relation to functional ability would reduce substantially the number of early school leavers.

We recommend that interclass grouping be practiced, that multiple curricula, graduated in levels of difficulty, be instituted, and that vocational and technical programs be expanded.

We also propose an extension of the practice of differentiated diplomas and certificates of attendance, giving appropriate recognition to the kind of educational program completed.

[8] Stuart E. Dean, *Elementary School Administration and Organization*, U.S. Department of Health, Education and Welfare. Washington, D.C.: Government Printing Office, 1961, p. 27.

[9] Martha Smelker, "School Progress in a Highly Transient Area," unpublished master's thesis, Ohio State University, 1960.

Chapter 3

Nongraded School Organization: The Elementary School

The Nongraded Elementary School—A Reality

William P. Colbert

There are many teachers in our schools who have developed a remarkable sensitivity to the needs of children. Sometimes, they have received a considerable amount of help from the supervisory and administrative personnel in their schools in attending to these needs. They have, for example, been allowed to set aside the standard content and texts designed for specific grade levels and work entirely on the basis of the kinds of things the pupils were ready and eager to learn. At other times, unfortunately, these teachers have found their efforts thwarted by a number of predetermined arrangements which, ironically, were once intended to expedite the process of educating our children. Some crucial questions before us at this point seem to be: Is the graded elementary school, with the administrative and curricular procedures which are so typical of this type of school organization, one of these outmoded arrangements? Does the graded school actually discourage teachers from developing the kind of sensitivity and creativity needed for working with today's children who will be senior citizens in the twenty-first century?

In one sense, the nongraded school has always been a reality. Children have always differed one from another. And even today, in this age of uniformity and the assembly line, children are more different than alike. To find evidence of this fact, we need only to move to the nearest school and look. When we get there, we might find ourselves looking at a group

Written especially for this book. William P. Colbert is Assistant Professor of Education, University of North Carolina, Greensboro.

59

of children who are alike on two counts. They may, for example, be all nine years old and in the fourth grade. If we are looking at this group with the idea of helping them learn, we will probably find a common starting point difficult, if not impossible, to come by because of the vast range of differences that prevails. Tim, Mary and Sue might have not only different grade equivalent scores in reading, but their strengths and weaknesses may also be in different reading skill areas. To deal with these children as though their reading problems were identical is at least a waste of time. The more time we spend looking for differences within any given age or grade group of children, the more we are bound to find. For the purposes of teaching, then, the graded school is more of an illusion than a reality.

The present-day system of school organization known as the nongraded school certainly warrants the examination and study of all those who are interested in dealing with the realities of helping children learn. In this chapter, the reader will find some of the more important statements which have been made concerning its definition, value and prospect for the future. In the first article, Marian Franklin has done an excellent job of defining some important terms that are continually used in discussions concerning nongrading. She has also put forth some very concise answers to the questions that constantly recur concerning the total nongrading concept. A reading of this selection will help the reader gain a fuller understanding of the articles that follow.

Louis DiLorenzo and Ruth Salter, in another article in this chapter, are especially concerned with the reality of nongrading and what they refer to as, "the actual differences between graded and nongraded primary schools." Their summary of the findings of some comparative research studies that have been done will give the reader some leads as to the kinds of research efforts that have been attempted in this area.

The kind of teaching competence required in nongraded schools is identified by Madeline Hunter. Perhaps some readers will be surprised to learn that it is the same type that has been advocated and discussed for years in professional circles. The reason for this, as Mrs. Hunter points out, is that "teaching a nongraded group is based on the same learning principles as good teaching in any group." The significant difference may well be that learning principles get more of a chance to function as guides for action in schools with fewer predetermined arrangements such as grade lines.

Nongraded Schools

Marian Pope Franklin

Nongrading is a plan for classifying students and moving them through a school program. It is primarily an administrative arrangement that recognizes individual differences; meets a student where he is; provides for his continuous progress at his own speed; makes suitable provision for him in the teaching, the grouping arrangements, the curriculum, and the materials; discards grade labels (i.e., first, second, third, etc.); replaces grade standards and uniform academic requirements with sequential subject-matter levels; permits inter- and intra-class grouping and movement; rewards the efforts of students; strives to challenge each student; develops a sense of adequacy in students; provides a reporting system consistent with its philosophy; eliminates failure and social promotion.

Both graded and nongraded schools have a plan for assigning students and teachers. Students may be grouped homogeneously on the basis of a single factor such as chronological age, IQ score, or achievement score. This decision is made in both graded and nongraded schools.

In addition to deciding whether students are grouped homogeneously or heterogeneously it must be decided how they will be taught. In a typical elementary school during the first half of the 20th century, students were taught in self-contained classrooms and had a single teacher all day. Sometimes they had specialists for their art, music, or physical education classes. A few elementary schools had a departmentalized teaching arrangement with specialists teaching each subject. Pupils thus had four or five teachers under such a plan. In still other schools, students were in core classes and had a teacher who combined two of their subjects such as English and social studies or mathematics and science. Such students had two or three teachers. In the last half of the 20th century team teaching was introduced in some elementary schools. Under such an arrangement students were taught by teachers with different staff functions. Junior and senior high schools were also similarly organized horizontally; however, the typical arrangement was departmentalized for these older students.

The vertical arrangement of a school is either graded, nongraded, or

Reprinted from *Educational Forum* 30:331–334, March 1966, by permission of the publisher, the author, and Kappa Delta Pi, An Honor Society in Education, owners of the copyright. Dr. Marian Pope Franklin is Professor in the School of Education at The University of North Carolina in Greensboro.

some combination of these two arrangements. This is where the philosophy of a graded and nongraded school differs. In a nongraded school students are assigned to classes on criteria other than chronological age. In some cases it is on the basis of achievement in a subject. On the primary level of the elementary school, for example, reading achievement appears to be the main basis for grouping students. In a few cases students are grouped on their social maturity, emotional maturity, or interests. In the nongraded junior and senior high, students are usually grouped for each class on the basis of their achievement in each subject.

A nongraded primary unit replaces the traditional kindergarten through grade three of a graded school. Some pupils may complete the work of the primary unit in less than four years while others might need more. Students in a nongraded primary unit may cover the same content as those in a graded unit. However, there is no calendar date when it must be "passed." Instead, there are differentiated rates of academic progress. Nongraded primary units in Milwaukee, Wisconsin; Cedar Falls, Iowa; and Westport, Connecticut, permit limited acceleration (approximately one semester) for students who learn rapidly. If there is an intermediate unit, the accelerated pupils are moved to it. If there is not, pupils start the fourth grade a semester early. Other school systems, such as Edmonds, Washington; Park Forest, Illinois; and Pontiac, Michigan, plan enrichment activities for those who finish the work of the primary unit early.

Most of the school ungrading is currently at the primary level. In 1960, the primary nongraded unit existed in almost one-fifth of the urban centers in the United States. Another additional 13 per cent of the urban centers indicated its possible future adoption.

An intermediate nongraded unit replaces the traditional grades 4-6. Again, a student progresses at his own rate. He may progress faster or slower than the equivalent of one grade per year. He has no grade expectations which he must reach or against which his teacher must pace him. Instead, the teacher tries to keep him working up to his capacity. Fast learners are usually given enrichment activities or are accelerated. Slower pupils are given additional time. All types of students are assured of success with appropriate rewards as long as they diligently pursue work that fits them.

Some schools that originally operated a primary nongraded unit experienced enough success to extend the plan. This happened in California at Emeryville, Marysville, and Pleasanton; in the state of Washington at Bellevue, Aberdeen, Highline, Edmonds, and Lynwood; in Shawano, Appleton, and Fond du Lac, Wisconsin; in the Douglas School System at Ellsworth Air Base, South Dakota; in the Wasatch School in Provo, Utah; in Elmira Heights Central School at Horseheads, New York; in the Emerson Elementary School at Dayton, Ohio; in the public schools of Chicago, Illinois; in the Elmhurst School in Greenville, North Carolina; and in the schools in San Angelo, Texas.

There are several schools that are nongraded above the sixth year. Nongraded junior high schools exist at Dutch Neck, New Jersey; Setauket and Greenlawn, New York; Mason City, Iowa; Newton Centre, Massachusetts; Kalamazoo, Michigan; and Chattanooga, Tennessee. There are nongraded high schools at Eau Gallie, Fort Lauderdale, Melbourne, Satellite Beach, and Tallahassee, Florida; Franklin and Treadwell, New York; Newport, Rhode Island; and Pittsburgh, Pennsylvania.

Professional literature contains many commentaries, testimonials, and subjective judgments as to the strengths and weaknesses of the nongraded school. Unfortunately, there is only a limited amount of research with an adequate design (i.e., matched experimental and control groups and adequate statistical treatment of data). It must be concluded, therefore, that the effectiveness or ineffectiveness of the nongraded organization has not been established.

A comprehensive survey of the literature clearly indicates that those individuals and groups who are experimenting with the nongraded plan are generally enthusiastic with their results. Statements such as the following are typical:

> "The primary nongraded system is working well." Manor Plains, Huntington, New York
>
> "According to Stanford Achievement Test results, pupils in nongraded units were significantly higher in all language arts and reading achievement." Washington Elementary School, Flint, Michigan
>
> "Many slow learners who were allowed to progress at their own rate accelerated during subsequent years, regaining time lost in the early stages." Christ the King School, St. Xavier College, Chicago
>
> "The ungraded primary benefits all children. Gifted children are not allowed to underachieve, nor are slow learners frustrated by repeated failure." Mary Skapski, Burlington, Vermont
>
> "Ungraded primary results so far have been fewer complaints from parents, greater teacher satisfaction, and the elimination of boredom on the part of bright pupils." Vestal Central, Vestal, New York
>
> "There is no failure and no boredom. The arrangement has special advantages at an age when children often progress in spurts, and it virtually assures a successful experience in early school years that will shape a wholesome attitude toward school in the future." Public Schools, East Williston, New York

"Nongraded grouping practices, based on planning for continuous, sequential growth, tend to encourage increased pupil achievement and improved pupil attitude." Betty Ann Ritzenheim, Detroit (Michigan) Public Schools

"The entire junior high of 300 pupils works without grades. The full three-year program consists of a series of twelve separate steps in each subject. This last step is equivalent to the tenth grade or higher. Pupils can move from one to the next at any time according to achievement." Public Schools, Setauket, New York

"Students at Melbourne High have been reclassified in line with their level of achievement and assigned to fluid learning situations in each subject on the basis of their need. Spurred by the increased intellectual excitement of their students from nongraded high schools, colleges too will turn to the nongraded systems." Dr. B. Frank Brown, Melbourne, Florida

"This educational program is truly tailored to individual needs and brings into practice the theory of 'taking each student as far as he can go.'" Burt Kaufman and Paul Bethune, Nova High School, Fort Lauderdale, Florida

The Ungraded Primary School in Milwaukee

Florence C. Kelly

The ungraded primary school program was organized in the Milwaukee Public Schools in January, 1942, under the direction of the late superintendent Lowell P. Goodrich (1942–1949). It was an attempt to solve the problem of the traditional pattern of promotion-failure which assumed, among other things, that all children were fundamentally alike and which ignored in practice the findings of research on child development. Since its initiation in one school in 1942, the ungraded program has been adopted on a voluntary basis in 115 of the 116 elementary schools. This progress has taken place because the Board of Education, principals, teachers, parents, and the general public have come to recognize and appreciate the values inherent in the ungraded primary school structure. By now it is more than a theory; it is an established fact.

In order to understand the program as operating in Milwaukee, certain areas need to be considered. This article will attempt to explain

1. the basic philosophy underlying the plan,
2. some desirable classroom practices which help its implementation,
3. the process of recording and reporting progress,
4. the orientation program for teachers and parents,
5. an evaluation—a look at ourselves as we work,
6. a look to the future.

PHILOSOPHY

The ungraded primary school organization is a means of making functional a philosophy that has been talked about for years. It is a most effective way of adjusting teaching and administrative procedures to meet the individual and irregular development of each child. It permits adaptation to the variations in pupils' mental ability and readiness, physical capacity and social adjustment. The ungraded primary school plan is not a method of teaching but rather an administrative tool to encourage and promote continuous and steady growth according to each child's own pattern.

At an early age and throughout each school year, the rate and pattern

Reprinted from *Delta Kappa Gamma Bulletin* 29:49–57, Summer 1963, by permission of Delta Kappa Gamma Society International and the author. Until her retirement, Florence C. Kelly was Director of the Division of Primary Curriculum and Instruction for the Milwaukee Public Schools.

of learning of each child are carefully studied; and soon parent, teacher, and child become aware of these patterns. Progress, however slow or fast, is recognized and the rate is maintained in keeping with the child's potential, readiness, and learning pattern. Teachers feel free to concentrate on these areas because academic pressures have been removed. Blockings, frustrations, confusions which can develop under the scheme of grade groupings, artificial standards, and promotion-failure practices are reduced and often prevented.

ORGANIZATION OF CLASSES

Milwaukee Public Schools operate on a semester basis and time spent in the primary school is recorded in terms of semesters beyond the kindergarten rather than grades. Since these children never have been graded, it is simple for them to fall into the ungraded sequence.

How does it work? Children who indicate a readiness to leave the kindergarten enter the primary school as Primary[1], P^1, which means they are in the first semester beyond the kindergarten. They then progress to Primary[2], P^2, (second semester), Primary[3], P^3, (third semester), and so on through P^6, P^7, P^8, as the case may warrant before entering the fourth grade. These designations P^1 through P^8 serve only as convenient indicators of how many semesters a child has been enrolled in the primary school. These symbols do not show academic achievement or performance. Academic progress is measured by achievement in reading, language arts, arithmetic, and other areas of learning rather than by the amount of time spent in the primary school. Since the curriculum is fluid and flexible with no areas or skills allocated to any one semester, the readiness and academic differences for learning can be adjusted to the child's needs and pattern.

Within the beginning group, just out of kindergarten, the teacher soon becomes aware of various maturation levels and growth patterns. She realizes that she must adapt her handling of these children to their special needs and must provide developmental experiences. This study and analysis of children continues through the primary school years. With proper guidance many children who otherwise would have been repeaters or skippers in the traditional graded structure make satisfactory adjustments.

Some children need more time, others less to satisfy their growing and learning needs before going into fourth grade. No amount of pressure beyond their ability will develop desirable learnings, attitudes, interests, and habits. This thinking carries through to the entire primary school experience—a respect for the growing power with all of its irregularities.

Most children complete the primary school in six semesters, but rapid and slow achievers are given special consideration. They find themselves in groups geared to their particular problems. If retardation appears, indicating that a child may need seven or eight semesters to find himself before entering the fourth grade, his experience will be extended accordingly. No child is asked to repeat what he has already learned, but he is helped to adjust his learning to his own slower pattern and thus progresses with a sense of interest and achievement rather than one of frustration or failure. Serious retardation is detected early and is handled through special channels.

A child who is maturing rapidly also gets attention. His program of acceleration must be interesting and challenging and may result in a shorter time for him in the primary school. He may enter the fourth grade from P^4 or P^5. His program is adjusted so that there is no break in his learning, no skipping as was the traditional method for the rapid learner. With both of these groups, slow and rapid achievers, the parents are contacted early and are made aware of the situations. These contacts result in better understanding and cooperation with the homes and schools.

The total length of time any child spends in the primary school depends upon his potential, accomplishment, and overall readiness for the fourth grade. However, no child ever remains in the primary situation longer than four years.

GROUPING PRACTICE

Many of the administrative and teaching problems have been eased by the cooperative planning of principal and staff within each building. This pre-planning done at the close of each semester provides a workable program for the coming semester. Principals and teachers study adjustments of children and decide on grouping and placements for the new term. Because of their contacts with and analysis of children in and out of the classroom, teachers are valuable persons at this time. They are the ones who really know the children and can bring to the "staffing" recommendations for wise placement.

What areas are considered at these staffings? Decision usually centers around items that will include the following:

1. Social grouping—sometimes determined by semester levels—so that children will be neither too young nor too old for working together. They must experience security and importance;

2. Teaching-learning grouping—determined among other things by readiness level, interest and performance, skills in other areas, work habits, interest and attitudes. Children need a lush environment and a range of learning opportunities and experiences within the group to provide for explorations and growth;

3. Adjustment grouping—considered for individual children who have personal problems that require consideration.

At all times the principal and the teachers are aware of flexibility in establishing these groups. If they find later that a child needs to be shifted from one room to another, this is done. The staffing judgments are not always final. Allowances must be made for error and for the possibility of change and variation in a child's developmental pattern. This adjustment from room to room is no problem. Door cards for classroom identification help. These cards are labeled "Primary School, Miss . . . . ," with no indication of the semester groupings within.

When the staffing is over, each teacher may find herself with several semester groupings—for example P³, P⁴, P⁵—as well as several learning levels within her classroom. As she begins to adjust curriculum content, materials, and experiences to her group, she finds a range of learning pattern and interest. Because of careful planning during the group staffing, she is not overwhelmed with a cumbersome range of learning and soon sets up her tentative working groups. As stated elsewhere, there is no curriculum material allocated to any one semester so the children really set their own starting point—where they are.

This is especially true in the field of reading. To provide for continuity in the developmental program of reading and related skills, a pattern of twelve progressive levels of achievement has been established. These levels provide for reading performance, for word analysis, and for other study skills. The teacher recognizes that the children will be at different stages of development and in setting up her working groups considers the range of potential and achievement. Since there are no reading levels as *musts* for any one semester, children advance from level to level regardless of semester. Evaluation of growth includes the total program of reading performance, skills, interest, and wide independent reading.

To meet the range of reading abilities and interests within the primary school, a variety of reading materials is provided. No one series of books is adopted as a *must*, but small sets of many different books, classified according to reading levels, are made available. Each teacher is free to select reading material from a list of many titles. Books for developmental and independent reading are supplied in abundance. This means that all children need not read the same book nor the same number of books. The type of book read, the interest and attitude displayed, and the effort put forth by a child are better indications of reading power than is the number of books read.

An individual reading record sheet shows the twelve levels of reading, and beginning with level three lists the available developmental books by levels. No child is ever expected to read *all* the books on a level nor is he asked to read a certain number of books before going on to the next level.

His readiness to advance is the determining factor. Books that are not used in group work may be read independently at any time. Teachers within each school building cooperate in analyzing and organizing reading materials. This enables the entire primary staff to know the available books and to make wise selection in the purchase of new books for additional or replacement purposes. The teacher checks the books read by each child and the semester in which he read them. In so doing she prevents a break in the continuity of the developmental reading program. She knows what books the children have read during previous semesters and is able to challenge and interest her groups with new materials. This record accompanies each child through his primary school years and into fourth grade.

A progress report is sent three times a semester to parents of primary school children. For parents' information, under growth in learning skills it states: "This form of progress report covers the years in the primary school. It takes time to recognize the learning power of each child. In these early years, growth may be rapid during one period and slow during another. Therefore it seems wise to use a narrow marking system—two symbols—until the growth and power can be more definitely determined. In the beginning each child will be marked in some areas but not in others." The two symbols used are "C"—is making progress—and "D"—needs to improve. Each child is marked on the basis of his own ability and effort and not in comparison with other children.

Specific items under *Personal and Social Development* are checked, not marked or graded, when a child needs to improve. This card also notes with a check mark, any special interest that a child may display in arts and crafts, music, stories and poetry, science, creative activities, and the like.

Reading progress is also included in this report. A chart of the twelve levels of reading carries with it a space for a date after each level.

The following statements printed on the report help parents to understand and interpret the data on the Reading Progress Chart:

1. As children progress from Level 1 to Level 12, the reading material becomes more difficult.

2. The latest date indicates the level on which the child is reading. A final hint to the parent states that a conference between the parent and the teacher is desirable.

ORIENTATION PROGRAMS—PRINCIPALS, TEACHERS, AND PARENTS

Principals, teachers, and parents are important in this child-interest organization and must be involved. The success of the primary school depends upon their understanding and acceptance of the underlying philosophy procedures and classroom practices.

In initiating the program in each school, the faculty must understand and accept it before meetings can be planned for parents. The program involving all the administrative details as portrayed in this article is carefully considered and discussed. No pressure is used and at times more than one meeting is held before a decision is made. It might be stated here that the method of moving slowly from one semester to the next in this initial period has often been a determining factor in the final affirmative decision.

It is well to remark also that if the philosophy of this early period is to carry into the upper elementary years, the entire faculty of a school should be present at these meetings. Mr. Goodrich once remarked: "Unless an entire faculty accepts the philosophy within which each teacher becomes an expert with respect to children of similar maturity, the real objective of the program may be sacrificed."

Once the primary faculty has consented to make the shift into the ungraded primary, meetings are set for parents of the children involved. The same problems that were presented at the teacher meetings are discussed with parents. Their "Yes" is considered as important as the teachers' vote. Both groups feel a sense of ownership and genuine responsibility because each has made its own decision.

Following these initial meetings, yearly or semester meetings for both teachers and parents have been held. With many new teachers and new parents of children leaving the kindergarten and becoming P¹ in the primary school, orientation meetings are necessary for them.

Through the years these meetings have developed good parent understanding and have contributed much to the success of the undertaking. Each parent group has been eager to have its children participate in the program and at no time has there been evidence of a desire to return to the traditional structure. In most elementary schools today the parent gathering, especially for those whose children are entering P¹, is standard procedure. Attendance is excellent and most encouraging. These splendid cooperative efforts of faculty and parents result in good working relations. Parents are free to come to school at any time and are invited in small groups to watch and follow the progress of children at all levels. This makes for smoother conferences at times of decisions in retardation, acceleration, a temporary disturbance, or a problem of a serious nature.

The planning, cooperation, and participation involved in these orientation programs require real work, but the result more than compensates for the effort expended.

SUCCESS AND SHORTCOMINGS

Does the philosophy outlined above work as easily as it writes and talks? The answer is *"NO"*—but the satisfaction and success compensate for the pitfalls and shortcomings. A gratifying amount of success is forth-coming when the practices recommended in this article are followed. One thing is certain. There can be good teaching without the ungraded primary school, but there is better with it.

The weaknesses and shortcomings have developed mainly because of lack of understanding and because of faulty interpretation of language used. The most serious have been due to the following practices:

1. Poor grouping—
   Piling up or bunching of problems; slow learners, social misfits, and the like at the end of the six semester period. These should have been adjusted earlier.
   Too wide a range of learning levels within one room.
   Advancing all children from one room to another as an entire group.
2. Misuse of language—
   Attempting to convert semesters into grades.
3. Pressures—
   Pushing some children too hard and others not enough.
4. Faulty interpretation of progress card—
   Reading growth not understood, changing date and advancing children too rapidly or retaining children too long on one date.
5. Poorly planned or skipped orientation programs for parents and teachers.

These and some others have not been too serious—and no one in itself would have been too disturbing—but if allowed to accumulate or if left unexplained they could have produced serious situations. Through clarification of faulty concepts, these shortcomings have been converted into assets.

A LOOK AHEAD

What about tomorrow? As new parents, children, and teachers, new global discoveries and happenings, horizons, curricula, and materials; new theories, concepts, and research findings confront the educational world, the personnel of this world are pledged to carry on and expand the activi-ties—vertically and horizontally—that offer so many challenges for chil-dren. A few of these challenges are:

1. *Extension and expansion of the program beyond the primary years.*
   Dr. John Goodlad[1] states in a recent article:

   At present the nongraded scheme is most prevalent at the pri-mary level. A few plans extend into the upper elementary grades.

[1] John I. Goodlad, "Inadequacy of the Graded Organization," *Childhood Education*, February, 1963, p. 277.

In an isolated community or two, consideration is now being given to the possibility of nongraded junior and senior high schools. There is no reason why the nongraded concept cannot be extended from kindergarten through the entire twelve—or—thirteen year structure of education. In fact the very logic of nongrading leads to a continuous stream of elementary and secondary education.

2. *New and more effective instruments or programs for measuring growth, not standardized achievement tests as we know them today.*

A prominent educator once remarked:

The day you assess the worth of your primary school with a battery of achievement tests you are putting back on the jacket you are attempting to take off.

Milwaukee uses no such battery in its primary schools but relies on teacher judgment, child performance—not just academics—and overall maturity in looking for growth and progress.

3. *Some criteria for analyzing elements in social maturity:*
   What is social maturity?
   How and when should it be measured?
   What should a teacher or parent look for?
   Not a check list of items!

4. *More effective grouping patterns:*
   What criteria should be used here?
   If education means the process of developing individual persons, then grouping practices need more study.

In one area especially individualizing instruction is being discussed, written about, experimented with to such an extent that the teacher must have help today with its interpretation. Where and how can she adjust the practical items when establishing working groups within her room?

There are other areas of concern, of course, but in due time they will be explored. As a child passes through developmental stages to reach maturity, so too goes the primary or ungraded school through its stages, slowly but positively, step by step, day by day. And so—on to another day!

Co-operative Research on the Nongraded Primary

Louis T. DiLorenzo and Ruth Salter

In the current welter of new directions and innovations in education, the nongraded primary unit stands out as a prime contender for attention at the elementary level. The most complete commentary on nongrading—as well as the most impassioned plea for it—is found in Goodlad and Anderson's book, *The Nongraded Elementary School* (1). A number of articles in school publications have described the operation of nongraded programs in individual communities, and various educational journals have reported the trend toward this plan of school organization.

Here we would like to give a composite picture, based on the literature, of the primary school without grades, to indicate the extent of research on nongrading and to describe a cooperative experimental study comparing graded and nongraded schools now in operation.

While the nongraded approach to the organization of early school life has come into prominence in just the past four or five years, it is not new. Milwaukee began its Primary School, the oldest existing nongraded program, in 1942. Moreover, the nongraded-primary plan is only one of many attempts to counteract the rigidities of the graded system that dominates American education at both the elementary and the secondary levels. Since the middle of the nineteenth century, when grades became the standard pattern for school organization, the individualization of instruction, which is the basic concept of nongrading, has been proposed in various guises—the philosophy of John Dewey, the Batavia plan, the Winnetka plan, the Dalton plan, and many others.

DEFINING THE NONGRADED UNIT

The nongraded unit has been defined as a pattern of elementary school organization designed to insure full recognition of individual differences in the instructional setting by the elimination of arbitrary grade classifications and grade expectations. The nongraded unit has also been described as an organizational arrangement that permits continuous educational progress for all by providing individual children opportunity to

Reprinted from *Elementary School Journal* 65:269–277, February 1965, by permission of the publisher and the authors. Louis T. DiLorenzo and Ruth Salter are with the New York State Education Department.

work at their own rates of speed without fear of failure. The nongraded unit is, in short, an administrative device for putting into practice a democratic philosophy that emphasizes the value of the individual child (2).

The nongraded unit is based on the following assumptions (3, 4):

1. The school program should be flexible so as to meet the varying developmental needs and growth patterns of individual children.

2. Each child should have the opportunity to achieve at his own rate.

3. Learning should be continuous.

4. Greater achievement results when children experience success in school.

5. Larger blocks of time for maturation and development will improve pupils' personal-social adjustment.

These assumptions reflect the results of studies of human development which have shown that not all children mature at the same rate, that they do not learn at the same rate, and that their rate of learning and accomplishment may not be the same in all areas or at all times. These assumptions are also consistent with those learning theories which assert that individual potential is subverted by failure, unnecessary restraint, or inadequate stimulation.

The reasons most frequently cited for the change from a graded to a nongraded plan are, in fact, increased emphasis on individual differences and research that purports to show the detrimental effects of nonpromotion (2).

Concern for achievement in reading is another recurrent reason for adoption of a nongraded plan, reading achievement being the most common basis for class assignments and for intra-class grouping in nongraded primary systems.

THE NONGRADED PRIMARY IN OPERATION

Goodlad and Anderson once arbitrarily defined the nongraded school as one "where grade levels have been removed from a minimum of two grade levels" (5). The need for an arbitrary—and somewhat mechanical—definition is evident. A survey of the current writings on the nongraded unit shows that while there is a certain consistency in the philosophy behind the various attempts to eliminate grade barriers, there is great variety in the scope of the efforts and the practices and procedures employed. However, some generalizations are possible.

The nongraded unit usually replaces Grades 1, 2, and 3; kindergarten may also be included. In some localities, nongrading has been extended to the intermediate years of the elementary school and, in a few instances, to the junior and senior high schools as well. Generally, there is a distinct cleavage between the primary and the upper elementary levels. Our concern here is the primary unit, which is also known as the primary progress plan, the primary block, the primary school, or the primary cycle.

Theoretically, a nongraded primary program, regardless of its name tag, has these characteristics (2, 4):

1. There are no grade labels.

2. The curriculum is organized in sequential work units which are units of achievement, not units of time.

3. Promotion is based on individual progress, not on time spent in a grade.

4. Intra-class grouping and movement between classes are flexible.

5. Good school-home communication is emphasized.

The most immediate physical sign of a nongraded school is the absence of the customary classroom labels. The signs "Grade 1," "Grade 2," and "Grade 3" have come down, and all rooms of the unit bear the single designation "Primary."

Generally, the initial primary class assignment is made at the end of the kindergarten year. Factors considered in this assignment are reading readiness, personal maturity, social adjustment, and mental ability as determined by tests and teachers' evaluations. Children in a given class vary in ability, but the range is narrower than that found under heterogeneous grouping. Goodlad and Anderson have recommended that there be three ability gradations in each class and some overlapping of ability levels in different classes so that there may be an easy transition from one to another (1, 4, 6, 7).

Under a nongraded primary system, the curriculum is divided into levels—a series of short stepping-stones that vary in number from seven to as many as thirty-two. Levels are most frequently described in terms of reading achievement. In a few systems, levels have also been established for arithmetic and spelling, but this arrangement is far less common. At each level, certain skills are to be acquired. Progress to a succeeding level depends on attainment of these skills. The time required for completion of a given level depends on pupil capacity; there is no penalty for failure to achieve in a stated time span; each child works at his own rate. Pupils may be transferred from one class to another at any time in accordance with their learning pace and other individual needs (1, 3, 4, 8).

Thus, in a nongraded primary unit, a slow child may take four years to cover the work the average child does in three, while the academically talented child may cover the same work in less time. The slow learner does not repeat work because of nonpromotion, and the bright child neither skips material by jumping grades nor becomes "bored and lazy" waiting for less able pupils to catch up with him (6, 9).

Most descriptions of nongraded units indicate that a child who has remained in the primary program for four years is moved on after that time regardless of his achievement. There seem to be three possibilities for the child who spurts ahead of his classmates: If he is mature socially and emotionally, he may be moved on to the fourth grade; he may be given fourth-grade work while remaining with his age peers; or he may be given enrichment material. In some plans, certain levels (say the fourth and the ninth of a nine-level sequence) are designated as enrichment levels and are covered only by the brighter children (7, 8).

The elimination of grades calls for a new system of reporting pupil progress. This is done in various ways. General trends are the abandonment of numerical (per cent) grades, the increased use of report forms that incorporate check lists or descriptive comments, and heavy reliance on teacher-parent conferences. Often teachers maintain files of samples of pupils' work. Skill cards may be used to show pupil achievement in a number of areas over the course of the primary unit. Accomplishment is measured in terms of individual capacity rather than grade standards (2, 6).

Under a continuous-progress plan, there are no annual promotions. The child returning to school after summer vacation resumes his studies at the point where he left them in June. In some systems, pupils have the same teacher for the entire primary sequence.

THE REALITY OF NONGRADING

While the number of nongraded programs is steadily increasing, the literature evidences some doubt about the actual differences between graded and nongraded primary schools. There is a growing suspicion that nongrading has no reality—that it is merely a change in vocabulary which is not accompanied by any change in teaching practices, in what happens to the child in school, or in what is expected of him. To rephrase this doubt in the words of our initial definition of nongrading, the grade labels are eliminated, but the grade expectations remain; there is no more individualization of instruction than before adoption of the plan.

This doubt is reinforced by some of the written descriptions of nongraded programs. At Chicago's Tesla School, for example, children in the nongraded elementary units are given dual ratings. A letter indicates their grade or level standing; a numeral, the degree to which they use their innate ability. An article extolling the Tesla plan proudly states that the school uses two sets of graded reading textbooks; the article then reports that the supplementary reader serves both as an additional basic textbook for those who have not mastered the necessary skills and as enrichment material for the more able (4).

The notion of continuous progress is seemingly contradicted by the inclusion in many nongraded programs of "enrichment" levels covered only by the brighter pupils. These children are, in effect, marking time until others catch up with them or until they reach a certain age level.

It might be expected that a plan for continuous progress with recognition of individual differences would result in interage classes, but such classes are rare. Age itself, or length of time in school, which is closely related to age, is considered in making class assignments. Only one system mentioned the possibility of early school entrance. In Appleton, Wisconsin, children who will have their fifth birthday in September, October, or November, after the regular cut-off date, may, at the request of their parents, be tested for admission to kindergarten. The observation was made that this program is "moving slowly toward eliminating age barriers, but rapidly toward respect for individual differences" (7).

Once class assignments are made there is apparently little movement between classes. In Chicago's Tesla School, for example, there is provision for transferring pupils to different classes during the year, but transfers are "more or less the exception" (4). Completion of the primary program in less than the usual three years seems also to be more or less the exception. It is estimated that only 2 per cent of nongraded pupils do this; similarly, only 2 per cent spend a fourth year in the primary unit (10). One must wonder whether such a small proportion of the pupil enrollment could not be served by plans that require something less than the total reorganization of the elementary school.

A curious exception to this avoidance of interage groups is suggested by a report on an "Achievement Grouping and Teacher Specialization Plan" used in East Brunswick, New Jersey. Here, nongraded homogeneous grouping (in Grades 4, 5, and 6) has produced classes of equal size, and the plan is seen as a happy solution to the problem of adequate space and staff that can arise with a graded system and variation in grade populations (11). In this case, one form of contrived uniformity may be replacing another.

The beneficial effects of any new program, any new ways of doing things, are generally recognized. Administrators have reported that the institution of nongrading has stimulated teachers, increased their emotional involvement in their teaching tasks, and drawn their attention to curriculum development and content. One must ask, however, whether such reports are descriptions of the Hawthorne effect in operation, reflections of the administrators' hopes, or genuine evidence that nongrading has brought change.

RESEARCH ON THE NONGRADED PRIMARY

In 1958 Goodlad wrote, "Nongrading is supported by some plausible-sounding claims and theories rather than by research" (5). In 1959, with Anderson he wrote in regard to the comparative achievement of pupils in graded and nongraded schools, "there is no evidence to suggest anything. We have little more than inadequate firsthand impressions to go on" (1). From 1959 to the present, eight comparative research studies have been reported (12–19). We shall summarize the findings but make no attempt to evaluate the relative quality of the investigations.

Six studies made comparisons in reading achievement primarily in Grades 3, 4, 5, and 6. Four studies (13, 16, 18, 19) found the performance of the nongraded pupils significantly superior to that of the graded pupils; one (15) found no difference; and one (12) found the graded control group significantly better than the nongraded experimental group. Of five studies that compared the two kinds of organization on arithmetic achievement, four (13, 14, 17, 19) found statistically significant advantages in favor of nongrading; the findings of the other study (12) favored graded classes. All three comparisons (13, 16, 19) on spelling achievement favored the nongraded pupils.

The findings cited here are hardly conclusive; they would not warrant a decision to adopt a nongraded organization. Most of the studies were based on new or relatively short experiences with nongrading. The variations in the programs make it impossible to treat them as eight replications of the same treatment.

MULTIDISTRICT STUDY

Since the basic claims of the nongraded plan still needed testing, the New York State Education Department decided to conduct an investigation that would not only build on the previous data, but would also overcome the limitations that faced the previous investigators.

One of the first steps taken was to determine the extent to which the nongraded primary unit was being used in New York State. A survey of the 861 operating districts in the state, conducted in 1963 by the Division of Research, yielded a response of 521 returns and the data reported in Table 1. These findings are remarkably similar to those of a nationwide survey conducted in 1959 by the NEA Research Division. In the NEA study the 71 school systems that reported use of the primary block constituted 8.6 per cent of the 819 districts responding (9, 20).

The number of nongraded programs in New York State and the number of districts interested in cooperating in research with the State

TABLE 1

Responses of 521 New York State School Districts to Questionnaire on Nongraded Elementary-School Programs

Response	Number	Per Cent
Nongraded program in operation one, two, three, or more years	50	9.6
No nongraded program but planning one for 1963-64	9	1.7
No nongraded program but desire help in becoming nongraded	2	.4
No nongraded programs past, present, or anticipated	449	86.2
Nongraded program discontinued	3	.6
Respondent confused nongraded program with ungraded program for retarded	8	1.5
	521	100.0

Education Department on such programs were sufficient to warrant a study of the nongraded concept and practice.

Before the 1963–64 school year, the department employed Robert H. Anderson, a strong proponent of nongrading, as a consultant and invited the chief administrators of sixteen school districts to explore the possibility of a cooperative study of nongradedness under Experimental Programs, a special state-aid program to encourage research for the improvement of instruction.

In an initial work conference, Anderson stated that the emphasis in nongrading is on individualizing the educational program and that the behaviors of pupils and teachers are the chief measures of nongradedness. Efforts to define nongrading resulted in a suggestion that it has three aspects:

1. A philosophy or value system with individualization as its foundation.

2. A distinctive administrative framework including school organization, structure, and nomenclature.

3. Special operational elements—teaching materials, curriculum, teaching procedures, public relations, and reporting practices.

The relative significance of these aspects was debated. Attention centered on how much individualization can be achieved without abandoning traditional terminology.

At a second work conference, attention was given to the specification of essential characteristics or minimal conditions of nongradedness. These conditions were:

1. An adaptable curriculum—operationally defined.
2. Inventorying and diagnosis for teaching.
3. Individualized instruction (for example, subgrouping).
4. Non-forced and unobstructed learning.
5. A reporting system consistent with the philosophy.
6. A nongraded program in both reading and arithmetic.
7. The absence of grade labels and related machinery.

Three aspects of nongraded programs were considered appropriately subject to variation: teacher utilization, pupil grouping, and policies on interclass transfers. Possible variations under teacher utilization are team teaching, self-contained classrooms, the use of special teachers, and teacher cycling. Pupil grouping might be homogeneous, heterogeneous, or interage.

In the discussion of objectives and methods of operation, there was considerable agreement among the districts on reasons for change. The reasons, in order of priority, were more individualized instruction, more continuous progress, elimination of holdovers, and better mental health of pupils.

Most of the districts that wished to participate in the experimental program had been operating one school or more on a nongraded basis for a number of years. Several had, in fact, pioneered the movement in New York State, but a few of the districts were just beginning the transition to a nongraded organization. The schools were to spend the 1963–64 school year in working toward the minimal conditions of nongradedness to qualify for participation in the evaluative stage of the research in the 1964–65, 1965–66, and 1966–67 school years.

To assure the attainment of the minimal conditions, the school districts called on college and university specialists to lecture, conduct workshops, hold conferences, and provide consultant services for their administrators, teaching staffs, and parents. Thus faculty members at Boston University, Fairleigh Dickinson University, Harvard University, Hofstra University, Hunter College, New York University, Queens College, the State University of New York at Buffalo, Syracuse University, and the University of Rochester became involved in the project. University assistance was also sought for the over-all research design, the construction of tests, and the planning of classroom observation procedures for the study.

At the end of the year, twelve districts were selected for the evaluative phase of the study: Bainbridge, East Irondequoit, Glen Cove, Hastings-on-Hudson, Marion, Maryvale, Niagara Falls, Plainedge, Port Washington, Vestal, West Irondequoit, and Yorktown Heights.

In the present study special attention will be given to a question which was not considered in any of the earlier studies. That is, to what extent are the desirable outcomes a function of the teacher's commitment to a nongraded philosophy, irrespective of the school's graded or nongraded designation? The study will test the assumption that teachers in a graded school may also offer individualized instruction. At the same time, teachers in a nongraded school may adhere to a graded philosophy. Teachers will be tested on their knowledge of and attitude toward a nongraded philosophy, and comparisons will be made of teachers' scores in graded and nongraded schools.

Taking into account the claims and counterclaims of nongraded and graded schools and the strengths and the limitations of past research, the present study will attempt to provide an empirical basis for an important decision—not the decision to elect or reject the nongraded school, but the decision to adopt the critical features essential in realizing the principle of individualized instruction, whether they be common to graded or nongraded schools.

REFERENCES

1. John I. Goodlad and Robert H. Anderson. *The Nongraded Elementary School.* New York: Harcourt, Brace and World, 1959.

2. Lillian Gore. "The Nongraded Primary Unit," *School Life,* XLIV (March, 1962), 9–12.

3. Hugh V. Perkins. "Nongraded Programs: What Progress?" *Educational Leadership,* XIX (December, 1961), 166–69+.

4. Jerome H. Gilbert. "Multigraded Developmental Plan Focuses on Pupil Achievement: Tesla School Breaks through Traditional Graded Structure," *Chicago Schools Journal,* XLIII (February, 1962), 209–14.

5. John I. Goodlad. "Classroom Organization," pp. 221–26. *Encyclopedia of Educational Research.* New York: Macmillan Company, 1960 (third edition).

6. Florence C. Kelly. "Ungraded Primary School," *Educational Leadership,* XVIII (November, 1960), 79–81.

7. Arthur D. Morse. *Schools of Tomorrow Today,* pp. 27–40. Albany: University of the State of New York, 1960.

8. Thomas Ultican. "Blue Springs Reports on First-Year Experiences with the Ungraded Primary Plan," *School and Community,* XLVIII (October, 1961), 22, 46.

9. National Education Association, Research Division. *Nongrading: A Modern Practice in Elementary School Organization,* Research Memorandum 1961–37. Washington, D.C.: National Education Association, 1961.

10. Celia B. Stendler. "Grouping Practices," *Those First School Years,* 1960 Yearbook of the Department of Elementary School Principals, National Education Association. *National Elementary Principal,* XL (September, 1960), 147–65.

11. Richard C. Anderson. "The Case for Nongraded Homogeneous Grouping," *Elementary School Journal,* LXII (January, 1962), 193–97.

12. Robert F. Carbone. "A Comparison of Graded and Non-Graded Elementary Schools," *Elementary School Journal*, LXII (November, 1961), 82–88.

13. Joseph W. Halliwell. "A Comparison of Pupil Achievement in Graded and Nongraded Primary Classrooms," *Journal of Experimental Education*, XXXII (Fall, 1963), 59–64.

14. Richard H. Hart. "The Nongraded Primary School and Arithmetic," *Arithmetic Teacher*, IX (March, 1962), 130–33.

15. Kenneth D. Hopkins, Malcolm L. Williamson, and O. A. Oldridge. "An Empirical Study of the Comparative Reading Achievement and Sociometric Status of Pupils in Ungraded and Graded Schools." Paper presented at the annual meeting of the American Educational Research Association, Chicago, February 15, 1963.

16. Vivien Ingram. "Flint Evaluates Its Primary Cycle," *Elementary School Journal*, LXI (November, 1960), 76–80.

17. Malcolm M. Provus. "Ability Grouping in Arithmetic," *Elementary School Journal*, LX (April, 1960), 391–98.

18. Mary K. Skapski. "Ungraded Primary Reading Program: An Objective Evaluation," *Elementary School Journal*, LXI (October, 1960), 41–45.

19. John R. Zerby. "Comparison of Academic Achievement and Social Adjustment of Primary School Children in the Graded and Nongraded School Program," *Penn State Review of Educational Research*, XIII (May, 1961), 33.

20. National Education Association, Research Division. *Administrative Practices in Urban School Districts, 1958–59*, Research Report 1961–R10. Washington, D.C.: National Education Association, 1961.

Teachers in the Nongraded School

Madeline C. Hunter

Changes and new decisions bother all of us. I was beset with misgivings the moment I found that the ignition switch on my new car was on the left instead of on the right side of the steering wheel as it had been in my former car. These uneasy feelings started to compound as I began to suspect manufacturers of sadistic perverseness. The drive selector on this car was also in a different place, the drive positions were not what I was used to, and I had to set the emergency brake by hand instead of by foot.

As I fought through the maze of new "feels" and places for my hands and feet, with typical human resistance to change, I regretted turning in my comfortable old model. It was too late to reverse my decision, however, so with the skills (and attitude) of a six-year-old with mixed dominance I decided to take my elderly mother for a ride while I got used to the recalcitrant mechanical monster.

"Whatever are you doing?" Mother asked in amazement as I lost my usual complacency and muttered a string of descriptive phrases which are best forgotten.

"I'm trying to decide which drive position to use," I explained snappishly.

"I'm glad that when I was learning to drive, the horse made most of those decisions," she said, primly smoothing her skirts.

Horse sense indeed! But oh how much more comfortable and effective is my new car, now that I am used to it.

I had the same problem of adapting to change when I first started using the "gear selectors" of nongrading. As a teacher in a nongraded school, it was up to me to make recommendations as to how each individual in my present class should be placed next semester. Which of my fellow teachers would bring out the best in Johnny? Should Mary and Sally continue to be in the same group or should they be separated? This decision-making brought into devastating visibility my lack of knowledge of that great middle group in my class—those children who learned just enough and conformed just enough that they never had received my full educational concern.

Reprinted from *NEA Journal* 55:12–14, February 1966, by permission of the publisher and the author. Madeline C. Hunter is Principal of the University Elementary School, University of California, Los Angeles.

Once the students were assigned to instructional groups, major learning decisions became the responsibility of individual teachers, rather than of the curriculum council or the textbook committee. No longer could the same graded materials be dealt out to an entire class; every teacher had to make professional judgments as to which book and which level of content was appropriate for each child in his class.

The use of educator decisions rather than system decisions is the hallmark of the truly nongraded school. Why do I say "truly nongraded"? Because if you are a teacher in an elementary school that assigns students to a levels program or that groups learners in different classrooms according to ability and achievement, you have eliminated astrology as the guiding principle for placement of children, but you have substituted something not much better. In place of numerals representing the date of birth, you have substituted the numerals from the score of a reading, general achievement, or intelligence test. Such a score is designed to give normative data for large groups; it is not supposed to yield diagnostic data relevant to the optimal placement of individual children in instructional clusters.

Each September, those of us who teach in a nongraded school greet a group that differs radically from those in most other American classrooms. The boys and girls have not all been born within a certain twelve-month period and teachers, therefore, do not have to depend on some fortuitous juxtaposition of the planets at the time of their birth for all to go well. Learners assigned to any one teacher have been diagnosed as responding well to that teacher's style of teaching. Likewise, the sociometric composition of each group has been designed to foster the optimal growth of individual members.

What a refreshing relief it is for teachers to know that each child is beginning the year with a fresh start; that they don't have to brace themselves in anticipation of one of those class groups that moves as an indigestible lump through the school.

Decisions regarding teaching style and peer group that have already been made about class membership help to eliminate such undesirable stereotypes as "worst reader," "poor sport," or "sloppy worker." Similarly, positive reputations such as "best reader," "most popular girl," and "team captain" need to be re-earned in the new group, thereby strengthening an ability that has been manifested.

Everything possible has been arranged in advance to optimize learning and now it's up to the teachers. It is quite a responsibility! No longer can anyone take refuge in the excuse, "He didn't even have fractions in *her* room so what do you expect *me* to do?" Teachers are expected to teach each pupil from wherever he is to as far as they can take him.

No longer is the goal to cover certain material (much of which should be "covered" and appropriately laid to rest). The question changes from, "Has the student done it?" to "Has the student learned it?" We, as teachers, must be able to confidently answer "yes" before moving on.

Selecting for the learner an appropriate task at the correct level of difficulty is the responsibility of each teacher in the nongraded school. This implies assessing the effectiveness of each day's teaching—a task not always conducive to the well-being of one's ego. The fact that a teacher thinks he has taught base ten gives him no license to go on unless he is sure it has been learned.

In a nongraded school, teachers facing, for the first time, a three-year age span of learners are appalled by the anticipated range of abilities. After a few weeks they are further shaken by the realization that they do not know which children are the youngest and which the oldest without looking it up.

After changing to nongrading, one experienced first grade teacher came to her principal complaining, "I can't teach five-, six-, and seven-year-olds in the same class. Why, some of them are not even ready to read, two can read at a third grade level, and one can read at a fifth grade level."

Upon investigation it was discovered that those not ready to read and those reading at third and fifth grade level were all six-year-olds. In the typical first grade class the wiggly, twitchy little six-year-old boys would have been "excused" from the reading group. ("John, take your book and sit over there until you can listen.") The able six-year-old readers would have willingly read "Run, Sally, run" to please such a nice teacher.

Because this teacher was in a nongraded classroom she was forced to the disquieting realization that the typical first grade reading program is inappropriate for some six-year-old children, yet perfectly appropriate for some five- and seven-year-olds. Nongrading does not necessarily assure a wider range of abilities; it does inexorably force teachers to make educational provision for the range they have.

Placement of children, using the criteria of teaching style and peer group composition, presents a new and often unexplored area of decision-making for teachers.

When a teacher in a nongraded school was asked what instructional group she would recommend for seven-year-old Howard in the coming year, she replied, "Give him a teacher who will really get after him. His mother has babied him so that he needs someone who means business."

The next day, however, Howard's teacher amended her recommendation by saying, "I've been watching Howard. When I ran late in my art period and started snapping out orders for cleanup, he just went to pieces. I've decided that he needs a teacher who is not too strict and who will give him support. At the same time, he needs a peer group that will really push him intellectually. He has such a quick mind that the children in his present group never challenge him enough to force him to refine his ideas."

The following day, Howard's teacher came to the office a third time. "Someone told Howard, 'Gee, that was a lousy picture you made' and Howard burst into tears, so I guess he's not ready for too much challenging." She concluded with, "You must think I can't make up my mind, but I'm not used to making these kinds of decisions."

None of us is used to making these kinds of teaching decisions. They represent a new and rigorous dimension in the process of education. These decisions, also, represent the impact of recent research which indicates that a powerful educational environment can make significant and pervasive changes in the individual.

It is not easy to assume the responsibility called for in a nongraded classroom. No longer can the teacher go to the textbook room and check out a set of fifth grade math books. He must begin by assessing at what point each child is able to function, and build the next appropriate skill on a stable foundation. In doing this, the teacher has the satisfaction of knowing that he is not making mathophobes out of the children who are not ready for fractions and that he is not developing indolence and indifference in those children for whom fractions are too easy.

When I used to teach in a graded classroom, I always existed in a frenzy of apprehension for fear I couldn't get place value taught to Johnny before his mother found out he wasn't having long division with the rest of the group.

In a nongraded school, we never have the rigid floors and ceilings of expectations that existed in the traditional graded materials. In a nongraded room, those graded books with dots on the back don't have the power to say, "Everybody should be here." Consequently, children do not need to experience failure and they cannot attain success without effort. As a result, they should become more self-propelling in their learning.

Teaching a nongraded group is based on the same learning principles as good teaching in any group. Teachers present appropriate material at the correct level of difficulty for each child. The difference is that in a nongraded school they do it openly, for it is what they are expected to do, whereas in a graded group some teachers have to bootleg appropriate learning opportunities.

It is easy for a teacher to get caught in a platitudinous trap and wail, "I can't prepare thirty different lessons for thirty different children!" No one expects him to. The tailored education of nongrading does not mean a different lesson for every child, but rather an appropriate lesson for each. With practice, teachers develop skill and facility in modifying academic content and teaching strategies so that they will be in keeping with realistic but rigorous expectations for children. (You should see me drive my new car now!)

Selected Bibliography

Nongraded School Organization:
The Elementary School

"Albany Plan of Primary School Organization." *Elementary School Journal* 36:413–416, February 1936.
> *Describes plan based on chronological age and reading readiness used in Albany, New York in 1936. There was no repeating or skipping but continuous progress through achievement levels at varying rates. Article is of historical significance.*

Anderson, Robert H. "Organizational Character of Education: Staff Utilization and Deployment." *Review of Educational Research* 34:455–469, October 1964.
> *Points out a school experiment usually involves many changes. Nongrading, for example, stimulates interest in team teaching. Discusses team teaching, sub-professional personnel, the flexible school, nongrading, grouping, flexible scheduling, and technology.*

Anderson, Robert H. "Some Types of Cooperative Teaching in Current Use." *National Elementary Principal* 44:22–26, January 1965. Included in Chapter 8.
> *Gives examples of team teaching, of nongrading, and of experiments designed to overcome disadvantages of the traditional graded school.*

Anderson, Robert H. *Teaching in a World of Change.* New York: Harcourt, Brace and World, 1966.
> *Includes chapters on organization of schools, nongraded school, cooperative teaching, and school library and materials center.*

Association for Childhood Education International. *Toward Effective Grouping.* Bulletin 5-A. Washington, D.C.: the Association, 1962.
> *Shows impact of cultural change on school grouping practices. Describes programs in Appleton and Milwaukee, Wisconsin, and Salt Lake City, Utah.*

Austin, Kent C. "The Ungraded Primary School." *Childhood Education* 33:260–263, February 1957.
> *Describes the Continuous Progress Primary at Westwood School, Park Forest, Illinois. Gives the orientation plan, school procedures, and a summary of the community evaluation.*

Austin, Kent C. *The Ungraded Primary Unit in Public Elementary Schools of the United States.* Doctoral Dissertation, University of Colorado, 1957. Also in *Dissertation Abstracts* 19:73–74.
> *Used a questionnaire to gather information on the objectives, development, operation, professional staff, and public relations of the ungraded primary unit.*

Austin, Mary C. and Morrison, Coleman. *The First R: The Harvard Report*

on Reading in Elementary Schools. New York: Macmillan Company, 1963.
Recommends flexible grouping to provide for individual differences. Says the ungraded approach, at least in reading, should be tried so pupils will be free to progress according to their ability.

Beggs, David W. and Buffie, Edward G. (Editors). *Independent Study*. Bloomington, Indiana: Indiana University Press, 1965. pp. 68–82.
Describes the independent study programs, facilities, and instructional materials for the elementary school.

Bethune, Paul. "The Nova Plan for Individualizing Learning." *Science Teacher* 33:55–57, November 1966.
Describes nongraded continuous progress science program for the elementary and secondary years developed at Nova School, Fort Lauderdale, Florida.

Bishop, C. W. "Role of the Local Administrator in Reorganizing Elementary Schools to Test a Semi-Departmentalized Plan." *Journal of Educational Sociology* 34:344–348, April 1961. Also see references by Heathers, Stoddard, and Trachtman.
Describes the elementary school Dual Progress Plan at Ossining and Long Beach, New York. Half of the day is in a graded arrangement and half in a nongraded.

Black, Hillel. "A School Where Children Teach Themselves." *Saturday Evening Post* 11:60–85, June 19, 1965.
Describes Valley Winds Elementary School in suburban St. Louis, Missouri. Nongrading, team teaching, and independent study are featured.

Blackstock, C. R. *A Field Study to Initiate an Ungraded Primary School in Brazesport*. Doctoral Dissertation, University of Houston, 1961. Also in *Dissertation Abstracts* 22:2258.
Concludes ungraded primary, when properly introduced, merits close attention for its overall advantages to teacher and pupils.

Bockrath, Sister M. Bernarda. *An Evaluation of the Ungraded Primary as an Organizational Device for Improving Learning in Saint Louis Archdiocesan Schools*. Doctoral Dissertation, St. Louis University, 1958. Also in *Dissertation Abstracts* 19:2819–20.
Compared reading test scores of students in graded classes with those in ungraded. Found ungraded students had a median reading increase of five months over that of graded. A questionnaire further revealed overwhelming majority of primary teachers in St. Louis Archdiocese favored ungraded program.

Brickell, Henry M. *1961 Catalogue of Educational Change*. Albany, New York: State Department of Education, October 1961.
Survey of changing instructional practices and description of programs in public and non-public elementary and secondary schools of New York State. Includes nongraded references.

Brossard, Chandler. "A School for the Future." *Look* 29:55–56, March 9, 1965.
Description of the Garden Springs Elementary School in Lexington, Kentucky. Nongrading and achievement level grouping are features.

Buffie, E. G. *A Comparison of Mental Health and Academic Achievement; The Nongraded School vs. The Graded School*. Doctoral Dissertation,

School of Education, Indiana University, 1962. Also in *Dissertation Abstracts* 23:4255.
Measured mental health and academic achievement in four graded schools with that of four nongraded schools. All differences favored nongraded.

Carbone, Robert F. *Achievement, Mental Health, and Instruction in Graded and Nongraded Elementary Schools.* Doctoral Dissertation, University of Chicago, 1961.
Showed clear-cut models of grading and nongrading were not yet available. The curriculum practices and the goals of instruction in some of the nongraded schools in his study appear graded even though they were labeled nongraded.

Carbone, Robert F. "Non-Graded School: An Appraisal." *Administrator's Notebook* 10: September 1961. Also see *Elementary School Journal* 62:82–88, November 1961.
Reports study of the relation between organizational structure and instructional practices. Schools designated as nongraded were accepted for study. No criteria had to be met. Concludes a change in school organization will not produce higher academic achievement unless it is accompanied by appropriate adaptations in the instructional practices.

Chadwick, Ruth E., *et al.* "The Report Card in a Nongraded School." *National Elementary Principal* 45:22–28, May 1966.
Describes the efforts of an elementary staff in a nongraded school to design a report card consistent with its philosophy.

Chastain, C. S. *An Experimental Study of the Gains in Achievement in Arithmetic and Reading Made by the Pupils in the Intermediate Grades in the Rangeley, Colorado, Elementary School Who Were Introduced in Traditional Classrooms, in Achievement Platoons, and in Nongraded Classrooms.* Doctoral Dissertation, Colorado State College, 1961. *Abstracts of Field Studies on the Degree of Doctor of Education* 23:75–79, 1962.
Compared test scores of pupils in arithmetic and reading in grades 4–6 with students of achievement-platoon classes and nongraded classes. Concluded no significant differences in achievement due to grouping homogeneously by achievement and/or ability. Teacher opinion poll revealed most parents, pupils, and teachers preferred the nongraded school and it was better for all three.

Clara Francis, Sister and Mary Loretta Rose, Sister. "Ungraded School System Offers Greater Advantages Than the Graded School System." *National Catholic Education Association* 60:429–436, August 1963.
Debate by two supervisors whether teachers in a graded or nongraded school system can give more attention to individual differences.

Cowles, Gardner. "Speech at Annual Meeting of the National School Boards Association." *Education USA*, April 8, 1965.
Editor of Look *points out the importance of early years of schooling. Recommended first three grades be organized into ungraded units.*

Dean, Stuart E. "Nongraded Schools." *Education Brief.* U.S. Department of Health, Education, and Welfare, Office of Education. Brief OE 20009. Washington, D.C., July 1964.
Describes graded and nongraded structure and curricular implications. Gives pros and cons, evaluation, research results, etc. Reports studies with contrasting findings.

Dean, Stuart E. "Nongraded Schools: Is There Magic in It?" *School Life* 47:18–23, December 1964.
Summarizes growth, development, and application of nongrading. Gives pros and cons of plan.

Drinkard, Mary Barbara. *A Comparison of Achievement in Skills of Written Expression Between Third Year Children in Nongraded and Graded Elementary Schools.* Master's Thesis, University of North Carolina, 1963.
Compared written skills of 30 graded pupils with those of 30 nongraded. Differences favored nongraded.

Dufay, F. R. *The Development of Procedures for the Implementation of the Nongraded Primary School in Central School District No. 4, Plainview-Old Bethpage, New York.* Doctoral Dissertation, New York University, 1963. Also in *Dissertation Abstracts* 25:2311.
Recommends adopting nongraded plan at a gradual pace, modifying existing grouping to allow some interage mixing, and changes in promotion policy.

Dufay, F. R. *Ungrading the Elementary School.* West Nyack, N.Y.: Parker Publishing Company, Inc., 1965.
Defines ungraded school. Gives preludes to starting an ungraded program in a Long Island elementary school. Describes the role of specialists in art, physical education, music, etc. Reports techniques tried.

Edgerton, Alice K. and Twombly, Ruth W. "Programmed Course in Spelling." *Elementary School Journal* 60:380–386, April 1962.
Report of a third grade spelling experiment in Weston, Massachusetts. Has implications for individual work in graded, nongraded, or multigraded schools.

Enevoldsen, C. L. *An Evaluation of the Ungraded Primary Program in Selected Schools in the Lincoln, Nebraska Public School System.* Doctoral Dissertation, University of Nebraska Teachers College. 1961. Also in *Dissertation Abstracts* 22:3054.
A study to determine the degree of success of the ungraded primary program in Lincoln showed there was very little difference in basic structure between the graded and the ungraded. It was logical, therefore, that the researcher found no significant difference in academic achievement. Reports principals, teachers, and parents still favored the ungraded plan.

Estes, Nolan. "Nation's School of the Month: Valley Winds Elementary School, St. Louis County, Missouri." *Nation's Schools* 75:61–64, March 1965. Also see Hillel Black. Other references by Estes in *School and Community* 51:8–9, May 1965 and *Audiovisual Education* 10:142–143, February 1965.
Describes outstanding school with nongraded, team teaching program.

"Explorations in Education." *School Management* 3:58, February 1959.
Reports the extension of an ungraded plan from grades 1–3 to 4–8 in Edmonds, Washington.

Ferguson, D. A. and Neff, N. "The Nongraded School Administers to the Dull-Normal Child." *School and Community* 47:16–17, October 1960.
Identifies advantages of nongraded plan for the slow learner.

Ford, J. P. *An Analysis of Organizational Structure and Peer Status in a Nongraded School.* Doctoral Dissertation, University of California, 1965. Also in *Dissertation Abstracts* 26:5578.

Analyzed relationships between formal organization (team teaching and self-contained classroom) and the informal organization (peer status and the characteristics attributed to it). Tested five hypotheses.

Franklin, Marian Pope. "Nongraded Organizational Patterns: Theory and Practice." *Virginia Journal of Education* 56:11–13, April 1963.
Describes nongraded philosophy, organization, and practice.

Frazier, Alexander. "Needed: A New Vocabulary for Individual Differences." *Elementary School Journal* 61:260–68, February 1961.
Points out nongrading frequently results in the modification of only one dimension, rate of learning.

Glogau, Lillian and Fessel, Murray. *The Nongraded Primary School: A Case Study.* West Nyack, N.Y.: Parker Publishing Company, 1967.
Describes operation of a nongraded primary. A "how we did it book," written by the administrators.

Goldberg, Albert L. "Programmed Spelling: A Case Study." *Audiovisual Instruction* 8:94–96, February 1963.
Report of the development and successful use of first grade programmed spelling in Livonia, Michigan. Has implications for graded, nongraded, or multigraded classrooms.

Goodlad, John I. "Individual Differences and Vertical Organization of the School." *Individualizing Instruction.* Sixty-first Yearbook of the National Society for the Study of Education, Part I. Chicago: University of Chicago Press, 1962. pp. 209–38.
Discusses form and function of vertical school organization. Gives ways to modify the graded structure. Describes and appraises some nongraded plans.

Goodlad, John I. "Meeting Children Where They Are." *Saturday Review* 48:57–59, 72–74, March 20, 1965.
A classic in nongraded literature in which the author compares graded and nongraded concepts.

Goodlad, John I. and Anderson, Robert. "Education Practice in Nongraded Schools: A Survey of Perceptions." *Elementary School Journal* 63:33–40, October 1962. Also see *Elementary School Journal* 62:261–269, February 1962; and *Education Digest* 31:8–11, May 1966.
Surveyed reasons for introducing nongrading and the changes effected by the authors.

Goodlad, John I. and Anderson, Robert H. *The Nongraded Elementary School.* Revised Edition. New York: Harcourt, Brace and World, Inc., 1963.
Describes the philosophy underlying nongrading and gives the details of putting the plan into action. Includes chapters on curriculum, reporting pupil progress, mental health, and organization.

Goodlad, John I. and Hunter, Madeline C. "The Big-City School—Problems and Prospects." *PTA Magazine* 59:81–90, April 1965.
Shows children from harsh environments began school with handicaps. Points out characteristics of adequate schools and suggests nongraded organization can help meet them.

Goodlad, John I. and Rehage, Kenneth. "Unscrambling the Vocabulary of School Organization." *NEA Journal* 51:34–35, November 1962.
Points out need for a common vocabulary in describing school organization.

Goodrich, L. P. "Organization and Individual Progress in the Primary School." *Wisconsin Journal of Education* 65:232, January 1933.
Reports schools in Fond du Lac, Wisconsin abolished graded system in the primary years in favor of a primary school. Reading achievement was the chief grouping criteria. Article is of historical interest.

Hanson, Lincoln F. "Schools Using Programmed Materials." *Audio-Visual Instruction* 8:101–103, February 1963.
Reports grade level listing of school systems using programmed instruction. Useful for planning independent study activities in graded, nongraded, or multigraded schools.

Heathers, Glen. "Dual Progress Plan." *Educational Leadership* 18:89–91, November 1960. Also see articles by Trachtman, Stoddard and Bishop.
Description of Dual Progress Plan in grades 3–8 in Long Beach and Ossining, New York. All teachers are full-time specialists in one of seven curricular areas—language arts, social studies, mathematics, science, physical education, arts and crafts, and music.

Hickey, Sister Mary Paul. *Analysis and Evaluation of the Ungraded Primary Program in the Diocese of Pittsburgh.* Doctoral Dissertation, Fordham University, 1962. Also in *Dissertation Abstracts* 23:2817.
Study of 754 ungraded and 603 graded primary students favors ungrading.

Hillson, Maurie. *Change and Innovation in Elementary School Organization.* New York: Holt, Rinehart and Winston, 1965.
A selection of readings concerned with ability grouping, departmentalized and semi-departmentalized plans, team teaching, dual progress, multigrading, and nongrading.

Hillson, Maurie, *et al.* "A Controlled Experiment Evaluating the Effects of a Nongraded Organization on Pupil Achievement." *Journal of Educational Research* 57:548–550, July–August 1964.
A report of an experiment with 26 students in a graded arrangement and 26 in a nongraded to discover the effects of such organization on reading achievement. Study favors nongrading.

Hoflich, Right Rev. Msgr. J. E. "Ungraded Primary." *National Catholic Education Association Bulletin* 57:8–25, November 1960.
Describes the ungraded primary grouping arrangement in all the elementary schools of the St. Louis, Missouri Archdiocese. Reports failure pattern has been cut 10–15 per cent since program has been functioning.

Hunter, Madeline C. "Dimensions of Nongrading." *Elementary School Journal* 65:20–25, October 1964. Also in *Education Digest* 30:35–38, November 1964.
Describes nongrading as a plan that forces decisions concerning the educational opportunities that most successfully advance the learning of each student.

Hunter, Madeline C. "When the Teacher Diagnoses Learning." *Educational Leadership* 23:545–549, April 1966.
Points out the importance of diagnosis and prescription for all learners. Article has implications for teachers of graded, nongraded, and multigraded classrooms.

Hunter, Madeline C. "You—as a Diagnostician." *Instructor* 76:31, 126, February 1967.

Asks teachers to determine appropriate learning tasks and instructional materials on the basis of a diagnosis of each student's present knowledge in each subject. Such diagnosis is absolutely essential for prescribing in nongraded or multigraded schools. It should also be true of graded ones.

Ilg, F. L. and Ames, L. B. "Viewpoint on School Readiness." *School and Society* 92:397–402, December 26, 1964. This article is Chapter 1 of their book *School Readiness: Behavior Tests Used at Gesell Institute,* Harper, 1964.

Advocates nongrading and grouping on the basis of developmental readiness through junior high.

Jaffa, N. Neubert and Brandt, R. M. "Approach to the Problems of a Downtown School." *National Elementary Principal* 44:25–28, November 1964.

Account of nongraded organization, team teaching, and in-service education in a Baltimore elementary school.

Jaquetta, F. C. *A Five Year Study to Determine the Effects of the Ungraded Classroom Organization in Reading Achievement in Grand Junction, Colorado.* Doctoral Dissertation, Colorado State College of Education, 1959.

Found pupils from ungraded schools made significantly higher scores at the 1% level of confidence in mean reading achievement than the pupils from graded schools.

Johnson, Glenn R. "Lots of Smoke but Little Fire." *Educational Forum* 29:159–164, January 1965.

Questions evidence supporting claims made for the nongraded school. Gives 10 guidelines for implementing new elementary school organizational structure.

Keller, Charles R. "History and Social Sciences: Selections and Recommendations." *Journal of Secondary Education* 37:263–270, May 1962.

Says the curriculum should be kept flexible so it will fit the nongraded elementary and secondary school. Suggests scope and sequence.

Kelly, Alice Jo. *The Ungraded Primary Program: An Analysis of the Plan with Emphasis on Its Use in North Carolina.* Master's Thesis, University of North Carolina at Chapel Hill, 1963.

Identifies organization and basic philosophy of the ungraded primary unit and the use of the plan in North Carolina.

Komoski, P. Kenneth. "Programmed Instruction: New Technique for Independent Study." *PTA Magazine* 56:15–17, March 1962.

Recommends programmed instruction for homework assignments at every level.

Kvaraceus, William C. "The Behavioral Deviate in the Culture of the Secondary School." *Frontiers of Secondary Education, Proceedings and Conferences on Secondary Education.* Syracuse: Syracuse University Press, 1958. pp. 18–27.

Points out age-grade grouping implies to teachers and pupils an equality and homogeneity that does not exist and leads to undifferentiated instruction through use of the single text and identical assignments. Recommends broader grouping by overlapping age membership in some classes and ability achievement grouping in others.

Mary Alice, Sister. "Administration of the Non-Graded School." *Elementary*

School Journal 61:148–152, December 1960. Also see *Elementary School Journal* 57:268–271, February 1957.
Account of nongraded classes at St. Xavier College Elementary School in Chicago. Discusses use of teaching teams and teaching aides.

Moore, Daniel I. *Pupil Achievement and Grouping Practices in Graded and Ungraded Primary Schools.* Doctoral Dissertation, University of Michigan, 1963. Also in *Dissertation Abstracts* 24:32–33.
Investigated the differences in reading and arithmetic achievement between pupils in an ungraded primary and a conventional graded organization in four schools in Wayne, Michigan. Mean score of graded pupils exceeded that of ungraded in nearly all measures of achievement.

National Council of Teachers of English. "Topics of Current Interest." *Education* 84:313, January 1964.
Briefly describes continuous Progress Primary Plan used in Philadelphia, Pa. since 1961.

National Education Association, Department of Elementary School Principals. *Elementary School Organization: Purposes, Patterns, Perspective.* Forty-First Yearbook. Washington, D.C.: the Department, 1961. pp. 78–92, 115–125.
Gives report of history, current trends, and future development of elementary school. Discusses vertical school organization and team teaching and gives its merits and disadvantages.

National Education Association. Project on Instruction Report. *Planning and Organizing for Teaching.* Washington, D.C.: the Association, 1963. pp. 53–92. Filmstrip and accompanying record available.
Concise discussion of vertical and horizontal school organization. Recommends nongrading and team teaching.

National Educational Association. *Project on Instruction: Schools for the Sixties.* New York: McGraw-Hill Book Co., 1963. pp. 71–98. Also summary report in *NEA Journal,* January 1964.
Overview volume of publications of the Project on Instruction. Gives thirty-three recommendations for improving school curriculum, the classroom, materials, etc. Encourages nongrading.

National Education Association, Research Division. *Nongraded Schools.* Washington, D.C.: the Association, Research Memo. 1965–12. Also see *NEA Research Bulletin* 43:93–95, October 1965.
Survey revealed more than half of the largest school systems (enrollment of 100,000 or more) are using nongrading in one or more schools. Cites advantages and disadvantages.

National Elementary Principal. December 1961 and May 1966.
Entire issue of magazine devoted to either school organization or report cards. Has implications for graded, nongraded, or multigraded schools.

National Society for the Study of Education. *Individualizing Instruction.* 61st Yearbook, Part I. Chicago: University of Chicago Press, 1962. pp. 239–264.
An analysis by Robert H. Anderson of the nature of individual differences between and within pupils and of school practices that encourage individualizing instruction. Describes teacher orientation necessary to make individualizing effective.

National Society for the Study of Education. *The Changing American School.*

65th Yearbook, Part II. Chicago: University Press, 1966. pp. 32–84 and 110–134.
Includes two chapters by John Goodlad on the changing role of the teacher and the curriculum and a chapter on school organization by Glen Heathers.

"One-Room Schoolhouse." *Time* 77:41, May 5, 1961.
Describes nongraded cluster grouping in an elementary school in Carson City, Michigan.

Peters, Kenneth L. "Achievement Levels: Easy Half Steps to a Nongraded Plan." *Nation's Schools* 74:32–33, July 1964.
Report of a nongraded elementary plan in Beverly Hills, California.

"Planning and Operating the Middle School." *Overview* 4:52–55, March 1963.
Upper elementary grades (5–6) were combined with junior high grades (7–8–9) at Bedford School in Mount Kisco, N.Y. Subject matter ungraded as rapidly as possible. Organized around teaching teams.

"Plan Takes Lockstep and Buries It in Space." *Nation's Schools* 72:86–89, October 1963.
Presents nongrading and team teaching as practiced in the Josiah Haynes Elementary School, Sudbury, Massachusetts. School was planned and built for nongrading and team teaching.

Pratt, H. Milton. "Space—A Plan to Meet Children's Needs." *Instructor* 76:19, January 1967.
Principal from Cocoa, Florida describes operation of nongrading and team teaching in Brevard County. Says the administrators, supervisors, and teachers say it has enhanced education in Poinsett Elementary School.

Prince, Thomas C. "Trends in Types of Elementary School Organization." *American School Board Journal* 106:37–38, June 1963.
Brief report of status and trends.

Ritzenheim, Betty Ann. *Survey of Personnel Perceptions of Selected Factors in Nongraded Programs in Eight Detroit Elementary Schools.* Doctoral Dissertation; Wayne State University, 1963. Also in *Dissertation Abstracts* 25:5645.
Results from two questionnaires from 52 teachers and 8 principals identifies personnel perceptions concerning nongraded procedures and operation.

Roberts, G. M. *Case Studies of Two Nongraded Elementary School Programs.* Doctoral Dissertation, University of Tennessee, 1964. Also in *Dissertation Abstracts* 25:2830.
A study of achievement grouping in reading at a nongraded elementary school in Brevard County, Florida and ability grouping at nongraded elementary school in Sarasota County, Florida. Team teaching was used in both situations. Gives conclusions.

Russell, James N. *Change and Challenge in American Education.* Boston: Houghton Mifflin Co., 1965. Chapter 4.
Says neither team teaching nor nongrading arrangements fit the entire elementary school but each has a place. Believes elimination of grades fits the early elementary years and specialization and departmentalization fit the upper elementary.

Sanders, David C. "School Organization—How Do You Decide?" *National Elementary Principal* 42:25–28, September 1962.
Describes internal organizational questions facing schools such as: de-

*partmentalization, team teaching, self-contained classroom, etc. Gives a
rationale for making decisions.*

Shane, Harold G. "We Can Find Better Ways of Grouping Children." *Childhood Education* 36:350–351, April 1960.
Suggests a partial solution to the grouping problem can be found in introducing more kindergartens for four-year olds and considering age four and five as an ungraded period of school living for all boys and girls.

Sloan, F. A. "Nongraded Social Studies Program for Grades Four, Five, and Six." *National Elementary Principal* 45:25–29, January 1966.
Proposes nongraded social studies curriculum for middle grades based on concepts.

Smith, Lois. "Continuous Progress Plan." *Childhood Education* 37:320–3, March 1961.
Describes "Continuous Progress" in Appleton, Wisconsin and compares it with the traditional graded structure.

Snyder, Edith Roach. *An Evaluative Study of a Developmental Elementary School Program.* Doctoral Dissertation, Wayne State University, 1957.
Describes nongraded primary plan at Webster School in Pontiac, Michigan.

Stoddard, George D. "Dual Progress Plan in Elementary Education." *Educational Forum* 25:271–6, March 1961. Also see references by Heathers, Bishop, and Trachtman.
The author of the Dual Progress Plan outlines its rationale and describes experience with it in two Long Island schools.

Stoddard, George D. "Dual Progress Plan." *School and Society* 86:351–352, October 11, 1958. Also see the book, *The Dual Progress Plan: A New Philosophy and Program in Elementary Education.* New York: Harper and Brothers, 1961.
Gives details of Dual Progress Plan. Half of the elementary school day includes instruction in social studies and language arts in a graded situation. The rest of the program is nongraded with specialist teachers.

Taylor, Toni. "Look What Two Teachers Have Done in the Little Red Schoolhouse." *Grade Teacher* 82:32–37, 121–122, September 1964.
Report of primary nongrading and team teaching in Gloucester, Massachusetts.

Tewksbury, John. *Nongrading in the Elementary School.* Columbus, Ohio: Charles E. Merrill Books, Inc., 1967.
Deals with the meaning of nongrading, its teaching procedures, curriculum levels, report forms used, etc.

"Topics of Current Interest: Continuous Progress Primary." *Education* 84:313, January 1964.
Brief explanation of the Continuous Progress Primary Plan begun in Philadelphia Public Schools in September of 1961.

Trachtman, G. M. "Role of an Inservice Program in Establishing a New Plan of Elementary School Organization." *Journal of Educational Sociology* 34:349–354, April 1961.
Reports the use of inservice education in preparing for the Dual Progress Plan in Long Beach, New York.

"Ungraded Primary—Has Your Staff Considered It?" *School Management* 3:40–44, 97–98, November 1959.

Details of ungraded programs given in a tape recorded interview with two administrators from Hillsboro, Oregon.

Wilson, Donna. "Pre-Recorded Tapes Teach a Whole Class." *Grade Teacher* 83:41–42, 130, January 1960.
Report of use of tapes in teaching at Norwalk, Connecticut. Has implications for graded, nongraded, or multigraded schools.

Woodring, Paul. "Reform Movement from the Point of View of Psychological Theory." *National Society for the Study of Education.* 1963 Yearbook, Part I. pp. 286–305.
Describes nongraded plan as one of the reforms designed to promote effective teaching and learning.

Zerby, John Richard. *A Comparison of Academic Achievement and Social Adjustment of Primary School Children in the Graded And Nongraded School Program.* Doctoral Dissertation, Pennsylvania State University, 1960. Also in *Dissertation Abstracts* 21:2644.
At end of primary period, nongraded children were eight months advanced over anticipated achievement. Graded primary children exceeded anticipated achievement by five months. Results of sociometric measures were similar. Fewer "isolates" were found in nongraded school.

Chapter 4

Nongraded School Organization: Junior and Senior High Schools

Coping with Individual Differences in the Secondary School

William P. Colbert

In the one-room, nongraded school that once dominated our educational scene, teachers had little choice but to make some effort to deal with individual differences. It was, for example, almost impossible for these teachers to offer the same learning experiences to those children who were just beginning school as they offered to the children who were about to terminate their school career. When our schools became more consolidated, teachers and school administrators found they had many children of the same chronological age. They therefore entered into a grouping arrangement on this expedient basis. The process of placing children to work in various groups was relatively simple. If the child was six years old he was in the first grade, tackling the set curricular tasks for that grade whether or not the tasks were appropriate for him. The following year he would proceed to the second grade and tackle those curricular tasks, unless of course he failed to receive a passing grade in all his work during his first year in school. The underlying belief in this type of arrangement seemed to be that children of the same age are, for educational purposes, more similar than dissimilar.

It didn't take long of course for perceptive teachers to realize that pupils of the same chronological age were hardly similar—at least for the

Written especially for this book. William P. Colbert is Assistant Professor of Education, University of North Carolina, Greensboro.

purpose of teaching. Nor did it take long for teachers to realize that the more time groups of children spent making their way through the graded structure, the more different they became one from another. By the time groups of children reached the secondary schools, the problem of dealing with individual differences became so acute that many secondary school teachers found themselves almost overwhelmed by it. Perhaps many secondary teachers are still at this point. If the reader finds himself among this group, a reading of the contributions in this section will surely move him on.

Does the nongraded secondary school really offer some vehicle for dealing with the vast range of differences one finds at this level? This question can only be answered by the individual reader after he has read and pondered both sides of the question. Some good source material for reading and thinking is provided in this chapter. The article by Abraham Lass and Jerome Bruner is most interesting and presents the two separate views of these most capable discussants and writers. Accounts of two widely celebrated nongraded, secondary school plans are also included. One is, of course, B. Frank Brown's describing the Melbourne, Florida, High School plan and the other is by Burt Kaufman and Paul Bethune which discusses "The Nova Plan." The selection by James McCullough not only discusses the educational program of the Dalewood Junior High School in Chattanooga, Tennessee, but also describes the physical arrangements in a new school building built with the idea of a nongraded program in mind. After the reader has exhausted the sources in this section he will want to examine the excellent bibliography which has been compiled by Marian Franklin.

Chattanooga Builds a Nongraded Junior High School

James D. McCullough

The concept of nongraded programs of instruction is not new to Chattanooga public schools. Pilot programs in elementary schools have been in operation since 1959, but the junior and senior high schools followed the Carnegie one-grade-a-year approach until September, 1963. When it became apparent that a new junior high school was needed in North Brainerd, a rapidly growing suburban area east of Missionary Ridge, the instructional staff began studying the feasibility of extending the nongraded program to the junior high level. The Chattanooga board of education has always followed the philosophy of planning and building its schools in accordance with the needs of the community they are to serve. One nongraded-type elementary program had already proven itself in the Brainerd community. The idea of extending this program to the junior high school was presented to various groups in the community and a preliminary nongraded curriculum was developed by the Division of Instruction for purposes of study.

SPECIALISTS ASSIST IN PLANNING

For the past three years, the board has retained the services of the School Plant Planning Division of the University of Tennessee which operated under sponsorship of the Educational Facilities Laboratory. Specialists in school construction and curriculum from the university worked with the instructional staff and teachers from the school system for a study of feasibility. After it was decided to construct a building flexible enough to accommodate a nongraded program and also to house the more traditional program, the consultants assisted in preparation of educational specifications. It was the desire of the board to design more efficient buildings than those previously constructed in this area. Therefore, the objective of the planning committees was a compact building providing the combination of a nongraded program and a building with minimum corridor space. Plans to air-condition also suggested the practicality of a compact building with reduced glass areas.

Reprinted from *American School Board Journal* 148:71–74, February 1964, by permission of the publisher and the author. James D. McCullough is Assistant Superintendent for Business, Chattanooga, Tennessee, Public Schools.

The services of Butler, Wilhoite & Hildebrand, a Chattanooga architectural firm, were retained by the board prior to preliminary planning of the building. This was consistent with board policy to employ its architects as soon as the need for a school becomes apparent in order that their advice will be available in selection of the site. The architects worked closely with the planning committee. They postponed developing preliminary plans for the building until they had thoroughly acquainted themselves with the concept of the nongraded program and with the philosophy of the board and staff as well as with the recommendation from the consultants representing EFL. The Dalewood building literally was planned from the inside out.

The first schemes that were developed were sketches of areas—science and mathematics, social studies, physical education, fine arts. Acceptable arrangements for these spaces were developed and were studied by the planning committees before an attempt was made to combine them into a building. After several weeks of planning, the staff developed comprehensive educational specifications which they transmitted to the architects for final study. Again the architects spent time studying and analyzing specifications. Only then did they begin to make line drawings which they felt would accommodate the program outlined in detail.

Statistics of the building reflect efficiency in the form of very little corridor and lobby space and a considerable amount of flexibility available to the staff in the form of folding partitions. The unusual shape of the classrooms originated from a sketch submitted by a group of teachers working on the mathematics area. These teachers suggested a small instructional materials center where a team of teachers could work and plan together, store materials, and share ideas as well as pupils. The proposal proved to be in keeping with the compact approach and was incorporated as a general arrangement for one side of the building.

THE EDUCATIONAL PROGRAM

The language arts-social studies block of time is scheduled for all pupils during the first two hours of the day. Mathematics and science are scheduled during two hours in the afternoon, with half the pupils in mathematics and the other half in science; obviously, these groups exchange places midway of this block of time. All exploratory and enrichment courses are scheduled during the middle of the school day, with physical education receiving heavy emphasis during the seventh or last period.

The purpose of this type of schedule is to provide the flexibility required by a nongraded program. To clarify, pupils at varying instructional levels in the language arts-social studies field can be moved with little difficulty from one level to another as the need occurs. Similarly, pupils moving from one level to another in mathematics can do so without disturbing their time schedules.

Achievement of pupil mobility within an instructional area does not depend entirely upon such a schedule, but it is facilitated by a schedule involving the total student body—or half the student body—in the same area.

Natural questions arise as to teacher competency and building efficiency in such an arrangement. Leaders are those teachers with certificates in the instructional area, and their associates have completed more than the average amount of work in the area. Teachers of exploratory courses, all of whom have minors in other areas, are members of either the language arts-social studies teams or the mathematics and science teams. Individual teachers have the experience of taking leadership roles in one area and cooperating roles in another. Planning periods of team members are an essential part of the nongraded program.

The total building is used, though in what might be termed a decidedly nonconforming fashion.

The instructional program is designed for young adolescents of the usual junior high school age range and specifically provides for all boys and girls at whatever achievement levels they find themselves. The goal is continuous growth at the individual's best pace.

CLASSROOMS IN CLUSTER ARRANGEMENT

The four clusters of rooms at the north end of the building serve as the regular classrooms for what might be termed normal use in the core subjects of language arts-social studies, mathematics, and science. These rooms circle the materials center which is immediately available to all of them. A wealth of instructional tools and their ready accessibility are essential features of the nongraded program. Small conference rooms and individual study spaces provide for special teaching-learning activities which are not "special" in this program.

The materials center and the adjacent commons, or cafeteria, are actually in the middle of the four incomplete hexagon-shaped clusters of trapezoid classrooms. These two areas serve for large-group instruction for any of the core subjects. A recent afternoon visit to the school found half the student body—those taking science while the other half were studying mathematics—viewing an appropriate film which was to be discussed subsequently by the students grouped according to their varying levels of science sophistication. The students were comfortably seated in the gay-colored commons which had been speedily and easily converted from eating hall into viewing room. Promptly after the film, the students fanned out into classrooms in two nearby clusters.

The materials center serves as the heart of the educational program. Physically, it has the usual large room of any school library, with bookshelves around the walls and a limited number extending into the reading room. In addition to the main area, there is a rectangular area which can easily seat a class coming from any of the clusters; it provides amply for library research activities without interfering with other students working individually in the library. The study room and two conference rooms in the materials center enable small groups of students to do library research, view projected materials, plan special projects, and carry on other instructional activities under the supervision of the librarian. The audiovisual room is a well-organized storage space, not a viewing area; portable projectors and related equipment are handled by a group of pupils under direction of the librarian. A second storage room, for printed materials and smaller instructional tools, is a librarian's dream come true; it houses those expensive materials frequently needed in the classroom but not required at all times. An upstairs storage room accessible by means of a disappearing stairway expands the provisions for a multiplicity of instructional tools which can be protected when not required for immediate use. A preparation room available to all faculty members is located between the materials center and the commons; here teacher aides and teachers prepare all sorts of projecturals, including transparencies for overhead projectors regularly used in large-group instruction.

Pupils needing developmental reading instruction remain in the language arts-social studies block during the third hour and these include the majority of boys and girls normally designated as seventh and eighth graders. Special grouping is provided for educable mentally retarded pupils. Pupils at the top of the "spiral" or in the upper levels of achievement in these areas have choices among many electives, including two modern foreign languages, vocal and instrumental music, art, mechanical drawing and shop, typewriting, and home economics.

Exploration is the emphasis at the fourth period. All pupils have experiences in the areas where electives are offered at the third period, with the exception of pupils at the top of the spiral who have participated in similar courses during the preceding hour; they have physical education and health at this time.

MUSIC CENTER

The music center, consisting of two main rooms, five individual practice rooms, a music library, and an office provides for general music,

DALEWOOD JUNIOR HIGH SCHOOL
STATISTICS AND COSTS

Plot Area: 20.73 acres

Building Area: 79,494 sq. ft.

Units: 13 Classrooms

1 Outdoor classroom

4 Instructional material centers

1 Material center with audiovisual and teachers' workrooms

1 Staff lounge

1 Commons and kitchen

2 Science classrooms

1 Science laboratory with project room

1 Typing and business classroom with storage rooms

1 Home economics (multipurpose)

1 Choral room

1 Band room with music department office and library

4 Practice rooms and instrument storage

1 Art

1 Planning

1 Shop with finishing and project storage rooms

1 Exercise room

1 Weights room

1 Gymnasium with showers and locker rooms, first aid

1 Boiler room with heating and air-conditioning equipment

1 Administrative with health clinic, conference and offices

Auditorium to be constructed at a later date

Construction Cost:

General	$ 932,212
Kitchen	28,205
Architect's fees	57,625
Concrete testing	1,125
Insurance and legal fees	1,500
All equipment	98,000
Total cost of project as of October 31, 1963 . .	$1,118,667

vocal and instrumental. It is in heavy use at third, fourth, and seventh periods and is also available for correlated activities at the language arts-social studies block in the morning. While music for all students receives major emphasis, performing groups come from pupils at the top of the fine arts spiral.

The home economics and industrial arts quarters provide for unit teaching in the former and general shop and mechanical drawing in the latter. Special teachers are in charge of the instructional program, and they also serve as members of teaching teams for language arts-social studies or for mathematics and science.

The seventh period, following the mathematics and science classes, finds most of the pupils in physical education and health, while those who have achieved high levels in the various instructional levels—the "Quest" group—are engaged in a variety of independent and special group activities, including work on the newspaper, participation in dramatics and a host of other clubs, and research in any of the subject-matter fields. Most of the staff members are necessarily engaged in physical education with the student body though certified personnel are in general charge of the instruction. An important by-product is the different type of relationship established between teachers and pupils when those teachers usually associated with so-called academic areas discover superior achievement among all levels of pupils. Much emphasis is placed on the health aspect of the physical education program, with unusual support coming from the competencies of these "other" teachers including a science teacher who is a registered nurse. The schedule is so arranged that about 75 boys and 75 girls at a maximum are on the gymnasium floor at any time, with three teachers assigned to each group of 75 pupils.

Courses of study as such are not equated with requirements for given grade levels. The sequence of skills, values, and concepts is identified, and pupils move upward in the various sequences at their own pace. The building accommodates this type of spiral mobility, and boys and girls "latch" on at the level where their maturity of understanding and achievement permits. Of particular significance to this type of continuous progress, as far as the physical plant is concerned, are the facilities of the materials center and the relationship of the four clusters of classrooms to each other and to the materials center and commons.

Gradeless Classes

James C. Sandilos

As a school board member or professional school executive, have you ever wondered whether grade designations serve the purpose of teaching a child according to his capacity and achievement?

At West Windsor Township, New Jersey, serious consideration was given to this question, and in the fall of 1956, the curriculum committee of the board of education, in cooperation with the staff of the Junior School, began a study of the curriculum offered to the sixth, seventh, and eighth grades. As a result of the study, a change in the Junior School curriculum was proposed to the board of education. After careful study, the board approved the new program for the Junior School. The program, instituted in September, 1957, provides for a change in scheduling and in the courses of study.

GRADES DONE AWAY WITH

Each pupil is permitted to pursue schedules based on his or her abilities, aptitudes, skills, and interests in the major subject-area fields. Every pupil has the opportunity to select, with teacher and principal guidance, certain additional areas of learning that will be of benefit to his educational progress. Furthermore, the program permits a more valuable use of teacher skills, knowledge, and time devoted directly to the instructional program.

The new curriculum is planned to provide more individual attention to all pupils, but especially to those who have ability and the desire to increase their educational opportunities in any area of learning. The Junior School has done away with grades as such, and the stereotyped levels of sixth, seventh, and eighth grades have given way to new group identities. Each child's mental ability, his present and former achievements, and his social adjustment are considered carefully before he is placed in any particular group.

Reprinted from *American School Board Journal* 136:55, February 1958, by permission of the publisher and the author. James C. Sandilos is Superintendent of Schools, East Moline, Illinois and was formerly with West Windsor Township Schools, Dutch Neck, New Jersey.

To secure the best possible placement for the individual child, a series of tests is administered by the teacher. The series includes a mental maturity battery from which the child's IQ is obtained, and a battery of achievement tests from which reading, spelling, English, and arithmetic grade levels are determined. If any inconsistency in the actual test results and the predicted ones appears, retesting is scheduled by the school's psychologist before final placement is determined.

In connection with the tests, conferences are held within the Junior School faculty. Every possible consideration is given to each individual child before definite placement is made.

WHEN PROGRAM FUNCTIONS

After placement of all pupils is completed and the program begins to function, constant evaluation of each pupil's progress is maintained. The schedule is so fluid that a child may be readjusted according to his progress with a minimum of difficulty. Thus, a child in a lower group may, with a little initiative on his part, advance to the next higher group. A child may also be dropped to a lower group.

The screening of pupils from every available angle results in the formation of homogeneous groups that can work together and attain maximum benefits to be derived from *planned placement*.

A pupil is exposed to new work as rapidly as he can successfully absorb it, regardless of his chronological age. He is guided and urged to move forward at his own individual speed that is both challenging and profitable to him. It has been necessary to replace the stereotyped grade level identities, such as sixth, seventh, and eighth grades, with a new group identity because pupils frequently cross the grade lines into other groups. For instance: Group C-5 is made up of former seventh and eighth graders. Group H-23 is a class composed of former sixth and seventh graders, and so on. These groups permit pupils of like abilities, interests, and capacity, to work as a unit so that maximum benefits will result.

ENRICHMENT AREAS

A program such as this necessarily must have enriched areas over and above the required academic field. To meet this need, a series of electives has been developed from which the pupil may choose electives under proper guidance. The additional areas of learning in the elective program are: French, the World Today, History in the Making, the Nature of Government, an Initial Course in Local, County, State, and National Government, music appreciation, advanced science, advanced literature, reading for enjoyment, mechanical drawing, and consumer education for intelligent and resourceful buying.

In addition to the elective areas, remedial courses in reading and mathematics are given to pupils who need this work to maintain their rightful places in their group.

Under this program, the teachers find that they too benefit, because they can cope more effectively with groups with similar abilities, interests, and achievements.

The parents and pupils have reacted favorably to the program. The pupils' adjustment and enthusiasm have been most rewarding. The transitional period from the previous program has been much shorter than anticipated.

The fine cooperation and enthusiasm that has been given this program by the board of education, the staff, the parents and pupils, indicate that the experiment will be adopted as a permanent curriculum of the Junior School.

The Non-Graded High School

B. Frank Brown

> We have not journeyed all this way across the centuries, across the oceans, across the mountains, across the prairies, because we are made of sugar candy.
> —Winston Churchill

What the space age needs educationally is a crack public school system designed to educate more youngsters than ever before and do the job faster and better. The components for the kind of school needed are inventiveness, flexibility, and quality.

These qualities are prominent in the nongraded high school, an innovation now beyond the hothouse stage. But the nongraded high school is an iconoclasm, and the conventional school administrator fears it. When he considers it at all, he thinks of it as involving an esoteric organization suitable only to unique situations. In reality there is nothing mysterious nor singular about it. It is a clear, crisp, logical arrangement by which schools can take off the academic bridle which restrains youngsters intellectually.

If the public schools in America are ever to achieve the ideal of having each youngster progress at his best rate of learning, then some form of nongrading must be instituted. This leads to the shattering implication that within the next five years every intellectually respectable high school will have some degree of nongradedness. For the grade is a trapping of the outworn past. It was first conceived during the Middle Ages in a *gymnasium* at Stuttgart, Germany, and has grown sterile in the age of universal education and the hydrogen bomb.

The durable attractiveness of the grade lies in its administrative convenience. It serves as a comfortable holding pool in which school administrators can and do throw youngsters for custodial purposes and forget them for a year. By comparison, nongrading is an administrative prickly pear constantly needling for attention to the learning needs of youngsters.

The schools have been both the inheritors and the prisoners of the grade tradition. In an era of invention and change, educators must overcome inhibitions against breaking the grade lockstep. With it will go

Reprinted from *Phi Delta Kappan* 44:206–209, February 1963, by permission of the publisher and the author. B. Frank Brown is Principal of the Melbourne, Florida, High School.

some of the obsolescence which has been built into the curriculum with the grade.

The logical basis for nongraded education was clearly stated recently by Henry Dyer, vice president of the Educational Testing Service. In an address before the tenth College Board Colloquium, Dyer reported that the practice of measuring students intellectually by the grade they have reached is not even remotely reliable. He asserted that the grade average is only an event at best and no measure of achievement at all.

The academic design should be reduced from the current seventeen fragmented divisions of learning (K-12 plus four) to five general areas with learning continuous within each. Trends today suggest that the school of the future will be composed of the nongraded primary curriculum, the nongraded intermediate curriculum, the nongraded junior high curriculum, the nongraded senior high curriculum, and the nongraded college curriculum.

Space limitations prohibit treatment of the entire nongraded spectrum. Consequently, this article will deal only with the nongraded innovation of the secondary school, with the exception of a brief word about the implications for colleges.

We realize that bringing about change in the college curriculum is somewhat like moving a graveyard, but the impact of students educated without the academic bridle is already bringing a new respect for change in higher education. Spurred by the increased intellectual excitement of their students from nongraded high schools, colleges too will turn to the nongraded system. One result will be that college students in far greater numbers will enter graduate school.

TO RECOVER FROM DISASTER

The first step in recovering from decades of intellectual disaster wrought by the grade must be to reclassify youngsters for learning on the basis of their achievement rather than the grade to which they have been chronologically promoted. They must be fanned out in a new design. This is accomplished by clustering students intellectually on the basis of their performance on nationally standardized achievement tests. The intelligence quotient, which has been a primary measure in the past, is of little or no value in the nongraded school.

The results of standardized achievement tests dramatically reveal the fallacy of continuing to group students into grades. In the average grade in high school, only half the youngsters have the required knowledge to be in that particular grade. For example, the dispersal of achievement among students in a tenth-grade class in English will range from grade three through grade thirteen, which is the first year of college. The scatter is equally great in most other subjects. It is even greater in mathematics.

Youngsters at Melbourne High School have been reclassified in line with their level of achievement and assigned to fluid learning situations in each subject on the basis of their needs. Through selective acceleration, some students begin college level work when they arrive as tenth graders. By the same token, some students in the twelfth grade receive greater amounts of remedial work in areas in which their achievement is below standard.

The plan for continuous learning at Melbourne accommodates youngsters by placing them in temporary learning situations from which they can move at any time. These *ad hoc* learning arrangements are called phases. A phase is a stage of development with a varying time element. One student may remain in a low phase indefinitely; another may progress rapidly into higher phases.

When students enter Melbourne High School they are sorted on the basis of nationally standardized achievement tests. They are then clustered into a new spectrum in line with their various aptitudes and abilities.

Phase 1—Subjects are centered around remedial work.

Phase 2—Subjects are concerned with basic skills.

Phase 3—Subjects are designed for students seeking an average education.

Phase 4—Subjects are available for students desiring education in considerable depth.

Phase 5—Subjects are open to students who are willing to assume responsibility for their own learning and plan to go far beyond the boundaries of a single course.

Phase Q—Students whose creative talents are well developed in special areas should give consideration to this "Quest" phase of the curriculum. This is an important dimension of the phased organization designed to give thrust in the direction of individual fulfillment. In this phase a student may research an area in which he is deeply and broadly curious, either to develop creative powers or in quest of knowledge. A student may spend from one to three hours a day in Quest.

Phase X—Nonacademic subjects which do not accommodate student mobility; e.g., typing, physical education. These subjects are ungraded but unphased.

This realignment of students brings about a major difference in course content between the nongraded and conventionally graded school.

The motion of the nongraded curriculum compels the school to resort to a much wider range of materials. No standard textbooks are used in any phase. A multiplicity of material has replaced them. A gradeless curriculum designed for student mobility must be saturated with variegated materials.

The effect of nongrading is to change the educational process so that students are accelerated through subject matter on a continuing rather than yearly basis. Learning is both more appropriate and more viable when children of comparable academic accomplishment and pace are grouped together.

There are no study halls in the Melbourne plan for a nongraded school. The study hall, like the grade, belongs to the remote past. In a nongraded curriculum students are expected to take responsibility for their own learning and the monitored type of study hall becomes a useless appendage.

All students at Melbourne High are registered for six subjects. Subjects do, however, vary greatly in depth. For example, in a phase one mathematics class the concepts studied are fundamentals which the student should have been required to learn in the elementary school. At the other end of the scale is phase five, which encompasses calculus during the third high school year. This kind of flexible and mobile curriculum is rewarding to both the untalented and the multitalented. Equalitarianism wrongly conceived ignores differences in both achievement and native talent.

The following are typical schedules of three students of the same age but of widely varying abilities.

Student A		Student B	
	Phase		Phase
English	1	English	3
Mathematics	3	Mathematics	2
World History	2	Amer. History	4
Biology	3	Chemistry	3
Phys. Ed.	X	Band	X
Typing	X	Art	4

Student C	
	Phase
English	4
Differential Equations	5
History of Asia	3
Physics	5
Spanish	4
Probability & Statistics	Q

CHANGES WROUGHT BY THE GRADELESS PLAN

What are some of the changes that have taken place at Melbourne High School after three years of gradeless learning?

First, it is evident that a nongraded school is different from a graded school in more ways than just a reranking of students. Some classes must be smaller; others must be larger.

A subject in which class size has been dramatically increased is typing. Typing classes have been expanded to 125 students per class. The surprising thing is that we never thought of this before. The typewriter is a gadget and students attempting to master a mechanical device can be taught in classes of almost unlimited capacity. Space and administration are the only considerations. The teacher needs merely to be equipped with a first-rate public address system and a transistorized neck microphone without wires, so she can move freely about the room. One typing teacher at Melbourne easily instructs 625 typing students a day in five classes of 125 students each.

Since we have found that students can be taught typing in classes of 125 as well as in classes of thirty, three teachers are released for assignment elsewhere in the school program.

Typing and similar subjects at Melbourne High School which are ungraded but do not permit student mobility are scheduled as phase X. The student remains for a semester or even a year in phase X classes.

The nongraded high school as developed at Melbourne stands squarely on the concept of basic education first. This requires that youngsters coming into the high school who are weak in the basic subjects of English and mathematics devote double time—two periods a day—to each of these subjects until such time as they are up to the standard we set. The nongraded innovation, while embracing flexibility, is centered on a tightening and toughening of the academic sinews.

The gradeless curriculum at Melbourne High is also founded on an awareness that each of the school's students is different. The program of studies is designed to accommodate these variances in individuals.

The curriculum, which has a degree of flamboyance and at first seems complex, is merely unrestrained. It is designed to offer a bountiful academic fare on a wider range than is conventionally permitted when students are chronologically grouped in grades ten, eleven, and twelve.

Since English is the most widely studied subject in any school, perhaps the strategy of the Melbourne curriculum is best understood through this subject and what happens to a student who enters Melbourne High in the tenth grade.

Many tenth grade students are hampered by an inability to read at what is called the tenth grade level. These handicapped students rarely finish school. Truancy to them is a matter of self-preservation. In an effort to meet this problem, the teacher time gained from consolidating typing classes is used to reduce loads in classes for students in need of remedial work (phase one). These classes contain a maximum of fifteen students. They are designed so that each student may be involved in a personal engagement with learning.

Remedial students are taught to read through phonics. Students who have not learned basic skills are vigorously confronted with basic education and each phase increases in depth. At the other end of the spectrum is phase five English, which is an open-ended advanced placement college program in which the student can study and learn for three years. The intent here is to do something for students who can "run a faster mile."

In order to avoid repetition in literature and accommodate up-phasing of students, all phases of English study the same literature in a given year. One year all phases study American literature, the next year English literature, and the third year world literature.

Another reform which is spurred by non-graded education is a change in the function of the teacher. Students who are unbridled intellectually are no longer content with a passive "telling" kind of education. Teachers must throw out the old kit bag.

Gradeless schools are moving from memorized learning and simplified explanations to the process of inquiry for each individual. What is inquiry? In its simplest form, inquiry is curiosity linked to action. It means newer and deeper perceptions for the individual. In its ultimate form, it leads to the developments of traits of imagination and creativity and eventually to new discoveries for science and the humanities.

In the nongraded school, the intellectual pace of various students is more separate and unequal than in graded education. As the curriculum is expanded and becomes variegated, achievement becomes a hallmark of the school. The illusory aim of evenness in achievement which is characteristic of graded schools is not evident here.

Rebellion against the grade lockstep is one of the missed revolutions of our time. Still poised and full of ferment, it may never occur, although the grade curtain which was rung down around learning has been pierced by a new system of learning where the flashpoints are phases instead of annual promotion.

As Philip Coombs said when he was executive secretary of the Fund for the Advancement of Education, "What the schools need is not simply more money from the outside but sweeping changes on the inside." Sweeping changes do take place in a nongraded school, and without an increase in the budget.

The Nongraded High School: Two Views

ONE: Imaginative, Dynamic, But Unproved

Abraham Lass

What's wrong with our present-day high schools? Plenty, says Dr. B. Frank Brown, author of *The Nongraded High School:*

They aren't turning out students who are prepared "for jobs which do not now exist and for professions which cannot be described."

"Educators are timid, pedestrian, unimaginative, shackled to outmoded traditions and procedures . . . window-shade and chalkboard men rather than dynamic leaders."

In an effort to meet the demands of a curriculum which is suddenly being pushed "from auto mechanics to celestial mechanics and from terrestrial geography to celestial geography," schoolmen are "taking baby steps where giant steps are needed."

The school has become a "citadel of routine," "a bureaucracy for children." The curriculum is "narrow, rigid, obstinate, and far from first rate."

Students have little opportunity to experience the excitement of exploring or discovering either themselves or the world around them.

The conventional high school organized by grades or years is a Procrustean bed on which both the slow and the bright are broken. Here the bells ring on time. The classes change on time. And everyone advances and grows or doesn't advance and doesn't grow on time. At least this is the comforting delusion most schoolmen share.

Dr. Brown finds nothing in the conventional high school worth saving or commending. If we are going to get to the moon first, master our space technology, produce the men and women who will control the mechanisms of our wildly automating civilization, it will, he is sure, come only through "an imaginative organization and dynamic process of educational enterprise," like the ungraded Melbourne, Florida school he presides over with such dynamic distinction. Here, out of his intense convictions, driving

Reprinted from the *Saturday Review* 47:70–74, January 18, 1964, by permission of the publisher and the authors. Abraham Lass is Principal of the Abraham Lincoln High School in Brooklyn, and Jerome S. Bruner is Director of the Center for Cognitive Studies at Harvard University.

energy, and deeply felt commitments, Dr. Brown has forged what he passionately believes to be the only kind of school that provides the proper intellectual climate, facilities, organization, curriculum, staff, and community support necessary for high' school students to learn, live, and grow into a full awareness of themselves, their time, and their responsibilities.

In *The Nongraded High School*, Dr. Brown sets down in some detail what the ungraded high school is like, how it is organized and taught, and how it differs from the conventional high school.

At Melbourne, students are grouped according to their achievements and readiness for future learning as determined by such objective criteria as placement on national standardized achievement tests. There are no conventional "grades" or "forms" or "terms" at Melbourne. The IQ—as too frequently misused—plays no role in determining where a student begins, how fast he progresses, when he is "promoted" or graduated. Each area of learning is organized into five phases for students of varying abilities and achievements: the slow, the marginal, the average, the bright, and the very superior. The content and pace of the instruction in each area is geared to what the student needs and can absorb. When the student has mastered whatever "phase" of a subject he is in, he goes on to the next phase or area. Thus the bright ones are not held back by the slower ones; the slow students are not compelled to essay the impossible.

The emphasis throughout the Melbourne plan is on the individual student, on designing for him the program he can best cope with and master. All programs are tailor-made. There is no "block" programing at Melbourne. A poor or mediocre mathematics student may thus find himself in a very small Phase 1 class in mathematics where he will receive intensive remedial instruction. Being a gifted English student, he will be programmed for a Phase 4 or Phase 5 class, where he may be working on an independent project for part of the time, meeting with a small group in a seminar setting, conferring with the teacher at other times.

Other features of the Melbourne plan include:

Exciting opportunities for academically gifted students to engage in honors, "depth," and independent study in advanced placement, college level courses.

Team teaching.

Classes of variable size to meet the students' special needs.

The single textbook does not dominate Melbourne's classes. It has been replaced by a multiplicity of relevant materials and learning devices.

There are no monitored study halls at Melbourne. Study time is for studying, not for sitting in "study halls."

For the "academically able," class attendance is voluntary. An A student in physics need not attend classes. He may give this time to subjects he is less proficient in. But he is still responsible for his physics course. He paces himself and budgets his own time.

Periodically, students get "throw-away report cards." It is assumed that they show these to their parents. The school does not collect these report cards or require parents to indicate that they have seen the reports and understand what they mean.

Is the ungraded high school doing everything Dr. Brown says it does? Is it educating more students faster and better? Is it giving them everything they need when they need it, and how they need it? Dr. Brown says it is. But he is extremely long on assertion—disquietingly short on proof. Here he is in good, or at least numerous, company, with all those schools and school systems that have embraced (or find themselves in the embrace of) such exciting developments as closed circuit TV, team teaching, programed learning, foreign language laboratories, etc. There is an alarming lack of hard, reputable evidence (statistical or otherwise) that would lead one to conclude, even tentatively, that, under the new regime dominated by the new gadgetry, our children are learning more, learning it better and faster, liking it more, or retaining it longer in a more meaningful context. We are occasionally visited by a disturbing, albeit only fleeting, thought that all over this country we are in various degrees committing a whole generation of boys and girls to new curricula, schema, and methodologies, without any really firm and sure indication that we are leading them down the right path, in the right way, to the right goals. No one questions Dr. Brown's intentions. But we would feel more comfortable about his and his community's total commitment to the ungraded high school if we had something more substantial than his zeal, sincerity, intelligence, and devotion to go by.

Is the ungraded high school, Melbourne style, the answer to the big city school problems? Not very likely—certainly not for overcrowded, multiple-session schools with substantial numbers of culturally disadvantaged minority groups, poorly motivated or unmotivated students. And not very likely either for schools with large masses of "slow," average, non-college-bound students. For though Dr. Brown says that Melbourne is as good for the slow and average as it is for the academically bright and gifted, his illustrations are almost invariably studded with references to independent study in the library in special carrels, research in depth, projects of startling sophistication, college level courses, Advanced Placement, College Entrance Examinations, etc. Every sign seems to point to Melbourne as a predominantly college-oriented school and community. We find in Dr. Brown's account of the Melbourne experience none of the overwhelming student, community, and staff problems that bedevil the high schools in large cities—and even in the not-so-large cities. There may be some facets of the Melbourne plan that could with profit be adapted to individual schools similar to Dr. Brown's, but it seems doubtful that the ungraded high school can meet the big city challenges as patly as it has done at Melbourne.

What does the ungraded high school add up to? A vigorous, uncompromising, imaginative, brave tale about a rare kind of educational adventuring. It is a bold, free-wheeling challenge to everything traditional. Some readers may find Dr. Brown's hopped-up metaphors and occasionally overheated prose a bit hard to take. But only the blunt and captious can fail to appreciate the tonic quality of his mind and approach. Melbourne High School is his creation—his and the dedicated band of teachers and parents he has gathered around him. Not to read *The Nongraded High School* is to have missed a stirring account of one of the most arresting experiments on the contemporary educational scene.

TWO: A Vivid Glimpse of the Future

Jerome S. Bruner

This courageous book is a report of an experiment in pedagogy at a high school in Melbourne, Florida. As such, it might merit no special attention, but the experiment is so daring and so general in its applicability that Melbourne High School earns its right to special attention for the feel it gives of the future. To call it all a "report on the nongraded high school" is to do the venture a grave injustice—in much the same way that it would be an injustice to call the American Constitution an experiment in non-monarchical government. What turns out to be so deeply important about abolishing grade levels in a high school is that it forces a complete rethinking about what one is trying to accomplish in the high school years. It is not that a Procrustean system of grouping students according to their "year" was abolished, but that there was erected in its place something new and challenging and full of promise. The bare statistics of accomplishment hardly do it justice—reduction in dropouts from a normal 30 per cent to 4 per cent between 1958 and 1962, or an increase in college enrollment of graduates from the usual 40 to 70 per cent. That could have been accomplished by several strokes of good fortune. It is the process of change and all that it liberated in the students, the teachers, and the town that is striking.

There was good reason behind the decision to abolish the usual system in which a student enters as a "freshman" and pursues a "freshman" course all that year, going almost automatically to "sophomore" courses the next year, and on to the end, step by step. To begin with, there is the obvious fact of variability. Some students can go faster than their age-mates—phenomenally faster whether because of capacity or the fortune of background. If one demands a standard amount of work from all in any given grade, may we not be robbing the student of the opportunity of learning and using his own pace? Some will inevitably feel a sense of failure, however hard they try, while others will squirm their way through a year of unchallenged freedom. If a student can do college work in mathematics or history in his freshman year in high school, Melbourne argued, let him take Advanced Placement courses in those subjects from the beginning right to his last year. And if another student needs extra, remedial work in mathematics his freshman year, let him not be dumped into a regular or even a "slow" algebra course to do his best—ending, likely, by memorizing matters that make no sense to him. Give him a course in the fundamentals he will need before launching him into algebra. These were the kinds of considerations that led to the decision to "ungrade" Melbourne.

As I read Dr. Brown's introductory indictment of the deadening effects of a graded system (where failure is punished by having to repeat the same work over), my first thought was that this was going to be another book of deploring. But it soon became clear that this was not what the book was about at all. School grading is simply a poor piece of technology for using the resources of a school, one that has to be removed if the next step is to be taken. It is like nothing so much as the replacement of the top hitch by the horse collar during the medieval period. Up to the introduction of the horse collar, the weight to be hauled was attached to the top of a yoke by a strap that passed over the horse's back. When the horse pulled, the yoke pressed against his windpipe in a self-choking manner. The innovation was a simple one: pass the strap under the horse's body and attach it to the lower part of the collar. With thrust, the collar would press against the horse's strong neck and shoulders. He could, then "put his back into it."

And so with the graded high school. The eager student pressed against the system and found himself stifled by the requirements of his grade. Soon he regulated his thrust to suit the system. What often resulted was boredom for the swift, bewilderment for the slow, and a general surrender of intellectual aspirations to what teacher wanted.

Seeing a difficulty clearly often requires that one see an alternative to it. Frank Brown saw an impressive number. Let me note only briefly what has replaced the older, graded system at Melbourne. It is the real story.

Courses were reorganized into a system of "phases" that reflected not the grade in which they were being taught, but the student's ability to grasp the subject and his willingness to throw his weight into the task. Phase 1 was remedial, for students who needed special assistance in small classes. When a student feels ready to try something more advanced, he is encouraged to set forth to the next "phase." His willingness is a major criterion. Phase 2 is for students who need more emphasis on the basic skills of a subject. Phase 3 is for those who are ready to have a go at the major substance of the curriculum in the field—about which more in a moment. Phase 4 is the subject in depth and with concentration. Phase 5 is independent study for the exceptional student willing to assume responsibility for his own learning and ready to use all available resources in doing so. He is supervised by a teacher with whom (as in any tutorial system) the student makes an appointment when he has finished a stint of work.

The phase system operates in four basic intellectual disciplines: mathematics, science, English, and history. They are at the core of the school's offering. Freed from the old pattern, Melbourne was now in a position to innovate. Virtually every one of the major curriculum efforts of the last decade has been incorporated and fitted to the school's needs—the Physical Science Study Committee course, the Chemical Bond course, the Biological Sciences Curriculum Study, several experimental mathematics programs, and some home-grown innovations in social studies and humanities. Courses have had to be adapted to different phase levels, and I wish more had been said on what this entailed.

"This realignment of students on the basis of achievement brings about a major difference in course content between the nongraded and the conventionally graded school. The motion of the nongraded curriculum compels the school to resort to a much wider range of materials than is used in the graded school. Standard textbooks aimed at a grade level are inappropriate and have been abolished. A multiplicity of materials has replaced these media." But there is more to it than that, something in the system that seems to challenge students to reach. Brown suggests it: "Motion itself is not the cure for monotony in the schools; liveliness of image is the key. The flexibility of the nongraded structure gives a new image to both the learning process and the educational establishment." The new "image" has the effect of making the student decide his pace, whether to get into a next phase, whether to undertake independent studies.

There are many little things that make up the image of mobility, things that individually are shrewd, but in aggregate make educational wisdom. For one thing, Melbourne boasts that it is the only high school in America that has a library larger than its gymnasium. For another, the student who is doing independent studies or who is in pursuit of some special topic, is given a key to the school building and to the library or laboratory or studio where he is working. For another, the library is not built around the old system of study tables, but consists of carrels for individual work. If the ardor produced is "just Hawthorne effect," and I doubt it, then maybe Melbourne should go all out for a permanent Hawthorne effect. It may have to, for the system seems to require chronic innovation by its very nature. Team teaching, for example, is a necessity. Phase organization of courses requires that teachers take a hand in a course, depending on what they do best. And as students move, prepare special papers, or pursue independent studies, they are encouraged to see the teacher who knows the topic best.

Such "reforms" have a way of sounding too administrative. There is obviously something far deeper than administrative skill or decisiveness in the Melbourne arrangement. At the heart of the matter is a sense of intellectual style, a confidence in the ability of students to learn, and a respect for the disorderly ways in which people come by their insights. Dr. Brown describes the curriculum as "concept centered." "The primary purpose of education is the development of the intellect. All other aims and objectives are subordinate." The courses are hard and challenging, and achievement is emphasized. Sir Richard Livingstone is quoted with favor: "Facts and theories are . . . counters with which he learns to use his brains . . . to distinguish the relevant from the irrelevant." The courses explicitly encourage the use of heuristics, the arts of inquiry.

What has happened at Melbourne is not really "just something local." Frank Brown and his teachers—and now his students—are a reflection of something that is new on the national scene. I do not wish to diminish my praises in saying this. I agree with the author when he says that a school will not change unless its administrative head wishes to take the gamble. Frank Brown was man enough to change the pattern radically. When he did so, he was able to use the new, rich resources that have come out of the last decade of curriculum development. Yet it goes deeper than that. For not only is there more material available today—a joint product of university scholars and school teachers—but there is a new daring in our definition of what is pedagogically possible. The pace of "subject coverage" seems to be lifting; the grip of "the textbook" is loosening; the myth of uniform progress is being replaced by more challenging premises that place on the student the responsibility for his own progress. Even the handling of report cards at Melbourne provides room for thought. The parent is not required to sign it, though the student, it is expected, will take it home. The school argues that the student's relation with his parents is his private affair. This too is part of Melbourne's intellectual image or style.

A book of this kind is bound to leave many questions unanswered. To what extent does a program of this kind require especially gifted teachers? Upon reflection, I realize that while one is prone to ask this question, it is probably meaningless. Middling teachers would be the better for similar innovations, but surely they would handle it somewhat differently in the light of their own backgrounds. Or, how much does it cost? Again, I suspect that cost would place limits on how ambitious one might get. But surely, one could do considerable without much expense. Ironically, the most interesting experiments in education—including much in curriculum development—are considerably less costly than even modest bricks and mortar. Finally, would one get support for such a program in a community less gifted than this town housing an extraordinary number of professional scientists and engineers from Cape Kennedy? Probably not, but only a few such communities have to take the leap.

I find one special lesson in Frank Brown's report. Many of the best curriculum projects have rested their case on the importance of inquiry, structure, discovery, and independent thinking. Drop a bright new curriculum into a dull school atmosphere, and its glint can be quickly tarnished. Melbourne is one high school that has changed the atmosphere of learning to conform to the spirit of the new curricula—from keys to the library to report cards that are your own to dispose of. Inventions have a way of cultivating support. The nongraded high school is one that supports the inventive new work on curricula going on around the country. Like all social inventions, it has a power to liberate human energy to an astonishing degree—and it is this that makes it so promising.

What's Brewing in Bassett

Edward Eisman

Something new has been brewing in Bassett. It is an experiment to see how our California school district—and by extension, any comparable school district—can offer a twentieth-century educational program in the twentieth century. This endeavor does not seem to ask too much. Let's see what is involved.

We all know that American public education has been criticized persistently from the time of the neighborhood dame school. Sometimes constructive and sometimes ill-founded and malicious, this scrutiny and criticism have been among the forces that have helped shape our present system of free public education.

The school system is still being sharply criticized both within the profession and in most communities. What do we do to eliminate the basis for any justified fault-finding? To measure up better to the school's real job now?

The officials of the Bassett Unified School District, under the leadership of Superintendent James C. Ketcherside, decided to go to the source and find out what the community wanted in its schools and why they wanted it. A citizens committee was formed and asked to draw up a list of desirable educational objectives for the new Bassett High School which [opened] in the fall of 1964. This group met with Assistant Superintendent Robert E. Walker and eventually submitted a long list.

In this list, two threads ran throughout: these parents wanted their children educated up to their individual capacities, and they also wanted the school to help develop in each child a sense of individual responsibility.

Recognizing that these goals were sound educationally, the district administration sought an organizational framework that would best realize them. It was here that the difficulty arose.

The district administrators faced two alternatives: in formulating plans for the new high school, they could concentrate either on devices or organization. In other words, they could build a conventional school and

Reprinted from *Audiovisual Instruction* 8:136–137, March 1963, by permission of the publisher and the author. Edward Eisman is with the Parks Job Corps, Pleasanton, Calif., and was formerly Research Coordinator in the Bassett, California, Unified School District.

try to utilize those instructional materials and devices that would contribute to the development of individual capacities, or they could seek to reach these goals through a new organizational pattern—plus varied instructional resources including audiovisual materials and devices.

The criticisms of education from both the profession and lay public pointed to difficulties that were plainly organizational in nature. The district administration recognized that—regardless of the methods used and the aids—certain restrictions are inherent in the conventional educational framework. These authorities, therefore, decided first to investigate schools and school systems that were designed specifically to meet individual differences, and then to incorporate into the new Bassett High School those technological developments that were relevant.

BASSETT SEEKS OUTSIDE HELP

With this in mind, the Bassett District contacted the School Planning Laboratory at Stanford University and requested that it work with the District in developing a high school program. An agreement was reached whereby the Bassett District would invest $5,000 and the School Planning Laboratory would secure $8,500 from the Educational Facilities Laboratories (a branch of the Ford Foundation) to approach this problem jointly.

A professional committee was formed involving the Bassett Board of Trustees; Superintendent Ketcherside and his administrative staff; representatives from Schoolhouse Planning (a branch of the California State Department of Education); representatives from Flewelling, Moody, and Horne, the architects serving the District; and representatives from School Planning Lab.

This committee investigated various school programs and interviewed a number of people who had helped develop them. Recognizing that all these programs had something to contribute, but also feeling that none of them individualized the curriculum to the desired degree, the committee eventually came in contact with the work of Edwin A. Read of Brigham Young University, borrowed and adapted his chief educational design.

Dr. Read has developed what he calls "The Continuous Progress School" (a term that has also been used in reference to other programs). Its principles have been applied in teaching mathematics and English in the Laboratory School at Brigham Young University for the past three years.

The rationale for the Continuous Progress School is that learning is an individual matter, and that it suffers when external agencies impose restrictions upon the learning processes. To apply this theory to schools, we can see that we place many impediments in the way of learning. Grade levels, time schedules, etc., are all artificialities that we have been utilizing for convenience but that have no other value in education.

In a Continuous Progress School, an attempt is made to break down the artificial barriers that interfere with maximum learning. This undertaking calls for an individualized approach to education that places the major responsibility for learning on the student himself.

The core of the plant is the Instructional Materials Center (IMC). Immediately adjacent are the study units, each containing studio offices and a large group of individual study carrels—student stations. (Originally, carrels were monks' alcoves for study and meditation.)

In the Bassett Continuous Progress High School, assignment to each study unit will be on the basis of one professional teacher and one paraprofessional (teacher aide) for every 60 students; each unit, consequently, will house 300 students. Peripheral to the IMC and study units will be provision for those activities that will not lend themselves readily to individualized instruction (band, physical education, industrial arts, etc.).

STUDENTS ARE TESTED FIRST

When the program is inaugurated in the fall of 1964, each student will have participated in an extensive testing program and will develop certain objectives for the semester or year. (For example, in 20 weeks he expects to complete Algebra II, Spanish I, or World Literature.) He will then be provided with a personal program—a prepared sequence of activities—to help him reach these objectives. Incorporated into the program will be directions for use of auto-instructional materials, programed textbooks, study kits, books, audiovisual aids, and a variety of technological teaching devices.

The home base of the student will be his carrel (individual study station). It will be a work area including provision for a television receiver and the facilities for scheduling or dialing videotape lectures and demonstrations. It will also include an electronic communication system whereby the student can communicate with the paraprofessional or master teacher and vice versa.

Each day the student will fill out a brief card indicating his progress in his program and also whether or not he needs help before he can continue. The paraprofessional will group these cards on the basis of common needs and will give them to the master teacher. The master teacher will then meet with the students who need help, either individually or in small groups.

The student will work on his own program in his own carrel. When he reaches a point where he needs additional help, he will inform the para-professional who will try to afford immediate assistance. If the student and paraprofessional consider still more clarification desirable, arrangements will be made for the student to confer with the master teacher.

The Bassett Continuous Progress program involves a systems approach to education: first, the essential concepts relative to specified educational goals have been analyzed; second, the Bassett High School is designed and will be equipped to provide experiences conducive to the development of these concepts. Where the printed word is appropriate, it will be used; where audio or visual experiences are desirable, they will be available; where manipulative experiences are called for, they will be incorporated into the program. Where group interaction or teacher involvement is desired, they too, will be integrated into the program. In other words, the individual student will be drawing upon and utilizing an entire instructional system with a wide range of media, and the rate and degree of his learning will be primarily up to him.

Limitation of space prevents further exposition at this time, although I am sure that at best I have only whetted the reader's interest. I would like to close with a pertinent quotation, and have two from which the reader can choose. One was phrased by Simon Ramo: "Don't be ashamed to propose a ridiculous idea. Though worthless today, in ten years it may be of no value whatsoever." The other is Herbert Muller's view that we must look forward to the future and not present "the curious spectacle of civilized man forever marching with his face turned backward—as no doubt the cave man looked back to the good old days when men were free to roam instead of being stuck in a damn hole in the ground."

Of the two quotations, we feel Muller's point is most appropriate to the Bassett Continuous Progress School where we are looking toward the future. History, of course, will be the final judge.

Automated Grouping

Sidney P. Rollins

Explicit in the philosophy expounded by public secondary school people, almost always, is a paean to the worth of "the individual." This is usually accompanied by a solemn pledge to cherish "individual differences"—that is, to provide for each youngster a curriculum which is best for him. Listening to the professional, an innocent might believe that through some mysterious process each youngster is offered an individualized curriculum suited to his interests, his needs, and his abilities. This is, indeed, an excellent and an important aim. But alas, it is too often true that the phrase "individual differences" becomes what Barzun has called a *thought cliché*—a nice idea. In practice the pupil is fitted into a preconceived curriculum. And there he remains.

Of course educators have made many serious attempts to individualize the curriculum. On the basis of careful testing and teacher analysis, pupils are "grouped" into "tracks." These tracks usually number from two to four, their intent being to place the pupil with other pupils of similar abilities. This idea is sometimes extended until as many as seven or eight different groups are manufactured (most often in English and the social studies) with the same intent—to place the pupil within groups of youngsters with similar abilities. Unfortunately, most youngsters' abilities vary from one subject field to the next, so that a youngster in one of the "top" groups in English may have difficulty in mastering mathematics.

Educators have made some serious attempts to solve this problem too. Pupils are occasionally grouped according to their measured abilities in *each* of the subject fields. In this manner a pupil may work with a "top" group in English, and an "average" group in mathematics. This more nearly approaches the philosophical ideal. But the fact remains that the groups themselves have been preconceived, thereby limiting the number of possibilities for individualization to the number of groups which have been organized in advance.

In defense of secondary school administrators, it must be admitted that until quite recently, as our school curricula are organized, little else was feasible. To build a curriculum for each youngster involves a hor-

Reprinted from *Phi Delta Kappan* 42:212–214, February 1961, by permission of the publisher and the author. Sidney P. Rollins is affiliated with Rhode Island College, and Director of the Middletown School Project, Middletown, Rhode Island.

rendous task of record-keeping, for it requires a continuous knowledge of the achievement of every individual in the school. But we no longer have the excuse that the record-keeping is impracticable, because the means of obtaining continuous checks on each pupil in each subject field are now available. And that brings us to the title of this article, "Automated Grouping."

An experiment in the use of IBM equipment for developing an individual curriculum for each pupil is in progress in the new six-year secondary school in Middletown, Rhode Island. This experiment is one aspect of the development of a total program for the Middletown School, which [opened] in September, 1961. The development of the total program, named the Middletown Project, is supported in part by a $20,000 grant from the Fund for the Advancement of Education and in part by a $10,000 grant from the town of Middletown to Rhode Island College, which provides the services of the project director.

The automated grouping experiment was a natural and concurrent outgrowth of the plan of curriculum organization developed through the Middletown Project. Investigation of means to implement curriculum plans seemed to indicate that electronic equipment offers many opportunities for adaptation to the problems of pupil scheduling and data-processing in the secondary schools. Unlike industry, public educational institutions have been slow to make use of electronic equipment. The IBM Corporation has produced machine systems which can be utilized in the schools, however, and new ideas in curriculum construction have been made feasible.

In Middletown the curriculum has been organized in terms of six or seven years of a subject field, rather than in terms of specific "courses." The content in each of the subject fields has been developed into a sequential pattern. All of the learning experiences to which a pupil is exposed during his career in the secondary school are identified; then they are taught in logical sequence. It is expected, of course, that the sequence will be evaluated (and probably modified) continuously.

Those staff members who developed the curriculum in each subject field first determined, with the help of the community, the administration, and qualified consultants, the purposes of teaching their particular subject fields. The teachers developing the curriculum then selected content which, consistent with their knowledge of their subjects and their knowledge of child growth and development, appeared to contribute to the achievement of these purposes. Naturally, traditional content which did not appear to contribute to the achievement of purposes was omitted. The sequence of curriculum content was organized on the basis of what each pupil requires, rather than in terms of a sequence into which each child grows as each calendar year passes.

It is quite possible for a pupil in what is ordinarily the ninth grade to need experiences which he usually meets in the eleventh grade, and automated grouping makes it possible for this particular pupil to study at what usually is called the eleventh grade level. (The reverse is also possible, and is just as likely to occur.) This means that a curriculum is developed for each child, as opposed to the generally accepted practice of placing a child in a prescribed curriculum.

This is the way automated grouping works: Skills, understandings, and concepts, having been identified, are listed sequentially. Those skills, understandings, and concepts which an individual pupil has not yet mastered are punched on the pupil's IBM card for each subject. Coding the items, once they have been placed in sequence, is a relatively simple matter. By using a sorter, it is possible to group pupils on the basis of those elements of a subject field which they have not yet learned. These groups are organized into classes and assigned to teachers who are already aware of the needs of the pupils in their classes. In this way the pupil's progress is measured in terms of what he has learned rather than in terms of the number of courses he has passed. A quick look at a pupil's IBM card reveals at once what he has already learned and what remains to be learned.

For each subject field there will be as many groups as the total enrollment in that subject field divided by 25—the average number of pupils in a standard class. Hypothetically, each class may be at a different point on the sequential continuum for each subject field. It is possible, too, but extremely unlikely, that all of the classes may be attempting to learn material at the same point on the sequential continuum. What is important, here, is that automated grouping is based on the achievement of the youngsters, and not on any preconceived grouping system.

Pupils within each class must be given an opportunity to progress at their own speeds. Clearly, automated grouping by itself does not eliminate the responsibility of the teacher to concern himself with the differences which will appear among pupils in a particular classroom. Each teacher must encourage and stimulate each pupil to learn as much as he is capable of learning. As each semester terminates, each pupil will be rescheduled on the basis of his progress during the past semester. Under ideal conditions there would be a constant evaluation of a pupil's work, and as he gained competencies he could be re-grouped into another class. Presently, however, it is possible to evaluate pupils only twice each year.

The idea of automated grouping is based on the premise that it is possible to place into a logical sequence all of the experiences to which pupils are exposed in each of the subject fields. In Middletown, we think that it is possible. We think, too, that an intelligent, considered organization of content into an articulated sequential pattern is preferable.

The Middletown Public Schools are committed to a genuine consideration of differences among individuals, and to the development of a curriculum organization which will, in fact, provide individual programs for each pupil. Automated grouping is one of the means adopted to fulfill this commitment.

Here are some questions on automated grouping with answers by Mr. Rollins:

Q. *Do you know now what the additional costs of installing and maintaining automated grouping will be?*

A. Not exactly. IBM equipment will be used for many other purposes (census, payroll, guidance, pupil records, grading, etc.). Because of this it will be difficult to obtain a breakdown to show cost for automated grouping. Rental of the required machines will run about $450 per month. We do not know now what salary we will have to pay an operator.

Q. *How large a system or school must one have in order for automated grouping to be feasible and economical?*

A. The Middletown Six-Year Secondary School will house 1,200 pupils. We do not consider the cost exorbitant for this size school. However, there are other ways to preserve the basic idea of automated grouping. In small schools where record-keeping is a lesser problem, other devices, such as the McBee Keysort cards, can be used.

Q. *Have you considered the possible psychological disadvantages of breaking up old groups and forming new ones each semester?*

A. Yes. Until fairly recently, secondary schools adjusted the schedules of individual pupils twice yearly (which was the reason for January graduations). Keeping secondary school youngsters in one class for a whole year is a relatively recent innovation. We have found little evidence to indicate specific psychological disadvantages in breaking up old groups and forming new ones each semester. J. Wayne Wrightstone writes, "Data regarding the effects of ability grouping upon personal characteristics are so inadequate or subjective in character that no valid conclusions can be drawn."[1]

Mr. Rollins welcomes questions and suggestions. Send them to the Graduate Office, Rhode Island College, Providence 8, R. I.

[1] In *Class Organization for Instruction* (Washington, D.C.: Dept. of Classroom Teachers, American Educational Research Association, NEA, Bulletin 13, May, 1957), p. 8.

Nova High Space Age School

Burt Kaufman and Paul Bethune

The Nova High School, which opened in September, 1963, is an initial unit of the South Florida Education Center, an educational complex imaginative in design and advanced in concept. Eventually this complex will house tax-supported schools encompassing kindergarten through junior college, plus a private university with a graduate school. This long-range program, when completed, will present a continuous integrated process of learning unparalleled in education history. Known as "The Nova Plan," this new approach may well develop a model educational system for the county, state, and nation.

In March, 1960, Dean Dessenberger, then chairman of the Broward County Board of Public Instruction, looked at Forman Field, a 545-acre government surplus airfield, and envisioned this exciting experiment in education. Tireless efforts by the school board and Broward's professional educators resulted in a government gift of 320.5 acres and the purchase of the remaining land. After months of research and intensive planning, construction of Nova began in August, 1962.

What makes Nova High School different? It is not experimental in curriculum but in concept. Its construction features, equipment, teaching aids, and instructional methods have been tested and proved in other school systems. In fact, the director of Nova High School, Arthur B. Wolfe, spent three full years visiting outstanding schools of the United States in order to incorporate the best of modern educational methods in the Nova plan for instruction. The educational specifications were completed in their entirety before the first brick was laid.

Nova is a space age school. Its philosophy is based on a concept best described as scientific learning for a scientific age. Interestingly, to achieve the goals of such a philosophy, there has been a return to a "hard-core" curriculum. Each Nova student pursues a schedule of studies which includes mathematics, foreign language, English, science, social studies, technical science, special studies, and physical education. A student may choose a foreign language from among Latin, Spanish, French, Russian,

Reprinted from *Phi Delta Kappan* 46:9–11, September 1964, by permission of the publisher and the authors. Burt Kaufman is Coordinator of Mathematics, and Paul Bethune is Coordinator of Science at Nova High School, Fort Lauderdale, Florida.

and German. His choice of a technical science or special studies course comes from electronics, mechanical and scale drawing, music, home economics, art, personal typing, mechanical technology, safety and driver education, physiology, and home nursing. A student who chooses a foreign language in one school year may elect two courses from technical science; a student who does not may elect five for that school year.

Despite the seeming rigidity of this curriculum, there is flexibility within its framework. Nova is a nongraded school and this is the main feature of its program. It is possible for seventh-year students to be studying math with tenth-year students, science with eighth-year students, and English with seventh-year students. In other words, a nongraded program allows complete homogeneous grouping within each subject area without any regard to age or year in school. This educational program is truly tailored to individual needs and brings into practice the theory of "taking each student as far as he can go." For example, the mathematics department strongly believes in vertical acceleration for the gifted. The nongraded organization allows this to be done with ease. It is expected, therefore, that many students will study college mathematics courses such as abstract and linear algebra, calculus, and probability and statistics, beginning these in some cases as early as the ninth and tenth year in school. It is anticipated that, in the future, mathematically capable students will be able, prior to their graduation from high school, to complete what is now considered a very strong undergraduate math major in leading universities. At the same time, many of the less capable students will not get through the normal high school curriculum, even though all students will study mathematics as long as they are in school.

Each discipline has identified the approach its faculty thinks best suited to remove extraneous retardation in the case of the gifted and relaxation of time pressures for the less able. The idea here is predicated on the fact that each student should go as far as his capabilities will carry him without pressures to complete material for the sake of artificially set standards which do not take into consideration the individual differences among students.

Instead of being promoted a grade level each year, students progress through a series of achievement levels called "units" in each subject area. At the end of each unit a test is given which determines whether the student may continue to the next level. A student performing below minimum levels on the test must repeat that unit satisfactorily before being allowed to advance. Thus no student ever fails a whole year's work in any subject. At graduation time it is not expected that all students will have completed the same amount of the curriculum. However, a student who reports for a certain unit is expected to have a set of values, skills, and knowledge in common with others who are promoted to the same units. The identification of material within a unit allows for ladder-like steps upon which the student is constantly building and will use in later units.

When students enter Nova they undergo area examinations and all information coming from their former schools is considered. The student is then placed in the appropriate units *in each discipline.* The class to which he is assigned may have students at various levels within the unit. For example, some students in the group may be working to considerably more depth than others in the same group. This is not intended to retard the more able students but rather to meet individual needs and interests. Some students need depth in chemistry; some do not. Even though the student does not elect major studies, he does in practice exercise control over a portion of his education.

A student whose interest is in science may elect to go far beyond what is required, while in English he may pursue a less time-consuming pattern. On the other hand, he may devote extra effort to languages and do a minimum of science and math.

As the student progresses through the sequence, he is aware of his status within the sequence. The units require approximately one month of time for the average student, about six weeks for the less able. During a major reporting period of seven and a half weeks a typical student would have completed at least one and often two units. Each student receives a quality grade and a quantity grade. These are recorded on the report card and averaged for a final grade for a period.

Students are encouraged to do independent study and research in every discipline. The student is taught from the very beginning that he is the person primarily responsible for his education. Far more freedom is allowed students at Nova than at traditional schools, the goal being to help students develop mature study habits before they enter college. It is expected that Nova students will find the transition from Nova to college a smooth one.

The end of one trimester and the start of another means very little to the individual student or teacher. It calls for no major rearrangements. The one exception to this is the end of the third trimester, when the students embark on a one-month vacation. At this time we try to finish a unit so that the students will be mentally free for their vacation.

Nova is not attempting to become an educational racetrack. Students may apply for early graduation, but each case will be judged on its own merit. Ultimately, Nova will hold three graduations a year, to coincide with the student's entrance into the junior college or to one of the universities.

The newest and best of educational techniques and media are utilized at Nova. Among these are team teaching; closed-circuit television; overhead projectors in every room; reading laboratory; science and language laboratories; and large group, medium group, and small group instruction. There is also wall-to-wall carpeting throughout the school, resource centers equipped with a large number of reference books, microfilm readers, teaching machines, and tape recorders. At hand is also a complete data-processing center. The closed television system permits telecasting throughout the school as well as the making of video tapes of lessons and lectures for reshowing at a later date. Nova is completely air-conditioned. These innovations were financed by the omission of facilities which have long been considered as standard equipment in conventional schools. Nova has no large auditorium and no expensive kitchen or cafeteria. Students either bring their lunches or buy food at snack bars which are supervised by a dietician. The students eat outside in a protected area.

Nova has already become an educational showcase in its own locale, Broward County, and is rapidly becoming a national mecca for educators hoping to see the newest ideas in practice. It is anticipated that many of the ideas and practices alive at Nova will be adopted elsewhere.

Math Education in an Eleven-Month Nongraded Secondary School

The educational program at Nova High School embodies many of the new ideas that educators have been talking about in recent years—including nongraded grouping in all subjects, closed-circuit TV, an overhead projector in every room, the use of clerical aides and teaching assistants, team teaching, and an 11-month (220 day) school year.

All these factors have enabled the school to offer an outstanding math curriculum geared to the individual needs of all students. Slow learners are stimulated to work beyond their capabilities and faster students challenged to study what has traditionally been considered college level math.

The school opened as a Grade 7-10 institution in September of 1963. This year an 11th grade was added. Next September the school will become a full-fledged 7-12 school and a new adjoining elementary school with the same educational philosophy and advantages will be opened.

School is open from September 1 to July 30 and operates on a trimester schedule. The school day consists of five 70-minute periods and runs from 9 a.m. until 3:45 p.m.

NONGRADED GROUPING

The most important single factor in the Nova program is the nongraded grouping. Students are grouped only by ability and not by age or grade levels.

"The nongraded program allows us to move students as rapidly or as slowly as it is necessary for them to learn mathematics or any other subject properly," says Burt Kaufman, mathematics coordinator. "Not being concerned with a student's age or year in school allows us to truly accelerate the gifted and also removes much of the time pressure which normally impedes the work of the slower student. Last year, for example, we had 12 seventh grade youngsters who were able to complete the SMSG Algebra I course and gain about two years' acceleration in their mathematics studies.

"On the other hand," Mr. Kaufman continues, "instead of giving 10th graders who are extremely weak in mathematics a course in geometry, we placed most of them at the seventh grade level where they can get a

Reprinted from *Updating Mathematics* 7:2-3, November 1964, by permission of the publisher. Copyright, Croft Educational Services, 1964.

worthwhile background before taking more advanced courses. I'd say the real advantage of the nongraded program is to break the lockstep in teaching."

Mr. Kaufman explains that acceleration in math at Nova is vertical. There are no enrichment units as such. Pupils move ahead as rapidly as they can. This is possible because the curriculum is based on units. As soon as a student passes a test on one unit, he moves on to the next. Under this system, no youngster repeats a full year's work, although he may have to repeat a unit. And at the beginning of a new school year, the students merely pick up the unit on which they left off the preceding July 30. At year's end there is no such thing as final or comprehensive exams in a course. The final exam comes when students are ready to complete one course and move on to the next.

Grouping is homogeneous and determined entirely by the teachers. That is, a boy in Grade 7 may study math with 10th graders, science with 8th graders, English with 9th graders.

TEAM TEACHING

At Nova a modified team teaching approach is used in math. However, Mr. Kaufman does not believe that large group instruction is feasible in mathematics on a regular basis. For this reason Nova doesn't have too many math classes in which two or three instructors teach one large group.

"We do, however, use team teaching to some degree," Mr. Kaufman says. "All math instructors teaching the various levels of each course meet to plan each unit cooperatively and design their unit tests together. They continually evaluate themselves and each other as well as their students and move students from one level to another according to their evaluation of each student's work and ability. Whenever possible we try to use the special talents of an individual teacher with a large group of students."

The math staff at Nova includes 10 full-time teachers in addition to Mr. Kaufman. In addition the department has two clerical aides—to relieve the teachers of nonteaching chores such as taking the roll, keeping records, collecting money, and duplicating materials—and several teaching assistants to grade papers, tutor slower students, and perform similar duties. There is also a full-time Ph.D. in research on the school faculty who evaluates the program and determines its effectiveness.

RESOURCE CENTER

"Each department has its own building equipped with a resource center that includes a large collection of reference books, tape recorders, microfilm readers, and similar materials," Mr. Kaufman says. "We also have a closed-circuit TV, overhead projectors in each class, and 15 study carrels equipped with TV monitors and ear phones so that students may individually watch reruns of lessons we video tape or any of the educational TV channels in our area.

"Eventually we plan to develop most of our math units by means of study guides and TV video tapes," Mr. Kaufman continues, "so that students can truly work at their own pace. When we accomplish this the teacher will be able to devote less of her time to classroom teaching and more of it to working with individuals who need extra help. Teachers will also be able to spend more time improving the curriculum, revising and making new tapes and become real resource persons."

CAMBRIDGE REPORT

In September of 1965, when the elementary school is open and the 12th grade is added, Nova will have an integrated 12-year math program under Mr. Kaufman's direction.

"Since I will have full responsibility for the development of the elementary and secondary math curriculum, there will be 100% coordination from one level to the next," he says. "This fact alone, we feel, will enable us to develop a program along the lines suggested by the Cambridge Conference report. Our efforts last year and so far this year have been toward developing a curriculum that best fits the needs of our present-day students, as well as developing ideas that will enable us to create a truly modern K-12 program to be started with our kindergarten class in September of 1965. We are receiving valuable help in this regard from an advisory group of college and university math educators."

The present program for Grades 7–11 is designed to give the student as much math as he is capable of learning. In the future, many students will complete such college mathematics courses as abstract and linear algebra, calculus, and probability and statistics, beginning these in some instances as early as the ninth and 10th grades. Mr. Kaufman believes that many of the more brilliant students will be able to complete what is now considered to be an undergraduate college math major.

"In the same vein," he says, "many of the less capable students will not get through the normal high school curriculum even though all students will study mathematics as long as they are in school. The idea is to have each student go as far as his capabilities will carry him."

At present about 25% of Nova's students are in the talented category, about 60% are average students, and about 15% are slow. Mr. Kaufman believes that the percentage of talented students will rise as the years go on.

Mr. Kaufman concludes with the following observations: "At present our poorest students and the ones really having trouble adjusting to our program are those who started in Grades 9 and 10. They came from different schools with many divergent backgrounds. Many of them had developed poor study habits that we are having trouble breaking. We find that those students who started with us in Grade 7 seem to adjust to our program quite easily and are eager to move ahead at their own pace. In the years to come, when we have students going through our program beginning in kindergarten, we should really be able to accomplish a great deal with students of different ability."

Nova's 7-12 Math Curriculum

By 1966, Mr. Kaufman expects the following curriculum to be fully operative. Generally speaking the below average math student will take courses I-V in order during his secondary school career; the average student will take courses II-IV, and VI-VIII; the talented student will take courses II-IV, and IX-XII—and from there the horizons are unlimited.

I. Fundamental Mathematics—A course for nonachievers.

II. Elementary Contemporary Mathematics I—A pre-algebra and pre-geometry course introducing some elementary algebraic concepts together with intuitive geometry. Included is the study of numeration systems other than base 10, sets, properties of whole numbers, points, lines, curves, planes, factoring, prime numbers, finite mathematical systems, and measurement.

III. Elementary Contemporary Mathematics II—A continuation of the previous course. It includes a study of integers, congruence, construction, circles, exponents and scientific notation, rational numbers, area, regular polygons, circle graphs, solving equations, polynomials over rationals.

IV. Elementary Contemporary Mathematics III—Completes the elementary algebra series and includes two more units in intuitive geometry. Includes polynomials in several variables, number sentences, logic, elementary set theory, system of real numbers, geometry in three dimensions, radical notation, relations, functions, probability, numerical trig.

V. SMSG (M) Geometry—A course for the less talented mathematics student including the items studied in Course VI in far less detail.

VI. SMSG Geometry—For the average student who completes Course IV. It will include a study of geometric figures, congruences, properties of perpendiculars and parallels, geometric inequalities, similarities, areas of polygonal regions and circles, volumes and surface areas of solid figures and spheres, characterization of sets, plane coordinate geometry.

VII. Introduction to Modern Algebra—Includes real numbers and fields, linear equality and inequalities, number theory, polynomials, quadratic polynomials, complex numbers, algebraic structures, functions.

VIII. Introduction to Advanced Mathematics—Begins with a review of logic followed by study of the algebra of sets.

IX. The Number Systems of Algebra—Develops rigorously the number systems of algebra beginning with the postulates for the natural and whole numbers, the integers, rationals, ordered fields, the algebraic extension of the rationals with $\sqrt{2}$ adjoined, real numbers, roots, exponents, radicals, quadratic equations, the complex number system, and systems of equations and determinants.

X. Elementary Geometry From An Advanced Standpoint—A college level course for the gifted student who has completed Course IX. It includes everything covered in Course VI plus a rigorous treatment of the real numbers, an introduction to the Hilbert approach to Euclidean geometry, absolute plane geometry, parallel projections, the construction of an area function, rigid motions, an introduction to hyperbolic geometry, consistency of the hyperbolic postulates, countable and uncountable sets.

XI. Abstract Algebra—A college level course for the gifted student who has completed course X. It includes algebraic structure, mapping, isomorphisms, homomorphisms, rings, integral domains, fields, group theory, a formal development of the reals beginning with the Peano Postulates and concluding with Cauchy sequences, polynomial theory, rational functions, vector spaces, linear transformations, matrices and similar material studied in linear algebra.

XII. Calculus—Follows Course XI. Emphasizes such topics as the Mean Value Theorem, the Intermediate Value Theorum, the Fundamental Theorum of Calculus, Bolzano-Weierstrass Theorum, Reimann's theory of integrations, Taylor series, and the theory of infinite series.

Selected Bibliography

Nongraded School Organization: Junior and Senior High Schools

Alexander, William M. "The Junior High School." *Bulletin of NASSP* 49:277–285, March 1965.

Says a continuous program must be planned for junior high. Describes the possibilities for curriculum differentiation in the emerging middle school. Encourages nongrading and team teaching.

Asbell, Bernard. "Cape Kennedy's High School for Sky-High Learning." *PTA Magazine* 58:14–18, January 1964. Also in *Education Digest* 29:26–28, March 1964.

Account of a nongraded high school at Melbourne, Florida. Grouping is based on achievement in each subject regardless of year in school.

Other descriptions of Melbourne program in *Bulletin of NASSP* 46:127–134, January 1962; 47:67–68, May 1963; *Delta Kappa Gamma Bulletin* 30:22–25, Spring 1964; *Parents Magazine* 37:46–47, September 1962; *Newsweek* 60:109–112, October 8, 1962; *Scholastic Teacher* 83:18–T–19–T, October 4, 1963; *Saturday Evening Post* 235:75, 78, December 15, 1962; *Phi Delta Kappan* 47:43–46, September 1965; *School and Community* 49:20–21, September 1962; *Nations Schools* 74:10, 12, December 1964; *U.S. News and World Report* 54:80–83, February 19, 1962; and *The Changing Curriculum* by Kimball Wiles, pp. 313–321. Also check writings of B. Frank Brown.

Baker, W. Bradley. "Break-through in Brevard." *Florida Education*, September 1963. pp. 9–12.

Points out changes in Brevard County School System that have taken place since the advent of Cape Canaveral. The system has changed from graded to nongraded for all twelve years.

Beggs, David W. and Buffie, Edward G. (Editors), *Independent Study*. Bloomington, Indiana: Indiana University Press, 1965. pp. 83–217.

Describes school programs, facilities, instructional materials, team teaching, and flexible scheduling. Has implications for graded or nongraded schools.

Brickell, Henry M. "Dynamics of Change." *Bulletin of NASSP* 47:21–28, May 1963.

Explains the shifts in the major structural elements of a school which are necessary in order to introduce innovations such as team teaching, ungraded classes, use of para-professionals, flexible scheduling of large and small groups, etc.

Broudy, Harry; Smith, B. O.; and Burnett, Joe. *Democracy and Excellence in American Secondary Education*. Chicago, Illinois: Rand McNally and Company, 1964. pp. 248–255.

Proposes a high school curriculum which is appropriate for a nongraded high school.

Brown, B. Frank. "An Answer to Dropouts: The Nongraded High School." *The Atlantic* 214:86–89, November 1964.
Describes nongraded Melbourne High.
Other references by B. Frank Brown in *North Central Association Quarterly* 38:238–244, Winter 1964; *Journal of Secondary Education* 37:368–375, October 1962; 40:195–200, May 1965; *Bulletin of NASSP* 45:349–352, April 1961; 46:127, January 1962; 46:164–166, May 1962; 47:46–64, May 1963; *Overview* 2:61, May 1961; 4:68–69, June 1963; and *American School and University* 38:41–43, November 1965.

Brown, B. Frank. *The Appropriate Placement School: A Sophisticated Nongraded Curriculum.* West Nyack, N.Y.: Parker Publishing Company, Inc., 1965.
Proposes a spiral curriculum plan of schooling for kindergarten through high school. Calls for a nongraded phased organizational structure and curricula for K-12. Emphasizes team teaching and independent study. Includes chapters on school buildings, the library, dropouts, and disadvantaged students.

Brown, B. Frank. *Nongraded High School.* Englewood Cliffs, N.J.: Prentice-Hall, 1963.
Gives details of nongraded Melbourne High School organized in 1958. Discusses organization, independent study, small and large group instruction, advanced placement, expanded curriculum, ability grouping, and interest grouping.

Brown, Charles E. "The Schools in Newton: Experiment in Flexibility." *The Atlantic* 214:74–78, October 1964.
Gives a brief report of nongrading in several elementary, junior, and senior high schools in Newton, Massachusetts. Describes school-within-a-school plan used in a junior and senior high. Briefly describes mathematics, social studies, and vocational curriculum.

Carlsen, G. Robert and Conner, John W. "New Patterns for Old Molds." *English Journal* 31:244–249, April 1962.
Describes English program practiced at University High of State University of Iowa.

Clark, Gwyn R. and Noall, Matthew F. "Better Staff Utilization in Hurricane High School Through Language Arts Reorganization." *Bulletin of NASSP* 45:223–227, January 1961.
Reports homogeneously (achievement) grouped nongraded English classes for the 10–12 years resulted in gradual student improvement. Teachers rotated among various sections and taught as a team.

Clark, Leonard. "Ability Grouping—A Third Look." *Bulletin of NASSP* 47:69–71, December 1963.
Reminds the reader that ability grouping and curriculum tracks are not the only devices for providing for individual differences. Recommends grouping within the secondary school class, differentiated assignments, individualized instruction, flexible promotion system, nongraded school, etc.

Cochran, John R. "Grouping Students in Junior High School." *Educational Leadership* 18:414–419, April 1961.
Reports flexible grouping arrangement in a Kalamazoo, Michigan, junior

high school. Found the grouping did not greatly change students but did seem to influence the procedures used by teachers.

Dean, Stuart E. "Nongraded School." *School Life* 47:19–23, December 1964.
Summarizes growth, development, and application of nongrading. Gives pros and cons.

Dean, Stuart E. "Nongraded Schools." *Education Brief OE20009.* U.S. Department of Health, Education, and Welfare, Office of Education, July 1964.
Describes graded and nongraded structures, curricular implications, pros and cons, evaluation, research results, etc.

DiPasquale, Vincent C. "The Relation Between Dropouts and the Graded School." *Phi Delta Kappan* 46:129–133, November 1964. Included in Chapter 2.
Advocates abandonment of gradedness and its single standard of achievement for each grade and each academic subject. Believes this would reduce the number of dropouts. Recommends interclass grouping, multiple curricula that is sequential in levels of difficulty, and expansion of vocational and technical programs.

Docking, R. and Hogan, D. "Breaking Grade Barriers." *Michigan Education Journal* 42:16–17, January 1965.
Describes nongraded arrangement, team teaching, and independent study at a Michigan high school.

Eilers, Wm. Jr. "San Angelo's Three-Rail Program." *American School Board Journal* 149:11–12, September 1964.
Organized the first six years of the San Angelo's school system on a nongraded basis in 1962. Grades seven through twelve have three levels of instruction: slow students are in a terminal program, college-preparatory students have a middle-of-the-road program, and gifted students have a program designed to challenge them.

Figurel, J. A., et al. "Emerging Instructional Procedures in English." *Education* 85:249–265, January 1965.
Describes team teaching, nongrading, and other experiments at the high school level.

Filbin, Robert I. "Continuous Progress for All: Implications for the High School." *American School Board Journal* 143:11–14, October 1961.
The principal of a nongraded elementary school in Lincoln, Massachusetts presents his view of continuous progress plan and gives its implications for grouping in high school.

Franklin, Marian Pope. "New-Type School Promising." *Greensboro Daily News*: June 14, 1964.
Reports innovations at Nova High nongraded school at Fort Lauderdale, Florida.

Gelinas, Paul J. and Lacoste, Aime. "Setauket Junior High School." *Bulletin of NASSP* 47:68–69, May 1963.
Plan does away with traditional grade lines. Uses homogeneous achievement grouping in each subject area. Study shows by end of freshman year 40% of students had earned one or more sophomore credits.

Gran, Eldon H. "Ungrading the Secondary School." *SDEA Journal* 15–16, January 1964.
Gives plan for ungrading seventh and eighth grades.

Hay, Morris E. "Effective Learning Through Grouping in Junior High School." *California Journal of Secondary Education* 32:4–13, January 1957.
Found there was wide divergence within groups despite homogeneous ability grouping. Faculty decided to ungrade junior high arithmetic as a result of finding.

Hoban, F. and McManus, B. J. "How to Nongrade a Small High School." *School Management* 9:79–81, September 1965.
Description of nongraded English and social studies plan in a high school for 100 students in Tuxedo Park, N.Y. Students are sectioned on the basis of ability.

Hooten, Joseph P., Jr. "Trimester Year-round Operation of the University School." *Florida Education* 40:7–8, November 1962.
Describes nongraded school, 1–12, at University School, Tallahassee, Florida.

"How Nova Learning Levels Work." *Nation's Schools* 73:84–88, April 1964. Also see *Science Teacher* 33:55–57, November 1966.
Describes nongraded levels, team teaching, flexible scheduling, and lengthened school term at Nova High in Fort Lauderdale, Florida.

Howard, Eugene R. "The School of the Future—Now." *Bulletin of NASSP* 46:256–267, May 1962.
Superintendent of Ridgewood High School in Norridge-Harwood Heights, Illinois describes its organization. Team teaching, large and small group instruction, grouping across grade lines, and other practices are described.

Ilg, F. L. and Ames, L. B. "Viewpoint on School Readiness." *School and Society* 92:397–402, December 26, 1964. This article is Chapter 1 of their book *School Readiness: Behavior Tests Used at Gesell Institute*, Harper, 1964.
Advocates nongrading and grouping on the basis of developmental readiness through junior high.

Keller, Charles. "History and Social Sciences: Reflections and Recommendations." *Journal of Secondary Education* 37:263–270, May 1962.
Recommends curriculum be kept flexible so it will fit the nongraded elementary and secondary school. Suggests scope and sequence. Recommends advanced placement for grade 12.

McPherran, Arch. "A Multitrack English Program." *Journal of Secondary Education* 37:206–208, April 1962.
Describes English program for grades 10–12 in Beatrice, Nebraska. Students are grouped on the basis of standardized achievement test and teacher recommendation.

National Education Association. Project on Instruction Report. *Planning and Organizing for Teaching.* Washington, D.C.: the Association, 1963. pp. 63–228, 147, 169.
Concise discussion of vertical and horizontal school organization. Recommends nongrading and team teaching.

National Education Association. *Project on Instruction: Schools for the Sixties.* New York: McGraw-Hill Book Co., 1963. pp. 63–98. Two 18-minute color filmstrips and accompanying records available.
Gives thirty-three recommendations for improving schools. Includes nongraded recommendation.

Niess, Charles. "A Nongraded Program for the Small High School." *Bulletin of NASSP* 50:19–27, February 1966.
Describes nongrading with 7th & 8th year students at Roosevelt Jr.-Sr. High, Second Laboratory School of Kansas State Teachers College. Students placed in one of three achievement levels in each area of learning.

Noall, Mathew and Nuttall, Maurice. "Hurricane, Utah, High School Ungraded English Project." *Bulletin of NASSP* 185:192, January 1962.
Gives details of a plan designed to improve language arts for sophomore, junior, and senior years. Students are grouped homogeneously in five sections according to ability and skill in English language arts rather than on their class. Each teacher instructs in only one area: (1) literature; (2) grammar aid usage; (3) composition; (4) speech; or (5) reading.

Oestreich, Arthur H. "New Chrome or a New Bus?" *American School Board Journal* 149:19–20, September 1964.
Reports the Division of University Schools of Indiana University is exploring nongrading at the early primary and the junior high level. Cites some of the problems staff has recognized.

Pearson, John C. "Certainly We Group Our Students." *Phi Delta Kappan* 39:358, May 1958.
Deer Path Junior High School of Lake Forest, Illinois combines homogeneous and heterogeneous grouping. In the academic areas (English, science, mathematics, and social studies) students are grouped according to achievement on standardized tests and teacher-evaluation. In non-academic areas students are grouped heterogeneously. The Junior High School is completely departmentalized.

"Planning and Operating the Middle School." *Overview* 4:52–55, March 1963.
Report of Middle Schools for grades 6–8 at Mount Kisco and 5–9 in Sarasota County, Florida. Nongrading and team teaching featured.

Rifugiato, Francis J. "Special Courses for the Ability Student." *Bulletin of NASSP* 47:26–33, March 1963.
Report of innovations at Schenley High School in Pittsburgh including six experimental courses, college guest teachers, selected high school students attending University of Pittsburgh part time, and nongrading in some areas.

Rollins, Sidney. "High School Where No One Fails." *School Management* 5:77–79, May 1962. Also see *Time* 80:70, October 12, 1962; *Bulletin of NASSP* 47:70–72, May 1963; and *Nation's Schools* 73:110–130, April 1964.
Reports program in a six-year secondary school in Middletown, Rhode Island, featuring nongrading, achievement grouping, team teaching, and flexible scheduling. Each student learns at his own speed.

Rollins, Sidney. *The Middletown Project: Development of a Nongraded Secondary School.* Providence, Rhode Island: Division of Graduate Studies, Rhode Island College, 1962.
Gives resume of Six-Year Secondary Nongraded School at Middletown, Rhode Island. Includes a statement of philosophy and purposes; a description of the school as it now exists with no grade designations; curriculum organization in terms of six or seven years of a subject field and a flexible schedule. Cites unsolved problems, such as pupil evaluation and in-service education.

Whitmire, Janet. "The Independent Study Program at Melbourne High." *Phi Delta Kappan* 47:43–46, September 1965.

Describes organization, facilities, admission procedures, course requirements and independent study programs followed by Melbourne High students. Has implications for graded and nongraded schools.

Chapter 5

Multigraded
School Organization

Facilitating Effective Teaching and Learning in the Elementary School

William P. Colbert

At one time mention of the term "elementary school" brought to mind pictures of thirty or so children of approximately the same age sitting quietly in graded classrooms working at specific tasks that were synonymous with that grade. First grade children, for example, were hard at work trying to master first grade reading, writing and arithmetic, while fifth grade children were attempting to master fifth grade reading, writing and arithmetic, along with the fifth grade course of study in history, geography and science. Sometimes children who demonstrated sufficient mastery of the curricular tasks for a specific grade level were rushed on to a higher grade level before the school term was over regardless of their age, size, or ability to relate to the older pupils in the higher grade. At other times, however, children remained in the same grade no matter how well or how fast they performed the specific tasks assigned to that grade. At still other times children who were unable to do all the work of a specific grade were retained in that grade to work until they completed all or most of the task assigned to that grade.

While this picture of the elementary school might still be prevalent in the minds of many laymen, teachers at least know better. They know that children have specific strengths in specific areas and specific weaknesses

Written especially for this book. William P. Colbert is Assistant Professor of Education, University of North Carolina, Greensboro.

in other areas. They know that no child is average in all things at all times. They know, too, that learning tasks cannot be arbitrarily assigned to grades and that it is better by far to do careful diagnosis of individual pupils to discover what kinds of learning experiences are appropriate for specific learners. Hopefully, then, a picture of the elementary school today might show some pupils in a specific grade working at tasks that were once assigned to either a higher or a lower grade level. In short, all grades in our graded school system are in a sense multigraded because of the nature of the pupils.

Authors of selections in this chapter describe with favor multigraded school organization as an administrative plan, and ask some searching questions concerning the value of continuing the more prevalent system of graded schools in light of all we have learned from years of research in psychology and education. In the first article Marian Franklin helps us with the definitions of some terms that are commonly used and locates many of the school systems in the United States that are experimenting with this plan. J. H. Hull describes a three-year study of multigrade teaching in a California school system, the findings of which were decidedly in favor of this plan. In describing the operation of multi-age classes in Appleton, Wisconsin, James Retson cites twelve distinct advantages of the plan in addition to the fact that the system compels teachers and administrators to treat learners as individuals. Lillian Glogau also underscores this point in a very amusing account of a rapid change-over from a graded to more of a nongraded structure in a Plainview, New York, school. Another research study by Carmen Finley and Jack Thompson focuses on the achievement of multigraded and single-graded rural elementary school children. Dr. Franklin's bibliography which concludes this chapter offers further leads to exploration in this area.

Do successful teaching and learning still depend on the teacher? Of course! Perhaps, however, some ways of organizing facilitate more effective teaching and learning for more children than do others.

Multigrading in Elementary Education

Marian Pope Franklin

An elementary school multigraded class is one that is composed of students from two or three grade levels. It is a vertical administrative arrangement that:

> groups students on the basis of differences rather than on similarities;
>
> provides flexibility for the students;
>
> requires differentiation of instruction;
>
> modifies the traditional elementary graded school.

Multigrading is a well established arrangement at the secondary level, particularly in elective classes. French, for example, is often made up of students from several of the high school years (freshman, sophomore, junior, or senior). At the elementary school level, however, a multigraded class is usually an exception. This paper is concerned with the multigraded arrangement in the elementary school.

Are multigraded and nongraded plans similar?

There are many similarities between multigrading and nongrading.

Both attempt to break the lockstep of the graded school and eliminate its failures and frustrations.

Both attempt to recognize and plan for a wide range of pupil abilities.

Both provide for differentiated rates of pupil progress.

Both adjust to individual mental, emotional, physical, and social needs.

Both require a curriculum study and extensive curricular modifications.

Both are vertical dimensions of school organization.

How do multigraded and nongraded classes differ?

Multigraded classes are composed of students of several ages, abilities, interests, and grades. Each student considers himself in a specific grade,

Reprinted from *Childhood Education*, Vol. 43, No. 9, May, 1967, by permission of the publisher and author. Dr. Marian Pope Franklin is Professor of Education at The University of North Carolina in Greensboro.

but he is also a member of a class that has one or two other grade levels. Multigraded grouping, sometimes called interage or intergrade grouping, is based on the assumption that students are better off when they are grouped on the basis of differences rather than on similarities. The plan operates within a framework of a graded system and it retains grade labels. Nongraded classes, on the other hand, have grade labels and grade barriers removed. The curriculum, the materials, the activities, and the instruction are all ungraded to provide for the continuous progress of each student.

What are the horizontal organizational arrangements in multigrading
    and nongrading?

The horizontal organizational alternatives for grading, nongrading, and multigrading are the same. Each school staff makes horizontal decisions in terms of its value system. Choices lie between the self-contained classroom, departmentalization, team teaching, or some combination of these horizontal arrangements. Then, there is a further choice between homogeneity or heterogeneity on some factor. These horizontal decisions are made in graded, nongraded, and multigraded schools.

What is a multigraded unit?

A primary class in a multigraded unit has approximately an equal number of first-, second-, and third-grade students. An intermediate multigraded unit has approximately an equal number of fourth-, fifth-, and sixth-graders. Grouping within the classroom cuts across grade level lines. Within the class, students move from one grade to another in subject matter. Nine-year-old Johnny, for example, may be working at grade four in reading, five in science, and six in mathematics in an intermediate multigrade unit. He is able to study at a level that fits him, and he advances at different speeds in various aspects of his learning. All the while, he experiences a reasonable amount of success in his endeavors. Multigrading is a facilitating arrangement and the plan focuses on the needs of the learner rather than on grade level standards.

A student begins a multigraded unit as one of the youngest ones in the class. The second year he is in the middle group and the last year he is the oldest. The pupils are motivated academically by those above them and supported emotionally by those below. The psychological processes of socialization and identification are probably facilitated by such an arrangement. Ties of affection and admiration for older students and protective attitudes toward younger ones develop. Attitudes, values, and beliefs are extended. Meanwhile, each student is tackling subject matter that fits him regardless of its grade level.

The membership of two-thirds of the group is the same each year in a unit that has three grades. The older third moves on to another class, and a new third joins the group. In some schools, the teacher spends more time than a year with each unit, and so she has a real opportunity to become very familiar with the students and their needs. The students, in turn, have an excellent opportunity to identify with the teacher.

What does research say?

Because there are so few multigraded units in the elementary schools, studies of them are still very limited. In the findings that are available, results indicate that continued experimentation is justified and should be encouraged.

A three-year study was launched in 1955 in Torrance, California by Walter Rehwoldt and Warren Hamilton. Data reveal multigraded groups exceeded single-graded groups in reading, arithmetic, and language. In 46 out of 48 statistical comparisons, multigraded pupils also showed greater gains in personal adjustment, social adjustment, social maturity, and behavior characteristics. The researchers concluded:

that academic achievement in most grade levels was favorably influenced in multigraded classes;

that membership contributed to greater personal adjustment;

that social adjustment was improved;

that pupils at five of the six grade levels made greater improvement in certain aspects of maturity;

that oldest pupils consistently made significantly greater gains;

that pupils at all levels made greater improvement in certain aspects of behavior;

that pupil attitudes toward school were better in multigraded groups;

that parents expressed strong support of such grouping and evidenced better attitudes toward school than did parents of single-grade pupils;

that pupil-pupil relationships within multigraded classes were very similar to those in single grades;

that teachers and administrators of multigraded classes expressed agreement with 13 of the 14 hypotheses in support of multigraded grouping;

that there was considerable acceptance between pupils of different ages and grades.

For over 15 years Appleton, Wisconsin has had nongraded grouping. The Language Arts Consultant at Appleton indicates one group of teachers identified the next step was multigrade grouping. A pilot multigraded arrangement and study was begun. The consultant reports in an ACEI publication, *Toward Effective Grouping:*

> We have noted the development of a fine spirit of responsibility and leadership, a minimum of emotional and behavior problems, and an easy orientation of the youngest children into good work habits. On standardized tests, the children in the "mixed primary" room have exceeded those in the control group in every area of learning. On the basis of these observations, we are continuing our two primary groups and setting up two pilot classrooms on the same plan at the intermediate level for the coming year.[1]

At the University of Utah Campus School teachers, parents, and pupils are enthusiastic about interage grouping. Achievement, as determined by standardized tests, is high.

Other schools with multigraded classes are in Franklin, Oyster Bay, New York City, and Schenectady, New York; Lynwood, La Mesa, Culver City, Borrego Springs, Whittier, Carlsbad, Merced County, and Claremont, California; Englewood, Florida; Minneapolis, Minnesota and Chicago, Illinois.

---

[1] Lois Smith, "Continuous Progress Plan," in *Toward Effective Grouping* (Washington, D.C.: Association for Childhood Education International, 1962), p. 44.

Grouping Within a School

John M. Bahner

Mary was the brightest girl in the classroom. A few desks away sat Johnny, the slowest in the class. These two children were almost as different as day and night, yet there were also thirty other unique individuals in the classroom and only one teacher. Furthermore, every teacher in Englewood School was faced with the same problem. As individual teachers they had already adjusted their methods of teaching in an attempt to provide for these differences in children; but, if every teacher had the same problem, perhaps some schoolwide solutions should be attempted.

Throughout their experience, these teachers observed that the individual children and groups of children had a range of academic abilities and attainments that extended over at least several years. Thus, they could state with firm conviction that a single grade designation could never adequately describe the achievement level of either a single class or a single child. It seemed obvious that some children were going to need a longer period of time than six years to achieve most of the goals of an elementary school program and, conversely, that others would be ready to profit from the next unit of school organization after only five years in the elementary school.

HETEROGENEOUS GROUPING IN COMBINATION GRADES

These observations indicated a need for a type of organization that would enable all children, fast and slow, to move smoothly through the school at their own rate without either skipping or repeating. Both an ungraded structure and an increased use of combination grades were discussed. The school already had a combination second-third-grade room and a fifth-sixth-grade room. The two teachers who had these combination grades expressed satisfaction with them and reported only minor problems of parental understanding. Since none of the staff had the benefit of any experience in an ungraded system and since it was doubtful that such a plan could be presented adequately to the community before the end of

Reprinted from *Childhood Education*, April, 1960, Vol. 36, pp. 354–356, by permission of the Association for Childhood Education International, 3615 Wisconsin Avenue, N.W., Washington, D.C. 20016. John M. Bahner is Associate Superintendent of Schools, Miami, Florida.

the school year, it was decided to organize classes for the following year as follows:

> Kindergarten—two sections (Financial conditions necessitated having only one teacher for the two sections.)
>
> Grade 1, 1, 1–2, 2–3, 3–4, 3–4, 4–5, 5, 5–6, and 6
>
> A line over a number indicates the section where the three or four most advanced children of a grade were placed; a line below a number indicates where the three or four most retarded children were placed.

This plan was followed to prevent a teacher from having to work with the extremely accelerated and the extremely retarded in the same classroom, yet heterogeneity is still retained—a condition which the staff felt was important. At the same time, placing the extremely advanced or retarded in specific rooms reduced the range in any given classroom to a point where a *teacher with a combination class could see no difference in the range of abilities as observed the preceding year with a single grade level per classroom.*

As the staff seized every opportunity to explain the reasons behind this type of organization through parent-teacher meetings, study groups and individual conferences, parents began thinking of children of a given age level as having a wide range of abilities. They realized that a child's reading ability is most apt *not* to be the same as his ability in arithmetic. For the most part, they accepted as perfectly natural that some children (not theirs, of course) need longer than six years to move through the elementary school program. Even for those who do not accept this, the various combination grades will probably obscure the movement of a child sufficiently so that only his parents will realize if he takes more than six years in Englewood School.

> Johnny is a boy of low scholastic aptitude. All the evidence gathered during his two years of school indicates he will profit by having seven years in the elementary school. This year Johnny is in a 2–3 class. Next year he will be in a 3–4 class, the following year probably in a 4–5 class, and the year following perhaps in a straight fifth grade. Thus he will have taken three years to cover what is typically known as the third and fourth grades.

Of course, if Johnny's ability has been misjudged or if his growth pattern changes to a point where it no longer seems desirable to have him spend seven years in the elementary program, he could be placed in the sixth grade three years from now without any dislocation in his progress. In either event, there will be no social stigma attached to his decelerated rate of progress. There has been no boring repetition of a grade; he is making numerous friends among his somewhat younger classmates who are achieving at various levels along the learning continuum.

Through a similar use of the combination grades, an extremely mature, "gifted" child goes through a typical three- or four-year grade span in one less year and completes the elementary school program in five years. There is no skipping of any essential skills or being thrust suddenly into a group one year older chronologically.

Mary, who is in her fourth year of school beyond kindergarten, is an academically advanced child with high social and emotional maturity. This year she is in a 4–5 class and next year will be placed in a 5–6 class. At the end of next year she will probably be passed on to the junior high school, thereby completing the last three grades in a two-year period. If she does not live up to this expectation, she will be placed in a sixth grade at the end of next year.

TEAM TEACHING

The graded structure of the elementary school was not the only tradition put under scrutiny by the Englewood School faculty. Another obstacle to better provision for individual differences seemed to lie in the traditional concept that a single teacher must work always with approximately thirty pupils. This seemed to be too restrictive. Therefore some of the faculty decided to plan and work closely together in teams of two or three teachers. During that same year in which the school planned having combination grades, one of the closely knit teams in operation involved a woman teacher with a third-fourth grade combination and a man with a fourth-fifth grade combination.

The typical day for this team began with a fifteen- or twenty-minute planning period during which each group discussed with its teacher the day's general plan and individual work. Reading groups then occupied the next hour and one-half. Each teacher had from two to four groups (this varied as the need arose throughout the year) composed of children with similar reading achievement levels from both rooms regardless of their grade placement.

Next came a short break for the morning fruit juice, followed by the physical education period when the two classes combined. The teachers planned this period together. Then one assumed responsibility for the total group while the other took a break, collected materials, evaluated the work of pupils, or performed other needed tasks. After the physical education period, these sixty-five children remained together for a story period, music or art. The teacher who had the preceding half-hour away from the class assumed full responsibility now, while the other teacher had an unscheduled period of approximately twenty minutes.

From this point until lunch, the sixty-five children were divided into four arithmetic groups on the basis of achievement—again without regard to their grade placement. Each teacher worked with two groups.

The program after lunch varied considerably. Often there was some type of project going on, with the two classes sometimes combined and sometimes working separately. Special interests and abilities of the two teachers often determined just how the two classes operated. For example, both classes worked together on an electricity unit with the man assuming the major responsibility for planning the lesson, gathering the materials and doing the group instruction. The woman member of the team performed as an aide during this project, helping individuals and small groups. Later on, the teachers reversed their roles while undertaking a unit on space.

Although sometimes taught as separate entities, social studies, science, music and art were integrated during the afternoon period. Of course, individual work going on during reading groups was often based on the units or projects then in progress.

MODIFYING TRADITIONAL PRACTICES TO FIT BELIEFS

The variations of team teaching being practiced at Englewood School are too numerous to describe in this article. However, these descriptions are not so important as the fact that this staff has shown that professionally-trained teachers, given freedom to develop improved educational practices, rise to the occasion and modify traditional practices in line with their educational beliefs.

Further faculty effort undoubtedly will modify present innovations in grade organization and teacher utilization. The traditional grade structure is fast being replaced by the ungraded concept. New insights into team-teaching techniques are emerging. The Englewood faculty is pleased to join company with other groups who are seriously questioning long-established practices of grouping children within a school.

Multigrade Teaching

J. H. Hull

The one-room school had something. In an experimental program in the unified school district of Torrance, Calif., we have been able to recapture that "something"—increasing the spread and speed of learning through a grouping of grades.

Our three-year study has dealt with the multigrade system, and the results indicate that under this type of organization more learning takes place than under the traditional system of single grades.

In fact, in the three skill subjects scored in this experiment—reading, arithmetic and language—multigrade learning clearly exceeds single grade learning experiences insofar as can be measured by the standardized test procedures available.

Our findings to date further show that, in addition to gains in the three skill subjects listed, the multigrade pupils in 46 out of 48 statistical comparisons showed greater gains in four other areas: personal adjustment, social adjustment, social maturity, and behavior characteristics. In addition, the multigrade pupils have shown a better attitude toward their school work and toward their peers than have the single grade pupils.

Observations in the Torrance study also indicate that not only have children an improved rate of growth in learning but also there is a remarkable improvement in the quality of instruction and even in the creative personality of the teacher. What's good for one seems to challenge and improve the other.

The originator of the study was Walter Rehwoldt, then director of instruction in Torrance and now assistant superintendent in Barstow, Calif. Experience as a country school teacher, the frustrations of the graded system, and the desire to find the next step after the self-contained classroom, all contributed to the idea.

Dr. Rehwoldt and I and Warren Hamilton, my collaborator,* had many discussions over a period of a year on the approach we might take. We agreed upon certain points for the protection and welfare of the

Reprinted, with permission, from *The Nation's Schools*, 62:33–36, July 1958. Copyright 1958, The Modern Hospital Publishing Company, Inc., Chicago. All rights reserved. Dr. J. H. Hull is Superintendent of the Torrance Unified School District, Torrance, California.

* Rehwoldt, Walter, and Hamilton, Warren: An Analysis of Some of the Effects of Interage and Intergrade Grouping in an Elementary School, doctoral dissertation, University of Southern California, January 1957.

school district. Welty LeFever of the doctoral committee of the University of Southern California advised on the design of the experiment.

We decided that existing district policy would prevail. This included:

1. The board must unanimously endorse the plan.

2. Participation would be voluntary. Obviously, parent education would be required. It so happened that only one parent meeting was required to establish a waiting list of those who wanted their children in a multigrade.

3. The plan must have potential for improving instruction and for benefiting the children, and it must not lead to excessive costs.

4. The plan must qualify under the existing written policies of the school system, many of which have to do with educational philosophy.

From time to time as the planning for the experiment progressed, we briefed the board of education. Then it made a decision, and in 1955–56 the experiment began at Walteria School. We formed seven classes in two multigrades, with each class consisting of approximately 33 children. The primary multigrade classes—four in all—contained 11 children from the first grade and the same number from Grades 2 and 3. The intermediate multigrade classes—three in number—contained 11 children each from the fourth, fifth and sixth grades.

Teachers for the classes were drawn from a hat containing the names of all the teachers in the school system. Supervision was by the building principal and was the same as that afforded regular grade classes.

MANY REQUESTS FOR CLASSES

Last year, the second year of the establishment of the classes, parental demand was sufficient for an eighth class. In fact, there were requests to fill an additional ninth class, but we did not add one until this year.

In February of this year, the board approved a plan whereby several Torrance schools may carry on the multigrade class organizations on a voluntary basis on the primary and intermediate levels, as is being done at Walteria School. Children will be placed in these classes only upon the request of the parents.

Before this step toward extension of the plan was taken, I called a conference at which were present the principal and all teachers of multigrade classes at Walteria and to which were invited several staff members and some of the elementary school principals of the district.

WHAT MULTIGRADE TEACHERS SAY

At this conference we asked the multigrade teachers and the Walteria principal, Don Mullaney: "What do you regard as the most important aspect of the multigrade program?"

Some of the replies were these:

"There is no important difference between a multigrade and a straight grade."

"Individual differences get more attention in the multigrade setup."

"You can go much more into depth and detail with the older and more gifted pupils."

"If you have a multigrade, you'll become a better teacher. It gives you problems; it makes you think. You make the work more effective for all."

"I'm doing nothing that I shouldn't have been doing in a regular grade classroom. Yet what has happened to me is important in terms of professional growth. The solving of problems and the interchange between teachers improve our teaching."

"I've never before done so good a job with bright children."

"After three years as a multigrade primary teacher, I now have more materials to cover the spread of interests and abilities. I would probably teach a straight grade the same way now."

RESULTS IN NEW LEARNING

Another teacher said the multigrade plan results in a spread of activities that causes a lot of new learning on the part of everyone.

We asked the teachers about peer rivalry. They said that after three years it was about the same as in a regular grade, although tests showed that there was less and the teachers said there was less in the multigrade rooms the first year of the experiment.

All the teachers thought it would be a mistake to drop the program, and most of them didn't know which straight grade they would want to teach after teaching a multigrade.

AVOID COMPARISONS

Principal Mullaney of Walteria School advised against having a minority of straight grades in any school in the district. Under such conditions any comparisons that are made are too easy to identify, and this affects the morale of the straight grade teacher, he declared. As a starter in the other schools, he suggested two teachers at each multigrade level.

"It's more work to administer a school that is divided on a half-and-half basis," Mr. Mullaney declared, but he admitted that the constant stream of visitors to his school created part of that feeling.

ANALYSIS OF FINDINGS TO DATE

Why do these multigrade pupils have better attitudes, have better personal adjustment, better social adjustment, and even tend to do better work in academic areas? Our study does not provide the answer. Some of the factors that probably have an effect on the findings are:

1. Older children seem to gain from helping younger children.
2. Younger children seem to learn from older.
3. Wider range of experiences and interests stimulates all.
4. Teacher attitude when faced with three grades seems to include a do-something-about-it attitude.
5. Peer rivalry may to some extent be replaced by friendly acceptance of difference when the grade level loses its significance through spread of ability and interests.
6. Children gain the advantage of experiencing being in the younger, middle and older group in successive years rather than always having to view the situation from one position year after year.

As Table 1 indicates, so far as the three skill subjects are concerned, of the 18 tests in subject areas, 11, or 61.6 per cent, favored multigrade and only seven, or 38.8 per cent, favored straight grades. Further refinement revealed that of the 11 favoring multigrade, five were statistically

TABLE 1

Mean Differences in Gains Between Multigrade Pupils and Their Matched Partners in All Areas in Which Comparisons of Gains Were Made

Area of Comparison	Grade Level					
	1	2	3	4	5	6
Reading	0.46**	−0.25	0.20	0.14	0.55*	−0.47
Arithmetic	0.30**	−0.21	0.38*	−0.12	0.85**	−0.13
Language	0.25	−0.11	0.17	−0.24	0.11	0.28
Personal Adjustment	2.0	3.1**	4.0	1.8	0.7	0.3
Social Adjustment	2.7	3.9	4.6*	0.2	4.5	5.0
Social Maturity	3.3	11.5*	18.3**	0.3	−13.9	20.5**
Behavior Characteristics	5.9	11.3*	6.5	14.8	21.9*	15.0

*Significant at the 5 per cent level.
**Significant at the 1 per cent level.
Note: The negative differences favor the regular grade pupils.

significant at either the 1 per cent or the 5 per cent level while none was statistically significant in the regular or control classes. Hence, as far as the experimental and the control groups were concerned, multigrade learning clearly exceeds single grade learning experiences as far as they are measurable by the standardized tests that are available.

The school district, however, was not satisfied with stopping here, so the board of education financed a comparative statistical study involving all six grade levels at six other randomly selected schools in the district. This required thousands of careful computations and produced the following mean gain results shown in Table 2.

PRODUCED BETTER RESULTS

Table 2 shows clearly the same trend that the matched pairs in the experiment produced, namely, that multigrade classroom organization did produce more learning as measured by the testing instruments, both by area tested and by grade level of pupils. This result was obtained with

TABLE 2

Mean of Mean Gains by Grade Level of All Pupils in Subject Matter and Social Areas in Multigrade, Single Experimental, and Single Grades of Other Schools

Areas	Multigrade	Single Grade Experimental	Single Grade Other Schools
Reading	1.1	1.0	1.1
Arithmetic	1.4	1.2	1.2
Language	1.3	1.2	1.1
Personal Adjustment	3.9	2.8	2.0
Social Adjustment	2.1	−0.3	1.7
Social Maturity	16.5	11.1	7.6
Behavior Characteristics	6.1	−1.7	−0.2
Grade 1	4.7	4.1	1.4
Grade 2	4.7	2.5	2.0
Grade 3	5.7	1.9	2.4
Grade 4	5.2	1.7	2.5
Grade 5	4.2	3.6	2.3
Grade 6	3.1	1.8	2.1

teachers drawn by lot from a regular school faculty, with teachers untrained for specific multigrade teaching, with teachers given no special supervision for multigrade teaching, with pupils unselected and very comparable to the other half of the enrollees.

When only one mean of the mean out of 26 comparisons of single grades shows an equivalent result to the multigrade and all the rest show the multigrade to be superior, it appears that a fact has been established.

It is significant that the one area in which single grades equal multigrade is reading. This is the major area of emphasis in the minds of most school teachers. Reading is the area where grouping and individualized instruction is most highly developed. Reading is the area in which the techniques that have been developed by most classroom teachers most nearly parallel the kind of instruction that naturally develops in a multigrade.

If there is any importance to timing in providing learning opportunities for children, it is not unreasonable to assume that helping children to develop their own rate and timing will produce better results than attempting to make children develop at a predetermined rate and timing, which is exactly what the typical graded school did try to do, in the past at least. This does not mean that alert teachers cannot overcome grade level traditions, but it is more difficult than when they have the multigrade before them.

These results would indicate that there is something inherent in this plan of pupil grouping that educators should consider in organizing a school or in building faculty and parent attitudes, or in both.

Are We Back to the Little Red Schoolhouse?

James N. Retson

Are we returning to the era of the "Little Red Schoolhouse"? This question is frequently asked by parents of children in nine multi-age classes being conducted in Appleton's (Wisconsin) Huntley Elementary School.

Parents who ask this question may be partly right when they refer to this project in multigrading as "The Little Red Schoolhouse Experiment." Certain advantages for children were inherent in the old one-room country schoolhouse. We can capitalize on these if we add proven, up-to-date teaching methods in a modern city school setting.

Experts in child growth and development have been pointing out for many years that children are different. They have their own unique growth patterns—physical, emotional, academic, and social. Yet too many of us continue to place them in lockstep, graded school organizations that assume that all children, upon reaching a given chronological age, are ready to absorb a given instructional diet at the same rate.

Today, some schools are recognizing individual differences in children and are providing for these differences. There are differential materials, team approaches, homogenous groupings, elaborate "levels" systems of achievement, and various forms of "ungrading."

Educators in Appleton have, over the past 15 years, gone from a rather rigid "graded" philosophy to a more flexible nongraded concept. This is now known as the "Continuous Progress Plan."

Under the multi-age system, children are placed in classes on a heterogenous, random basis. Each primary class contains approximately 30 boys and girls who are six, seven, and eight years of age and who would be in first, second, and third grade in a graded school. The intermediate classes contain children of nine, 10, and 11 years of age who would have been in fourth, fifth, and sixth grade. Hence the tag, "Little Red Schoolhouse."

But why do this? What are the advantages? Isn't the spread of achievement too great to cope with? What textbooks are used? Isn't it a

Reprinted from *Grade Teacher* magazine 83:108–110, February 1966, by permission of the publishers and the author. Copyright 1966 by Teachers Publishing Corporation, Darien, Connecticut. James N. Retson, formerly Elementary Curriculum Coordinator of the Appleton, Wisconsin, Public Schools, is now at Arizona State University, Tempe.

great task for the teacher? Can a six-year-old function in the same room as an eight-year-old? These are questions frequently asked about our nine multi-age classes, and perhaps we can give some answers to them.

INDIVIDUAL NEEDS VARY

We are doing this because we feel this is a realistic way of recognizing and providing for individual differences in children. A teacher of a multi-age class can no longer think of a child in terms of chronological age or specific grade. Age and grade have little bearing on growth. Instead, a teacher must approach the child as a human being who wants and needs to learn just as much and as fast as his inborn capacity warrants.

Beside the fact that our system compels us to treat youngsters as individual learners, there are many other advantages inherent in this type of organizational structure. For example:

1. The teacher has (in most cases) a child for a longer period than one year and yet does not have the *same class* for three years. This allows for a better understanding of the child.

2. The teacher has only one-third of her class as "newcomers" each year, which can actually give her an opportunity to spend more time with the beginning students, who need it most.

3. This program allows the teacher much more flexibility in ability grouping within the class since the range of abilities is likely to be greater. A child can, therefore, work at his level of achievement in any subject area.

4. Stereotyping of students is eliminated. For example, the tallest, shortest, fastest, slowest, fattest, etc., does not necessarily remain in this position year after year in school. In the first year a child may be the smallest. The next year others will enter the class who may be smaller and so on.

5. Leadership qualities are developed. The shy child often comes out of his shell as he gets older and associates with some of the younger children in the room.

6. Better judgments can be made regarding acceleration or retention since the child can be observed over a longer period of time.

7. A more natural transition can be made for the child who is retained for an extra year and also for the child who is accelerated a year, since in neither case are they cast into a situation that is completely new to them.

8. Children are in a more natural, neighborhood-like social situation in a mixed group rather than being placed with all others the same age, which is an unnatural situation.

9. The attitude that an age or grade barrier exists is broken down in a mixed group. Children respect one another for their individual abilities and not for their ages or grades.

10. Six-year-olds learn and develop independent study habits earlier than is usually expected.

11. There is less time wasted for teacher and student in getting acquainted at the opening of each school year since two-thirds of the class are already accustomed to the procedures and expectations of the class.

12. Administratively, a better deployment of students is possible when mixed groups are used. Class sizes can be consistent and kept to any desired number that is felt necessary since all children of a single age group do not need to be placed in separate classes.

THEY LIVE TOGETHER NICELY

The spread of achievement is usually very great, but it can be coped with beautifully if the teacher has the proper attitude toward his pupils, employs methods of individualized instruction, plans with the entire class in mind, and allows for interplay and independent study when appropriate.

A must, concerning textbooks and materials, is that the teacher must have a variety, as much as is available, at his disposal. He must be able to draw what he needs and when he needs it to enhance a particular task for a given child or group of children.

We have observed that groups of children with a three-year age span live together very nicely. They seem to extend themselves to be cooperative and are more than anxious to offer help to another child in their room who may lack the maturity they have attained. This organization simulates a neighborhood or family setting.

We feel that after five years there has been a measure of success with these classes. When comparing the academic achievement of multi-age groups with their counterparts in graded classes, we find their gains to be significantly greater. We can make some subjective judgments, also, and state that these youngsters are more independent and self-directed. They also display more leadership qualities than we see in children of regular graded classes.

These gains are, of course, subject to the usual variable factors as teacher ability, parental cooperation, and each child's background, but generally we feel that more success has been gained through this approach than we had originally anticipated.

Mary Jo Weingarten, a teacher of a primary multi-age unit for the past four years, sums up her experiences with the following:

"Our classroom day is a flexible one. We go through a multitude of acts, a kaleidoscope of events, and numberless interplays, making any variety theater bill look stagnant in comparison. My role as a teacher is that of a planner, giving guidance, lending continuity, and helping direct our routine."

YOUNG ONES ARE EAGER

"I have found that the younger children can see a long-range growth process stretched out before their eyes. They are eager to push forward— with little motivation on my part. Phonetic skills, word syllabication, and number concepts are more easily approached because these children have had the experience of observing others mastering these processes.

"Because of the variety of activities and skills being developed, I have found large blocks of time to be more conducive for teacher-pupil planning. Multi-age grouping readily lends itself to individualization of instruction."

THEY WORK IN GROUPS

"The morning is devoted to the area of communicative arts. Listening, speaking, creative writing, and personalized or selective reading combine to make learning purposeful for the individual. Skill groups are based on the learner's need at his particular stage of development. Spelling and handwriting are an outgrowth of these areas, depending upon the child's readiness.

"Planning in the afternoon prepares us for arithmetic. Here children work according to their level of ability rather than that of age or grade level. Art, music, social studies and science are whole class projects; however, a problem may arise and interested groups may form to solve it.

"There are apparent advantages to multi-age grouping. Socially, the children choose friends because they like them, regardless of age. They donate their time and talents to whoever can make use of them. Academically, there is a constant interchange of help and direction. Emotionally, a mature stability in climate is provided, so that a teacher can more easily discern and lend help to those who are having difficulties.

"A mixed primary classroom can be a workable one. I believe the key to this most rewarding experience is that of flexibility. Use it, and you open the door to a fascinating and meaningful experience."

Make Me a Nongraded

Lillian Glogau

"Make me a nongraded." Boiled down to its essence, this was the message my boss and I received from the superintendent of schools a year ago this spring. "But," came our answer, "we need more time, time to educate our faculty, time to prepare our parents." "But me no buts," came the response, and what man know you who has ever butted a superintendent of schools—especially one who has a board of seven men tried and true awaiting the miracle?

Thus equipped with our own faculties, an outstanding teaching staff, a dedication to differentiated instruction and some excellent curricula, we were off. I don't recommend the crash program which I am about to describe as being favorable to ulcers or for that matter even to sanity, but I shall describe the process as closely as I can for one simple reason. I don't think that too many of our peers describe the desperate agonies of organizing a new program (there never seems to be the time) and I think our experiences (right and wrong) are invaluable. Perhaps our story may be helpful to others.

My boss, Mr. Murray Fessel, the principal of the school, and I began by restudying every available source of information in print on the nongraded school. We distributed material to the staff members. Impromptu, unrehearsed question-and-answer sessions took place all over the building. There were many questions, and not too many answers. We began a program of visitations to other schools which had operating nongraded primaries and to any and all conferences which had lectures scheduled on our topic. Most of our visits weren't too profitable until we happened upon P.S. 89 in Queens and the indomitable Rheba Meyers. This New York City principal and her teachers, who are operating an experimental nongraded primary, were a storehouse of good, practical, specific ideas which we carted back to our teachers with gratitude.

Finally, came the fatal day when Mr. F. and I sat down to hash out the philosophical basis for our program and the ground rules for its operation. It was a hard day for both of us because we were working under

Reprinted from *National Elementary Principal* 44:51–54, May 1965, by permission of the publisher and the author. Copyright 1965, Department of Elementary School Principals, National Education Association. All rights reserved. Lillian Glogau is Assistant Principal, Old Bethpage School, Plainview, New York.

extreme pressure. We were holding our formulation meeting with staff the very next day and our first orientation meeting with parents that same night. It was vital and essential to our future that we both completely understand what we were going to explain to the teachers and what we were going to promise to parents.

It was at this brainstorming session that Mr. F. and I made our first mistake, as you shall soon see. We committed ourselves to a specific grouping organizational pattern. Each class was to house (for the first year) children whose age span did not exceed two chronological years. Further, each class was to house three (contiguous) reading groups, each reading group capable of being instructed at approximately the same achievement level. We had seventeen teachers in the primary school and approximately twenty-five children in each class. (Incidentally, one excellent outcome of nongrading is a more equitable distribution of children.)

We began our meetings with teachers in the afternoon and parents in the evening. Mr. F. prepared an outstanding brochure on the nongraded primary which was distributed to all the parents of the school (graded classes, too). We answered questions. We clarified. We mollified. Throughout it all, the teachers were a source of strength and reinforcement.

To aid us in the grouping of children, we used a profile card for each youngster entering our primary school. It was a fairly comprehensive card indicating special characteristics which need watching in any youngster's placement (emotional, physical, social, mental). Each card also indicated the reading instructional level of the child as determined by individually administered independent reading inventories. For the youngsters in kindergarten, we used the percentile the youngsters achieved on the Metropolitan Reading Inventory as a guide for placement in primary school.

Mr. F. and I drew up a "master paper plan" for grouping in each class based on the cumulative totals now available from the profile cards (i.e., twenty-seven youngsters to be instructed at level eight in reading, etc.). It was a beautiful plan, if I do say so myself; we even used different colors to designate different chronological ages. Each class had three contiguous reading groups, and no class had an age span of more than two years as per our predetermined agreement.

We called our first grouping meeting with teachers. The purpose of the meeting was to designate actual class placement for real children according to the "master paper plan." All hell broke loose. Our heretofore well-mannered, staunch friends panicked. For the first time the specter of actual, real honest-to-goodness interage grouping reared its head, and they weren't having any.

The school psychologist, normally quite busy with final reports at this time of the year, was now quite busy holding the hand of almost every teacher in the building. The news spread quickly. Mr. F. and I closed the door, took out pipe and cigarette, respectively, and talked. We both went home and chewed the cud some more. Mutual decision next morning: scotch our beautifully colored "master paper plan" and start from scratch. The "master paper plan" we developed the next day (Want to talk about producing under pressure?) kept us to the same basic grouping structure but reduced our original seventeen interage classes to six, leaving eleven classes without interage groups. Mr. F. and I, realizing full well that we hadn't been allowed sufficient time for "selling," had goofed. We got the word out fast—only six interage classes. The building visibly relaxed, nerves untensed, and smiles returned once more to the faces of our friends.

We started grouping in earnest: three contiguous reading groups, distribution of leadership qualities, and attention to special problems. These were our major criteria. We held many small group meetings with teachers, reviewing and analyzing our class placements. In all cases, the child's current teacher groups him for the next year. Good teachers are like mother hens when it comes to the placement of their children, and what with the nongraded looming on the horizon for the upcoming year, our teachers were exceptionally cautious. This is a tribute to their devotion and their love of children.

Finally, after much agonizing and superhuman labor, we closed the school for the summer. Came September, all too soon, and the doors of our nongraded primary were officially open. Once again, all hell broke loose. The parents who sweetly consented to the organizational change in the spring balked in the fall. We were barraged with telephone calls and visits from anxious mothers and even some worried fathers. Everyone wanted his son or daughter out of the interage class. For self-preservation we quickly established a rule for ourselves—no changes except when warranted for sound educational reasons. It's a good rule, but it took a good deal of time and effort to convince our parents.

It wasn't until after the first six weeks of school that the tide ebbed. The complaints waned. We held an evening parent education meeting, called it Nongraded—Progress Report #1, and answered the remaining "doubting Thomases." Eliminating the grade concept is difficult when parents are steeped in this tradition, and we are far from achieving total acceptance, but the early panic is subsiding for one reason. "A rose by any other name will smell as sweet," and the parents now know that our children are still getting a sound education—the nongraded plan notwithstanding.

The youngsters themselves are responding well to interage grouping. Many of our uncertainties are being eliminated through conscientious planning by the teachers. At the start, the program was carefully detailed to include lessons appropriate to the achievement levels of the youngsters. No child was given instruction which was too difficult or too easy for him in any curriculum area. This reassured the youngsters. Social intermingling has begun, and the children are adjusting nicely to the age differences in their rooms. As time passes, many of the advantages of interage grouping (the literature abounds in examples) are becoming evident. The kids are enjoying each other and mixing quite naturally.

A particular technique which we borrowed from Rheba Meyer was the center of interest (a topic for the day, or a few days) as a unifying device at the start of each day. We find this a most effective technique and are now exploring other types and kinds of experiences which can be utilized for the center of interest. The spectrum is quite broad.

An important technique which we use to great effect, and which we cordially recommend to all schools reorganizing for any reason, is the weekly meeting with small groups of teachers. We divided our seventeen primary teachers among three groups, the teachers in each group having classes with similar grouping patterns and therefore similar problems. We have open-ended meetings with these groups every week. The agenda items come from the teachers, the psychologist, the speech teacher, the special teachers, the administrator, or anyone directly connected with the primary school. The purpose of these meetings is expressly the improvement of instruction. They constitute a supervisory technique which we cannot recommend too highly. We know of no other procedure which has reaped the harvest these meetings have for all of us.

First, and most important, these meetings are the arena for surgery. It is here that we dissect, chew, cut up, and try out every idea and thought each of us has about our new program. Second, they are the arena for therapy. We are all under extreme pressure, and it is at these meetings that we let our hair down and confess our fears and our triumphs, our anxieties and our accomplishments. It is here that we hold each other's hands. Third, it is at these meetings that we get a real look at the total picture of our program, its weaknesses and its strengths. We determine where we need further work and where we are successfully on the way. Fourth, these meetings provide time to examine individual children and what we at school should be doing for them. Fifth, the meetings open new avenues for us to explore.

A few topics selected at random from our minutes may give a taste of the work we have been doing: the thinking process; creative music;

flow sheets for recording each child's achievement in various curriculum areas; criteria for levels of achievement in each curriculum area; the unit approach to the teaching of social studies; individualizing instruction. It is especially interesting to note that many of the agenda items at our weekly meetings have been expanded to become the subjects of full-fledged workshops or study programs designed to explore specific problems as we meet them. Our meetings with the primary teachers reflect the heartbeat of our school this year. The pulse of the school can be told by reading the minutes of each group's weekly meetings. We consider these sessions the core of our new program, and we can't imagine operating without them.

One of the most delicate matters in the organization of the nongraded school is the on-going evaluation of children and their regrouping whenever it becomes obvious that they are instructional isolates in their current classroom situation. Criteria for movement of youngsters are being carefully developed, and these criteria are explored in relation to each youngster at our primary meetings. Before making final decisions, both the receiving and sending teacher are consulted as are other appropriate faculty members (psychologist, reading consultant, etc.). Movements are made at any time in the school year, and this is one of the greatest advantages of the nongraded program for us. Parents are made aware of changes, and conferences are held with them if necessary. In general, surprisingly, we are finding, to date, that movement of youngsters is accepted graciously with only a phone call by the teacher to parents.

We are "making a nongraded." We're sure the pace called for could have been slower, but all things considered, maybe more time really might not have altered appreciably the emotional reactions of some of our parents or teachers.

We have been learning a great deal. We feel very positive education is taking place. The odd thing about our total experience so far is that most of the changes of which we are proudest are not apparent to the eye. If you were to visit our building, you would find no fireworks shooting off the roof and no Chinese gongs chiming in the halls. The changes are subtle. They represent refinements in teaching techniques and learning situations which only the very trained observer could note during a classroom visitation. Yet there have been changes, and they are continuing every day in every way.

The essential truth of what has happened, as we see it, is quite simple and can be easily stated. The basic structure of the nongraded program forces the classroom teacher to note the differences among children in a way graded structure does not. She sees each child as an individual with special needs, problems, hopes, and learning rates. When the teacher recognizes and accepts these differences, she begins to make changes in her curriculum, her patterns of interacting with pupils, her teaching techniques, and her instructional materials in order to accommodate these differences. The process is slow, tortuous, and wearying, but unbelievably rewarding.

A Comparison of the Achievement of Multigraded and Single-Graded Rural Elementary School Children

Carmen J. Finley and Jack M. Thompson

School district reorganization in California and elsewhere in the nation progresses slowly. It has been shown that there is an optimal size range which promotes efficient administration and a good instructional program. Support for this program of reorganization can be demonstrated on the basis of a lower unit cost and added services such as transportation, hot lunches, instrumental music, nursing services and the like. Are these advantages reflected also in higher achievement for children in larger schools? This is the question with which this paper is concerned.

It is recognized that this particular issue of achievement can only be narrowly investigated with the present available testing instruments. However, with current interest in the ungraded primary class or multigraded grouping in larger schools, the question arises as to whether the one- and two-room schoolhouse may not have been forced into a desirable curriculum grouping years ahead of its time.

The hypothesis of this study is that there is no difference in the achievement in basic subjects of rural children in multigraded classrooms as compared with children attending single-graded classrooms.

A review of the research studies in this area shows conflicting results. Drier (3), Adams (1), McIntosh and Schrammel (7) and Nelson (8) found no significant differences in achievement between children educated in single-graded and multigraded classes. Martens (6), Foote (4), Clem and Hovey (2) and Wilson and Ashbaugh (9) found differences favoring children educated in a graded school. On the other hand, Hull (5), in evaluating multigraded teaching within a graded school system, found differences favoring the multigraded group.

Some of the above studies have certain limitations. McIntosh and Schrammel (7) and Foote (4) used no tests of significance. McIntosh and Schrammel (7), Clem and Hovey (2) and Nelson (8) did not equate the multigraded and single-graded groups. Hull's (5) conclusion of higher achievement for the multigraded group might be questioned as statistically

Reprinted from *The Journal of Educational Research* 56:471–475, May–June, 1963, by permission of the publisher and the authors. Carmen J. Finley and Jack M. Thompson are both with the Sonoma County Schools, California.

significant differences were found for only five of the 18 tests made in achievement areas.

METHOD

Grades three and five were chosen for investigation. Both multigraded and fully-graded populations consisted of all pupils at these grade levels in Sonoma County, California. The third graders must have been in attendance at school the two previous years (as first and second graders). The fifth graders must have been in attendance at the school the three previous years (as second, third, and fourth graders). For the purpose of this study, the multigraded school was defined as a school with four teachers or less.

The fully-graded population consisted of children attending a school large enough to have at least one teacher per grade level. The size of the fully-graded schools ranged from 300 to 1,322 average daily attendance.

The two groups were matched on the following basis:

1. Sex
2. IQ within five points
3. Chronological age within three months
4. Participation in the yearly county-wide group testing program. Since the fall testing program usually extends from September through December, it was further required that a given pair must have taken the achievement test within a month's time of each other (differences in opening dates of schools accounted for). Each member of the pair also must have taken both the achievement test and the mental ability test during the current year.

The mental ability test used was the California Short Form Test of Mental Maturity. The achievement test used was the California Achievement Battery Form W.

After children were matched on the above criteria, their achievement records were investigated for the following test areas:

1. reading vocabulary
2. reading comprehension
3. arithmetic fundamentals
4. arithmetic reasoning
5. mechanics of English
6. spelling
7. battery

Mean differences and t-values were computed for boys, girls and total group. The five percent level was defined as indicative of statistical significance.

SUBJECTS

The subjects for this investigation consisted of 53 paired boys and 51 paired girls at third-grade level and 62 paired boys and 46 paired girls at fifth-grade level who met the criteria for matching. The multigraded group was drawn from 28 schools with no more than 12 of the total 212 coming from any one school. The fully-graded group was drawn from 23 different schools with no more than 21 coming from any one school. Table I shows the ability level and the chronological ages of the groups.

RESULTS

Table II summarizes the results.

Third Grade: Boys.   It may be seen that boys in fully-graded classrooms in larger schools tend to score better, on the average, in reading vocabulary, mechanics of English and spelling, while boys in smaller multigraded schools score better, on the average, in reading comprehension, arithmetic reasoning, arithmetic fundamentals and on the composite battery score. However, none of the differences are large enough to be considered statistically significant. The largest t-value was found in arithmetic fundamentals with a probability of a difference this great occurring by chance between five and ten times out of a hundred.

Third Grade: Girls.   As may be readily seen, there is a consistent tendency for girls in the larger, fully-graded classrooms to score higher, on the average, than girls in small, multigraded situations. With the one exception of arithmetic fundamentals, all differences favor girls in fully-graded schools. However, none of the differences were large enough to be considered statistically significant. The one area in which multigraded girls excelled fully-graded girls, arithmetic fundamentals, produced the highest t-value and most nearly approached statistical significance. The probability of obtaining a difference this large by chance is between five percent and ten percent. The only other area which approached a difference this great was spelling.

Third Grade: Total Group.   When boys and girls are considered together, the differences found in reading comprehension, arithmetic reasoning and total battery tend to balance out. However, in the case of arithmetic fundamentals where the direction of the difference is the same for both sexes, one supports the other to produce a difference which is significantly in favor of third graders in the multigraded school. The remaining

TABLE I

Ability and Chronological Ages of Fully-Graded and Multi-Graded Groups

	I.Q.			N	Chronological Age		
	Range	Mean	S.D.		Range	Mean (in yrs.)	S.D. (in mos.)
Third Grade							
Fully-Graded Boys..	74-130	104.28	14.33	53	7-11 to 9-7	8.47	4.49
Multi-Graded Boys..	75-132	104.30	14.49		7-10 to 9-7	8.49	4.83
Fully-Graded Girls..	81-141	107.08	14.22	51	7-10 to 9-0	8.29	3.20
Multi-Graded Girls..	80-142	107.10	14.28		7-10 to 8-10	8.28	3.10
Fifth Grade							
Fully-Graded Boys..	72-142	100.56	13.74	62	9-11 to 11-9	10.40	4.70
Multi-Graded Boys..	70-143	100.40	13.87		9-10 to 11-9	10.38	4.91
Fully-Graded Girls..	78-134	106.33	13.79	46	9-10 to 11-9	10.40	4.00
Multi-Graded Girls..	77-134	105.93	13.66		9-9 to 11-10	10.42	4.36

TABLE II

Results Obtained on 53 Paired Boys and 51 Paired Girls at Third-Grade Level; 62 Paired Boys and 46 Paired Girls at Fifth-Grade Level

Subtest	Boys			Girls			Total		
	Mean			Mean			Mean		
	Fully-Graded	Multi-Graded	t	Fully-Graded	Multi-Graded	t	Fully-Graded	Multi-Graded	t
Third Grade									
Reading Vocabulary	3.04	2.86	1.02	3.60	3.42	1.07	3.31	3.13	1.49
Reading Comprehension	2.89	3.03	.93	3.67	3.48	1.17	3.27	3.25	.18
Arithmetic Reasoning	2.78	2.92	—1.09	3.39	3.27	.86	3.08	3.09	—.11
Arithmetic Fundamentals	3.02	3.19	—1.79	3.13	3.26	—1.78	3.08	3.23	—2.50*
Mechanics of English	2.78	2.59	1.41	3.24	3.12	.80	3.00	2.85	1.50
Spelling	2.71	2.66	.40	3.35	3.16	1.73	3.02	2.91	.89
Battery	2.88	2.91	—.29	3.40	3.29	.90	3.13	3.10	.38
Fifth Grade									
Reading Vocabulary	5.08	4.83	1.18	6.09	5.85	1.06	5.51	5.27	1.56
Reading Comprehension	4.88	4.67	1.04	5.76	5.63	.65	5.25	5.08	1.19
Arithmetic Reasoning	5.12	5.13	—.05	5.40	5.42	—.10	5.24	5.25	—.07
Arithmetic Fundamentals	5.16	4.86	2.29**	5.18	5.19	—.08	5.17	5.00	1.79
Mechanics of English	4.60	4.74	—.78	5.91	5.98	—.28	5.16	5.27	—.75
Spelling	4.71	4.57	.61	5.74	5.95	—.80	5.15	5.16	—.06
Battery	4.93	4.81	.83	5.69	5.68	.07	5.25	5.18	.67

* Significant at .02
** Significant at .05

areas of reading vocabulary, mechanics of grammar and spelling tend in the direction of favoring third graders in fully-graded situations. However, the differences are not great enough to be considered statistically significant.

Fifth Grade: Boys.   As in the case of third-grade boys, fifth-grade boys tend to score better in reading vocabulary, although the difference is not great enough to be significant in either case.

For reading comprehension, the situation is reversed. While third-grade multigraded boys tend to score better than their matched pairs, fully-graded fifth-grade boys tend to score higher. However, again, neither difference is great enough to be significant.

The most interesting situation is seen in arithmetic fundamentals. For fifth-grade boys, this is the only area in which a significant difference is found, the direction favoring boys in fully-graded schools. At the third-grade level, the difference was in favor of multigraded boys, and although the difference was not significant, it was the one of the two subtest areas which most nearly approached significance.

Other differences for fifth-grade boys are negligible.

Fifth Grade: Girls.   Fifth-grade girls show negligible differences for the most part, the highest t-value being found in reading vocabulary in favor of fully-graded girls. However, the difference is non-significant.

Fifth Grade: Total Group.   When fifth-grade boys and girls are treated as a group, no significant differences are found. However, the subtest which most nearly approaches significance is arithmetic fundamentals and is in favor of fully-graded children.

DISCUSSION

The results of this study support the stated hypothesis. There is no difference in the achievement of rural children, whether they are educated in a single-graded or multigraded school unit. Arithmetic fundamentals was the only subtest area which showed a statistically significant difference between the two groups. However, this difference was not consistent so that it is not possible to make any real generalizations in this area.

The findings in this study are in line with those of Drier (3), Adams (1), and McIntosh and Schrammel (7), while in conflict with those of Martens (6), Foote (4), and Clem and Hovey (2). Differences in design and statistical procedures and measures of achievement used may account for the differences in the findings.

One of the basic problems in a study such as this one lies in the definition of level of achievement. It is obvious that any achievement test can only measure a part of a child's educational achievements. Thus, any generalizations made on the data have to be in terms of the test instrument used as the measure of achievement.

Another problem is in the definition of a large district. By some criteria none of the schools in this study could be classified as large districts. However, in a predominantly rural community, the difference is often related to having enough teachers so that each may teach a single-grade level, rather than the multiple grades taught in schools of four teachers or less. The results may well have been different if a large district were defined as one having 5,000 or more average daily attendance.

One of the uncontrolled variables in the present study is the competency of the teacher. It is a fact that on the average, less adequate salaries are paid in districts having one, two, three or four teachers. One would expect a positive relationship between teacher competency and salary, although there may be exceptions. On the other hand, one is also likely to find a lower pupil-teacher ratio in these schools, and hence the child may be more likely to receive greater amounts of individualized instruction. These two factors may compensate for one another.

In this study, no consistent difference in achievement between multi-graded and single-graded rural children was found. On the basis of these findings, one would not expect to find differences in achievement for similar populations utilizing the same measure of achievement.

SUMMARY

A comparison of the achievement of multigraded and single-graded rural school children was made. Matched pairs of 53 boys and 51 girls at the third-grade level and 62 boys and 46 girls at the fifth-grade level comprised the samples studied. Arithmetic Fundamentals was the only subtest area which showed a statistically significant difference. This difference was not consistent. The findings of this study support the stated hypothesis that there are no differences in the achievement of rural school children, whether they are educated in a single-graded or multigraded school environment.

REFERENCES

1. Adams, Joseph J. "Achievement and Social Adjustment of Pupils in Combination Classes Enrolling Pupils of More Than One Grade," *Journal of Educational Research*, XLVII (October 1953), pp. 151–55.

2. Clem, Orlie M., and Hovey, Chester W. "Comparative School Achievement of Village School Pupils and Rural School Pupils," *Elementary School Journal*, XXXIV (December 1933), pp. 269–72.

3. Drier, William H. "Differential Achievement of Rural Graded and Ungraded School Pupils," *Journal of Educational Research*, XLIII (November 1949), pp. 175–86.

4. Foote, John M. "A Comparative Study of Instruction in Consolidated and One Teacher Schools," *Journal of Rural Education*, II (April 1923), pp. 337–51.

5. Hull, J. H. "Multi-Grade Teaching," *Nation's Schools*, LXII (July 1958), pp. 33–6.

6. Martens, Clarence C. "Educational Achievements of Eighth Grade Pupils in One-Room Rural and Graded Town Schools," *Elementary School Journal*, LIV (May 1954), pp. 523–25.

7. McIntosh, H. W., and Schrammel, H. E. "Comparison of the Achievement of the Eighth Grade Pupil Both in Rural Schools and Graded Schools," *Elementary School Journal*, XXX (December 1930), pp. 301–06.

8. Nelson, Thomas L. *A Comparison of the Achievement of Pupils in Schools of One or More Teachers With That of Pupils in Schools of Eight or More Teachers*, unpublished doctoral dissertation (University of California, 1932).

9. Wilson, W. K., and Ashbaugh, E. J. "Achievement and Rural and Consolidated Schools," *Educational Research Bulletin*, VIII (1929), pp. 358–63.

Selected Bibliography

Multigraded School Organization

Adams, Joseph J. "Achievement and Social Adjustment of Pupils in Combination Classes Enrolling Pupils of More than One Grade." *Journal of Educational Research* 47:151–155, October 1963.
Found fifth-grade students in combination classes achieved as well as fifth-grade pupils in regular classes.

Association for Childhood Education International. *Toward Effective Grouping.* Bulletin 5–A. Washington, D.C.: the Association, 1962.
Describes interage grouping (or multigrading) in the Upper Elementary School at the University of Utah. Includes a discussion of multigrade philosophy by Warren Hamilton.

Bahner, John M. *An Analysis of an Elementary School Faculty at Work: A Case Study.* Doctoral Dissertation, University of Chicago, 1960.
Reports the efforts of the Englewood, Florida, staff in reorganizing the elementary school to a multigraded arrangement.

Bahner, John M. "In Grades Four Through Six." *Reading Instruction in Various Patterns of Grouping.* Proceedings of Annual Conference on Reading. Chicago: University of Chicago, 1959. pp. 95–98.
Explains the reading program in Englewood, Florida. Grouping is multigraded.

Beauchamp, Mary. "How Should We Look at Levels—From the Psychology of Learning." *Childhood Education* 32:164–167, December 1955.
Urges a reconsideration of grade-level grouping. Advocates multigraded arrangement for elementary school.

Bienvenus, Harold J. and Martyn, Kenneth A. "Why Fear Combination Classes?" *American School Board Journal* 130:33–34, 98, April 1955.
Says combining two grades into one class has advantages for teacher and students.

Brickell, Henry M. *1961 Catalog of Educational Change.* Albany, New York: State Department of Education, October 1961.
Reports results of a survey of new programs in the public and nonpublic elementary and secondary schools of New York State. Includes references on multigrading.

Carlson, Wesley H. "Interage Grouping." *Educational Leadership* 15:363–368, March 1958.
Describes attempts to provide for individual needs by combining graded and nongraded grouping into interage primary grouping. Gives the advantages in terms of five factors needed for a good elementary program.

Chace, E. Stanley. *An Analysis of Some Effects of Multiple-Grade Grouping in an Elementary School.* Doctoral Dissertation, University of Tennessee, August 1961. Also in *Dissertation Abstracts* 22:3544.
Conducted a study in Tennessee evaluating classroom results in which two to four different grade levels were taught by one teacher compared

181

to matched single-grade groupings. Found students in multiple-grade groupings showed a slight but consistent advantage over students in single-grade groupings in academic achievement and a slight advantage in personality and social development. Also found parents accepted the theory of multiple-grading; however, they did not care for its practice.

Chicago Board of Education, Nikola Tesla Elementary School. *Multi-Graded Developmental Plan Handbook for Parents.* Chicago Board of Education, 1961.

Chicago Board of Education, Nikola Tesla Elementary School. *Multi-Graded Elementary School: An Experimental Program for Educating the Culturally Deprived.* Chicago Board of Education, 1963.

In a low-income area of Chicago, the kindergarten through the third years were ungraded. Classes were composed of students from two or three grade levels in a deliberate attempt to break the lockstep of the graded school.

Clausen, Robert. "Grouping for Continuous Learning." *Childhood Education* 36:352–353, April 1960.

Discusses several grouping possibilities such as the school with the ungraded system, the combination-grade classroom, and team teaching techniques.

Douglass, Malcolm P. "Reading and Nongrading in the Elementary School." *Claremont Reading Conference 26th Yearbook*, edited by Malcolm P. Douglass, 1962. pp. 85–95.

Discussion of five major patterns of school organization that have implications for reading: departmentalization, staggered sessions, continuous progress, departmentalization within a teaching team, and multi-age grouping. Describes multi-age grouping at the Sycamore School in Claremont, California.

Drummond, Harold. "Grouping: A Preliminary Statement." *School Life* 45:9–10, June 1963.

Reports conference of the Office of Education. Predicts multigraded grouping will return. Makes other predictions concerning teaching, learning, and grouping.

Franklin, Marian Pope. "Vertical, Horizontal or in All Directions." *North Carolina Education Journal* 32:12, 34, 35, December 1965. Included in Chapter 1 as "Vertical and Horizontal School Organization."

Describes vertical organizational alternatives: grading, multigrading, and nongrading; and horizontal alternatives: self-contained classroom, departmentalization, and team teaching.

Gilbert, Jerome H. "Multigraded Development Plan Focuses on Pupil Achievement, Tesla School Breaks Through Traditional Graded Structure." *Chicago Schools Journal* 43:209–14, February 1962.

School principal explains activities of school changing from a graded to a multigraded organization. Describes primary and elementary multigrading at Tesla School in Chicago, Illinois.

Gilbert, Jerome H. "Tesla School Breaks the Lock Step." *Elementary School Journal* 64:306–309, March 1964.

Report of the continuous development program at a Chicago school located in a slum area. Curriculum is nongraded and sometimes grouping is interaged for the primary years.

Goodlad, John I. and Anderson, Robert H. *The Nongraded Elementary School.* Revised Edition. New York: Harcourt, Brace and Company, 1963.
Major coverage of the nongraded school. Includes philosophy and details of multigrading.

"Gradeless School." *Newsweek* 52:76, September 15, 1958.
Reports ungraded primary at Port Washington, New York; Westport, Conn.; and Waldwick, New Jersey; ability grouping at Galveston, Texas; Philadelphia, Pa.; and Dade County, Florida; and multigraded arrangement at Torrance, California.

Hester, Kathleen. "Every Child Reads Successfully in a Multiple-Level Program." *Elementary School Journal* 53:86–89, October 1952. Also in *Readings on Reading Instruction* by Albert J. Harris. New York: David McKay Company, Inc., 1963. pp. 156–160.
Advocates multiple-level reading programs for elementary school instruction. Pupils join any group or groups within the self-contained classroom.

Hamilton, Warren W. "Multigrade Grouping: With Emphasis on Differences." *Toward Effective Grouping.* Washington, D.C.: Association for Childhood Education International, 1962. pp. 54–64.
Superintendent of Schools of Torrance, California describes the multigrade plan of grouping in the elementary grades. Cites research evidence to show success of the arrangement.

Hunter, Madeline C. "Teachers in the Nongraded School." *NEA Journal* 55:12–15, February 1966. Included in Chapter 3.
Cites new kinds of decisions required of teachers in nongraded programs. Describes three-year age span of learners arrangement which is multigrading.

Imhoff, Myrtle. *Early Elementary Education.* New York: Appleton-Century-Crofts, Inc., 1959. Chapter 7.
Discusses three types of school organization in practice at the early elementary level: the primary unit, the graded plan, and the multigraded or interage plan.

Laas, Maria. "The Multi-Grade Room Concept at Prairie Lane School." *1964 APPS Yearbook.*
Describes graded and ungraded programs in Omaha, Nebraska in large room with 4–6 teachers and students.

Lane, Howard A. "Moratorium on Grade Grouping." *Educational Leadership* 4:385–395, March 1947.
Discusses graded concept of school grouping. Recommends interage grouping.

Lane, Howard and Beauchamp, Mary. *Human Relations in Teaching.* Englewood Cliffs, New Jersey: Prentice-Hall, Inc., 1955. pp. 298–303.
Recommends class groups have a wide range of ages, cutting across several grade lines. This is multigrading—sometimes called interage grouping.

National Education Association, Department of Elementary School Principals. "Toward Improved Vertical Organization." *Elementary School Organizations: Purposes, Patterns, Perspectives.* Forty-First Yearbook. Washington, D.C.: the Department, 1961. pp. 78–92, 115–125.
Gives report on history, current trends, and future development of elementary school. Discusses vertical school organization and team teaching and gives the merits and disadvantages.

National Education Association. Project on Instruction Report. *Planning and Organizing for Teaching.* Washington, D.C.: the Association, 1963. pp. 53–92.
Concise discussion of vertical and horizontal school organization.

National Education Association. *Project on Instruction: Schools for the Sixties.* New York: McGraw-Hill Book Co., 1963. pp. 71–98. Summary report in January 1964 *NEA Journal.*
Overview volume of the Project on Instruction. Gives thirty-three recommendations for improving school curriculum, the classroom, materials, space, etc.

National Education Association, Research Division. *Nongraded Schools.* Washington, D.C.: the Association. Research Memo. 1965–12.
Cites advantages and disadvantages of nongrading. Briefly describes multigrading.

National Society for the Study of Education. *Individualizing Instruction.* 61st Yearbook, Part I. Chicago: University of Chicago Press, 1962. pp. 239–264.
Study of the nature of individual differences between and within pupils, school practices that encourage individualizing, and teacher orientation necessary to make it effective.

Otto, Henry J. and Sanders, David C. *Elementary School Organization and Administration.* Fourth Edition. New York: Appleton-Century-Crofts, 1964. pp. 112–114.
Discusses multi-age grouping and graded placement.

Polkinghorne, Ada R. "Grouping Children in the Primary Grades." *Elementary School Journal* 50:502–8, May 1950.
Describes multigrading in the primary years at the University of Chicago Laboratory School. Presents data from a questionnaire designed to locate other plans.

Polkinghorne, Ada R. "Parents and Teachers Appraise Primary-Grade Grouping." *Elementary School Journal* 51:271–78, January 1951.
Also see *Elementary School Journal* 50:502–508, May 1950.
Author questioned 130 parents at the Laboratory School of the University of Chicago, and found the ungraded approach had proved popular with both parents and their primary children. Parents believed children had been helped significantly in making adjustments to the third grade.

Rehwoldt, Walter, and Hamilton, Warren W. *An Analysis of Some of the Effects of Interage and Intergrade Grouping in an Elementary School.* Doctoral Dissertation, University of Southern California, January 1957.
Reports findings of a study on interage and intergrade classes in Torrance, California. Studied pupils' learning and personal adjustment in multigrade classes. Evaluated additional factors such as parental attitudes toward multigrade classes, teacher and administrator opinion of such classes, and pupil-pupil relationships within multigrade classes. Study favors multigrading.

Rehwoldt, Walter, and Hamilton, Warren W. "Why Group By Grade Levels?" *Grade Teacher* 76:18–19, 75, January 1959.
A consistent pattern of gains, greater than that of children in single-grade classes, was observed in multigrade classes in academic achievement, per-

*sonal and social adjustment, and maturity and desirable behavior charac-
teristics.*

Theman, Viola. "Continuous Progress in School." *Childhood Education* 18:21–
23, September 1941.

*Recommends: (1) the teacher continue with a group for more than one
year; (2) small groups of three or four teachers cooperatively plan the
six or eight year program of a given group of children; (3) each group of
children have an age range of several years (multi-age); and (4) grouping
be based on ability to live together with profit to each student.*

Weaver, J. Fred. "A Non-Grade-Level Sequence in Elementary Mathematics."
Arithmetic Teacher 7:431, December 1960.

*Reviews the report, "A Non-Grade-Level" by Glen Heathers and Samuel
Steinberg and gives seventeen major levels of their non-grade-level sequence.*

Weiss, Bernard J. "Reading: Blind Alleys and Fruitful Byways." *Education*
84:529–532, May 1964.

*Discusses attempts to improve reading instruction such as organizational
changes (nongraded primary, team teaching, "levels" approach by reading achievement); methods; and materials and aids (workbooks, laboratories, junior-edition periodicals, etc.).*

Wolfson, Bernice J. "A Look at Nongradedness." *Elementary English* 42:455–
457, April 1965.

*Advocates multi-age classrooms and "adapting curriculum and instruction
to foster both individual and group development." Cites research by John
Goodlad, Robert Anderson, Louis DiLorenzo and Ruth Salter. Gives a list of
minimal conditions of nongradedness; and discusses the individualization
of instruction.*

Wolfson, Bernice J. "Multi-Grade Classes." *Elementary English* 38:590, December 1961.

*Describes Torrance Unified School District, California, volunteer program
of multigrade grouping in twenty-six of its thirty elementary schools.
Warren Hamilton, coauthor of the original study, says the multigrade
pupils demonstrated greater personal and social growth.*

SECTION III

Horizontal School Organization

Chapter 6

The Self-Contained Classroom

The Self-Contained Classroom: Myth or Reality?

Marian Pope Franklin and Frances Kennon Johnson

For years one of the issues of elementary education has been whether to have self-contained or departmentalized classrooms. It has been debated many times yet the question remains unanswered in the sixties.

Actually, the term self-contained classroom used to describe an arrangement in the elementary school approaches being a myth. Few, if any, elementary classrooms are actually self-contained today. The survey reported in the reading by Oscar Jarvis reveals only 12 per cent of 64 metropolitan elementary school districts have only one teacher to handle all instruction for a class. Elementary classrooms have music, art, physical education, library, guidance, and remedial specialists helping with instruction and with special services. Some so-called self-contained classrooms have all of these helpers. It is not possible, then, to call such a classroom contained. Furthermore, students are in contact with bus drivers, guards, aides, secretaries, lunchroom workers, nurses, and janitors. Each of these persons may, and probably does, have an impact on students. In some respects, then, the issue of the self-contained classroom vs. departmentalization is largely one of lack of precision in terms.

For years the elementary school self-contained classroom has been advocated on the basis of assumptions such as: it enables students to identify with small groups; it gives an opportunity for coordinating the total program; it promotes closer teacher-learner relationships; and it

Written especially for this book. Dr. Marian Pope Franklin is Head of the Guidance Department at The University of North Carolina in Greensboro, and Frances Kennon Johnson is Assistant Professor of Education, University of North Carolina in Greensboro.

provides greater flexibility in the daily program. Each of these conditions may or may not exist in a self-contained classroom. They also may, or may not, occur in other arrangements. Unfortunately the present research is not conclusive so one can not say with authority whether any of the assumptions are true.

The issue of self-contained vs. departmentalized classrooms does not exist in the high school or in higher education. There, departmentalization has been a well established fact except for an occasional use of core curriculum.

Readings in Chapter 6 have been selected to show views of both the proponents and the opponents of the elementary self-contained classroom. Lobdell and Van Ness present a brief history of departmentalization and note a present trend toward it. They, however, make a case for the use of the self-contained arrangement. George Ackerlund reports the results of his survey of elementary-school teacher attitudes toward the self-contained classroom. On the basis of his study he also reports strengths and weaknesses of the arrangement and says school staffs should try to preserve the values yet seek to solve the problems. He says team teaching may be a promising alternative. Arthur Morse, CBS Staff Producer, attacks the assumptions of the self-contained arrangement and the role of the teacher in it. He effectively pleads for flexibility and innovation. Daniel Tanner labels the self-contained classroom an evil for upper elementary students, age nine and over.

The bibliography at the close of the chapter will lead the reader to further references on the self-contained classroom. References on departmentalization will be found at the close of Chapter 7.

The Self-Contained Classroom in the Elementary School

Lawrence O. Lobdell and William J. Van Ness

In many school systems the basic organizational unit is known as the self-contained classroom. In the true self-contained classroom, the children are taught all subjects by one teacher. In actual practice, however, certain subjects—usually art, music, and physical education—are often taught by special teachers, and the regular classroom teacher has the children for all other school activities. This arrangement, sometimes referred to as the modified self-contained classroom or the coordinated classroom, is as far as many elementary-school officials are willing to depart from the pure self-contained classroom.

The antithesis of the self-contained classroom is departmentalization, a program "in which children move from one classroom to another for instruction in the several subject fields by different teachers" (1: 146).

There are, of course, degrees of departmentalization. One, two, or more academic subjects may be taught by special teachers. Some educators consider the modified self-contained classroom a degree of departmentalization, and undoubtedly it is. Actually, the self-contained classroom and departmentalization may be thought of as being at the opposite ends of a continuum; any deviation from the pure self-contained classroom represents a point on the continuum in the direction of departmentalization.

Discussions between the proponents of the self-contained classroom and the proponents of departmentalization in the elementary school have been going on for at least half a century, according to Goodlad (2: 223). From 1910 to 1929 there was a growing interest in departmentalization, and during these years it was on the increase; from 1930 to 1939 there was constant debate between those who favored departmentalization and those who favored the self-contained classroom, with each side claiming the same advantages; between 1940 and 1949 more schools were reported as giving up departmentalization than adopting it, although in more and more schools art, music, and physical education were being taught by special teachers; finally, in the decade from 1950 to 1959, departmentali-

Reprinted from *Elementary School Journal* 63:212–217, January 1963 by permission of the publisher and the authors. Lawrence O. Lobdell is Principal of the Clear Stream Avenue School, and William J. Van Ness of Shaw Avenue School is Elementary Consultant, both in Union Free School District 30, Valley Stream, New York.

zation again seemed to be increasing, mostly in the intermediate grades and especially in school systems where the 8–4 pattern was in effect. Today there is some departmentalization in the primary grades, but not a great deal.

After sifting recent research, Shane and Polychrones concluded that

> departmentalization is widespread, that such organization *per se* is neither demonstrably helpful nor definitely harmful to children, and that while there may be a trend to the unit [self-contained] classroom, it is not a massive trend [3: 427].

However, it should be noted that these authors included in the term *departmentalization*, the teaching of art, music, and physical education by special teachers. If they had counted schools that had this arrangement as non-departmentalized schools, as is often done, the number of departmentalized schools reported by these researchers would have been smaller.

It is in the area of definition that confusion arises. While Shane and Polychrones use the word *departmental* to describe the Tulsa type of elementary-school organization, Broadhead, for example, uses the word *semi-departmental*. Broadhead wrote:

> The child receives instruction from the homeroom teacher for half the school day in the basic subjects of reading, writing, spelling, arithmetic, language arts, and social studies. During the remainder of the school day, the child receives instruction in other classrooms from various other teachers who have had specialized training in science, art, music, speech, physical education, or library science [4: 385].

This semi-departmentalization, it should be noted, is not departmentalization at all in academic areas other than science. It is difficult to see how the Tulsa findings can be used to support academic departmentalization or teacher specialization in the teaching of the academic subjects, as Anderson seems to attempt to do (5).

While research that deals directly with departmentalization is inconclusive, authorities in other areas suggest implications that favor the self-contained classroom. Under departmentalization, when each subject is taught by a different teacher, integration of children's educational experiences into a meaningful whole becomes difficult, if not almost impossible. What Blough says about science may well be applied to all subject-matter areas:

> A basic premise underlying the science program is that it should be in harmony with the total program of education. This implies that elementary science is an integral part of the fabric

which includes social studies, language arts, music, mathematics, art, and health education. Science brings new strength to the elementary schools. Its methods, its approach to problem-solving, and its informational content enrich the whole program and give it new scope and depth [6: 122–23].

If this premise applies to science, it also applies to every subject area and every skills area. Each has its important contribution to make to the elementary-school program. Reinforcement of learning often occurs when a concept is applied to areas other than that involved in the teaching of the moment. It is difficult to see how this kind of reinforcement, this mutual enrichment, this integrative process, can take place as effectively outside the self-contained classroom as in.

While not mentioning either departmentalization or the self-contained classroom by name, Tyler says:

> From the standpoint of achieving desirable organization, any structural arrangement that provides for larger blocks of time under which planning may go on has an advantage over a structural organization which cuts up the time into many specific units, each of which has to be planned with some kind of transition and consideration of the work of other units [7: 123–24].

How will teachers in the departmentalized school find time to get together to provide these transitions and considerations?

In support of Tyler's position on the difficulty of achieving integration in a departmentalized situation, Elsbree and McNally state:

> If one holds an organismic point of view with respect to learning, and believes that education should be life-problems centered rather than subject-centered, a considerable number of objections will be raised against departmentalization. It will be pointed out, for example, that its approach to learning is fragmentary and disintegrative, discouraging of unity and wholeness in the learning program. Even with sincere attempts at "integration" the separate subjects will tend to be discrete and relatively unrelated in the minds of pupils [8].

Another weakness of departmentalization, as opposed to the self-contained classroom, is the disruption of continuity when each activity is cut off arbitrarily at the sound of a bell.

The organization of the elementary school and its curriculum must be a means to an end, not an end in itself. It must take into consideration the feelings not only of the educators but of all those who are concerned with any aspect of the development of children.

With regard to what is known about how children grow, develop, and learn, Hamalainen finds the self-contained classroom superior to departmentalization:

> Departmentalization disregards the fact that the individual is an organic being who cannot be farmed out piecemeal to many persons. He must be seen and reacted to as a whole being if the most effective learning is to occur.
>
> *   *   *
>
> In the self-contained classroom the teacher is thought of as the guide and counselor, the coordinator with the children of the experiences most meaningful to them. Because of the length of time he spends with the children he has the opportunity to know individual children in the class and thus better understand their needs [9: 272–74].

In view of the lack of any conclusive research evidence in favor of departmentalization, and in view of the knowledge we have of children's growth, learning, and needs, it is difficult to account for the trend toward departmentalization noted by Shane and Polychrones.

There are a number of excuses, unfortunately often offered as reasons, for entering into departmentalization. First, there is the willingness to experiment and, second, the submission to the hysterical pressure to do something. Experimentation may be a defensive hedge behind which to hide; yet it would seem unnecessary to experiment further with a device that was tried so widely a few decades ago that platooning (a form of departmentalization) was found in 1,068 schools in forty-one states (10: 379). Submission to the *do-something!* hysteria is indefensible; educators have no moral right to take action for this reason alone.

A third excuse often offered for departmentalizing the elementary school is that junior high schools are departmentalized and elementary schools had better follow suit to "get the children ready" for junior high schools. One of us recently heard a school official defend departmentalization on the ground that the junior high schools will not modify their organization to the extent of undepartmentalizing the seventh and eighth grades. Therefore, he said, the elementary schools should departmentalize in the upper grades to "prepare" the children, even though departmentalization might not be the best arrangement for them. This line of reasoning, followed to its logical and ridiculous conclusion, would end only with the departmentalization of the kindergarten.

A fourth, and common, excuse given for departmentalization is that it allows each subject to be taught by specialists. This practice might be praiseworthy if the teachers were truly specialists in the best sense of the word; but there would seem to be a world of difference between one who merely specializes in teaching a given subject and one who has had both pre-service and in-service preparation in the area of specialization. We suspect that many elementary-school "specialists" are specialists by virtue of their teaching assignments only, not by virtue of their preparation. A true specialist is not made simply by changing a teacher's assignment.

Perhaps the best picture of what the self-contained classroom can mean to elementary-school children is that drawn by Koopman and Snyder. The self-contained classroom, these writers say, is

> a workshop in which the principles of child development come into play. It is a home away from home—a living room for learning. It is a base of operations out of which a group of children (ideally no more than 20) work all day, every day, for a year or more with one teacher.
> . . . the *responsibility* for organizing and coordinating the educational experiences of a group of children is [the teacher's] alone [11: 18].

This "living room" promotes an atmosphere in which all phases of the child's growth—intellectual, emotional, and physical—are provided for.

The authors describe a warm and colorful physical setting, appropriate furniture, all kinds of books, records, films, and materials, and small groups of children engaged in meaningful and worthwhile learning experiences. To cite one example:

> Four boys are in the far corner, where science materials are clustered behind a screen. They are involved with Tim, a turtle that Jimmy found on his way to school.
> Since no one, including the teacher, knows how to care for him or what to expect of him, two of the boys are reading up on turtles in the encyclopedia. One of the boys is writing down important things to remember about turtles. Jimmy is on his hands and knees watching with wonder and adoration as Tim explores his new surroundings . . . [11: 19].

After presenting additional examples of children busy in a variety of learning activities, the authors consider and dispose of a number of objections that are sometimes raised against the self-contained classroom. Good in-service programs may help overcome objections that not all elementary-school teachers are broadly educated and that some children might get a poor teacher. The children will not be deprived of instruction in the special fields if special consultants are made available to work with—not in place of—the teachers. Fundamentals may be developed in various organizational plans, always provided that the teaching is good. As for the objection that children in self-contained classrooms do not meet enough people—

children and adults—Koopman and Snyder state: "The principle of emotional security implies that learners don't grow well in a swirling crowd of people. They need the homeroom base" [11: 20].

It would seem that such a base, rather than departmentalization, would make possible the establishment of group membership as described by Gibb:

> The process of establishing membership in a classroom group is the process of both finding a niche in a group and also finding enough freedom to move in and out of the niche to build rich relationships with other members of the classroom group. The mature instructional group can provide rich internal resources that maximize learning outcomes [12: 135].

In the end, however, we suspect that the basic issue may not be the choice between departmentalization and the self-contained classroom. Educators must be concerned with organization and with organizational patterns; but they must likewise be constantly on guard lest concern for organization obscure the element for which all else exists: the child. Dean issues a clear warning to this effect:

> The structural plan of operation of a school is not an end in itself; its value lies in the effectiveness it contributes to the improvement of the quality of classroom education. Since the teaching-learning relationship is the heart of any school program, campaigns to improve education should be focused on the classroom, not on the administrative design [13: 9].

If the focus should be placed on the classroom, then it is safe to say that sharpening the focus should result in concentrating on the most important element of the classroom, the child. Dean implies this:

> There is . . . danger of oversimplifying the issue, of abandoning the psychological studies being made of child growth and development or of not using the knowledge such studies have made available, and of casting aside the basic purposes and programs of elementary education [13: 8].

Perhaps the need for considering educational theory and practice, not alone but in connection with all possible sources of information about children, is best summarized by Lanning:

> From guidance, from child development, from group dynamics, and from anthropology, new findings are coming that offer fresh understanding of the nature of the child and the dynamics of development. We can find in these rich resources

support for the view that if we have the best interests of the child at heart we will be concerned about the whole child [14: 286].

We agree with Lanning that the emphasis should be placed on the child. There may be danger in accepting a procedure simply because it works. Under the pressing demands that schools "Do something!" educators are discovering new facts, among them that some children apparently can learn subjects like algebra and geometry, generally reserved for the high-school years. But such discoveries are not really answers to anything; they simply pose the basic question: Granted that children can learn this and that, should they? Does this or that new proposal square with what is known—and is being discovered—about children's needs and characteristics? Is it in keeping with sound principles of guidance, psychology, and the learning process? Is its placement in keeping with the logical sequence of the development of the subject?

So with departmentalization, semi-departmentalization, and the self-contained classroom: the basic question is the same. Which of these administrative devices is true to all that we know about children? It is by this criterion that any educational program—including departmentalization—must be judged. Practicability alone is not enough.

REFERENCES

1. Harold G. Shane. "Elementary Schools Changed Only a Little During the Fabulous Fifties," *Nation's Schools*, LXV (April, 1960), 71–73, 146–48.

2. John I. Goodlad. "Classroom Organization," *Encyclopedia of Educational Research*, third edition, pp. 221–26. New York: Macmillan Company, 1960.

3. Harold G. Shane and James Z. Polychrones. "Elementary Education— Organization and Administration," *Encyclopedia of Educational Research*, third edition, pp. 421–30. New York: Macmillan Company, 1960.

4. Fred C. Broadhead. "Pupil Adjustment in the Semi-Departmental Elementary School," *Elementary School Journal*, LX (April, 1960), 385–90.

5. Richard C. Anderson. "The Case for Teacher Specialization in the Elementary School," *Elementary School Journal*, LXII (February, 1962), 253–60.

6. Glenn O. Blough. "Developing Science Programs in the Elementary School," *Re-thinking Science Education*, pp. 112–35. Fifty-ninth Yearbook of the National Society for the Study of Education, Part I. Chicago: Distributed by the University of Chicago Press, 1960.

7. Ralph W. Tyler. "Curriculum Organization," *The Integration of Educational Experiences*, pp. 105–25. Fifty-seventh Yearbook of the National Society of Education, Part III. Chicago: Distributed by the University of Chicago Press, 1958.

8. Willard S. Elsbree and Harold J. McNally. *Elementary School Administration and Supervision*, p. 91. New York: American Book Company, 1951.

9. Arthur E. Hamalainen. "Some Current Proposals and Their Meaning," *Educational Leadership*, XVI (February, 1959), 271–74, 328.

10. Henry J. Otto. "Elementary Education—III: Organization and Administration," *Encyclopedia of Educational Research*, second edition, pp. 368–83. New York: Macmillan Company, 1950.

11. Robert G. Koopman and Edith Roach Snyder. "Living Room for Learning—a Self-contained Unit," *NEA Journal*, XLVII (January, 1958), 18–20.

12. Jack R. Gibb. "Sociopsychological Processes of Group Instruction," *The Dynamics of Instructional Groups*, pp. 115–35. Fifty-ninth Yearbook of the National Society for the Study of Education, Part II. Chicago: Distributed by the University of Chicago Press, 1960.

13. Stuart E. Dean. "Organization for Instruction in the Elementary Schools," *School Life*, XLII (May, 1960), 8–9.

14. Frank W. Lanning. "The Plight of the Whole Child," *Elementary School Journal*, LX (February, 1960), 283–86.

Some Teacher Views On the Self-Contained Classroom

George Ackerlund

The self-contained classroom organization, in which one teacher teaches all subjects, seems destined for further critical examination. Although it is widely used, the self-contained classroom has some serious weaknesses which cannot be ignored. Failure to correct these shortcomings will prevent that improvement in both the quality and quantity of learning which is possible. It is also logical to assume that teacher morale could be improved if the self-contained classroom organization were revised.

Proponents of the self-contained classroom organization claim that it provides for greater teacher acquaintance with each child, more flexibility in time allotments, and better correlation and integration of subject matter. Moreover, it avoids the necessity of the child having to adjust to more than one teacher.

Those who maintain that the self-contained classroom needs re-evaluation argue that it requires teachers to be with children all day on a sustained basis without providing for the much-needed "breaks" permitted in other lines of work. They also believe that the subject-matter knowledge and skill in methods required to teach all subjects in elementary school are greater than can be adequately achieved by all who enter the field. Expecting all teachers to like to teach all subjects, they claim, is unrealistic —it ignores the factors of aptitude and interest and the scientific fact that people do better work when doing what they like and enjoy.

Recently the writer conducted a survey in a large school system to ascertain what elementary school teachers themselves think of the self-contained classroom organization. The questionnaire asked, "Do you believe the self-contained classroom, in which one teacher is required to teach all subjects, is the best type of organization for elementary education?" Teachers were asked to indicate whether they like to teach, neither like nor dislike, or dislike to teach the various subjects in the elementary school program. They were asked to indicate whether they considered themselves well prepared, moderately well prepared, or inadequately prepared in two areas: knowledge of subject and methods of teaching. Data

Reprinted from *Phi Delta Kappan* 40:283–285, April 1959, by permission of the publisher and the author. George Ackerlund, formerly Superintendent of the Quakertown, Pennsylvania, schools, is now at Southern Illinois University, Edwardsville, Illinois.

sought also included sex, marital status, years of experience, type of institution from which the bachelor's degree was received, grade now teaching, degree held, and the number of courses taken in high school and college which correspond to those taught in the elementary school.

Of those who responded to the question, "Do you favor the self-contained classroom as an organization for the elementary school?", 109

Teacher Attitudes Toward Teaching the Elementary School Subjects

Subject	Number of Responses	Like To Teach It	Neither Like Nor Dislike	Dislike To Teach It	Less Than Well Prepared in Content (in Per Cent)	Less Than Well Prepared in Method (in Per Cent)
Reading	256	223	27	6	61	65
Handwriting	254	208	44	2	48	50
English	254	208	44	2	26	30
Spelling	245	210	43	2	18	21
History	245	144	78	23	51	58
Geography	242	163	62	17	47	55
Arithmetic	253	222	21	10	18	24
Science	248	136	75	37	69	73
Art	257	158	65	34	61	64
Music	245	128	58	69	59	63
Health and Phys. Educ.	256	126	70	60	..	..

said "yes," 122 said "no," 11 gave a "qualified yes," 3 gave a "qualified no," 13 stated they were doubtful, and others gave no answer. The accompanying table shows the respondents' attitudes toward various subjects they teach.

A comparison of the group that favored the self-contained classroom and the group that opposed it showed no significant differences between teachers who like or dislike to teach various subjects, except in the case of science, history, art, music, and health and physical education. In these five subjects a greater percentage of teachers who opposed the self-contained classroom indicated a dislike for teaching these subjects than was the case among teachers who favored it.

Generally speaking, the teacher's subject-matter emphasis in high school and college did not affect her liking or disliking to teach similar areas in the elementary school. For example, the amount of science taken in high school and college did not seem to influence significantly the desire to teach, or not to teach, science in the elementary school.

Four teachers of the total number considered themselves well prepared in all subjects they taught. One of these favored the self-contained classroom and three opposed it. Twenty-one teachers stated that they like to teach all subjects, of which number fifteen favored the self-contained classroom and six opposed it. Only three stated that they like to teach all subjects and consider themselves well prepared to teach all subjects. One of these teachers favored the self-contained classroom and two did not.

In grades K-2, 51 teachers favored the self-contained classroom while 33 opposed it. In grades 3-4, 35 favored it and 40 opposed it. In grades 5-6, 17 favored it as against 37 who opposed it.

So far as sex and marital status are concerned, a significant difference appeared only between married women and single women. Among married women, 59 per cent opposed the self-contained classroom; only 44 per cent of the single women opposed it.

Among those holding bachelor's degrees, 71 favored the self-contained classroom, 88 opposed it. Twenty-two of those with the master's degree were opposed, and 21 were favorable. Those with no degree were evenly divided, eleven for and eleven against.

Those who received the bachelor's degree from a state teachers college numbered 151, of whom 71 favored the self-contained classroom and 80 opposed it. Eleven graduates of university colleges of education were favorable and fourteen were opposed. Graduates of liberal arts colleges divided fifteen for and eighteen against.

The number of years of college education appeared to have no relationship to teacher opinions on this subject. Those who favored the self-contained classroom had 4.05 years of college education while those who opposed it had 4.07 years of college training.

Drawing conclusions from this limited survey must be done with considerable caution, but a few statements can be made rather confidently.

1. Even though some teachers are well prepared to teach certain subjects, it is clear that they often dislike to do so. This suggests that it may not be wise to expect elementary teachers to be both competent in and like to teach all subjects in the elementary school program.

2. It seems clear that a higher degree of knowledge of content is required, especially in the upper elementary grades, than many realize.

3. The self-contained classroom does not give the teacher an opportunity to choose areas in which she likes to teach, as is the case in high school.

4. The self-contained classroom provides teachers with opportunities to emphasize or de-emphasize certain subjects, depending upon their likes and dislikes.

5. There is strong support for the self-contained classroom in grades K-1-2, but opposition to it begins in grade three and becomes increasingly greater in grades 4-5-6.

The basic philosophy of the self-contained classroom is excellent and probably should be retained, but it need not be sacrificed to bring teaching specialization into the elementary school. It is possible for three, four, or five teachers to work together as a team with a certain group of children, meeting once each week for planning. The unity of the self-contained classroom can be preserved, yet teachers can teach those subjects which they like to teach and in which they are highly competent. There is no evidence that adjustment to several different teaching personalities simultaneously is harmful to children; it could even be valuable.

Whatever one's attitude toward the self-contained classroom, it must be concluded that it has important advantages that should be preserved, but it must also be realized that it has serious weaknesses that should be overcome. How this can be done will vary among schools; the important thing is that administrators become fully aware of the problem and begin planning its solution where changes have not already been made.

Open Minds and Flexible Schools

Arthur D. Morse

"Find out and report on the most promising new approaches to education being tried in American public schools."

That, in brief, was the assignment I received recently from James E. Allen Jr., New York State Commissioner of Education.

In outlining my assignment, Dr. Allen explained that he wanted the public schools of New York State to have the benefit of the experience of other school systems throughout the country which had blazed new educational trails. Never before, he pointed out, have so many new approaches to educational problems been tried as in the past few years.

It was with these instructions that I set out on an exciting exploration of the frontiers of education in the nation's public schools.

What facts emerged from this study? One conclusion was that American education is showing signs of being lifted out of its rut. Resistance to change, an odd characteristic for a profession that honors the inquiring mind, is melting slowly under the heat generated by new ideas.

Another conclusion is that the process of change needs to be speeded up. The crisis is *now*, and there is dramatic need for action.

To an observer wandering through the nation's schools the conclusion is inescapable that the process will be speeded only when more parents, teachers, administrators, and school boards recognize the existence of the rut.

It is exemplified by the dulling uniformity of the typical elementary school. This consists of a cluster of identical classrooms, each presided over by a single teacher. Youngsters are grouped according to the magic number of the moment, say thirty to a teacher (in some places the magic ratio may be thirty-two to one, in others twenty-eight to one, provided the teachers and space are available). Pupils receive virtually all of their instruction from this single teacher—language arts, arithmetic, science, social studies, music, and art (with occasional visits from itinerant specialists).

The classroom teacher is omnipotent in a system which assumes that she is equally capable in each subject area, an assumption made by no other profession. This would be similar to making the assumption in medi-

Reprinted from *Saturday Review* 43:67–68, 90–92, September 17, 1960, by permission of the publisher and the author. Arthur D. Morse is a staff producer for "CBS Reports," and a free-lance writer.

cine that any physician is qualified to practice any or all of the specialties in his profession. The analogy is far-fetched only as we minimize the importance of the subject matter.

Decades of dreadful science teaching on the elementary level have stemmed from the assumption that any adult can teach science fundamentals to a child. It has taken a sky full of satellites to stimulate a re-examination of this tradition of ineptitude.

Since the elementary school teacher is all things to all boys and girls she must work all day or not at all. Part-time experts in various subjects are ruled out. Few school systems utilize the services of gifted and qualified women whose family responsibilities prohibit full-time teaching schedules.

The self-contained classroom with an unchanging group of thirty-odd youngsters is governed by the assumption that its pupils are more or less alike. The problem of individual differences is solved by so-called ability grouping. Room 12 may have the fast fifth-graders, Room 11 the average youngsters, and Room 10 the slowest group.

This conventional ability-grouping assumes that children of a high intelligence level will be exceptional in all subjects. This assumption is not warranted; in fact it often has socially undesirable effects. Ambitious parents, not quite able to afford wall-to-wall carpeting in their suburban garages, attempt to achieve status by pressuring the kiddies into the fast group. A child quickly becomes aware of his "niche," often an unreal measure of his potential.

The most common defect of ability grouping is its failure to accomplish its central purpose—to enable youngsters to work up to full capacity. When a "fast group" has completed its required program for the year, the typical teacher assigns more of the same sort of work to fill out the term. Thus fifth-graders read more and more fifth-grade materials instead of pushing ahead to more advanced work.

This system avoids the administrative complication of starting next year's program prematurely, with subsequent embarrassment for the principal, librarian, and future teacher. It also avoids the obligation of challenging the child. There is a phrase of purest educational jargon for this procedure—it is called horizontal enrichment.

The organization of youngsters into classroom groups of thirty-plus hardens the conventional school's rigidity. There appears to be no evidence that a fixed pupil-teacher ratio is ideal in all learning situations. The number of pupils who can benefit best from a lecture is quite different from the number who can participate effectively in a give-and-take session. Advanced lessons for gifted youngsters and remedial programs for slower learners illustrate the fallacy of rigid organization. The caliber of the students, the quality of the teachers, and the nature of the subject matter would seem to be ideal criteria for class size. They rarely are.

What is needed is flexibility, and flexibility is impossible when all subjects are taught by one teacher to classes of uniform size all day.

The traditional elementary school classroom has other rigid characteristics. The teacher tends to become isolated behind the closed doors of her exclusive domain. Her attributes and defects are largely unobserved and she becomes less and less inclined to adopt an open-door policy. Rarely, if ever, does she watch an outstanding teacher in action, though professionals in other fields draw inspiration from the work of their most gifted colleagues.

It is but a short step from the closed door to the closed mind. The tendency toward isolation is one of the most undesirable characteristics of the teaching profession and is completely at odds with the self-interest of the competent teacher. Personal fulfillment, greater prestige, higher salary, and community recognition flow from public and professional awareness of her gifts. How can she grow professionally behind those closed doors?

A teacher's ritualistic performance at "Open School Night" and her dutiful attendance at PTA meetings cannot communicate her worth. Nor does she have adequate opportunity to contribute creatively to the program of the typical elementary school. The mechanics of school operation dominate faculty meetings. Discussions about monitoring the cafeteria, problems of the playground, and the complexities of record-keeping are stressed, while the substance of education is left to higher authority. It happens usually that higher authority is also preoccupied with nuts and bolts and the complexities of record-keeping.

The teacher in this conventional environment is put upon to a degree undreamed of in other professions. Her work-load has increased staggeringly and with it her paper work. It has been estimated that a teacher spends up to one-fourth of her working day handling routine clerical chores. The world she lives in has automated but the teacher fills out the same forms and slips, collects the money for the various benevolent causes and school services, takes attendance, acts as charwoman, and performs tasks normally assumed by less educated clerks and stenographers—all this while we are told about an acute shortage of qualified teachers.

The teacher has little time to advance her own knowledge, to prepare materials, to consult with outside experts, to visit local resources for the improvement of her presentations. She may have one free period a day, but otherwise she is faced, hour after hour, with that standard group of thirty-plus. The world is dominated by change but the teacher is dominated by a relentless schedule that prohibits the reflection and study necessary to introduce change where it is most needed—in the curriculum.

To compound her travail, the gifted teacher tends to be unrewarded for her competence. The uniform salary scale has become an educational mystique without relevance to other professions or to the teaching demands of the 1960's. Good, bad, or indifferent, all teachers are paid alike except for adjustments based upon seniority and graduate degrees. This is one intellectual battlefield whose heights are dominated by mediocrity and longevity.

The gifted teacher with enough human traits to desire higher salary and/or recognition must become an administrator or spend the summer as a soda jerk or as a member of the Teamsters Union.

The rigid patterns of the elementary school are changed only slightly by our high schools. Here again, uniformity in numbers is the rule, and administrative convenience is the hallmark of scheduling. The same subjects, taught at the same time during the same days of the week to the same students, characterize secondary education. There is movement from room to room and teaching specialization, but that's about as far as the reed bends. The typical high school teacher has one free period each day, little or no time to prepare lectures, a heavy burden of paper work, and a constant conflict between his conscience and his instinct for survival.

The English teacher, for example, who wants to assign creative writing at least once a week faces the prospect of nightly toil after exhausting days. Who can blame this underpaid guardian of the flame of culture for limiting creative writing to a handful of superior students?

At this point, before venturing into the area of new ideas, let's consider the debt we owe teachers and administrators who have acquiesced in the old uniformity. It is one thing to suggest the new horizons which have opened and another to contemplate the problems of the educators who have dealt with the reality of life in America.

Schools do not function in a world apart from the societies in which they exist. To expect a standard of academic excellence, to demand an island of unselfish endeavor in a sea of materialism, is to ask the impossible. The achievement of our free, public schools is unprecedented. While other nations have educated a social elite, we have educated everyone. In the process of educating everyone we have short-changed our most capable youngsters. We have also underestimated the potential of our average students.

Today, at a time of unprecedented prosperity, as we lavish our national treasure in the pursuit of pleasure, we ask our schools to instill a durable ethic and a respect for learning which may be dissipated the moment the child returns home.

We ask our teachers to sacrifice every material convenience, every current symbol of success, as they attempt to inculcate in our overprivileged children the non-material values of the human spirit which set man apart from other animals.

If the teachers can't quite make it we should not be surprised. We are asking them to bear an enormous burden. They are expected to be our conscience, to live in a world apart, without acclaim, without recognition, without the resources even to indulge in a satisfying intellectual life. We are asking too much!

What is the cure for the educational malaise? It lies, I believe, in massive doses of new ideas and the realization by parents, teachers, school boards, and administrators that many of the old ways are inadequate, outdated, and stultifying.

During the past few years a ripple of innovation has been fanned into a national wave by foundations, imaginative local educators, independent citizens' committees, scattered school boards, a few (very few) state departments of education, individual teachers, and some death-defying principals.

Today a sense of adventure courses through the schools that have adopted these experimental programs. Clichés and stereotypes are losing their firm footholds. Tried and untrue formulae are being discarded "with all deliberate speed," and if the deliberateness usually exceeds the speed it doesn't halt the inexorable march of progress.

Magic numbers are on their way out. Experiments in all parts of the country have indicated that the traditional ratio of roughly thirty to one is in fact too large for discussion purposes, too small for lectures. Carefully organized research, in which identical groups of youngsters are matched, has revealed that the gifted lecturer can teach classes five times as large as the conventional group with approximately the same effectiveness.

Consider the far-reaching implications of this one breakthrough. The teacher who is capable of instructing five times the usual number of students frees four other teachers during that period. They can utilize this time in the preparation of their own subject matter, possibly for large-group lectures in areas of their own special competence. The four can meet for cooperative planning, a departure from the traditional isolation. The time can be used to harness community resources for a future presentation—to work with libraries, museums, laboratories; or industries that have vivid contributions for the classroom.

The teacher who reaches five times the traditional number of students casts new light on solutions to the teacher shortage and suggests some answers to the salary dilemma. When she enlists the aid of devices like magnetic tape, film slides, and overhead projectors that cast magnified images, she hurdles another educational rut. It is a curious paradox that the schools which stimulate their students' interest in new technology are themselves archaic technologically and are loath to adopt new techniques of communication. When our gifted, experimental teacher turns to television the revolution is complete, for now she reaches thousands of youngsters simultaneously.

"If we have a shortage of superior teachers, let's spread individual talents as far as possible," say the experimenters.

As of the Spring of 1960, 569 school districts and 111 colleges and universities were utilizing television for instruction. Great refinements have been made since the schools took their first hesitant and expensive steps in this direction.

Throughout the United States, teachers responded to the advent of classroom television as a threat to their security. The picture of an impersonal, robot-like communication between TV screen and child, eliminating the need for the teacher, was transmitted by word of mouth and by educational publications. A nation of pop-eyed, empty-headed children was in the offing. Gradually it became evident that television could provide scarce talents otherwise not available to school systems—conversational foreign language teachers for elementary grades; enthusiastic science teachers demonstrating equipment lacking in most schools; experts of national prominence; and, most important, superior teachers with that rare magnetic quality that holds and influences students.

Like the other new ideas, it held out the hope of an expanded horizon for the superior teacher. It offered too, the possibility of a rich working partnership between the classroom teacher and her television colleague. Comparisons of the achievement of youngsters receiving televised instruction with that of students in conventional classes have revealed little difference.

Obviously the mere use of television does not improve anything. A mediocre teacher on television has the power to spread her mediocrity like a brush fire. There are some schools using television as a "gimmick" and striving for theatrical effects at the expense of learning—but these are rare and cannot be cited fairly in an attempt to downgrade one of the most hopeful developments in education.

In its possibilities of reaching virtually limitless audiences, television represents another thrust at inflexibility in our schools.

Television reflects the end of the magic number approach to education and the adoption of new methods of organizing our schools. So does the concept of team teaching.

An elementary school may be divided into several teams, each consisting of several teachers and 100 or more students. A team may cross two or three grade levels. Liberated from the thirty-to-a-room rigidity, the teachers in each team plan flexible-sized classes, basing their size on the nature of the subject matter, the caliber of the students, and the type of presentation. Since the team extends beyond a single grade, children may be mixed chronologically. A youngster gifted in mathematics but lagging in language arts can work with an advanced group in the former and a special class in the latter. There is opportunity for large-group lectures, intimate seminar grouping, and independent study.

Youngsters are not penned in the same room with the same teacher all day. Instead, the skills of several teachers, specializing in the subject matter in which they are best qualified, are brought to bear upon each child.

Team teaching offers tangible rewards in salary and prestige for the demonstration of leadership and exceptional teaching skill. Each team is headed by a team leader and one or more senior teachers, who are paid additional salaries for their increased responsibilities. This kind of organization provides a new outlet for the gifted teacher who aspires to leadership in her profession and whose only alternative in the past was an administrative position removed from the classroom.

Each team is provided with clerical assistance to reduce paper work chores. All in all, the innovation represents a conscious effort to lift the level of teaching to that enjoyed by other professions, to stimulate the teachers' creativity and free them from drudgery while reorganizing classes to *take advantage* of the individual differences of children. Lexington, Massachusetts, and Norwalk and Greenwich, Connecticut, are among the communities currently experimenting with team teaching in their elementary schools.

There is a direct relationship between team teaching and the recruitment of high-quality teacher candidates. The top-notch liberal arts graduate will hesitate on three basic counts before joining the teaching profession. For one thing, teachers averaged $5,059 in earnings in 1958, less than half the average income in seventeen other professions. For another, the paths to advancement in teaching are unmarked. A third consideration, for those aware of the reality of teaching, lies in its frustrating limitations. Rigid school organization can stifle the creative mind.

Team teaching attacks on all three fronts. Its techniques are not limited to elementary schools but are also coming into wide use in high schools.

In the secondary schools, those citadels of Prussian scheduling, great strides have been made by experimentation. The Commission on the Experimental Study of the Utilization of the Staff in the Secondary School, directed by J. Lloyd Trump, has broken new ground in an effort to free high schools from their traditional shackles. The commission, appointed by the National Association of Secondary School Principals, and backed by the Ford Foundation and the Fund for the Advancement of Education, has supported experimental programs in about 100 junior and senior high schools.

As Dr. Trump writes in the commission's publication, "Images Of The Future":

> The secondary school of the future will not have standard classes of 25 to 35 students meeting five days a week on inflexible schedules. Both the size of the groups and the length of the classes will vary from day to day. Methods of teaching, student groupings, and teacher and pupil activities will adjust to the purposes and content of instruction.

It is significant that the National Association of Secondary School Principals, under whose aegis Dr. Trump has worked, is a department of the National Education Association. This most powerful of the nation's education groups numbers more than 700,000 members. It has a tradition of conservatism in the acceptance of new ideas, but once it supports innovation it can end the tragic twenty to twenty-five-year lag between the origination of an idea and its acceptance.

The NEA's Project on the Academically Talented Student, directed by Dr. Charles E. Bish and supported by the Carnegie Corporation of New York, is another example of its pioneering activities. Dr. Bish has developed a clearing house whose files include thousands of programs for the talented and a consulting service whose impact has been felt all over the United States.

In June his project released a report based on a conference held by the NEA and the Modern Language Association. The report recommended that the study of foreign languages begin in the elementary school, preferably not later than the third grade, and continue in "an uninterrupted sequence for ten years."

Coming on the heels of successful experimentation in the teaching of languages in elementary school, this report should help to administer the *coup de grace* to superintendents and principals whose apathy has slowed this obviously desirable development.

Another Carnegie Corporation grant, to the North Central Association of Colleges and Secondary Schools, is being used to improve practices in identifying, guiding, and motivating 18,000 students in 100 high schools.

The wave of experimentation throughout the nation is impressive, but it is, in fact, a drop in the bucket. There are about 45,000 school districts in the United States; only a relative handful are examining new ideas. Ingenuity, imagination, and tolerance are perhaps more essential to the resolution of our school crisis than is money.

Too few school superintendents, school board members, and government officials have kept pace with progress. The New York State Education Department's willingness to consider unorthodox programs, as attested by its commissioning of "Schools Of Tomorrow—Today," is a unique exception.

Progress is slowed, too, by the schools' frequent suspicion of the public. Faced with critical problems, one would expect that the schools would turn outward and welcome public participation in their solution. It is true that there is greater public interest and participation than ever before, but this falls far behind the need. Speaking in generalizations (for there are many exceptions to each of these points), the schools have been loath really to admit their patrons. On a superficial basis there is acceptance of the public's right to know, but few school systems have welcomed public suggestions in the crucial areas of programming, and critical appraisals are as welcome as the Asian flu.

Some of this reaction stems from the events of the early 1950's, when Senator McCarthy's influence had reached the schoolhouse door and irresponsible charges were leveled at textbook writers and school programs. At that time, some conservative, Republican textbook authors as well as liberals were pilloried because they discussed the New Deal era with objectivity, and there was frequent interference with teachers and with the principle of academic freedom.

Schools have always been harassed by the propaganda of pressure groups, those economic and political organizations which attempt to drive their partisan points into youngsters' minds. But it is quite easy to separate the self-seeking and the selfishly motivated pressure groups from the responsible citizens who have no axe to grind other than a demand for better schools. The independent citizens' groups which sprang up during the heyday of the National Citizens Commission for the Public Schools have been scrupulously non-partisan and, with groups like the League of Women Voters and the American Association of University Women, have made notable contributions to improved education.

Those principals and superintendents intelligent and open-minded enough to work with these groups can harness community opinion for better schools regardless of cost. But too many principals and superintendents are wedded to the status quo. They prefer to keep local PTAs in their hip pockets, concentrating on innocuous fund-raising drives and pleasant social events, rather than on searching self-examination.

Much of their reticence is easy to understand. In the "good old days" there was a great cultural gap between the teacher and the community, the teachers being the intellectual leaders of the herd. Today the lay leaders of community groups tend to be as well or better educated than many of the educators. A natural conflict has arisen. In addition, the dogma of seniority has frozen-in many second-rate school principals who are all too aware of their inadequacies and whose instincts for survival are understandably strong. They are as eager for change as building trades workers are for automation.

Philip H. Coombs, Program Director of the Ford Foundation's Education Division, has suggested that every public school system and every institution of higher learning appoint "a vice president in charge of heresy."

"His job," said Dr. Coombs, "would be to welcome fresh ideas, to encourage the trying out of new approaches in his school system or college, to evaluate the results, and to pass these on, good and bad alike, to colleagues in other school systems and colleges."

Dr. Coombs has pointed out that "what the advancement of education requires, just as much as more money, is a larger and more dynamic frontier of experimentation and new developments, and a pervasive professional mood which not only tolerates innovation, but which welcomes and encourages it. Herein lies today, I believe, education's greatest shortage."

This is one shortage we cannot afford. It can be ended by an informed public.

How Much to Teach?

Daniel Tanner

An avalanche of criticism has fallen upon our schools. Yet what is perhaps one of the most serious weaknesses in American public education today has been virtually ignored by the critics. This particular shortcoming, like so many others, is a consequence of a society which expects great dividends from meager investments in its schools. Astonishing as it may seem, the result, in numerous instances, finds us still groping with a structural vestige of the one-room schoolhouse. For in elementary schools throughout our nation hundreds of thousands of youngsters must rely on a system of classroom organization in which a single teacher is responsible for the total formal educative experience at each grade level. In other words, these children receive their instruction in all subjects in the same classroom and from the same teacher. Administratively, this plan is termed the "self-contained" or "unitary" system of classroom organization.

TREND TOWARD SELF-CONTAINED TEACHING

In the "self-contained" classroom, an individual teacher must provide the instruction in arithmetic, reading, writing, spelling, science, history, geography, art, music, physical education, and so forth. While not all elementary schools are committed to the "self-contained" plan, the U.S. Office of Education reports that the leaders in elementary education are endorsing this system, and that the national trend is swinging away from departmentalization by subjects to unitary teaching by grade. Although the "self-contained" program of classroom organization usually operates through grade six, in certain school systems it extends through grades seven and eight where youngsters as old as twelve and thirteen are dependent upon an individual teacher for instruction in virtually every area of the curriculum.

Back in the days of the one-room school it was assumed that a single teacher was capable of instructing throughout the entire spectrum of studies. The "self-contained" classroom of today places a given grade grouping of youngsters under the guidance and direction of a single teacher for the entire day and over the full school semester.

Reprinted from *American School Board Journal* 140:15–17, September 1960, by permission of the publisher and the author. Dr. Daniel Tanner is at The City University of New York, New York City.

Many professional educators contend that the "self-contained" class-room is the most desirable system of classroom organization at the elementary level. Such a classroom unit, they argue, provides for the fullest possible integration of learning experiences inasmuch as the youngsters are under the continuous guidance and supervision of a given teacher throughout the entire school day and school term. These educators also believe that this arrangement is more conducive to fostering desirable mental health factors in the teaching-learning process than any other system of instructional organization.

Advocates of this plan point out that mental health factors are best taken into account under this system since the "self-contained" teacher is concerned with the education of the whole child, rather than merely being concerned with the child's specialized competencies in a given subject field.

UNFAIR TO OLDER STUDENTS

It seems reasonable to assume that the "self-contained" plan is well suited to children at the early elementary levels when they need to develop stability and security by identifying themselves continuously with an individual teacher. But what about the older children who must rely on a single adult for the sum total of their learning experiences? Is it fair to isolate these nine, ten, and eleven year-old youngsters, and in some cases even twelve and thirteen year-olds, from the depth and breadth of educational experience which derives from contact with teacher specialists in the various fields of knowledge?

This writer has actually observed fifth- and sixth-graders whose knowledge of science markedly surpassed that of the teacher to whom they were assigned in the "self-contained" classroom. Can we honestly expect a teacher to be highly competent to teach such youngsters in every one of the subject fields? It is very unlikely.

Those who favor the "self-contained" plan ignore the very real possibility of detrimental effects on the mental health of a given youngster who might be the victim of a personality clash with the teacher, but who, nevertheless, finds himself confined to that teacher's "self-contained" classroom all day long for the entire school semester or year. Also ignored is the possibility of serious psychological harm being wrought by a particularly poor teacher in a "self-contained" classroom situation.

PROPER EQUIPMENT NECESSARY

Originally, proponents of the "self-contained classroom" conceived of a plan whereby specialists could be brought in systematically and at the discretion of the regular "self-contained" teacher. In actuality, due to personnel cost factors, very few school districts have been willing or able to provide adequately for these specialists and consultants. The consequence has been frustration for the regular teacher. Since it is not economically feasible to provide each and every "self-contained" classroom with the equipment, supplies, materials, and resources necessary for conducting an adequate instructional program in all of the subject fields, the teacher and children are compelled to get along with what little they have. The end result is that these teachers and youngsters cannot secure the full dimensions of enriched experience which a more specialized curriculum and teaching staff might afford. Most of these schools are devoid of a central library and are lacking in the specialized facilities and resources needed for the support of adequate instructional programs in science, art, music, physical education, and other areas of the curriculum.

Inasmuch as the "self-contained" classroom teacher is responsible for her youngsters during every minute of the school day, she is seldom allotted more than a half-hour for lunch—during which time she may be assigned "yard duty" in order to supervise the lunchtime activities of her charges. So vital is the custodial function of the "self-contained" classroom teacher that, in most cases, she is required to work the entire day without relief. There is no time during the school day for working on curriculum problems, planning lessons, grading papers, compiling records, or even taking a five-minute coffee break.

Although it was originally intended that the ideal "self-contained" classroom would have at its disposal all of the facilities and equipment necessary for instruction in each of the subject fields, such a plan of operation would be prohibitively expensive. But, in actual practice, the "self-contained" classroom effects a real economy in school operation because it is forced to function without these specialized resources. In designing and constructing an elementary school building under the "self-contained" plan, each classroom can be identical since there is no need to make special provisions for expensive science rooms, laboratories, libraries, music rooms, and other specialized instructional facilities. As a consequence, the "self-contained" classroom is actually the cheapest system of instructional organization. Undoubtedly, this is the prime reason for its widespread acceptance.

TEACHERS NOT CAPABLE

In many schools, the "self-contained" teacher is not only expected to handle all subject areas in the curriculum, but she also is expected to conduct the physical education program for her pupils. Now, a woman teacher at the fifth- or sixth-grade level is, for the most part, incapable of dealing adequately with the physical education activities of ten and eleven year-old boys. Therefore, the school rarely provides for the facilities and equipment needed for such actively growing youngsters. The "self-contained" woman teacher, consequently, engages her class in simple, childlike games. The result is a program that is utterly devoid of its original intent and purposes.

Because so much is expected of the "self-contained" classroom teacher, one wonders how it is possible to develop teachers who possess adequate levels of subject matter competency in all fields of instruction. Obviously, even in cases where the prospective teacher has the interest and desire to achieve such a wide range of competencies, it would require many years beyond the usual four-year teacher certification curriculum to approach such a goal.

"MASTER OF NONE"

The economies realized through the "self-contained" plan are so great that, almost without exception, the colleges and universities must yield to the demands of the many school districts for candidates prepared as "self-contained" teachers. And this must be accomplished within the limitations of the usual four-year baccalaureate sequence. With many educational theorists lending support to such programs, the teacher preparation curriculum rarely penetrates beyond the survey stage. To make matters worse, the various subject area departments at these colleges and universities frequently refuse to accept any real responsibility for teacher preparation in the respective subject specialties.

TEACHER PROGRAMS NOT AT FAULT

It would be unfair to condemn the various teacher education programs and their staffs for this superficiality, when many communities, for the sake of educational economy, demand this of our colleges and universities. And since the "self-contained" teacher must be prepared to teach in all subject areas, there is no opportunity for developing adequate specialization. As a result, the bachelor's degree program rarely amounts to more than a smattering of emphasis in each of many fields of study. It is no wonder then that recent research conducted by the College of Education at the University of Illinois revealed that elementary school teachers are, by and large, incompetent in the teaching of mathematics. The investigations showed that these teachers have a strong fear and disdain for the teaching of this subject.

In four or five years of college studies, it is difficult enough to develop adequate depth and breadth in one or two areas of subject-specialization. Yet we expect the prospective elementary teacher to build such specialization and synthesis through a smattering of many subject fields. This is an impossible task.

Youngsters at the upper elementary school level are curious, imaginative and eager to learn. They delight in the wonders of exploration and discovery. They ask more questions than most adults are willing or even able to answer. But we lose many opportunities in our elementary schools to stimulate and nurture the eagerness and creativeness of the child. Under the "self-contained" scheme, we confine the youngster to the influence of only one adult who is expected to develop the child's capacities in all phases of the learning spectrum. Then we fail to comprehend why teachers fall into the expediency of overemphasizing the shallow skills of memorization-regurgitation, while neglecting the deeper and more significant understandings and appreciations.

Despite the claims by proponents of the "self-contained" plan, there is no evidence to support the contention that limiting a youngster's contacts to a single teacher will result in a greater cohesion of educational experience for that child. One could just as well argue, on the contrary, that limiting the learner's educative experience to the jurisdiction of a single teacher under the "self-contained" plan would more likely result in a dissociated, fragmented, and one-sided education.

CHANGE NEEDED

In today's world, it is the rare individual indeed who is capable of teaching throughout the entire range of the educational spectrum, working singlehandedly in all fields of study with youngsters of nine, ten and eleven years of age. On the other hand, a competent and somewhat more highly specialized faculty at the upper elementary level, with unified and coordinated effort may be able to do a far better job of lending continuity and coherence to the learner's educative experience. This does not mean that the curriculum for the fourth, fifth, and sixth grades should be dissected or fragmented into an array of atomistic and unrelated courses under independently specialized teachers. It does mean that we must develop other patterns of preparing elementary school teachers, and we must experiment with and evaluate new approaches to curriculum organization in our elementary schools.

Moreover, our communities need to provide the elementary schools with adequate libraries, laboratories, and other needed resources and facilities for high quality instruction. And, of course, teachers must be given time each day for curriculum analysis and development, lesson planning, parent and pupil consultation, preparation of instructional materials—and even a few minutes for a morning coffee break.

The trouble with many of the elementary school programs throughout the United States today is that, under the "self-contained" classroom plan, each teacher has too much to teach.

Door Opens in Self-Contained Classrooms To Let in Specialists

Oscar T. Jarvis

Completely self-contained classes in intermediate grades have moved down to third on the list of most commonly used organization plans. Only 12 per cent of 64 metropolitan elementary school districts recently surveyed expect one teacher to handle all instruction for her class.

By far what is most common—in two-thirds of intermediate grades— are self-contained classes assisted by a special teacher.

Music teachers are the most popular specialists; they are assigned in 44 per cent of the schools surveyed (see chart below).

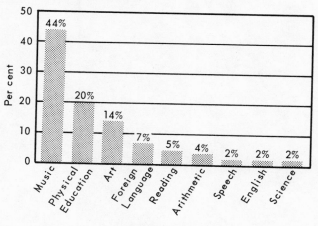

Types of Special Teachers

Further breakdown of the placement of specialists shows that in 20 per cent of intermediate classes physical education is taught by a special teacher. An art teacher teaches art to 14 per cent of fourth, fifth and sixth graders.

(The schools surveyed had from 500 to 150,000 in average daily attendance.)

Reprinted, with permission, from *The Nation's Schools* 74:33, December 1964. Copyright, 1964, McGraw-Hill, Inc., Chicago. All rights reserved. Dr. Oscar T. Jarvis is Assistant Professor of Education at the University of Georgia, Athens.

Making up the rest of the corps of special teachers in intermediate grades are teachers of foreign languages, remedial reading, speech, arithmetic, English and science. (The chart above gives exact percentages.)

Besides the self-contained classroom arrangements, departmentalization is found in intermediate grades; in fact, 17 per cent of intermediate classes are departmentalized—more than are totally self-contained. Five per cent of intermediate classes are combination plans of some type. The platoon system and Winnetka plan are among those used.

According to one educator,* basis for the trend toward specialists for elementary children comes from the behavior of children as they advance in grade. He maintained: "As children get into the intermediate grades they press for answers to technical questions and informational backgrounds that may be beyond the general classroom teacher."

---

* Otto, Henry J.: Elementary-School Organization and Administration, New York, Appleton-Century-Crofts, Inc., 1954.

Selected Bibliography

The Self-Contained Classroom

Analysis of a Team Teaching and of a Self-Contained Homeroom Experiment. Dearborn, Michigan: Public School District. 1962.
Account of experiment in Detroit, Michigan.

Anderson, Robert H. "Organizing Groups for Instruction." *Individualizing Instruction,* 61st Yearbook of the National Society for the Study of Education. Chicago: University of Chicago Press, 61:239–264, 1962, Part 1.
Gives historical background of ways of organizing classes. Includes discussion of self-contained classroom.

Association for Supervision and Curriculum Development. *The Self Contained Classroom.* Washington, D.C.: the Association, NEA, 1960.
Collection of articles advocating the self-contained classroom.

Badger, E. M. and Covell, E. M. "Teaching Music in the Self-Contained Classroom: Opinions Differ." *NEA Journal* 55:16–18, May 1966.
Gives two views of issue.

Bahner, John M. "Team Teaching in the Elementary School." *Education* 85:337–341, February 1965.
Points out strengths of the self-contained classroom and of departmentalization as claimed by their advocates. Says team teaching combines advantages of both plans.

Bennett, H. K. "Making the Transition Requires Administrative Planning, Courage, and Patience." *Nation's Schools* 49:60–65, January 1952.
Describes transition from a departmentalized elementary plan to a self-contained classroom arrangement at Dearborn, Michigan.

Brown, B. Frank. "Schools of Tomorrow—Today." *Bulletin of NASSP* 46:164–166, May 1962.
Advocates schools move from the self-contained classroom to the self-contained school, from gradedness to non-gradedness, from grouping of children toward their ungrouping, from grouping for all to solitude for many, and from education in the mass to education by appointment.

Burnsworth, C. C. "Self-Contained Classrooms Reconsidered." *Music Educators Journal* 48:41–42, November 1961.
Questions the practicality of music education in the self-contained classroom with the regular teacher.
Also see views expressed in Music Educators Journal 43:36–38, February 1957; 48:132–138, February 1962; 52:62–64, September 1965; 52:67–68, November 1965; and *NEA Journal* 55:16–18, May 1966.

Coffin, G. C. *The Effect of Departmental Teaching on Academic Achievement of Children in Grades Four, Five, and Six.* Doctoral Dissertation, University of Connecticut, 1963. Also in *Dissertation Abstracts* 24:4498.
Concluded there was no significant difference in the academic achievement of 590 fourth, fifth, and sixth grade pupils when participating in either a departmentalized or self-contained program. Reports pupils,

teachers, and parents who participated in departmentalized plan enjoyed it and would like to continue.

Dean, Ray B. "Team Teaching in the Elementary Schools." *American School Board Journal* 145:5–6, December 1962.
Opposes self-contained classroom. Describes team teaching plan in effect for thirty-two years in Sacramento, California.

Department of Elementary School Principals. "1954–1962 Resolutions." *National Elementary Principal* 42:33–48, January 1963.
Says the self-contained classroom is the best basic unit of organization yet devised.

Drummond, Harold. "Team Teaching: An Assessment." *Educational Leadership* 19:160–165, December 1961. Also in *Education Digest* 27:5–8, February 1962.
Gives examples of five meanings of the term "team teaching." Notes that the cost of team teaching personnel need not be higher than costs of a self-contained classroom even if differential salary scales are used for team members.

Echternacht, Charles and Gordon, Virginia. "Breaking the Lock Step in Arithmetic." *Arithmetic Teacher* 9:86–89, February 1962.
Describes changing arithmetic instruction from a self-contained classroom arrangement in grades 4–6 to a Joplin or departmental plan at Park School, San Mateo, California.
Also see further readings on Joplin Plan in arithmetic in *Elementary School Journal* 9:86–89, February 1962; *Arithmetic Teacher* 10:12–17, January 1963; and *Dissertation Abstracts* 22:2247.

Fordell, Patrick. "Self-Contained Classroom in Operation." *Nation's Schools* 49:55–57, January 1952.
Cites advantages of self-contained classroom.

Gibb, E. C. and Matala, Dorothy. "Study on the Use of Special Teachers of Science and Mathematics in Grades Five and Six." *School Science and Mathematics* 62:565–85, November 1962.
Describes a study of the merits of the use of special teachers in science and mathematics as compared with the use of one teacher in a self-contained classroom.

Goldberg, Miriam, *et al. The Effects of Ability Grouping.* New York, N.Y.: Teachers College Press, 1966.
Assesses the effects of ability grouping on the academic and personal-social learning of elementary school students. Findings raise some serious questions about the adequacy of the one-teacher classroom, especially for able pupils.

Halliwell, Joseph W. "Comparison of Pupil Achievement in Graded and Non-graded Primary Classrooms." *Journal of Experimental Education* 32:59–64, Fall 1963. Included in Chapter 2.
After a study of approximately 150 primary pupils in a nongraded unit and 150 in a graded self-contained unit, researcher concluded that a nongraded approach to the teaching of reading and spelling was most effective.

Hamalainen, Arthur E. "Some Current Proposals and Their Meaning." *Educational Leadership* 16:271–274, February 1959. Included in Chapter 7.
Gives pros and cons of departmentalization in the elementary school. Evaluates the self-contained classroom.

Heathers, Glen. "The Role of Innovation in Education." *National Elementary Principal* 43:9–14, September 1963.
Gives four claimed features of self-contained classroom and shows how they are challenged by new forms of classroom organization.

Hillson, Maurie. *Change and Innovation in Elementary School Organization.* New York: Holt, Rinehart and Winston, 1965.
A selection of readings concerned with ability grouping, departmentalized and semi-departmentalized plans, team teaching, dual progress, multigrading, and nongrading.

Hood, Adeline. "A Junior-High Division in the Elementary Schools." *Clearing House* 29:460–462, April 1955.
Describes growth and development of junior high students. Recommends a semi-self-contained class in the elementary school to meet the needs of students of grades 7 and 8.

Jackson, Joseph. "Analysis of a Team Teaching and of a Self-Contained Homeroom Experiment in Grades Five and Six." *Journal of Experimental Education* 32:317–331, Summer 1964.
Analyzed results from two teaching arrangements. Author labels one plan "team teaching," however, it is actually departmentalization. Used control and experimental groups. Concluded team teaching was beneficial.

Keliher, Alice V. "Team Teaching." *High Points.* 44:65–68, May 1962.
Expresses fear that team teaching is "band wagon." Calls for research studies. Presents case for self-contained elementary classroom organization.

Kemeny, John G. "The Mathematically Talented Student." *Bulletin of NASSP* 47:26–40, April 1963.
Describes the ways the imagination of mathematically talented grade-school students can be captured. Suggests it may be necessary to use arithmetic specialists in the graded school.

Koopman, G. Robert. "A Natural Pattern for Child Growth and Learning." *Nation's Schools* 49:50–54, January 1952. Also see *NEA Journal* 47:18–20, January 1958.
Recommends self-contained classroom for the elementary school.

Koury, Rose. "Elementary School Organization . . . What Direction Shall It Take?" *Education Briefs No. 37.* U. S. Department of Health, Education, and Welfare, Office of Education, 1960.
Gives a historical view of elementary school organization, current practices and experiments, and an evaluation of departmentalization and self-contained classrooms.

Kowitz, Gerald T. and Wahlferd, G. H. "The Gifted Child." *Overview* 3:37–39, August 1962.
Says programmed instruction gives support to the self-contained classroom in the elementary school.

Lambert, Philip, *et al.* "A Comparison of Pupil Adjustment in Team and Self-Contained Organizations." *Journal of Educational Research* 58:311–314, March 1965. Also in *Journal of Experimental Education* 33:217–224, Spring 1965.
After two-year study with 349 elementary students concluded there are no effects on pupil adjustment from either team or self-contained organization or else the personality scales used are not sensitive to such differences. Spring, 1965 article reports multigrade teams were formed for grades 1–3

and 4–6. *Found indications that achievement improved under a team organization that had been functioning longer than a year.*

Lounsbury, John H. and Douglass, Harl R. "Recent Trends in Junior High School Practices." *Bulletin of NASSP* 49:87–98, September 1965.
Reports increase in departmentalization.

Miel, Alice. "The Self-Contained Classroom: An Assessment." *Teachers College Record* 59:282–291, February 1958.
Gives pros and cons. Makes a case for self-contained classroom.

Moorhouse, William F. "Interclass Grouping for Reading Instruction." *Elementary School Journal* 64:280–286, February 1964.
Reports 1958 study in Laramie, Wyoming, of interclass grouping in reading in grades 4–6 in self-contained classrooms and in a Joplin Plan. Researcher suggests "Hawthorne Effect" may account for some gains in the experimental group in the early part of the study that did not exist after the initial motivation passed.

Morgan, Elmer F., Jr. and Stucker, Gerald R. "The Joplin Plan of Reading vs. a Traditional Method." *Journal of Educational Psychology* 51:69–73, April 1960.
Describes research using ninety matched pairs of fifth- and sixth-graders in a rural school. States pupils grouped by the Joplin Plan achieved significantly more than did pupils taught in the self-contained class.

National Education Association, Project on Instruction Report. *Planning and Organizing for Teaching.* Washington, D.C.: the Association, 1963. pp. 53–92.
Analyzes vertical organization in a school, graded, multigraded and nongraded structures. Also analyzes the horizontal organization including achievement grouping, ability grouping, self-contained classroom, team teaching and departmentalization.

National Education Association. *Project on Instruction: Schools for the Sixties.* New York: McGraw-Hill Book Co., 1963. pp. 94–96.
Points out possibilities for continuity and relatedness of learning inherent in self-contained organization. Says this is not its exclusive possession. Encourages flexibility and creativeness in finding and using means to attain this end.

Powell, William R. "The Joplin Plan: An Evaluation." *Elementary School Journal* 64:387–392, April 1964. Also see articles in *Elementary School Journal* 65:38–43, October 1964; *Journal of Educational Research* 55:567, August 1962; and *Dissertation Abstracts* 26:4342 and 25:1780.
Report of a study of reading achievement in Joplin or departmental plan and self-contained classrooms with fourth-, fifth-, and sixth-grade pupils. There were no significant differences in reading achievement.

Roff, Rosella. "Grouping and Individualizing in the Elementary Classroom." *Educational Leadership* 15:171–175, 1957.
Points out difficulties a teacher experiences in a self-contained classroom in trying to meet individual needs.

Sanders, David C. "School Organization—How Do You Decide?" *National Elementary School Principal* 42:25–28, September 1962.
Gives criteria which help administrators and staffs decide on school organization.

Shane, Harold G. and Polychrones, James G. "Elementary Education Organization and Administration." *Encyclopedia of Educational Research.* New York: Macmillan Company, 1960. pp. 421–430.
  Summarizes developments in structure and function of elementary school during the Fifties. Bibliography of 39 entries accompanies discussion of ability grouping, ideal class size, self-contained classrooms, and departmentalized classrooms.

Shaplin, Judson T. "Team Teaching." *Saturday Review* 44:54, 55, 70, May 20, 1961.
  Gives three alternatives to the self-contained classroom. Discusses advantages and disadvantages of team teaching.

Smith, Norvel L. "Primary Schools and Home School Relationships." *Educational Administration and Supervision* 42:129–133, March 1956.
  Concludes self-contained primary unit enriches school-home relationships. Says changes in school policies and procedures will have to be made to take advantage of the potential of self-contained classroom.

Spivak, Monroe L. "The Junior High: Departmentalized or Self-Contained?" *Phi Delta Kappan* 38:134–135, January 1957. Also see article in Chapter 7.
  Research evidence on forty-one matched pairs of seventh- and ninth-graders shows students do better in a self-contained class organization in junior high than those in a departmentalized arrangement.

Tillman, Rodney. "Self-Contained Classroom: Where Do We Stand?" *Educational Leadership* 18:82–84, November 1960.
  Cites seven promising practices promoted by the self-contained classroom.

"Toward Improved School Organization: Further Look at Horizontal Structure, The Self-Contained Classroom." *National Elementary Principal* 41:93–115, December 1961.
  Gives rationale, organization, administrative responsibilities, and professional reactions to the self-contained classroom.

Also check bibliography of Chapter 2 for readings on graded self-contained classrooms.

Chapter 7

Departmentalization and Semi-Departmentalization

The Departmentalized and Self-Contained Elementary School: How Much Do The Labels Tell Us?

William P. Colbert

Like so many things people discuss under the heading of specific labels, the departmentalized elementary school is perhaps less specific as an operative school unit than its label implies. One reason for this might be that the term is more often applied to the secondary school where there is a more common, widespread type of departmentalization. As the reader moves through this section, he will know of a departmentalized elementary school where teachers work in large blocks of time in rather general areas, with only twice as many students as they would in a self-contained organization. He will also find references being made to a departmentalized elementary school program where one specialist might work in more specific areas with many times this number of children.

As a label, the self-contained classroom might imply something more specific, but here, too, there are opportunities for meanings to become obscured unless some specific definitions are rendered. Sometimes, it is implied that the self-contained classroom is a place that is definitely off limits to specialists of any kind. At other times, we might hear of people describing schools that are self-contained except for the specialized teachers who work with children in the areas of music, art and physical education. Even in its purest form, there are probably, and hopefully, few teachers

Written especially for this book. Dr. William P. Colbert is Assistant Professor of Education, University of North Carolina, Greensboro.

working with children in self-contained classrooms who do not make use of outside resource persons.

Seldom, then, is the self-contained school entirely free of all of the features that might be more naturally ascribed to the departmentalized school. Perhaps, too, there are many advocates of departmentalized elementary schools that have attempted to gain some of the values that their opponents in the self-contained organization have claimed by allowing teachers to work in broad curriculum areas, such as social studies and language arts, rather than having a specialist work in history and another in geography and another in reading, etc. Working in these broader areas usually allows teachers to work in terms of larger time blocks and fewer numbers of children.

As a result of reading the contributions in this chapter, the reader will become aware not only of some of the degrees of difference in the definition of these ideas, but also some of the basic issues that professionals raise when they decide to support or adopt an organizational plan for the elementary school that is essentially more self-contained or more departmentalized. The articles by Arthur Hamalainen, Richard Anderson and Donald McCarthy do an excellent job of delving into the issues on both sides of the question. The research study reported by Monroe Spivak focuses on the academic achievement and the school adjustment of pupils who have gone through departmentalized seventh and eighth grades in the junior high school, compared to children who had attended elementary schools having self-contained seventh- and eighth-grade classrooms. Another study, reported by Roy C. Woods, investigated the results of these two types of organization in two elementary schools of strikingly similar environmental backgrounds. The reader will no doubt be interested in delving further into the research in this area to get a broader picture of the many assessments that have been attempted. The reader will also want to consider and compare the advantages claimed by the newer type of school organization—team teaching—that is discussed in Chapter 9 of this volume.

Some Current Proposals and Their Meaning

Arthur E. Hamalainen

Since 1950, universal military conscription, the tensions of the world situation, and the scientific advances of the Russians have brought about the formulation of certain proposals which clearly affect planning for integration and continuity in learning. The anxieties created by these various factors have led to a demand for a "hurry-up" process in education, an insistence that we all become linguists beginning in the kindergarten, a cry for more and better scientists, and an ultimatum to do more for the gifted child.

Such proposals take the form of adding special subjects such as foreign languages or science to the program and thus organizing the elementary school on a departmentalized plan from its simplest form to a dual or multiple track platoon system. Also, suggestions are made for homogeneous grouping and the earlier introduction of advanced work in the lower grades. These plans are presented as "new" and "tremendous strides" in education.

Forgotten is the thought that such proposals often represent a regression to procedures long discarded because they may be based upon an outmoded philosophy of education, and a mechanistic psychology of the teaching-learning process. If the same situation were to occur in the field of medicine, it would suggest that all medical doctors would turn their backs on the research of recent years and resort to bloodletting as a cure-all for their patients. In many situations where these proposals have been adopted, it is suspect that educators have done so not through conviction built on research but rather through community pressure, not through understanding of the ultimate effect of their practices upon children but rather through ignorance of the history of education and knowledge of how children learn in the light of the best evidence we have today. However,

Reprinted from *Educational Leadership* 16:271–273, February 1959, with permission of the Association for Supervision and Curriculum Development and Mr. Hamalainen. Copyright © 1959 by the Association for Supervision and Curriculum Development. Arthur E. Hamalainen is Principal, Plandome Road School, Manhasset, New York.

before we examine these proposals a restatement of the terms "integration" and "continuity" may be appropriate.

OBJECTIVES IN LEARNING

Integration, from both a psychological and biological approach, implies the harmonious development of the individual in all aspects of his development. As a process, it is the means by which the individual organizes his experiences in his own way to preserve his unity of self. We, normally, begin life as a unified, integrated personality. We spend the rest of our lives making every effort to maintain that original integration of self. Energy is directed by the individual to maintain this wholeness of personality, and the organism resists all attempts to thwart this unity of being. So strong is this urge to be an integrated organism that efforts to divert the individual in his striving to remain a unified, integrated being may result in abnormal or irrational behavior. The individual may resort to regressive or even infantile behavior to combat the demands placed upon him which threaten his unity of personality. He may break down completely, having found no "normal" means by which he can be himself. In practical terminology this behavior takes the form of problems in school discipline, dropouts, inattention, irrational behavior, or "misbehavior."

Continuity in the curriculum means that the individual is able to cope with problems of increasing difficulty more and more on an independent and mature level, that he is able to make more mature decisions, and that he understands the nature of himself and others and thereby develops his own self-image. "The principle of continuity of experience means that each experience both takes something from those which have gone before and modifies in some way the quality of those which come after."[1] It implies constant movement of the individual to higher levels of action. It meets the criterion of all education—that it end in action. In fact, continuity, if it means anything for the child, implies a share in the planning, the executing, the evaluation of the educative process through which he is going. Thus, what he studies has meaning for him and enables him to approach more difficult problems on a higher level with greater ease. It means concentrating on problems centered about his needs in the society in which he lives.

Based upon the philosophy of Peirce and Dewey these interpretations gained wide acceptance. The experiments of Lashely, Allee, and others, aided by the interpretations of such men as Hopkins appeared so sound

[1] John Dewey. *Experience and Education.* New York: The Macmillan Company, 1938. p. 27.

that the organization of the elementary school toward the self-contained classroom became quite apparent. Departmentalization in the elementary school as reported by Otto in 1950 was definitely on the decline. He further states that "A summation of the research evidence leads to the conclusion that no one of the claims made for departmentalization in the elementary school has been substantiated."[2]

DEPARTMENTALIZATION

Departmentalization disregards the fact that the individual is an organic being who cannot be farmed out piecemeal to many persons. He must be seen and reacted to as a whole being if the most effective learning is to occur. The teacher needs to observe and work with the individual in many circumstances and conditions in order that he can determine what materials and experiences the child needs for his fullest development. This is well exemplified in the films, "Skippy and the 3 R's" and "Passion for Life." To help the child maintain his essential unity and integration of self the teacher needs to know, not just one, but the many facets of his development. In addition, children learn best as they relate one to the other in the many phases of their development. Relatedness is only obtained as individuals spend extended time with other individuals in a setting in which there is freedom to interact. As the teacher thus works with groups of children over long periods of time she is able to help retain this essential unity of the organism and help children relate most effectively to each other.

One of the most obvious weaknesses of the departmentalized program is the very nature of the schedule itself. Continuity in learning is constantly interrupted, since it is impossible to pursue deep interests that have been developed in the classroom when the passing bell rings and the pupil must be in the next room within 3 or 5 minutes ready to switch his thinking to problems in an entirely different and unrelated field and setting. Impoverishment of the curriculum and the quality of experiences are evident when such rigid patterns of the curriculum are set. If learning is to be a continuous flow of experience, we defeat our very aims in attempting to segment it into specific, unrelated periods of the day under subject matter specialists. Otherwise, the individual is constantly left on a low plane of development which limits his capacity for growth and forms the basis of miseducation. The self-contained classroom appears to offer the more satisfactory answer to meet the criteria of high quality learning experience.

A first prerequisite of effective teaching is for the teacher to know the children quite completely. This is exceedingly difficult under a depart-

[2] Henry Otto. *Encyclopedia of Educational Research.* New York: The Macmillan Company, 1950. p. 379–80.

mentalized program, and impossible where a foreign language or science specialist may meet several hundred children each week for brief intervals of time. As a consequence, the teacher in the departmentalized program finds it very easy to become subject-centered in his teaching rather than being concerned with the uses of the subject to meet the needs of the children with whom he is working. This is certainly obvious in the high school, where departmentalization is most widely practiced. Here the perennial cry of administrators and of parents against the increasing amount of homework is so loud that rebellion is generally imminent. But the teacher, knowing that in the long run he will be evaluated on the achievement of youngsters in his particular area, gives increasing amounts of homework, while the integration of the individual and the continuity of his development are lost in the process.

Those who advocate the additive process as a method of curriculum improvement point out that the teacher in the self-contained classroom cannot be expected to know all subjects equally well and is thereby tempted to emphasize only the subjects he knows or likes best. It would be unrealistic to assume that each teacher knows all subjects with equal intimacy. It is probably more reasonable to expect the teacher to have more than a superficial, broad background and also a considerable depth of knowledge in the area of human growth and development.

In the self-contained classroom the teacher is thought of as the guide and counselor, the coordinator with the children of the experiences most meaningful to them. Because of the length of time he spends with the children he has an opportunity to know individual children in the class and thus better understand their needs. Through diagnostic procedures he is able to provide the experiences necessary for the child to meet these needs. In this way he is in a position to most adequately aid in the integration and continuity of experience for these children. At the time specialists are needed they may be brought into the particular activity the children are facing. To say that the teacher in the self-contained classroom will spend undue time on his own specialty or interest is less a criticism of the program as it is of the supervision or in-service training provided for the teacher of the self-contained classroom.

The teacher in a departmentalized program most often feels two needs: (a) a need to preserve the essential identity of the subject matter, and (b) a need to preserve the subject matter in its logical organization as determined by adults. These two concerns make any attempt at correlation or integration of subjects exceedingly difficult. Even in those cases where integration may be achieved the teachers find that the more completely they have integrated the subject matter the more difficult it is for the child to pull it apart to meet his own needs in this society. The integration of subject matter must be made by the individual himself, in his own way, and no one else can do it for him. Departmentalization, rather than facilitating this for the individual, actually hampers him in his attempts.

OTHER PROPOSALS

Although the discussion up to this point has concerned itself with departmentalization, there are other current proposals which affect integration and continuity of learning in the elementary school. In the limitations of this article only brief consideration can be given to these suggestions. Among them is the proposal for homogeneous grouping in order to provide more adequately for the talented or gifted child. In considering this proposal one should ask—grouping for what purpose? If the purpose is to meet the needs of the gifted, an examination of those needs reveals they are no different from the needs of every child. If the purpose is higher achievement, the research evidence does not indicate substantially higher achievement in segregated as opposed to unsegregated classes. However, if an objective of the elementary school curriculum is to help children learn to understand and show acceptance of each other, there is much to substantiate the need for heterogeneous grouping. If a major goal is to eliminate unhealthy competition, all children should be grouped together. If we segregate children one from the other and put them in groups more and more alike, we create a tense, unhealthy competition. If they are kept together where there are many differences, a helping atmosphere is created.

Finally the proposal is made that we hurry children through the elementary grades so that they will be prepared to enter high school and colleges at an earlier age than ever before. Suggestions are made that we begin reading in the kindergarten and that the reading readiness period in the first grade be considerably shortened. Other suggestions would have some of the junior high mathematics brought down to the 5th and 6th grade levels. In considering these proposals it should be recalled that play is the work of a five-year-old and to expect him to sit for prolonged periods at a desk doing paper and pencil work is contrary to the best that we know about this developmental level of children. It is through play and activity that five year olds are best prepared for the first grade. Consideration should be given, also, to the fact that children learn best that which they can relate to their own experiential background and that which comes within the phenomenological range of the individual. The more the subject matter or activities provided are outside of the individual's ability to integrate and assimilate the material, the more we must resort to artificial devices to stimulate learning. The more closely the materials are related to the individual's own life experience the less need there is for concern over the factor of motivation.

As the current proposals for integration and continuity are reviewed it seems that many of these are in the form of mechanical devices such as departmentalization, grouping, and acceleration. In general their proponents seem to avoid the real issue, which is that effective teaching is a matter of a high degree of interpersonal relationships between a teacher and a child and among the children themselves. This can only be achieved if we point out to the lay public the necessity of high professional standards for teachers, of small classes, and of adequate materials. The more vigorously we are able to impress upon the patrons of the school that these are the real issues, the more rapidly we will be able to discard, and the less need we will have to resort to mechanical devices to solve our basic problems in education.

Relative Merits of Departmental and Non-Departmental Elementary Schools

Roy C. Woods

For several years there has been a difference of opinion relative to the advantages and disadvantages of departmental and non-departmental teaching in the elementary schools. It was the purpose of this study to investigate the results of these types of organization in two schools of striking similar environmental backgrounds. In this study departmental teaching meant that a class had different teachers in each subject similar to the system used in high schools; whereas, the traditional or non-departmentalized teaching was the type where one teacher was responsible for all the subjects taught in a given grade.

Dougherty, Gorman, and Phillips[1] explained that:

> The characteristic feature of departmental instruction is that a teacher who is highly trained in a field of knowledge is assigned to teach English, which in the elementary school would include reading, writing, language, spelling, and literature; another teacher is assigned to the social studies, including history, geography, and citizenship in elementary schools; another to mathematics; another to natural science, etc. . . . This type of organization has been introduced somewhat extensively in the intermediate and grammar grades. . . .

Reavis, Pierce, and Stullken[2] described the traditional type of school as follows:

> The traditional or regular organization of the elementary school consisted of a group of classrooms with a teacher for each room who accepted responsibility for the complete education of the group of pupils assigned to the room.

Dougherty, Gorman, and Phillips[3] gave some arguments for and

Reprinted from *Peabody Journal of Education* 37:164–169, November 1959, by permission of the publisher and the author. Roy C. Woods is at Marshall College, Huntington, West Virginia.

[1] J. H. Dougherty, F. H. Gorman, and C. A. Phillips, *Elementary School Organization and Management*. New York: The Macmillan Company, 1936, p. 31.

[2] William C. Reavis, Paul R. Pierce, and Edward H. Stullken, *The Elementary School*. The University of Chicago Press, 1931, p. 7.

[3] *Op. cit.*, pp. 31–32.

against the departmental organization in the elementary school. Their statements are set forth in the following excerpt:

Some of the advantages claimed for departmental organization are that it (1) provides for more efficient instruction; (2) offers an enriched curriculum; (3) more highly trained teachers can be secured; (4) allows for concentration of equipment; (5) pupils may be promoted by subjects instead of grades; (6) pupils have contact with more teaching personality; and (7) both teachers and children in schools with departmentalization favor it.

The arguments against departmentalization are that (1) it overemphasizes subject matter; (2) teachers are only narrow specialists; (3) behavior problems are more difficult to handle; (4) it destroys the unity of school life for the pupil; (5) prevents integration of subject matter; and (6) the plan has been borrowed from secondary school practice.

Both School A in which departmentalization prevailed and School B organized on the traditional plan were located in the same area of an industrial development. The parents of both groups of children were economically dependent upon chemical and coal industries and were located in the same county with the same supervisory contacts and approximately the same quality of teacher preparation and experience. Table I shows how similar they are in socio-economic backgrounds. Table II shows that on mental ability the two groups were not equated and this point must be remembered in evaluating the final results of this study. The questionnaire was used to secure the necessary background of each child. A thorough survey of the social, cultural, economic, and health status of all the members of both eighth grade classes was conducted.

The questionnaire proved that the two communities were very similar economically, socially, culturally, and in matters pertaining to health. This and the permanent record and census cards furnished additional data. Personal interviews were used when necessary to secure needed data. The first test given to the eighth grade pupils of the two schools was the *Otis Quick-Scoring Mental Ability Test,* Beta, Form A.

This test was given September 23, 1949, by the principals of the two schools both of whom have had considerable experience in administering tests. They showed a keen and impartial interest, and the best of co-operation was given. Conditions prevailing at both of the schools were as nearly the same as was found possible, and the directions were followed implicitly.

Upon scoring and ranking the tests it was found that School A had a median chronological age of fourteen years and one month, had a median intelligence quotient of ninety-two, and a median mental age of thirteen

TABLE I
Socio-Economic Background

Factor	School A Departmental		School B Non-Departmental	
	Number	Per Cent	Number	Per Cent
Parents with Only Elementary Education	20	66.7	20	58.8
Those with High School Education or More	10	33.3	14	41.2
Five or Less in Family	13	86.6	11	64.7
More than Five in Family	2	13.3	6	35.3
Average Size of Family	4.49		4.65	
Chief Wage Earner was Father	10	66.8	12	70.6
Chief Wage Earner was Mother	1	6.7	1	5.9
Both Parents Worked	2	13.3	3	17.7
Step Mother and Father	2	13.3	1	5.9
Owned Homes	12	80.0	15	88.2
Rented Homes	3	20.0	2	11.8
Owned a Car	10	66.7	13	76.5
Bathroom in Home	10	66.7	7	41.2
Musical Instrument	8	53.3	10	58.8
Radio	12	80.0	15	88.2
Refrigerator	5	33.3	8	47.1
Telephone	11	73.3	10	58.8
Attended only One school ...	6	40.0	8	47.1
Attended Two Schools	5	33.3	5	29.4
Attended Three Schools	4	26.7	4	23.5

TABLE II
Mental Ability Status

Status	Departmental Class Medians School A	Non-Departmental Class Medians School B
Chronological Age (Years and Months)	14-1	14-9
Intelligence Quotient	92	78
Mental Age (Years and Months)	13-0	11-6

years; while School B had a median chronologically of fourteen years and nine months, had a median intelligence quotient of seventy-eight, and a median mental age of eleven years and six months. This gave School A an advantage of fourteen points in intelligence quotient and an advantage of one year and six months in mental age. Apparently School B should have been outdistanced considerably in achievement, but exactly the opposite happened as will be shown in the achievement tests.

The achievement tests were given under conditions very similar to those described in administering the mental tests.

The first of the achievement tests was administered in October, so as to establish a point from which to measure the gains in achievement. The test used was the *Stanford Achievement Test*, Advanced Battery—Complete, Form G.

It contained a total score of 550 points which was divided into ten parts under the following subjects: paragraph meaning, forty-five; language usage, one hundred; word meaning, fifty; arithmetic reasoning, forty; arithmetic computation, sixty-five; literature, fifty; social studies, Parts I and II, fifty each; elementary science, fifty; and spelling, fifty.

In analyzing the test results it was not considered necessary to compile tables of comparison on each of the ten parts of the tests for an analytical diagnosis of the achievements in the various fields, but the chief aim was to discover how the general achievements on the entire test compared. In the main, the object was to find, if possible, which type of school organization enhanced pupil achievement more academically.

The second achievement test which was given in May was the *Stanford Achievement Test*, Advanced Battery—Complete, Form D. It was very similar to the first achievement test given and was administered in the same manner and by the same people, but the results differed greatly and in an unexpected direction.

In this second achievement test the unitary School B had a median equated score of sixty-eight as compared to fifty-four and nine-tenths in the first test, a gain of thirteen and one-tenth points. Its age equivalent increased from ten years and ten months to thirteen years and six months which was a gain of two years and eight months. As to the grade equivalent median it was stepped up from the eighth month of the fifth grade to the fifth month of the eighth grade, a gain of two and seven-tenths grades.

The departmental school, A, made a median equated score of sixty-three and six-tenths as compared to fifty-eight and five-tenths in its initial attempt which was a gain of five and one-tenth points. The median age equivalent was raised from eleven years and five months to twelve years and five months, a gain of exactly one year; while the grade equivalent was increased from the fourth month of the sixth grade to the fourth month of the seventh grade, or a gain of exactly one grade.

In comparing the academic achievements of the two schools, it was found that School B apparently achieved eight points more in the equated score, one year and eight months more in the growth of age equivalent, and one and seven-tenths grades in grade development than did the departmental school. These facts will perhaps be better understood by a study of Table III.

TABLE III
Medians and Equivalents on the Achievement Tests

Test Number	School A Departmental			School B Non-Departmental		
	Equated Score	Age Equivalent	Grade Equivalent	Equated Score	Age Equivalent	Grade Equivalent
I	58.5	11-5	6.4	54.9	10-10	5.8
II	63.6	12-5	7.4	68.0	13-6	8.5
Apparent gain.	5.1	1-0	1.0	13.1	2-8	2.7

From this study it seemed that the learning process in the unitary school was, perhaps, more unified and continuous because the one teacher knew exactly what was being done in every subject. It was also found that assignments were more uniform, that is, distributed more evenly. On the other hand nearly all the pupils of the upper grades preferred departmental work, and it was apparent that the teachers in departmental work were more highly specialized in their particular fields. It was also noticeable that the departmental system lacked coordination in that one teacher knew very little concerning what the other teachers were endeavoring to teach at any particular time. That factor resulted in pupils having so much outside work to do on certain nights that they found it quite burdensome, while at other times they had little or nothing to do. The last mentioned factor could, of course, have been eliminated if there had been closer teacher contact and closer supervision on the part of the principal.

From these data the following conclusion seems reasonable. It must be understood however that this can only be said of conditions similar to those found in these two schools. No doubt variations in communities would affect the results.

1. Non-departmentalization in teaching seems to favor the poorer students since School B which had the lowest mental ability ratings made the greatest gain between October when the first test was given and May when the second achievement test was administred.

2. This may be due to the fact that the total learning process was better coordinated and integrated in the traditional and unitary type of school organization.

3. The unfortunate variation in mental abilities made an accurate estimate of this advantage impossible.

Science Specialist versus Classroom Teacher

Donald W. McCarthy

Science in the self-contained classroom versus science taught by the science specialist! Here's a topic sure to evoke heated discussions from either side. I even argue with myself! One side of me is for the science specialist, someone who has the interest and background to take responsibility for the science program of an elementary school. I call that side of me "Don." The other side of me is for the self-contained classroom teacher, where science is taught by the same teacher who teaches such subjects as reading, language arts, social studies, and arithmetic. I call that side of me "Mac." The argument usually goes something like this:

DON—Science is increasingly becoming a major part of American life.

MAC—You're right! And the elementary schools must accept responsibility for leading children to better understand their environments.

DON—Mac, don't you think it's time we gave up the assumption that the self-contained classroom is going to give the child the kind of science he needs?

MAC—I'm willing to examine the issue, but you know you are bucking an established pattern in 60 to 75 percent of the school systems.

DON—Just because we have it does not mean it's the best way. Interest in the science specialist is increasing. The lack of science background among elementary teachers is appalling. They admit themselves they are not prepared and they don't feel comfortable teaching science.

MAC—You've hit the key problem there, Don. We are getting a lot more scientific information thrown at us, but does the elementary teacher really need a competence so much greater than the well-informed layman? Isn't an acquaintance with the major generalizations enough?

DON—No. Our children need someone with more than a superficial grasp of the subject matter. Children can get tired of having their questions answered, "I don't know, let's look it up together." There's a lot of evidence to show that children can learn important material in embryology, astronomy, physics, and chemistry much earlier than we used to think. It takes a science specialist to know the material well enough to teach it.

Reprinted from *The Instructor* 73:51–52, 74, January 1964, by permission of the publisher and the author. Donald W. McCarthy is Staff Assistant to Assistant Superintendent–Instruction, Cleveland Public Schools, Cleveland, Ohio.

MAC—Besides the question of the advisability of including embry-ology in grade two, we have to ask if the science major coming into the elementary school is prepared to teach young children—is he able to "get down to the children's level"? I know elementary teachers with impressive numbers of hours in science who want to turn the science classroom into a lecture hall.

DON—They need in-service education.

MAC—Maybe that's all the teacher in a self-contained classroom needs. Give her appropriate background information and techniques of teaching elementary science through a good in-service program, and she can do the job.

DON—I'm glad you said "she." Most elementary teachers are women, and women are afraid of science—they want nothing to do with wires, bugs, and animals.

MAC—Yes, it's a cultural expectation that women are to be afraid of science. It's ironic, too—it's the women who are the gardeners, the moth fighters, and the dissecters of birds for the table. And who profits more from electric wires than the lady of the kitchen? It's only a step from these areas into the pure science of biology, chemistry, and physics. Women and girls should be as interested in science as men—it should be universal in its appeal.

DON—You'd have a real challenge there—changing these persons' attitudes.

MAC—The important attitude for the elementary teacher is that she have a sincere desire to provide the experiences that boys and girls need to develop their unique potentials.

DON—That's why I say get the specialist in there to develop that science potential. This concern for the individual child is not absent from the specialist—remember, the specialist will get to observe each child over a two- or three-year period, perhaps guide him into a science career.

MAC—Let's not put the specialist in a position where he is going to compete for talent.

DON—I didn't mean that, but certainly science-related occupations are requiring a larger and larger percent of the population.

MAC—It's because science is important for *all* children, not just the science-prone, that science belongs in the elementary school.

DON—Certainly, and it's important that all children get a true picture of science as a way of discovery as well as a body of information. Is the average classroom teacher equipped to teach science as "discovery"—a way of solving problems?

MAC—I think this discovery aspect of science teaching is its most exciting part; and it is so consistent with the true spirit of the elementary school, which involves children in the planning and execution of experiences and leads them to see the interrelationships of knowledge. This approach is most dramatic in science, but the inductive approach, leading children to arrive at generalizations for themselves, is also the emphasis within modern arithmetic, social studies—and even phonetic analysis in reading. We'd have better luck incorporating the discovery or problem-solving approach through the teacher in the self-contained classroom. The specialist might be so subject-centered he'd want to simply tell the answers or lecture rather than have children solve problems inductively.

DON—I want the specialist to have a good understanding of how children learn—he's going to have a good command of the inductive approach because it's part of scientific methodology. The inductive approach in science is specific enough to require much refining to master it. It requires deep understanding of science to provide the appropriate response to children's questions and comments and to recognize misinformation and faulty concept formation.

MAC—It also requires a good understanding of how children learn and how the individual child learns. In the self-contained classroom, a teacher has fewer children to get to know and can individualize instruction more effectively. Then, too, the children don't have to adjust to so many teacher personalities.

DON—Exposing the child to a variety of teachers may actually be desirable. The child can choose from more than one personality with whom he can identify. For example, a male science teacher would give a needed masculine balance to the school life of many children. The child would be exposed to a variety of techniques of teaching.

MAC—Many teachers have been able to start with science and draw experiences from it for other subjects—oral reports and supplementary book reading in language arts, scientific measurement in arithmetic, and social implications of science and technology in social studies.

DON—Yes, the typical elementary teacher, particularly the primary teacher, sees herself as a reading teacher and has to be sold on science.

MAC—I have to say that some primary teachers do a beautiful job of science teaching—I think they really enjoy watching children grow.

DON—Yes, perhaps the primary grades should be essentially self-contained, with the specialist acting as a consultant. But in the intermediate grades I think there should definitely be a special science teacher.

MAC—You know, the Great Cities Conference on departmentalization extends self-containment even farther. It has recommended the extension of self-contained classrooms into the junior high in culturally deprived neighborhoods, the argument being that these children need the security of their teacher in their classroom.

DON—That may be a special case, but there's little or no research evidence to indicate greater security of self-containment over departmentalization. All I'm asking for is to get upper elementary children exposed to someone who knows science and how to teach it.

MAC—There are some possibilities! I'll concede that the teacher gifted with the ability to lead children to discover the big ideas of science should be given more opportunity to teach more boys and girls. Educational television is exposing more children to the master teacher, although the major responsibility for helping children make their own discoveries rests with the classroom teacher.

DON—And team teaching places more children in a direct teaching situation with the science specialist.

MAC—Yes, but it can so easily become lectures and that's deadly. Coordination among the teachers takes much skill in human relations.

DON—Stoddard's Dual Progress approach offers possibilities.

MAC—Yes. Dividing subject matter responsibilities between two teachers probably permits a teacher to demonstrate greater competency, since she has responsibility for only half as many subject areas. But I resent Stoddard's designation of science as a "cultural elective."

DON—I do, too.

MAC AND DON (together)—Science is increasingly becoming a major part of American life and the elementary schools must accept responsibility for leading children to better understand their environments. Seems like that's how the whole thing started. . . .

CONTRASTING VIEWPOINTS

Area	Classroom Teacher	Science Specialist
Present Status	Undoubtedly the prevailing organizational pattern	Many teachers prefer departmentalization in upper elementary grades
Administration	No involved problems in scheduling room and teacher assignments	The authority and responsibility for science is delegated to one person
Time Allotment	Time is flexible so activities do not have to be completed in 40 minutes	Specialist insures certain amount of time devoted to science
Materials	Simple materials near at hand plus supplies from a central location are all that are necessary	New science activities require more elaborate equipment with a person in charge of it

Area	Classroom Teacher	Science Specialist
Problem Solving	Requires a deep understanding of individual children to know how to plan	Requires a deep understanding of science to know how to plan
Subject Matter	Competence required is actually little more than an informed layman has; in-service education can bring teacher up to date on new developments	Rapidly developing findings require a specialist to keep up to date and to correct children's misconceptions
Activities	Permits a rhythmic balance of stimulating and quiet activities	Provides a stimulating variety of techniques, personalities, activities
Integration of Learning Experiences	Promotes unity of knowledge, for the teacher can immediately relate science to language arts, arithmetic, social studies, health	The specialist is better able to see opportunities for extending learnings of science; lessons should be single-purposed
Individualization	By knowing his own pupils intimately, the teacher can "prescribe" appropriate activities	Through knowing the subject thoroughly, the specialist can select the important activity rather than the trivial
Teacher-Pupil Relationship	"My teacher" and "my classroom" give security; avoid "lost" feeling	Provides more than one adult model for the child

The Case for Teacher Specialization in the Elementary School

Richard C. Anderson

Most elementary schools in the United States have self-contained classrooms. Under this arrangement, one teacher is responsible for instruction in every area of the curriculum: language, literature, social studies, mathematics, the sciences, art, and music.

Only an extraordinary individual—a Leonardo da Vinci—could have an expert knowledge of all these areas. Conclusion: Most children in the United States are instructed by teachers who are not expert in every field they teach.

Daniel Tanner has aptly described the typical elementary school teacher as a jack of all subjects and the master of none (1). Most generalist elementary school teachers would probably agree with Tanner.

George Ackerlund made a study of teachers' attitudes on their competence to teach elementary school subjects. Of the 260 generalist teachers who took part in the study, 47 per cent felt that they were "less than well prepared" in content and method to teach reading, handwriting, history, geography, science, art, and music.

There were only three areas in which 70 per cent or more of the teachers felt competent in both content and method. These areas were arithmetic, English, and spelling. Only four of the 260 teachers considered themselves well prepared in all the subjects they taught (2).

Realistic plans of school organization take account of the fact that it is the rare teacher who has considerable competence in more than one or two areas of knowledge. The public schools of East Brunswick have recognized this fact by embarking on a program of teacher specialization.

The program is one phase of a new plan of elementary school organization, which we in East Brunswick refer to as the Achievement Grouping and Teacher Specialization Plan. The other major feature of the plan is nongraded, homogeneous grouping, which was discussed in the January, 1962, issue of the *Elementary School Journal* (3).

Teachers in East Brunswick who would ordinarily teach the fourth,

Reprinted from *Elementary School Journal* 62:253–260, February 1962, by permission of the publisher and the author. Richard C. Anderson is an Associate Professor at the University of Illinois, Urbana.

fifth, or sixth grade are now either language arts-social studies teachers or mathematics-science teachers. Each teacher instructs two groups of children a day in his special subjects. Teachers are assigned on the basis of academic background and the supervisor's estimate of competence. One more consideration is weighed in making assignments: whether the teacher works best with fast, average, or slow learners.

How competent should the elementary school teacher be in each area of the curriculum he is to teach? It could be argued that elementary school teachers need to be only somewhat more knowledgeable than their pupils. Proficiency in algebra, geometry, and calculus, it could be contended, is superfluous for the teacher of eleven-year-olds. This is a most insidious belief.

Anyone who has seen David Page, of the University of Illinois, or Robert Davis, of Syracuse University, teach a class of elementary school children realizes that there is a world of difference between the teaching of these men and typical instruction in arithmetic. One major reason why Page and Davis are extraordinarily successful teachers is that they have a thorough understanding of mathematics.

Other things being equal, the deeper the teacher's understanding of his subject, the greater the likelihood of excellent instruction. Some teachers who have mastered an area of knowledge may be able to lead their pupils to a comprehension of the basic ideas of the discipline. It is difficult to believe that a teacher who has only a superficial understanding of an area of knowledge could achieve such results. This is the key premise of the departmentalized school.

Specialization promises several other advantages. With specialization, teaching assignments can be more sharply focused, and sharply focused assignments make lesson planning easier. Specialization should make it easier for the teacher to keep in touch with developments in teaching methods, materials, equipment, and the professional literature. Surely it is easier to keep abreast of developments in one or two areas than in many areas.

In spite of the important advantages that specialization seems to offer, many educators object to specialization in the elementary school. At least three objections deserve serious consideration.

Some educators insist that it is of overriding importance that the teacher know the child. Under a departmentalized plan, the teacher comes in contact with more children than in the self-contained classroom. Therefore, some educators conclude, the teacher in a departmentalized school knows each child less well.

"Knowing the child" is a concept that has several levels of meaning. At one level, it refers to rapport. The teacher and the child are on friendly terms. The child feels free to approach the teacher. The teacher has a feeling for the child as a person.

In the East Brunswick Achievement Grouping and Teacher Specialization Plan, the teacher meets two classes of children during the school day, one class in the morning and the other in the afternoon. Almost any teacher should be able to develop rapport with most of his pupils if he sees them for half a school day throughout the school year. In this first sense of knowing the child, the departmentalized system used in East Brunswick should not prove inferior to the self-contained plan.

"To know the child" may also mean to have information about the child's health, his home background, his personality as revealed in inventories and psychologists' reports, achievement record and aptitude scores. In East Brunswick, where each teacher now instructs about twice as many children as he would in the self-contained classroom, to be well informed about each child is more difficult than in the self-contained classroom.

Still, within limits, the number of children that the teacher instructs may not be especially important in determining how well informed he will be about each child. Although most school systems collect and store huge amounts of information about pupils, one may wonder how many teachers, whatever the plan of school organization, are as well informed about their pupils as they could and should be.

To meet this problem, East Brunswick is developing an automatic school information system. Most educational bookkeeping will be handled by punch cards and high-speed data-processing equipment. One of the major purposes of this system is to increase the amount, the quality, and the relevance of information in the teacher's immediate possession. In addition, East Brunswick is attempting to improve the flow of current, anecdotal information to and from teachers. It is expected that these programs will increase the amount of usable information the teacher has about each child, even though the teacher must now keep informed about twice as many children as under the old plan.

Perhaps the most significant sense of knowing the child is understanding him in relation to his educational development. It is at this important level that the competent, specialist teacher has a big advantage over his generalist counterpart.

The teacher who has mastery of an area of knowledge has a frame of reference for evaluating the child's development. He can interpret the child as he is now in terms of how he should be when his schooling is complete. The teacher who knows his area well can conceive the details of today's lesson in terms of goals. The course of action of the less competent teacher is aimless or dictated by trivial, incidental considerations or by experts and curriculum guides that the teacher does not fully understand.

The teacher who is master of his area can read signs in a child's behavior, signs that tell him of the child's misunderstanding. The same behavior reveals little to the less competent teacher. He rarely sees that the root of a learning difficulty may lie in children's difficulty in understanding a concept. He is more likely to attribute children's difficulties to a short attention span, to laziness, to poor study habits, or to emotional disturbance—all factors that are comfortably distant from the teacher.

Many of the key concepts of every area of knowledge are elegant in their simplicity. Indeed, there are scholars who argue that a child can grasp the basic structure of most disciplines. Jerome Bruner has asserted in his exciting book *The Process of Education* "that any subject can be taught effectively in some intellectually honest form to any child at any stage of development" (4: 33).

But legions of generalist, elementary school teachers act on a contrary premise. Consider the great numbers of maps many elementary school children are required to color each year. Every point in the social studies curriculum is an occasion for mapwork. What of the concepts of political science, geophysics, history, economics, anthropology, sociology? Concepts in these areas, spokesmen for the generalist teacher assure us, are too abstract and too complex for the child to grasp. Is it possible that these people are speaking for themselves rather than children? A map is tangible. One can perceive it directly, while a concept is slippery and unreal to the teacher whose understanding is superficial. The limited intellectual perspective of many generalist teachers prevents them from knowing the child's intellectual limits.

To the teacher who must instruct children in an area in which he is poorly prepared, motivation is extrinsic to the learning task itself. Motivation becomes the bright, irrelevant wrapping that covers what, for the teacher, is sometimes a dull product. The generalist teacher is often incapable of leading his pupils to a sense of joy in learning and thinking because intellectual enterprise has never held any excitement for him.

The teacher who does not have an intellectual specialty can seldom know the child's eagerness to understand. He can seldom know the child as he struggles to develop skills and make sense of concepts. He can seldom know the limits of the child's ability to comprehend. He cannot know the child as he is in terms of intellectual goals. The typical generalist teacher can know the child in none of the most significant meanings of the concept.

Some educators argue that the child needs the security of studying with one teacher all day. They believe that the child suffers socially and emotionally from being subjected to the varying standards—behavioral and academic—of different teachers in a departmentalized school.

What evidence is there that departmentalization has undesirable effects on children's social and emotional adjustment? Little or no evidence is available. Broadhead wrote: "A thorough search of the *Education Index* and *Dissertation Abstracts* for the last ten years reveals no research indicating whether the semi-departmental type of elementary school organization promotes good or poor social adjustment among pupils" (5).

Broadhead has described a recently completed study of the adjustment of fifth-graders in the elementary schools of Tulsa, Oklahoma, where a semi-departmental plan of organization has been in effect since 1928. The results showed better than average adjustment for Tulsa fifth-graders.

The most pronounced advantage of the Tulsa fifth-graders was their adjustment to school, though the Tulsa group also showed significantly fewer problems in every other area (5).

As the Tulsa researchers recognize, the findings described here do not offer a base for firm conclusions, since norms on the SRA Junior Inventory do not comprise a satisfactory yardstick; nonetheless, the findings are suggestive. Livingston has stated that Tulsa is engaged in further research on the question (6).

The Experimental Teaching Center of New York University is now investigating the effects of the Dual Progress Plan on children's adjustment. This plan, which involves more departmentalization than either the Tulsa plan or the East Brunswick plan, also includes non-graded achievement-ability grouping of children who would traditionally be in Grades 3 through 6 (7).

Hopefully, these investigations will clarify the issue. On the basis of data now available, it must be assumed that the adjustment of children in departmentalized schools is, at least, not inferior to that of children in self-contained classrooms.

The results of the Tulsa study are not surprising. There are several reasons for believing that departmentalization will enhance children's adjustment. Good teaching involves a variety of techniques. There are limits to the methods and approaches that any one teacher can offer. Even the best of teachers is likely to have a single style of teaching, a characteristic approach to most topics of instruction. In contrast, variety is built into the departmentalized program. A pupil in the upper-elementary grades in East Brunswick receives substantial exposure to two styles of teaching every day. He receives instruction from the repertoire of techniques at the command of two teachers.

Greater variety may be valuable on two counts. First, not all children respond equally well to every technique and approach. The more techniques the class encounters, the greater the probability that some of them will be particularly well suited to each child. Second, a uniform environment is dull. Greater variety in the school day should make school more interesting. Children taught in departmentalized schools may well find learning more stimulating than children taught in self-contained classes.

Departmentalization may have another good effect on the adjustment of some children. No teacher—no matter how wise, mature, and emotionally suited for teaching—gets along with all his pupils. There are always a few pupils with whom the teacher has little patience. The teacher should find it easier to be patient with these pupils for a half day than for a whole day.

Identification with significant adult figures is important in socialization. For one reason or another, a child may not identify with a certain teacher. A departmentalized plan offers the child several models. The chances for identification are, therefore, better. Boys need adult males as role models. There is a better chance of getting a male teacher in a departmentalized school than in a school that has self-contained classrooms.

Aside from the child's social and emotional development, there is an ethical question. Is it fair for a school to impose a single adult personality, a single set of values, a single way of thinking upon the child? Within limits, the citizen in a democracy has the right to define life, liberty, and the pursuit of happiness as he sees fit. Shouldn't the child, as well as the adult, have this right? Indeed, if the child is not permitted alternatives, he may be incapable of choice when he reaches adulthood. Parents and clergy provide a counter-balance to teachers, and under the self-contained plan the child gets a new teacher every year. Even so, the teacher in the self-contained classroom is perhaps the most potent adult figure in the child's environment. Because every teacher attempts to mold his pupils in his own image, it is not safe to assume that one teacher will offer children live moral, emotional, and intellectual options. Educators should seriously consider the proposition that public schools have an obligation to provide children with more than one major teacher a year.

Integration of learning experiences is a third theme of those who favor the self-contained classroom. The theme is related to the concept of the "whole child." We are often lectured on the consequences of "fragmentation" by "narrow specialists." These phrases are the battle cry of many educators.

One may judge a concept by its fruitfulness. In terms of this criterion, "integration of learning experiences" must be regarded with suspicion. Where are the measures of integration? Where is the research on integration? Where are the theories that anchor integration to mechanisms of learning? *Integration* has been a byword for thirty years, yet it remains an article of faith rather than a utilitarian principle.

Those who see value and meaning in the concepts "integration of learning experiences" and the "whole child" must accept the challenge of sharpening these concepts, interpreting them precisely in terms of children's and teachers' behavior, and proving the ideas empirically.

Let us assume for a moment that the integration of learning experiences is a valuable idea. The elementary school curriculum presents countless opportunities for integration. For example, teachers could have children study folk music when they are studying the history and culture of a country. The children could learn folk songs and in doing so perhaps develop a better feeling for the culture of that country.

It would take special talent to conceive and successfully teach a series of lessons integrating music, history, and culture. The chances are that lessons prepared by a teacher who was a musician, a musicologist, or a student of the history of the country in question would be far more interesting and far richer in ideas than lessons prepared by a generalist teacher, who typically has a superficial understanding of most fields.

The principle holds for the integration of mathematics and consumer economics, mathematics and physics, geography and meteorology. Whatever the areas of knowledge to be integrated, the teacher who has considerable competence in one or both disciplines will in all likelihood do a better job than the teacher who is master of neither.

Departmentalization may result in the loss of some opportunities for integration. Is this a cause for worry? Perhaps not. The elementary school curriculum presents countless opportunities for integration. Almost every area of human knowledge can be related to many topics in American history, for example.

The real problem is to select appropriate occasions for integration. The generalist teacher is ill-equipped to make such decisions. Left on his own, the typical generalist teacher may stress trivial juxtapositions at the expense of more profound relationships.

If integration is important, decisions on what is to be integrated and how integration is to be accomplished cannot be left to chance or to the predilections of relatively untrained teachers. The specialist teacher seems to be in the best position to guide his pupils in an examination of the extensions and applications of his field. He can help pupils understand his specialty in the light of broader issues, and he can lead pupils in a consideration of problems that span several disciplines.

Thus far in this discussion of integration it has been argued that the generalist teacher is ill-equipped to conceive relationships between fields of knowledge. Integration can also be considered from another point of view. The practical vehicle for the integration of learning experiences is the multipurpose lesson. There are reasons for believing that the multipurpose lesson can be an unsound, ineffective instrument, although prospective teachers are instructed that the more goals a lesson serves, the better. Actually, some important goals may never come into sharp focus if they are imbedded in a multipurpose lesson.

Suppose that a class observes a science demonstration and that afterward each child is asked to write a brief report describing what he saw and presenting a plausible hypothesis to account for the phenomena.

If penmanship, spelling, grammar, punctuation, and capitalization are stressed in these reports—and the philosophy of the multipurpose lesson suggests that they should be—observational acuity and cleverness in hypothesis formation may be slighted. Praise for neatness may reinforce an inadequate description of the phenomena. It is possible that there would be negative transfer of the training in language usage to the science aspects of the lesson.

Compartmentalization and fragmentation may not be so evil as educational folklore would lead us to believe. Painstaking analyses of the concept of integration and of the multipurpose lesson are badly needed. Analysis may show departmentalized instruction in a better light than instruction in self-contained classrooms.

The argument for teacher specialists presented here has assumed that the children would be taught by highly competent specialist teachers. Deploying teachers in a departmentalized plan does not make them specialists. While some advantages result from departmentalization alone, major improvement depends on teachers who have mastery of a specialty.

What is a reasonable minimum standard for the elementary school specialist teacher? In terms of formal training, the prospective specialist should probably have completed with distinction an undergraduate major in his area of specialization. Furthermore, he should be highly intelligent and demonstrate a facile grasp of his area.

No one needs to be reminded that many persons with an expert knowledge of an area are not good teachers. The elementary school specialist should have a thorough understanding of children, of learning processes, and of teaching techniques. The elementary school teacher should be a specialist with a flair for teaching.

East Brunswick has embarked on an intensive in-service program to strengthen staff competence. A teacher recruitment campaign in which improved selection procedures are being used is also in progress. We hope to recruit outstanding experienced teachers as well as unusually promising beginners. The in-service program, the recruitment campaign, and the improvement of teacher-selection procedures should move East Brunswick toward its goal: a teacher with a mastery of an area of knowledge in every classroom.

Teacher specialization seems to make better sense educationally than the conventional plan of elementary school organization. For many pupils, teacher specialization could mean greater achievement, more profound learning, greater interest in learning, and better social and emotional development. None of these benefits will automatically result from teacher specialization. There are, however, reasons for believing that teacher specialization is a necessary condition or, at least, a facilitating factor in reaching these objectives.

REFERENCES

1. Daniel Tanner. "How Much To Teach?" *American School Board Journal*, September, 1960, pp. 15–17.

2. George Ackerlund. "Some Teacher Views on the Self-contained Classroom," *Phi Delta Kappan*, XL (April, 1959), 283–85.

3. Richard C. Anderson. "The Case for Non-graded Homogeneous Grouping in the Elementary School," *Elementary School Journal*, LXII (January, 1962), 193–97.

4. Jerome S. Bruner. *The Process of Education*. Cambridge: Harvard University Press, 1960.

5. Fred C. Broadhead. "Pupil Adjustment in the Semi-departmental Elementary School," *Elementary School Journal*, LX (April, 1960), 385–90.

6. A. Hugh Livingston. "A Study of the Relationship of Elementary Organization and the Personal Adjustment of Pupils." Tulsa, Oklahoma: Public Schools, 1960. Mimeographed report available from the author.

7. Glen Heathers. "The Dual Progress Plan," *Educational Leadership*, XVIII (November, 1960), 89–91.

Effectiveness of Departmental and Self-Contained Seventh- and Eighth-Grade Classrooms

Monroe L. Spivak

The problem of the investigation reported in this article may be stated thus: When children reach the departmentalized ninth grade of the junior high school, are the academic achievement and the school adjustment of pupils who have gone through the departmentalized seventh and eighth grades in the junior high school superior to the academic achievement and the school adjustment of children entering the same school from elementary schools having self-contained seventh- and eighth-grade classrooms?

Children entering the ninth grade of a junior high school in Newark, New Jersey, from elementary schools with self-contained non-departmental classrooms in the seventh and eighth grades were matched with children who had been in the completely departmentalized seventh and eighth grades of the junior high school. The records of the two groups in the ninth grade were then compared. It was hypothesized that two years spent in the departmental setup of the junior high school should have given the departmental children in this study the advantage, at least with regard to academic achievement and school adjustment, in the ninth grade at the same school.

The junior high school at which this study was made is in an underprivileged area of the city. Findings of similar studies in different socioeconomic areas might well be different from those reported herein.

FACTORS USED IN MATCHING

Matching factors used in this study were: sex, home room (in the departmentalized junior high school the home-room classes traveled as units), course of study, ninth-grade subject teachers, intelligence quotient, chronological age, eighth-grade academic record (teachers' marks), eighth-grade personality ratings (by home-room teachers), and a "family-score" derived from a simple, twelve-question questionnaire.

The mean scores for the two groups of children on the last five factors are shown in Table 1. Although socioeconomic status was not used as a

Reprinted from *School Review* 64:391–396, December 1956, by permission of the publisher and the author. Monroe L. Spivak is at Paterson State College, Wayne, New Jersey.

TABLE 1

**Mean Scores and Values of *t* on Factors Used in
Matching Forty-one Pairs of Pupils**

Factor	Mean Scores		Difference	*t*
	Depart-mental Pupils	Non-departmental Pupils		
Intelligence quotient	91.60	92.30	—0.70	—1.74
Chronological age as of September, 1954 (in months)	175.40	174.50	.90	1.61
Eighth-grade marks in English, mathematics, and social studies	3.32	3.41	— .09	— .27
Personality rating by eighth-grade teachers on co-operation, industry, emotional stability	4.27	4.61	— .34	— .89
Family score from family-life questionnaire	11.00	11.60	— .60	—1.71
Socioeconomic status, after a modification of the Sims Score Card.	21.54	20.59	0.95	0.69

matching factor, after the groups had been set up it was shown that the two groups were comparable in this regard, and the mean scores for this factor are included in Table 1. The last column in the table shows the *t* value for each comparison. Values of *t* of 2.02 or more would indicate differences that are significant at the 5 per cent level or less. It will be noted that none of the differences between the two groups was significant.

FACTORS USED IN MAKING NINTH-GRADE COMPARISONS

Academic achievement.   Forty-one pairs remained after all the matching criteria had been considered. These pairs were then compared as they went through the ninth grade at the junior high school. Their academic achievement was recorded in terms of teachers' marks in three major subjects at the end of each six-week marking period.

School adjustment.   School adjustment in the ninth grade was defined in terms of personality ratings by home-room teachers and a count of the number of children in the home room who named each child in the study as one of their "three best friends in the home room." School adjustment was negatively defined in terms of the number of school problems each child checked and in terms of the number of times each child was referred to the office or grade counselor for correction or advice. It was assumed that those who reported many problems and those who were referred frequently were poorly adjusted to the school situation.

The hypothesis adopted indicated that the departmental children should do better than their non-departmental mates. This means that their academic achievement scores should be higher, as should their personality ratings and peer-acceptance scores. On the other hand, to do "better" than their mates, these departmental children should report *fewer* school problems and should be referred *less* frequently than their non-departmental matchees.

FINDINGS FOR THE FIRST TERM IN THE NINTH GRADE

It will be noted from Table 2 that the hypothesis could not be accepted in any respect. In every respect examined, the mean score for the non-departmental children indicated their superiority to the departmental children. They made better academic records, received higher personality ratings (although, regarding this factor alone, the difference is no greater

TABLE 2

Comparison Data on Forty-one Pairs of Pupils for First Term of Ninth Grade

	Mean			
Factor	Depart-mental Pupils	Non-depart-mental Pupils	Difference	t
Academic record (teachers' marks in three major subjects):				
First marking period	2.56	3.61	—1.05	—2.06*
Second marking period	2.73	3.71	— .98	—1.71
Third marking period	2.93	3.93	—1.00	—1.94
Personality ratings by home-room teachers in January	3.39	3.73	— .34	— .74
Peer acceptance (number of times each child was chosen as "one of three best friends in home room"):				
In October	2.24	2.71	— .47	—1.10
In January	2.90	3.95	—1.05	—2.35*
Number of school problems checked:				
In October	6.02	4.88	1.14	1.38
In January	5.20	3.63	1.57	2.07*
Number of referrals to grade counselor and vice-principal (through January).	1.20	0.59	0.61	......

* Differences marked with asterisks are significant at the 5 per cent level of confidence.

than it had been in the eighth grade), had more friends, reported fewer school problems, and were referred to the office less frequently than were their departmental matchees. This was so in spite of the fact that the non-departmental children had moved to a new school situation and were facing a departmental situation for the first time.

The data, then, indicate that the hypothesis that the departmental children would do "better" than their non-departmental matchees in the ninth grade could not be accepted. As a matter of fact, the findings indicate that the non-departmental group in this study was actually superior to the departmental group in certain important ways. Differences of statistically significant size favored the non-departmental children in this study with regard to the ninth-grade academic record for the first marking period, the number of friends in January, and the number of school problems checked in January. This first-term record, then, indicates some important advantages for the non-departmental group in this study of ninth-grade academic achievement and school adjustment. An examination of the findings for the second ninth-grade term will serve to show whether this superiority was consistent and lasting.

FINDINGS FOR SECOND TERM IN NINTH GRADE

At the end of the first term, fourteen pairs were lost to this study for various reasons. Two departmental members and three non-departmental members changed to easier courses of study. One departmental member left school during the second term ("personal health" was given as the reason), and four non-departmental members moved out of the district at the change of terms. One departmental and one non-departmental member were changed to new home-room situations, and both pairs had to be dropped from the study. In addition, a non-departmental member changed to a harder program of courses and one non-departmental member was not promoted. These changes resulted in a reduction from forty-one to twenty-seven in the total number of pairs fulfilling all the criteria used in matching.

It was believed that some of these losses could be attributed to failures (partial or complete) on the part of the children involved. Leaving school because of "personal health," changes to easier courses, and term failures could be so classified. An examination of the first-term records of pairs lost for these reasons was made. It was found that non-departmental children who were rated low academically tended to change to easier courses more frequently than did lower-rated departmental children. Non-departmental children with lower first-term personality ratings tended to change to easier courses or to fail of promotion more frequently than did departmental children. Some of the more popular non-departmental children were lost at this point because their less popular matchees either changed to an easier course or left school.

This examination, too, led to the finding that the "nonconformists" (children who had been frequently referred for advice and correction) among the non-departmental children seemed to show much less staying power in this study than did nonconforming departmental children. These losses resulted in slight changes in the findings for the second term with regard to academic success, personality ratings, peer-acceptance scores, and referrals to the office.

Table 3 presents second-term data for the twenty-seven remaining pairs with regard to academic achievement, teacher-prepared personality ratings, peer acceptance, number of problems checked in June, and number of referrals to the office for correction and advice during the second

TABLE 3

Comparison Data on Twenty-seven Pairs of Pupils for Second Term of Ninth Grade

Factor	Mean		Difference	t
	Departmental Pupils	Non-departmental Pupils		
Academic record (teachers' marks in three major subjects):				
Fourth marking period	2.85	4.00	—1.15	—2.08*
Fifth marking period	2.78	4.15	—1.37	—2.41*
Sixth marking period	3.04	4.26	—1.22	—2.72*
Personality ratings by home-room teachers in June	3.00	3.74	— .74	—1.56
Peer acceptance (number of times each child was chosen as "one of three best friends in home room") in June	2.89	3.52	— .63	—1.30
Number of school problems checked in June	4.82	3.15	1.67	1.63
Number of referrals to grade counselor and vice-principal, February through June	1.04	0.19	0.85	4.08*

* Differences marked with asterisks are significant at the 5 per cent level of confidence.

term. Analysis of these scores indicates that some selective process had been operating. Both groups made better academic records than the larger groups had made for the first term. The differences between the groups for the second term, however, were greater. The non-departmental group was superior to the departmental group for every marking period during the second term by statistically significant amounts.

Because of the elimination of a larger number of low-rated non-departmental children than low-rated departmental children, the difference in personality ratings favored the non-departmental group more decisively in this regard. With regard to peer acceptance, it has been noted that some of the more popular non-departmental children were lost at the change in term because their departmental matchees had defaulted. The difference, however, still favored the non-departmental children.

Both groups reported fewer school problems in June than had the larger groups in January, but the advantage in this regard, too, remained with the non-departmental children. The difference in number of referrals to the office was more marked for this second term than it had been during the first term. There were, in all, twenty-eight such referrals among the departmental children remaining, and only five among the non-departmental children remaining in the study. The reason for the greater difference in this regard for the second term has been indicated earlier: the departmental "nonconformists" apparently had greater staying power than did the "nonconformists" among the non-departmental children. The non-departmental "nonconformists" were lost to this study, as were their more conforming matchees.

A confirmatory study.   A study comparing the increments in arithmetic growth and reading growth during the seventh grade in a self-contained classroom of one of the feeding elementary schools with these increments in the departmental classrooms of the junior high school was made. It was found that the children in the self-contained classroom gained more in these fundamental areas than did their matchees in the junior high school. However, the difference in increment was statistically significant only with regard to growth in arithmetic ability. Although the difference in reading growth favored the non-departmental group, this difference was not statistically significant.

RELATIONS AMONG FACTORS

Correlation coefficients were computed for some of the factors reported. Each of the matching factors (eighth-grade academic records, eighth-grade personality ratings, intelligence quotient, chronological age, and family score) was correlated with some of the ninth-grade comparison factors. Then each comparison criterion was correlated with the other comparison criteria.

Some coefficients were found to be significant. The highest of these was the coefficient of correlation (.717) between the eighth-grade academic record and the ninth-grade academic record. A high coefficient (.713) was also found between eighth-grade personality ratings and ninth-grade personality ratings. Both eighth-grade academic record (—.517) and eighth-grade personality ratings (—.607) were negatively correlated with the number of referrals to the office in the ninth-grade. In addition, the eighth-grade academic record was related to the ninth-grade personality ratings (.597), and the eighth-grade personality ratings were related to the ninth-grade academic record (.544).

There were two relations that appeared only in the departmental group of children. A negative correlation (—.437) was found between the eighth-grade academic record and the number of school problems reported in the ninth grade. There was a slight but statistically significant relation between eighth-grade personality ratings and the number of friends in the ninth grade (.342).

Chronological age was related only to the number of referrals to the office in the ninth grade (.401), and this was true only in the non-departmental group. The older non-departmental children tended to be referred more frequently than their younger colleagues. The intelligence quotient was related positively to ninth-grade academic achievement (.425) but only in the departmental group. Intelligence quotient was negatively related to the number of referrals to the office (—.337), but only in the non-departmental group.

Of all the matching factors used in this study, the eighth-grade academic records and the eighth-grade personality ratings were the most valuable predictors of ninth-grade achievement and adjustment.

With regard to interrelations between the various comparison criteria, there was a close relation (.692) between academic records in the ninth grade and personality ratings in the ninth grade. These two factors were correlated negatively (—.577 and —.608, respectively) with the number of referrals to the office in the ninth grade. In addition, there was a tendency for the departmental children with good academic (—.382) and good personality (—.394) ratings in the ninth grade to report fewer school problems.

A FOLLOW-UP STUDY

There were thirty pairs of children, of the original forty-one, who went on to high school at the end of the ninth grade. These pairs were followed up at the end of the first half of the first term in senior high school.

It was found that the children who had been referred frequently in the junior high school had already been referred to the office in the senior high school (with only one exception), while their more conforming matchees had not. The departmental group did slightly better than the non-departmental group with regard to teacher marks for the first marking period in the high school, but the difference was not statistically significant. An analysis of the pairs lost (of the original forty-one) before high school showed that this result was due to the loss of certain less successful departmental children. It is possible that their superior staying power did not last beyond graduation from the junior high school.

SUMMARY AND CONCLUSIONS

In this study of a junior high school in an underprivileged area in Newark, New Jersey, children who had been in a departmental setup in the seventh and eighth grades did not do better, academically and with regard to school adjustment, when they reached the ninth grade than did their matchees who had been in self-contained classrooms in the seventh and eighth grades. There was evidence that the children from self-contained seventh- and eighth-grade classrooms did better by statistically significant amounts in some areas: they did better academically; they made more friends by the end of the first term; they reported fewer school problems by the end of the first term; and they were referred for advice and correction less frequently than their matchees.

These findings raise questions about the desirability of continuing to operate junior high schools with completely departmentalized seventh- and eighth-grade classrooms, particularly in underprivileged areas similar to the one in which this school is located. Doubt is thrown on the readiness of seventh-grade children for full departmentalization in terms of what happens to them in the ninth grade. It is recommended that this study be repeated in schools representing various socioeconomic areas.

Selected Bibliography

Departmentalization and Semi-Departmentalization

Anderson, Lorena A. and Benson, Eunice P. "Organization of an English Department." *English Journal* 48:145–147, March 1959.
Suggests a way to organize a high school English department.

Anderson, Richard. "Case for Non-Graded Homogeneous Grouping." *Elementary School Journal* 62:193–197, January 1962.
Gives an account of nongraded homogeneous grouping for some classes and teacher specialization and departmentalization in others in the upper elementary school at East Brunswick, N.J.

Anderson, Robert H. "Organizing Groups for Instruction." *Individualizing Instruction,* 61st Yearbook of the National Society for the Study of Education, Part I. Chicago: University of Chicago Press, 1962. pp. 239–264.
Gives historical background of ways of organizing classes. Includes discussion of departmentalization.

Anderson, Robert H. "Some Types of Cooperative Teaching in Current Use." *National Elementary Principal* 44:22–26, January 1965. Included in Chapter 8.
Briefly discusses departmentalization and self-contained arrangements.

Bahner, John. "Team Teaching in the Elementary School." *Education* 85:337–341, February 1965.
Points out strengths of the self-contained classroom and of departmentalization as claimed by their advocates. Says team teaching combines advantages of both plans.

Barnes, R. E. "Survey of Status and Trends in Departmentalization in City Elementary Schools." *Journal of Educational Research* 55:291–292, March 1962.
Found the majority of 806 city elementary schools had not increased departmentalization in grades 1–6 during 1959. A counter trend was noted in schools in smaller cities where increasing departmentalization was noted.

Bellagamba, L. P. *A Study of Changes in Five Selected Junior High Schools, 1957–1962.* Doctoral Dissertation, Columbia University, 1963. Also in *Dissertation Abstracts* 24:5110.
Found increased departmentalization and grouping at the expense of block classes during the five-year period of the study.

Bennett, H. K. "Making the Transition Requires Administrative Planning, Courage, and Patience." *Nation's Schools* 49:60–65, January 1952.
Describes transition from a departmentalized elementary plan to a self-contained classroom arrangement at Dearborn, Michigan.

Bishop, D. W. "Role of the Local Administrator in Reorganizing Elementary Schools to Test a Semi-Departmentalized Plan." *Journal of Educational Sociology* 34:344–348, October 1962.

Gives details of Dual Progress Plan at Ossining and Long Beach, New York. Teachers are full-time specialists in one of six curricular areas.
Also see *Arithmetic Teacher* 6:302–305, December 1959; *Educational Leadership* 18:89–91, November 1960; *Educational Forum* 25:271–276, March 1961; *Journal of Educational Sociology* 34:349–354, April 1961; and *Science Education* 50:39–43, February 1965.

Broadhead, Fred C. "Pupil Adjustment in the Semi-Departmental Elementary School." *Elementary School Journal* 60:385–390, April 1960. Also see reference by A. Hugh Livingston.
Reports results with fifth graders in Tulsa, Oklahoma in semi-departmental arrangement.

Carson, Roy H. and Thompson, Jack M. "Joplin Plan and Traditional Reading Groups." *Elementary School Journal* 65:38–43, October 1964.
Reports experiment in Joplin (departmental) arrangement for reading instruction.
Also see *Journal of Educational Research* 52:228–231, February 1959; 56:317–321, February 1963; *Elementary English* 30:305–307, May 1959; 33:102–104, February 1965; *Elementary School Journal* 55:100–103, October 1954; 64:280–286, February 1964; *Journal of Experimental Education* 31:273–278, March 1963; *Saturday Evening Post*, October 27, 1957; and article by Richard H. Hart in Chapter 11 of this book for further discussions of the Joplin plan of reading instruction.

Chalender, R. E. "Desirable Degrees of Subject Departmentalization." *Bulletin of NASSP* 47:18–19, October 1963.
Summarizes one junior high staff's thinking on subject of departmentalization. Recommends it be used in music, art, homemaking, industrial arts, and physical education. Says self-contained classroom is needed in other subjects.

Coffin, G. C. "Are Your Elementary Grades Properly Organized?" *School Management* 5:61–62, December 1961. Also see *Dissertation Abstracts* 24:4498.
Found there was no significant difference in academic achievement of 4–6th grade pupils in North Reading, Massachusetts when participating in either a self-contained or departmental program.

Cox, Donald H. "The Cochrane Modification of the Joplin Reading Plan." *Canadian Education and Research Digest* 3:28–34, March 1964.
Reports Joplin or departmental plan for reading instruction has achieved a degree of success after three years of usage.

Davis, O. L. and Tracy, Neal H. "Arithmetic Achievement and Instructional Grouping." *Arithmetic Teacher* 10:12–17, January 1963. Also see *Elementary School Journal* 9:86–89, February 1962; and *Dissertation Abstracts* 22:2247 for dissenting views.
Compared effects of two grouping plans on arithmetic of 393 North Carolina pupils in grades 4–6. Report is unfavorable to Joplin or departmental plan.

Douglass, M. P. "Reading and Nongrading in the Elementary School." *College Reading Conference Yearbook*, 1962. pp. 85–95.
Traces departmentalization back to Gary Plan of 1907 and up to Joplin Plan. Gives assumptions of departmentalization.

Gibb, E. Clenddine and Matals, Dorothy C. "Study on the Use of Special Teachers of Science and Mathematics in Grades Five and Six." *School Science and Mathematics* 62:565–585, November 1962.
Describes study of the merits of the use of special teachers and departmentalization in science and mathematics as compared with the use of one teacher in a self-contained classroom.

Grant, Lester J. "The Principal Studies His Leadership Role." *Bulletin of NASSP* 43:61–64, February 1959.
Discusses roles of department head in curriculum improvement and in-service education.

Gumaer, H. T. "New Jersey Junior High Schools Question Emphasis on Departmentalization." *Bulletin of NASSP* 42:118–120, November 1958.
Reports status of departmentalization in New Jersey junior high schools. Gives recommendation to help junior high schools move away from this organization.

Gruman, Allen J. "Improving Instruction Through the Use of Department Heads." *California Journal of Secondary Education* 30:167–169, March 1955.
Gives desirable qualities of effective secondary school department heads.

Hagaman, Harlan. "Shall We Departmentalize?" *Nation's Schools* 28:30, July 1941.
Gives individual opinions of advantages and disadvantages of departmentalization.

Hanson, Earl H. "Let's Use Common Sense to End the Reading War." *NEA Journal* 51:41–43, February 1962.
Discusses grouping within the classroom, the Joplin Plan, and the individualized plan of reading instruction.

Hart, H. C. "Classroom Structures Rapidly Changing: Departmentalized Instruction." *Education* 86:200, December 1965.
Says departmentalization has been extended to the primary and intermediate years because of the introduction of modern mathematics and language. Many of the regular teachers are not equipped to handle this instruction.

Heathers, Glen. "Field Research on Elementary School Organization and Instruction." *Journal of Educational Sociology* 34:338–343, April 1961.
Discusses projects established to test experiments such as departmentalization, ability grouping, team teaching, cross grade grouping, etc.

Hillson, Maurice. *Change and Innovation in Elementary School Organization.* New York: Holt, Rinehart, and Winston, 1965.
Collection of readings on departmental and semi-departmental plans, team teaching, dual progress, nongrading, etc.

Jensen, Elizabeth S. "The Department Chairman: Why He Often Quits with Pleasure." *Clearing House* 23:284–286, January 1949.
Gives problems of high school English Department head and ways of resolving them.

Livingston, A. Hugh. "Does Departmental Organization Affect Children's Adjustment?" *Elementary School Journal* 61:217–220, January 1961.
Describes research study comparing the effects of semi-departmentalization and of the self-contained classroom on the personal and social develop-

ment of students in grades 1–5. Evidence reveals semi-departmental organization does not hinder the pupils' personal and social development.

Lounsbury, John H. and Douglass, Harl R. "A Decade of Change in Junior High Practices." *Clearing House* 40:456–458, April 1966.
Shows departmentalization was characteristic of junior high schools in study.

Madon, Constance. "The Middle School: Its Philosophy and Purpose." *Clearing House* 40:329–330, February 1966.
Describes philosophy of middle school (for grades 5–8). Partial departmentalization cited as one of the advantages.

National Education Association. "Departmentalization in Elementary Schools: Summary." *NEA Research Bulletin* 44:27–28, February 1965.
Located 97 large school systems that used departmentalization in 1964–65 in one or more elementary schools. Plan was most frequently used in grades 4–6 but was reported to some degree in every grade. Describes practices in Tulsa, Oklahoma; West Hartford, Connecticut; and Cleveland, Ohio.

National Education Association. Research Division, and American Association of School Administrators. *Departmentalization in Elementary Schools.* Washington, D.C.: the Association, Circular 7, October 1965. Details of study in *NEA Research Bulletin* 44:27–28, February 1965.

O'Reilly, R. C. "Generalist, Departmentalist, and Specialist." *Education* 83:295–297, January 1963. Also see *School Management* 4:38–40, December 1960.
Assesses role of generalist, departmentalist, and specialist in the elementary school. Concludes generalist has highest potential for success.

"Research on Departmentalization." *National Elementary Principal* 40:89, September 1965.
Reports results of three-year study of departmentalized and self-contained classrooms in grades 4–6 in Montgomery County, Maryland, Public Schools. Found departmentalization brought no gains in academic achievement. Pupils liked it and teachers felt they had an opportunity to exercise their skills in area of specialization. There was no significant difference in students' expressed perceptions of themselves as learners or in their feelings of satisfaction with their school situation between the two arrangements.

Rinker, Floyd. "The Department Head." *Bulletin of NASSP* 34:48–53, December 1950.
Enumerates duties of high school department head.

Robinson, G. "Principals' Opinions About School Organization." *National Elementary Principal* 41:39–42, November 1961.
NEA surveyed 721 elementary principals to learn what practices they favored. Responses indicated they favored an elementary school with 400–500 pupils in self-contained classrooms.

Shane, Harold G. and Polychrones, James Z. "Elementary Education—Organization and Administration." *Encyclopedia of Educational Research,* New York. Macmillan Company, 1960. pp. 421–430.
Summarizes developments in structure and function of elementary schools. Discusses self-contained classrooms and departmentalization.

Spivak, M. L. "The Junior High: Departmentalized or Self-Contained?" *Phi Delta Kappan* 38:134–135, January 1957.
Reports research evidence favorable to self-contained 7th and 9th grade arrangement.

Stephenson, C. E. "Departmental Organization for Better Instruction." *Bulletin of NASSP* 45:9–14, December 1961.
Discusses the role of the administrator, the department head, and the teacher in high school departmental organization. Attempts to show what departmental organization ought to be.

Stoddard, George D. "Dual Progress Plan after Two Years," in *Frontiers of Elementary Education.* (Edited by Vincent J. Glennon). Syracuse, New York: Syracuse University Press, 1961. pp. 1–12.
Describes Dual Progress Plan which uses teachers who are specialists in curricular areas.

"Toward Improved School Organization: Further Look at Horizontal Structure." *National Elementary Principal* 41:93–115, December 1961.
Gives rationale, organization, administrative responsibilities and professional reactions to departmentalization, self-contained classroom, etc.

Waskin, Leon S. "Organizing for Curriculum Study." *Bulletin of NASSP* 43:41–45, February 1959.
Summarizes ways of organizing high school staff for curriculum study.

Also check bibliography of Chapter 6 and Chapter 11 for further readings on this subject.

Horizontal Organization — Team Teaching

Chapter 8

Team Teaching: Theory

Team Teaching: Theoretical Conceptions

William P. Colbert

One thing is for certain: team teaching has captured the imagination and interest of a great many people, professional educators and lay citizens alike. Some members of the professional group, including teachers and administrators, representing every level of the educational system, have played a major role in bringing this idea to its present stage of development. The essential purpose of this chapter is to bring together some of the best recent thinking of this group in the hope that it may help teachers, administrators, students and others get a clearer picture of team teaching.

Those who are interested in an organizational analysis of team teaching will not want to miss the selection by Judson Shaplin. Nor will those who are interested in a recent appraisal of team teaching and the contribution it has made to education want to miss the article by Philip Carlin.

Perhaps one of the basic reasons for the increasing interest in team teaching in the elementary school is, as Stuart Dean points out, a result of the growing interest in subject matter. Elementary school teachers, working in teams, can specialize in various curricular areas and thereby gain greater control of the knowledge and techniques in these fields. While no one would quarrel with the idea of teachers becoming more knowledgeable in various curricular areas, we may hope that this idea carries with it the additional idea that teachers become more able diagnosticians—identifying individual pupil's learning needs in various areas—as a result of group or team efforts. Although Mr. Dean does give passing attention

Written especially for this book. Dr. William P. Colbert is an Assistant Professor of Education, University of North Carolina, Greensboro.

to this idea, much more needs to be said. Perhaps one position on each teaching team could be staffed with a person who was highly skilled in diagnosing pupils' learning difficulties generally. Perhaps, too, his main role could be that of helping other team members apply general principles of diagnosis to their work with individuals in specific curriculum areas.

Those who have accepted the challenge of team teaching are not without problems and concerns. This, most of the authors agree, is to be expected. After all, the entire current conception is, as Robert Anderson points out ". . . still in a formative if not primitive stage." Chief among the concerns of Arthur King are the human considerations and the kinds of relationships all the individuals—teachers, students, administrators and parents—involved develop with each other. Carl Olson is concerned with the kind of language we use when we discuss team teaching and suggests that loose use of the term does the whole concept an injustice. Shall there be a hierarchical arrangement of staff on the teaching team? This has been identified by some writers as the most controversial of all the questions pertaining to team teaching. Therefore, the reader will find a number of views put forth not only in this section, but in the one that follows which is concerned with practical programs. Readers who have concerns and misconceptions about the broader concept of team teaching are sure to find some answers to their questions and problems in this section. Readers who have a good grasp of the team teaching idea are sure to identify some new questions and problems as a result of this reading.

Cooperative Teaching: Definitions and Organizational Analysis

Judson T. Shaplin

My assignment in this article is to define and to describe the components of cooperative teaching, including team teaching. I will also attempt to make an organizational analysis of team teaching and to make comparisons with other types of school organization, both past and present. Finally, I will comment upon the future potential of team organization.

COOPERATIVE TEACHING

In this generation in American education, there appears to be a widespread increase in the amount of cooperative or collaborative activity among teachers, particularly of activity directly connected with classroom teaching. In the preceding generation, there had been a professional focus upon influencing teacher behavior through group activities: study committees, curriculum committees and workshops, in-service programs, etc. This approach persists, but with the added phenomenon of increased interaction between teachers at the classroom level. Though this collaboration and cooperation takes many diverse forms, there appear to be certain persistent themes, all of which reflect a deep discontent with the standard organization of the school on the basis of the self-contained teacher and the self-contained classroom.

One persistent theme is the desire of teachers to spend more time teaching those subjects or in those areas in which they are more interested, more highly specialized, or more talented. This leads to an *exchange of functions* between teachers; for example, one teacher may teach all of the arithmetic in two classes, the other might handle social studies.

A second theme is the desire of teachers to achieve greater flexibility in the grouping of pupils, at the same time maintaining economy of teaching time. This leads to the *exchange of pupils* between teachers; for example, the combining of the gifted students of two classes into a group

Reprinted from *The National Elementary Principal* 44:14–20, January 1965, by permission of the publisher and the author. Copyright, 1964, Department of Elementary School Principals, National Education Association. All rights reserved. Dr. Judson T. Shaplin is Professor of Education and Director, Graduate Institute of Education, Washington University, St. Louis, Missouri.

taught by one teacher, while the other teacher handles the rest of the children, or similar arrangements for handling reading groups.

A third theme is that of *efficiency of instruction* by *combining classes* for certain purposes. If two teachers are planning the same activity with pupils—and there is no apparent disadvantage in doing this in a larger group—why not combine the classes, releasing one of the teachers for other work? There may be a further advantage if one of the teachers has a greater talent for doing this particular task.

A fourth theme is a consequence of the first three. If teachers exchange teaching functions or pupils or combine classes, then there is a need for *joint planning and evaluation*. Two or more teachers are now teaching the same children, not entirely separate groups, and the teachers must plan the program together, develop a schedule, and share their evaluations of pupil progress within the areas of collaboration. As we examine this kind of cooperation or collaboration between teachers, we find every degree of organization from informal permissive cooperation, often ephemeral in time, to carefully defined formal organizations, the latter often labeled *team teaching*. Robert H. Anderson has recommended that the generic term *cooperative teaching* be applied to all these forms of cooperation and collaboration among teachers, including team teaching.[1]

TEAM TEACHING OR TEAM ORGANIZATION

Elsewhere, I have given the following definition of team teaching: *"Team teaching is a type of instructional organization, involving teaching personnel and the students assigned to them, in which two or more teachers are given responsibility, working together, for all or a significant part of the instruction of the same group of students."*[2] This definition was based on the common characteristics displayed by projects which called themselves team teaching and was intended as an inclusive, general statement. The wording of the definition was intended to carry rather specific meanings: that the team is an organization with formal, legitimate status; that certain responsibilities are delegated to the team, particularly the responsibility for the scheduling, grouping, and instruction of a shared group of students; that a team implies a close working arrangement between two or more professional teachers in planning, instruction, and evaluation; and that the relationship with the students is a sustained one, affecting a sub-

[1] Anderson, Robert H. "An Overview of Team Teaching." *Team Teaching at the Elementary School Level—Report of an Invitational Workshop Sponsored by The Perkins and Will Partnership, Architects.* May 1964. pp. 10–11.

[2] Shaplin, Judson T., and Olds, Henry F., Jr., editors. *Team Teaching.* New York: Harper and Row, 1964. p. 15.

stantial portion of the students' programs. The definition does not require specialization in teaching function, the hierarchical ordering of team personnel, the improvement of supervisory arrangements in teaching, the utilization of nonprofessional aides for teachers, or the expanded use of mechanical aids to teachers, though all these were noted as directions which many teams have taken.

A number of definitions of team teaching have now appeared in print, offering some disagreement with the definition given here. Goodlad has suggested that team teaching is characterized by three things: 1) a hierarchy of personnel, 2) differential staff functions, and 3) flexible kinds of grouping.[3] Anderson agrees that a hierarchical structuring of personnel is essential and adds that a minimum of three or more teachers is required to develop a team with sufficient maneuverability to make a difference.[4] Bair and Woodward also question whether two teachers, working together, can be called a team.[5] They prefer a description of team teaching given by Dean and Witherspoon which stresses "the essential spirit of cooperative planning, constant collaboration, close unity, unrestrained communication, and sincere sharing," rather than details of structure and organization.[6] Singer, affirming a size of two or more teachers, includes in his definition that the team must take advantage of the special competencies of the team members.[7]

Perhaps the resolution of these difficulties of definition and description comes with Paul Woodring's comment that team teaching is a misnomer because "the teaching, at any given moment, is done by an individual rather than by a team."[8] He suggests that team teaching might more appropriately be called "team organization and planning." I would shorten this to *team organization*, since planning is implied in the term organization. This renaming of *team teaching* to *team organization* fits my earlier attempt to develop a theoretical rationale for team teaching based upon

[3] Goodlad, John I. *Planning and Organizing for Teaching*. National Education Association, Project on the Instructional Program of the Public Schools. Washington, D.C.: the Association, 1963. pp. 81–82.

[4] Anderson, Robert H., *op. cit.*, pp. 14, 76.

[5] Bair, Medill, and Woodward, Richard G. *Team Teaching in Action*. Boston: Houghton Mifflin Company, 1964. p. 24.

[6] Dean, Stuart E., and Witherspoon, Clinnette F. *Team Teaching in the Elementary School*. U.S. Department of Health, Education, and Welfare, Office of Education, Education Brief No. 38. Washington, D.C.: Government Printing Office, January 1962. p. 4.

[7] Singer, Ira J. "What Team Teaching Really Is." David W. Beggs, III, editor. *Team Teaching—Bold New Venture*. Indianapolis: Unified College Press, 1964. p. 16.

[8] Woodring, Paul. "Reform Movements from the Point of View of Psychological Theory." *Theories of Learning and Instruction*. Sixty-Third Yearbook, Part I, National Society for the Study of Education. Chicago: University of Chicago Press, 1964. p. 292.

sociological and administrative theory and the effort by Olds to develop a taxonomy for the description of team teaching.[9]

THE TEAM AS A SMALL GROUP

Team organization involves the formation of small working groups, organized on a formal basis, for the accomplishment of certain goals. From a sociological view, teams are *secondary* or *instrumental* groups, in contrast to *primary* groups. In secondary groups, the emphasis is upon task orientation, and evaluation is based upon principles of universalism and achievement; whereas *primary* groups emphasize localism, friendship, kinship, and other personal factors. Viewed as a social system, following Getzels and Thelen, the *nomothetic* dimension, or rational organization of human behavior toward certain desired goals, is stressed in a working team.[10] Careful attention is given to the definition of goals and to the creation of positions and roles appropriate for reaching the goals. For a variety of reasons, it is possible for such a working group to change into a primary group with stress upon the affective needs of the individuals in the group, particularly if the goals are unclear or the related roles poorly defined.

Since teams in teaching are usually composed of a relatively small number of individuals, from two to six in most situations, they have capability for the accomplishment of only a small number of limited goals. One of the major confusions in the team teaching movement has been the tendency to claim all-embracing objectives and goals, on a grandiose scale, phrased in the most general terms. The goals of a team must be consistent with its size and capability. Given the multiplicity of goals available in American education, goals which are often conflicting, we can see that team organizations will vary significantly in their choice among these goals, with important effects, then, upon the structural variables chosen for the organization of the team.

It should be recognized, also, that there are almost infinite possibilities for the structural organization of small working groups in teaching. Olds has made a start in the analysis of the structural variables which can be chosen in developing a team organization.[11] The team, as a small group, is located structurally within a larger context, including such factors as

---

[9] Shaplin and Olds, editors, *op. cit.*, Chapters 3, 4.

[10] Getzels, J. W., and Thelen, H. A. "The Classroom as a Unique Social System." *The Dynamics of Instructional Groups.* Fifty-Ninth Yearbook, Part II, National Society for the Study of Education. Chicago: University of Chicago Press, 1960. pp. 53–82.

[11] Shaplin and Olds, editors, *op. cit.*, Chapter 4, "A Taxonomy for Team Teaching."

gradedness, departmentalization, and available financial resources, all of which place limitations upon the team. The amount of autonomy given to the team for the control of pupil and teacher assignments of time, tasks, and space locations may vary enormously, and the same restriction applies to the delegation of responsibility for curriculum decisions. Teams may also be organized on differing principles of authority structure, some emphasizing a hierarchical system of authority based on either decision-making processes or on substantive specialization and others maintaining equalitarian or collegial principles. Other important variables are the type and extent of procedural and substantive coordination built into the team organization.

Viewed in this context of the team as a small, goal-oriented, working group, the basic question confronting school administrators is "What problems can be approached through team organization?" not "Shall I *do* team teaching?" The selection of reasonable objectives and goals comes first, in the context of unsolved problems. We should proceed then to an analysis of the goals which have been stated for team teaching, remembering always that we are faced with a choice among possible goals and that no one system of team organization can encompass *all* of the goals discussed here.

Following Talcott Parsons, I have divided my discussion into two sets of functions and goals, the *managerial* and the *technical*, with the full realization that managerial and technical functions and goals are closely interrelated.[12] In the discussion, I will also relate cooperative teaching and team organization to other organizational plans, past and present.

POSSIBLE MANAGERIAL FUNCTIONS AND GOALS

The managerial functions we will consider here are of two types: first, those decisions regarding what educational services will be offered, what groupings of pupils will be made, and what the disposition of the teaching force will be with respect to pupil groups; and second, the decisions concerning what resources in the form of personnel, classrooms, books, and materials will be provided.

In most team organizations, there is a transfer of managerial functions from the principal and central staff to the team, particularly with respect to the grouping and scheduling of pupils and the assignment of teachers in accordance with their special interests and talents. This often leads to

[12] Parsons, Talcott. "Some Ingredients of a General Theory of Formal Organization." Halpin, Andrew W., editor. *Administrative Theory in Education.* Chicago: Midwest Administration Center, University of Chicago, 1958. pp. 40–72. (For an extended discussion, see Shaplin & Olds, editors, *op. cit.*, pp. 71–98.)

new divisions of labor, increased specialization, and a different distribution of authority. Exercise of these managerial functions requires skill and time on the part of team members. There are enormous increases in the amount of time required for planning, communication, coordination, and evaluation which may lead to a reduction in teaching time and productivity in dysfunctional teams.

Claims for enormously increased flexibility of pupil grouping and teacher assignments in teams are often greatly exaggerated. The basic restraints are the amount of school time, the number of pupils, and the number of teachers. These factors usually remain unchanged in team organization as compared with ordinary school arrangements, with the consequence that choice of one grouping arrangement within a team limits all subsequent choices. Rigorous priorities among choices are required, with a full knowledge of the consequences as compared with those inherent in possible alternative strategies.

In most of the major reorganization plans of the past, administrative control of pupil and teacher assignments was retained externally from the teacher group, and the teachers did not function in a team organization as here defined. In the platoon school or Gary Plan, developed by Wirt in 1900, teacher and pupil assignments were made by the administration. The same condition applied in the Winnetka and Dalton Plans developed in the 1920's, though the teachers were much more involved in applying the standards which moved the pupils on to new groups. The present Dual Progress Plan follows a pattern similar to these early plans. One exception is the Cooperative Group Plan developed by James F. Hosic in the early 1930's, which had a short life in the New York City schools and adjacent areas.[13] If this plan were in existence today, it would be called team teaching and would be outstanding in terms of its goals and detailed plans. The delegation of these managerial functions to the teaching force is a relatively *new* and *distinctive* aspect of team organization, with this one abortive predecessor, and has not been a persistent theme in American education. I believe this new theme is emerging because despite persistent shortages, our corps of teachers is now trained to the highest educational level in our history, and we can foresee a more effective use of this talent.

Let us now turn to the second type of management function, called by Parsons the *procurement* function, in which our concern is with decisions affecting personnel and material resources available for teaching. Here team organization is used by the administration to create more attractive careers within teaching, to recruit subprofessional technical and clerical

[13] Hosic, J. F. *The Cooperative Group Plan: Working Principles for the Organization of Elementary Schools.* New York: Teachers College, Columbia University, 1929.

personnel to relieve teachers from these duties, and to create units of sufficient size to allow the economical allocation of technical aids to teaching. The implications for learning by the children are more remote.

The creation of specialist posts within teaching and of a hierarchy of authority and responsibility within the teaching ranks accompanied by suitable rewards *might* make it possible for elementary and secondary school teaching to attract a higher proportion of able college graduates, particularly men, into long-term careers. The incentives offered in team organization, especially in hierarchical teams, differ from other schemes such as merit salary schedules in that increased rewards come with higher rank and position based on greater responsibility and specialization. A number of Eastern projects—particularly those involving the entire elementary school as in Lexington, Massachusetts, and Greenwich, Connecticut—have the creation of rank and position careers as important objectives.

Teams have also been used as a vehicle for attaching secretarial, clerical, and technical personnel to the schools on an economical basis, opening up a large reservoir of skilled labor for schools and relieving teachers of subprofessional duties. It is difficult to attach such personnel to individual teachers in an efficient, workable way; a team of some size— four or five members—is required to absorb an aide into a working, supervised situation without loss of teaching time or extra expense. Team organization is thus furthering the utilization of teacher aides started in Bay City, Michigan, and Fairfield, Connecticut, in the 1950's. A similar argument can be developed in regard to the use of audiovisual equipment and other technical aids to teaching. The difficulties of reaching individual classrooms with suitable equipment and materials can be overcome if a team is of sufficient size to command its own resources and provide economical utilization.

POSSIBLE TECHNICAL FUNCTIONS AND GOALS

Technical functions include the development of the curriculum, the organization of instruction, the specific methods of teaching, and the assessment of the needs and progress of the students. In this area, the team teaching movement has created few new functions and goals. Rather, it has proposed new ways of organizing for the promotion of long persistent aims in American education: particularly the aims of greater specialization in teaching, the promotion of continuous individual progress in students, the coordination of various elements of the curriculum, and the flexible grouping of students in terms of interest, ability, and common purposes.

Team organizations thus have close kinship with past and present innovations which have had the same purpose of breaking the lockstep pattern of the graded, self-contained classroom school. Some teams share the interest in continuous individual pupil progress so notable in the Pueblo, the Winnetka, the Dalton plans, the more recent Dual Progress Plan, and the nongraded school movement. Others share the objective of specialized teaching prominent in the Gary Plan, the Dalton Plan, the "cultural electives" sector of the Dual Progress Plan, and the movement toward departmental organization. Still others share the values of the Core Curriculum movement, stressing the interrelationships between the subjects. Team organization then becomes a way of organizing for the accomplishment of some combination of these objectives.

Perhaps the greatest innovation in technical functions promoted by team organization is in the area of supervision—supervision from within the teaching force rather than from the administration or a special supervisory staff. Within some hierarchical teams—particularly those involving beginning teachers, interns, and apprentices—it is possible to vary teaching loads in accord with the teachers' energy, ability, and experience and to provide immediate, on-the-job evaluation and help.

It should be clear from this analysis that team organization per se is of necessity incompatible with only one form of school organization—the self-contained, single teacher classroom—and with any instructional plan dependent upon that organization. Team organization can be adapted to further the objectives of most other forms of organization and instructional plans. Teams can be formed within departments or can be used to achieve a degree of departmentalization in the absence of departments. A nongraded school can be organized on the basis of teams, as can the Dual Progress Plan.

THE FUTURE OF COOPERATIVE TEACHING
AND TEAM ORGANIZATION

What, then, is the future of cooperative teaching? Are we faced with a fad, fed on the educational discontents of the present generation, or can we anticipate a long-range reorganization of the schools?

With respect to cooperative teaching as described in the first pages of this article, I am confident that we are engaged in a long-range trend destined to increase. The discontent with the rigidities of the graded school is endemic. I predict a continued and gradual increase in cooperative teaching, including all the elements of pupil exchange, exchange of teacher functions, combined classes, and joint planning and evaluation, much of it on an informal permissive basis stimulated by the needs of the teachers themselves. Cooperative teaching is already characteristic of the organization of nursery schools and kindergartens; it is common in college instruction, particularly in the sciences, the languages, and in general education or common studies programs; and it is increasingly common at all levels of the elementary and secondary schools.

With respect to team organization in the more formal sense developed here, the road ahead is still rocky and tortuous. Sand and Thompson in a recent review make the following statement: "These reviewers believe that the subject of this book—team teaching—is a relatively trivial issue when compared with the more fundamental problems of decision-making, establishing priorities for the school, selecting content, providing a balanced program, educating all youth including those not college bound, and improving the quality of learning experiences."[14]

I obviously do not believe that the issue is *trivial* relative to any statement of aims or objectives. When we talk of team organization, we are talking about the basic conditions of work for teachers, about the human organization for the accomplishment of objectives and goals, about the basic ways in which teacher and pupils will work together. Analysis of these issues cannot be trivial in any context, yet there are distinguished educators who state this view.

Sand and Thompson go on to place a very narrow interpretation upon team teaching, quite at odds with the positions taken in the book they were reviewing: "Specifically, it [team teaching] relates to horizontal organization, a system for dividing a given student population into instructional groups and allocating these students to teachers." This statement, of course, discards the richness of potential for organization in teams, which I have tried to convey in this article, and indicates a growing tendency to narrow and sharpen the definition of team teaching in order to give it a definite structure and place. Both Anderson and Goodlad, previously cited, show this tendency in their insistence upon hierarchical structure and role differentiation. If this tendency is accepted, and the hierarchical, specialized team becomes *the* model for team teaching, I predict that the movement will fall of its own weight, as did Hosic's Cooperative Group Plan and other highly specific and detailed plans in the past.

The issue here is fundamental: Are we talking about basic principles of human organization into small working groups adapted in personnel and resources to the tasks they undertake, or are we talking about a standardized approach of a highly structured, prescribed team organization? I envision a flexible development of team organization, comparable to the complex and variable small-group organizations characteristic of business and industry. Viewed in this way, I think team organization is viable—

[14] Sand, Ole, and Thompson, Margery. *Review of Team Teaching.* Judson T. Shaplin and Henry F. Olds, Jr., editors. *Harvard Educational Review* 34:601–02; Fall 1964.

it offers no specific answer but is a way of marshaling resources to tackle problems.

The most difficult problem facing the team teaching movement today is that of the clarification of goals. In the early stages of the movement, the tendency has been to claim that team teaching is the answer to the most general and all-encompassing problems: the teacher shortage, the improvement of instruction, the flexible grouping of pupils, and the proper utilization of teacher talent. As the bandwagon developed, schools have gone into team teaching for the sake of being in. Much of team teaching is organization for the sake of organization, with a mystical belief and confidence that team organization per se will solve problems, however undefined the problems may be. I am not sure that the movement has settled down to a more rational and sane course. In the present trajectory, it will become increasingly difficult to justify team teaching in terms of the learning by students.

Another ominous sign is the relative detachment of the team teaching movement from the various curriculum reform groups.[15] Team teaching organization is only rarely being used as a vehicle for the introduction of national curriculum reform programs or, if it is, this is not being reported. Characteristically, curriculum reform in teams is proceeding on a local basis, with enormous waste of energy. I doubt that the present pace, requiring herculean efforts by teachers, can be sustained on a long-term basis. We need to build the connections between team organization and curriculum reforms for their mutual benefit.

The concept of a hierarchical structure among teachers, based on team organization, is perhaps the hardest for the teaching profession to accept. Notions of autonomy in the classroom and equality among teachers are widespread and strongly held, and hierarchical team organization is often viewed as threatening. This situation is complicated by the fact that the talents required in a hierarchical team, specialization in decision making and supervision as well as in substantive fields, are often not yet fully developed in the teachers who hold the leadership posts, though these talents may be developing under the stimulus of the team.

In balance, I think that the future of team organization may be brighter than my pessimistic statements would indicate. The curriculum reform movement at the elementary school level is just gathering strength, and we still have a chance to use team organization for the implementation of the reforms. In addition, the overwhelming problems of educating the culturally deprived almost demand team organization, and a broad new front for team organization, with more specific aims and objectives, is opening. Team organization will have further chances to prove its worth.

[15] Shaplin, Judson T. "Team Teaching and the Curriculum." *Proceedings of the Annual Conference of the Educational Records Bureau*, October 1964.

A Current Appraisal of Team Teaching

Philip M. Carlin

And madly team.

We have embarked upon a sea of togetherness in education that has not been without its turbulence and calms. However, the fact of team teaching is upon us and we had better at least understand it or move in the eddies and shallows often allotted to those whose love of the tried and true has left no greater vision.

It is 1957, a few short years ago, and a new term appears in the literature (1). A crazy notion or a new technique? An ephemeral thing, some oddment to be whistled at, or the forerunner of a lasting efficacious educational change? Now we are bombarded in popular magazines and on TV with "team teaching," the thing to do, the panacea, the mark of status, whose coverage in the Sunday Supplement rivals that of the latest space probe.

The *Education Index* first lists eight articles on team teaching in the 1957–59 two-year compilation. The following two-year edition (1959–61) lists 72 separate entries and the subsequent (1961–63) edition bulges with 135 references. Last year alone there were 52 articles listed, with many mentions under various other subject listings.

Team teaching, it has been pointed out, is still a matter of controversy (2) revolving mainly around the several meanings of the term and the constitutional inclination of many educators to view with a jaundiced eye any innovation that has flash fire characteristics.

It must be noted, however, that the bandwagon syndrome cannot wholly account for the current popularization of team teaching; that schools and school systems, as is their wont, accept the new slowly in this area as elsewhere; that reaction on a large scale has yet to be experienced if, indeed, it ever will be; and that there is something in the direction of a substantial national commitment in terms of budgeted expenditures for team teaching (3, p. 1).

Some of the apostles of team teaching, however, are almost evangelistic in their advocacy. Is it a bird? Is it a plane? No, it's Superprogram come to do battle with all the knotty problems in education. People ask us, "When are we going to have team teaching in our school?" And we say, "Well . . . What merit has it? What empirical studies have been done to evaluate it? How can we best organize it? Where do we start? What is it?"

WHAT IT IS

A teaching team exists whenever two or more professional teachers, working together, assume joint responsibility for all, or a substantial part, of the instruction of a common group of children (3, p. 15). This definition, as is apparent, can be logically applied to myriad numbers of organizational plans.

If, however, the basic requisite of *joint* responsibility is not met, no matter how intricate the scheduling, how flexible the grouping, how collegial the supervision, there is no team teaching (in itself a misnomer since rarely, if ever, do teachers actually teach as a team). A London *Times* writer comments superficially on team teaching with the claim that Scotland has had it all along at the university level, mistaking lecture-quiz sessions, in which there is little or no joint planning, for team teaching (4).

The teaming process involves not only children, but primarily teachers. It is teacher oriented. Beyond this there may be as many types of team teaching as there are schools and school systems that employ it.

Its antecedents are many. As organizational plans, the Platoon System, the Winnetka Plan, the Dalton Plan, the Pueblo Plan—all were attempts at breaking the lockstep organization of the past. For primarily economic reasons the Lancastrian monitorial system of the early 1800's also attempted to team using pupils as teachers (3, pp. 24–26). Athletic programs have long had their coaching teams with a head coach and specialist assistants. Thus, the idea is not new, but the name and its popularity are.

RESEARCH SAYS

Contrary to the thinking of many educators not all is barren as far as research is concerned. Not all has been developed through popular media. Not all has been the result of promiscuous promulgation of a faddish idea neither new nor untried.

Experimentally team teaching has gone under the glass in a number of studies, most of which have adopted testing criteria based on pupil achievements and most of which have found no statistically significant differences in this area. More is being done, and it is too early to say definitely that there can be no improvement in pupil achievements.

Not enough has been done, however, in the study of certain aspects of teaching and learning that require less well established instruments than standardized achievement tests. Such areas as teacher job satisfaction, teacher education, in-service effectiveness, and pupil attitudes seem to be considerably enhanced. Much of what is casually observable as fact may prove to be erroneously so in the light of scientific investigation. Suffice it to say that we must consider and welcome much more research into these areas of team teaching.

If team teaching, properly understood, is to cost 10 to 15 per cent more for the operation of its schools (5) taxpayers may reasonably expect an additional 10 to 15 per cent increase in the product. (A few writers have extolled team teaching on its supposed virtue of actually saving money, mainly through large group instruction and reduced personnel costs. It is difficult to see how such programs can conceivably qualify as team teaching.)

The problem which is currently being researched to a greater extent lies not so much in pupil achievement test scores as it does in the vastly more complex "product" which might be measured. Much more needs to be done on a broad basis.

COOPERATIVE VS. HIERARCHICAL

One of the major areas of disagreement among proponents of team teaching is in the field of organization.

Many teams are organized informally with respect to each member's role, allowing the team to develop through working together. Leadership within the team, if any, often rotates from teacher to teacher. This represents one end of a continuum of organizational patterns that terminates at its other end in a highly structured hierarchical arrangement involving precise definition of roles and leadership, team leaders, senior teachers, regular teachers, teacher aides, student teachers, clerical assistants and the like (6).

Most team structures fall somewhere on either side of the midpoint of this continuum and all types have their adherents.

Concerning a cooperative team of equals it has been said that it is in fact leaderless, that it represents no more than a loose association of traditional teachers who may or may not exchange ideas and expertise. It is at best, according to detractors of the associative team, a half-hearted attempt at an organization which could be viable but is doomed to failure as an effective team structure.

Critics of the hierarchical structure complain that teachers react negatively to such categorization of their jobs; that it fosters a type of infighting and "Organization Man" sychophancy among teachers for the higher status, higher-paying jobs belonging to those higher up the hierarchical ladder; that it makes for unhealthy interpersonal relationships because of the premium placed on position in the team.

Ideally, of course, hierarchy in a team with its attendant gradations in status, prestige, and recompense must be counted as a chief factor in retaining good teachers as teachers without their having to leave the profession or become administrators to achieve these higher personal goals. Where good teachers can accept the challenge of team teaching and improve themselves as teachers without casting envious glances at those above them, hierarchy will succeed.

Also valid as a teaching team program is that whose leadership emerges from an associative type of team where it may be presently impossible to make pay or status differentials for degrees of leadership. It has been observed by the writer that in most such organizations leadership does develop within the team as one member chiefly influences decision making and is usually regarded as the leader.

ADVANTAGES FOR TEACHER EDUCATION

One of the more striking examples of team effectiveness is in the area of student teaching. All student teachers who have been assigned to teams within the school with which the writer is associated have found that this type of organization contributes immeasurably to their induction into the profession. Exposure to varying types of teacher personalities, teaching style, teaching techniques, and a multitude of teaching devices has given them an enduring introduction into teaching that many new teachers under traditional programs may take years to acquire.

Conant intimates that team teaching may very well be one of the answers to teacher education problems that result in the loss of so many competent young people from the profession (7).

TEACHING COMPETENCE

The area of teacher specialization at the elementary level has been accounted for in the past by departmentalization. Team teaching may offer the advantages of departmentalization without sacrificing the virtues of the self-contained classroom (8). Team teaching works no havoc on children's identity (9), nor does it submit a child solely to the constant inattention of a less-than-adequate teacher for a year or more.

Moreover, the mushrooming condition of knowledge today seems to make some teacher specialization imperative even at the primary level. There are eight-year-olds who can talk rings around some of us in some areas of science—space technology, for example. This used to be confined mostly to automobiles and batting averages. It is in self-defense that some teachers specialize. In team teaching, the job requires them to specialize.

The incompetent or poorly prepared teacher will find his position on a teaching team most unhappy, where his shortcomings become very apparent (10). His only recourse will be to improve (facilitated by easy and frequent observation of fellow team members' proficiency) or quit, to "shape up or ship out." In traditional programs a poor teacher may be suffered throughout an entire career through unspoken acceptance by the school of poor teaching as an educational fact of life.

PEER SUPERVISION

Then we are approached with the idea of improving instruction through the agency of the supervisor whose *raison d'etre* is, after all, only to fulfill the role of instruction improver. It so falls out that today we have principals to whom we consign this basic function but whose efforts in supervision are largely subsumed in administrative duties; whose many talents because of sheer constriction of time can be diverted only momentarily to the cursory visit and possibly the *ex post facto* alleviation of an uncomfortable, if not intolerable, teaching situation.

So why not tap that large reservoir of teacher know-how which has so long lain fallow in the supervisory field? Must it be necessary that the etymology of the word dictate its present function? Why not ask teachers to supervise each other? Must supervision come from above? Must the "improvement of instruction" be solely the duty of one whose ministerial function for so long may have taught him to effect change by fiat?

This is not to say that principals always are iron-handed in their leadership role. Quite the converse may more often be true, but the boss role too long built into the subculture of principaling has nourished in teachers a you-tell-me-how sort of regard for supervisory tradition of the principal who so frequently just does not have the time, the inclination, or, indeed in some cases, the competency to do it. This business of supervision is really a full time job for one person. So why not? Why not ask teachers to "supervise" teachers. It's called peer supervision.

What better way to improve the quality of what is being done in the classrooms; not in the clinical fashion of the over-worked medical analogy so much as frequent interclassroom and cross-team visitation, not to mention the day-in, day-out observations of team members who may assist, observe or minimally perform in large group instruction lessons?

We do not ask that the observed teacher appear before the green table staffed by fellow teachers and deliver humble *mea culpas,* nor do we schedule analysis sessions, wherein teachers expertly point out to a fellow teacher wherein he may improve what has transpired in the observed lesson.

Such programed peer supervision may ideally have value (11), but if experienced teachers unused to such a procedure have it imposed upon them, they may not have had the opportunity to develop the permeability necessary to be able to accept constructive and well-meant criticism. The potential harm inherent in seriously damaging a teacher's sense of self worth may easily negate whatever successes such a program may otherwise achieve. And you have a peeric victory, if you will. Team teachers must have a respect for the professional competence of each other.

We find instead the idea of peer supervision taking hold and wonderfully working by casual or scheduled gatherings, at lunch, at coffee, in passing meetings. We may hear, "Say, that was a terrific thing you just had, especially the way you introduced the lesson. But how about it if you were to ————." A suggestion. A critique for the improvement of instruction. Supervision.

TEAM TEACHING AND OTHER PRACTICES

Finally, let us say a word about team teaching as it affects some current practices. Perhaps the most important feature of team teaching lies in the fact that it qualifies not as a philosophy of education but as a vehicle for much that might be considered new and modern in educational change. It is not an end but a means.

Item: The non-graded school. Team teaching goes hand in glove with non-graded organization (12). Most proponents of the nongraded school cite team teaching as a highly desirable, if not necessary, concomitant. These two programs grew up and went to school together.

Item: Closed circuit television. The ideal in large group instruction functions best when it involves a teaching team.

Item: Merit pay. In a hierarchical organization team teaching provides pay differentials for teachers as teachers. It recognizes excellence in teaching and in leadership.

Item: Programed instruction. Most team programs provide larger blocks of time for independent study.

Item: Technological innovations. Team teachers can specialize in teaching devices and share their expertise with other team members and other teachers.

As Alexander Pope said,
> Be not the first by whom the new is tried,
> Nor yet the last to lay the old aside.

REFERENCES

1. Foster, Virgil E. "Teaching, by Teams," *International Journal of Religious Education*, Vol. 10 (March, 1957), pp. 18–19.

2. Hoppock, Anne. "Team Teaching: Form without Substance," *NEA Journal*, Vol. 50 (April, 1961), pp. 47–48.

3. Shaplin, Joseph T., and Olds, Henry F., Jr. (eds.), *Team Teaching* (New York: Harper and Row, 1964), p. 1.

4. "Team Teaching and All That: Scottish Experience," *The Times Educational Supplement* (London), Feb. 21, 1964, p. 446.

5. Morse, Arthur D. *Schools of Tomorrow—Today* (New York: Doubleday and Co., Inc., 1960).

6. Brownell, John A. *The Claremont Team Teaching Program* (Claremont, California: Claremont Graduate School, 1961).

7. Conant, James B. *The Education of American Teachers* (New York: McGraw-Hill Co., 1963), p. 147.

8. Dean, Stuart E., and Witherspoon, Clinette. "Team Teaching in the Elementary School," *Education Briefs*, No. 38 (Washington, D.C.: U.S. Department of Health, Education, and Welfare, Office of Education, Jan. 1962), p. 4.

9. Anderson, Robert H. "Team Teaching," *NEA Journal*, Vol. 50 (March, 1961), pp. 52–54.

10. Heller, Melvin P. "Qualities for Team Teachers," *Team Teaching: Bold New Venture*, Edward Beggs, (ed.). (Indianapolis, Ind.: Unified College Press, 1964), Chap. 10, p. 151.

11. Cogan, Morris L. "Clinical Supervision by Groups," *The College Supervisor: Conflict and Challenge*, Association for Student Teaching, 43rd Yearbook (Cedar Falls, Iowa: Association for Student Teaching, 1964), Chap. 11, pp. 114–130.

12. Goodlad, John I., and Anderson, Robert H. *The Non-Graded Elementary School* (New York: Harcourt, Brace and World, Inc., 1963), pp. 97–99.

Team Teaching: A Review

Stuart E. Dean

Of all the ideas to come out of the current reappraisal of the ends and means of the elementary school, one of the fastest to capture both professional and public attention is the idea of team teaching. In the ordinary meaning of language the term suggests merely a kind of cooperation among teachers; but in the meaning it is now being given, it is much more. It is a way of organizing a school, a way of utilizing staff, a way of using space and equipment. It is, in short, a considered and pointed response, from the organizational angle, to the nationwide cry for quality in education.

Because the term "team teaching" has come to mean so much, most of us are not clear on what it does mean; its meaning depends all too much on who is speaking—or listening. Until we can arrive at some degree of consensus on a definition, we can at least consider how the idea grew and why, what claims are being made for it, and how it is working in practice.

BEHIND IT, PROBLEMS AND QUESTIONS

Nearly every change in the schools, now as always, is in response to the demands of the times. Our times are full of change—social, cultural, technological, economic, and international—and it has driven us to scrutinize the fundamental values of a free and universal public education. We are also in one of those recurring cycles of disenchantment with the structural organization of the school which periodically send us into fresh debate on the virtues of the present pattern—a pattern which for us in the elementary school today is usually influenced by what we call "the self-contained classroom" (a term which can mislead but which means no more than a classroom in which a number of pupils at the same grade level are taught nearly every subject by the same teacher).

Much of the present querulousness over the self-contained classroom is the result of the growing interest in subject matter—the call for more science, more mathematics, more languages—and the growing worry about the talented student, who many fear will be a heavy loser if his teacher has to spread himself too thin over too many subjects and too much diversity

Reprinted from *School Life* 44:5–8, September 1961, by permission of the publisher and the author. Dr. Stuart E. Dean is the U. S. Office of Education Specialist for Elementary School Organization.

in pupil ability. As the stress on academic achievement has increased, the doubt has grown that one teacher can teach all subjects to all children with equal effectiveness and skill; and from that doubt there is only a step to the conviction that the subject-matter specialist has become necessary in the elementary school and that some way must be found to narrow the spread of capability in the group of pupils with which a teacher works.

The age-old questions about class size also have arisen: How large a group can a teacher handle effectively? Does not the optimum number vary with the circumstances? Are there not some subjects that can be taught just as effectively to many at a time as to few—and some that cannot?

And at the same time concern has grown over certain circumstances that make the teaching profession less than attractive to many talented and creative persons. Much attention has been spent on finding ways to relieve teachers of the endless clerical nonteaching chores laid upon them in most schools, and on devising an organizational pattern that will make it possible to promote to positions of leadership—and to remunerate financially—those teachers who show extraordinary skill and ability.

NO ONE DEFINITION

There are only a few definitions of team teaching available, and none of them say quite the same thing. Taken together, however, they suggest that for some of these questions and problems team teaching may have an answer. In effect they suggest that team teaching can take various forms, but that whatever its variations it is essentially a way of organizing the instructional program which is applicable at either the secondary or the elementary level. Teams may work "vertically" through the school, i.e., at all grade levels in a single subject or closely related subjects; or they may work "horizontally," i.e., at one grade level but in several subjects. For example, all teachers of the language arts may work as a team with all pupils from grade 7 through grade 12. Or all teachers in, say, grades 5 and 6 may work together, each one taking the chief responsibility for classes in his special field and probably doing most of the teaching in it but working always as a member of the team.

Even a small team has a leader, and many large teams have a hierarchy of levels that bestows different titles on its members—titles like "team leader," "master teacher," "senior teacher," "regular teacher," and "intern." Many teams also include nonprofessional people, such as aides and clerks to assist the teachers.

Team teaching as it is being defined today is certainly more than a group of teachers who have amiably agreed to work together. The heart of it seems to be an almost unprecedented kind of unity: members of the team plan together, collaborate constantly, communicate without restraint, and share sincerely and selflessly. Working together they can revise procedures and revamp programs to meet the educational needs of their pupils. In a sense the movement toward team teaching may be considered something of a revolt against the organizational restrictions of the past and a sharp reminder to all and sundry that the purpose of school administration is to serve the educational process, not to control it. One project director says: "We are questioning the status quo."

NEW, YET OLD

Is team teaching new? Yes—and no. The term itself is new; it first appeared in *Education Digest* in 1957. And there are inescapable signs of newness in current literature and in practices developing in some schools. History, however, reminds us of other forms of elementary school organization that began with the same goals as team teaching—the Platoon School, the Winnetka Plan, the Pueblo Plan, to mention a few. The Cooperative Group Plan, formulated in the 1930's by J. F. Hosic, who felt the same disquietude about elementary school structure that impels us to experiment today, is probably the most recent prototype; in this plan, small groups of teachers together organized the work for a group of children within a range of not more than three grades, and each group had its own chairman who also served in a supervisory capacity.

It is generally agreed, however, that the first recorded project in team teaching was begun in 1957 at the Franklin School in Lexington, Mass. This is one of the projects sponsored by Harvard University's School and University Program for Research and Development—SUPRAD—a program aimed at bridging the gap between university research and school practice.

The Franklin School project has been followed by many others in scattered parts of the country. Estimates of the number and substance of these experiments vary, but it seems fairly reasonable to say that they are to be found now in at least 100 communities, in both elementary and secondary schools.

Some of these projects have been much written about, in both professional and popular publications—for example, the projects in Norwalk, Conn.; Flint, Mich.; Baltimore, Md.; Jefferson County, Colo.; Evanston Township, Ill.; Ft. Wayne, Ind.; Newton, Mass.; Montgomery County, Md.; and Palo Alto, Calif. Some are linked with universities, such as Harvard, Chicago, Stanford, and Wisconsin. A great many of these have been encouraged and assisted by the Commission on the Experimental Study of the Utilization of the Staff in the Secondary Schools, appointed by the National Association of Secondary-School Principals and supported by the Fund for the Advancement of Education.

HOW ONE SCHOOL DOES IT

The very flexibility that characterizes team teaching makes it hard for any one to draw with firm lines a picture of how, precisely, a team works; it makes it in fact impossible, for no two teams are likely to work in the same way. That they do not is reenforcement for the point of view that team teaching is more of an organizational idea than a set of procedures and practices. It is moreover an idea which a group of teachers must understand and accept—to which they must in fact commit themselves—before they can work as a team; an idea which they must also adapt to their own personalities and abilities and to the personalities and needs of their pupils.

Claremont, Calif., has published a booklet which describes how its team-teaching project operates. But anyone who examines this project as an example should first remind himself that the Claremont way is not necessarily typical. From project to project teams differ both in the number of their constituents and in the way these constituents complement each other. In general, however, the following summary of the Claremont plan may be considered a reasonable review of how a team in an elementary school is organized and how it works.

Pupils.   For each team there are about 150 to 200 pupils, drawn from a particular age or grade group. For more flexible grouping of pupils and easier movements from one level to another, the school may be divided into 3 parts: early elementary, middle, and upper. But whatever arrangement the school makes for flexible grouping, the pupils assigned to each teaching team form a distinct group within the school organization.

Faculty.   Each team has 5 to 7 classroom teachers with both general and special abilities. The school tries to select teachers who have already specialized, or plan to specialize, in certain subjects in the elementary school curriculum. Some team members also specialize in certain skills, such as giving tests, interpreting results of group testing, and giving remedial instruction. Teams meet regularly to exchange ideas, share information, clarify their purposes, and organize their programs. They decide on the size of each instructional group and how the specialist will handle it.

Team leader.   The team leader, who is either elected or appointed, assumes responsibility for the way in which the team works and gives it leadership in improving instruction and guidance. He receives an additional stipend; and from time to time an auxiliary teacher relieves him of teaching, to give him time for his added responsibilities.

Auxiliary teacher.   The auxiliary teacher is a substitute teacher assigned specifically to the team. He not only substitutes for teachers when they are absent but also teaches approximately 20 full days a year to give teachers time for planning. His service makes the schedule more flexible; and, since he is a member of the team and attends all meetings, he is able to preserve the continuity of instruction in a teacher's absence.

Teacher aide.   The teacher aide does some of the clerical and routine work connected with teaching, such as correcting tests and marking papers, arranging for field trips, supervising study periods, and giving makeup examinations. Sometimes he tutors individual pupils or works with small groups, and does research for teachers on curriculum problems.

Citizens.   The team draws on citizens with special skill and knowledge. Scientists, mathematicians, story-tellers, children's librarians, artists, musicians, travellers, and others help the team enrich the curriculum; for example, they instruct small groups and lead discussions, either during school hours or at regular sessions after hours.

Intern teachers.   Intern teachers are an integral part of some teams. At the same time that they are being introduced to actual teaching, they are giving support to seasoned teachers.

BUILDINGS TO MATCH

The Claremont plan of team teaching—in fact any plan of true team teaching—obviously needs special arrangements in both space and equipment. Several observers already have commented on the limitations and restrictions the traditional type of school facility imposes on a full-scale program. "Conventionally constructed school buildings," a SUPRAD report says, "with their rows of equally sized self-contained cells divided by immovable partitions do not meet the needs of most effective team operation."

What kind of school will it have to be? One thing, for certain—a school with flexibility built into nearly every cubic inch. A number of actual and proposed plans for elementary schools and junior high schools can be found in *Schools for Team Teaching*, published by the Educational Facilities Laboratory; but the Laboratory does not say that they are final solutions to the problems posed by the team teaching. It calls them experiments, planned for an experiment, but goes on to say that "both the educational idea and the schools planned for it represent new and adventurous thinking, attempts to meet this country's mounting educational challenge." Among the schools it describes are the Estabrook Elementary School in Lexington, Mass., and the Dundee Elementary School in Greenwich, Conn.

Whether schools that fit team teaching cost more to build than the usual kind of school has not yet been determined, but informed estimates say they do. Robert H. Anderson of Harvard University, who directs the Franklin School project, says, "It is hard to predict whether the radically different buildings needed for team teaching will be more expensive. . . . My guess is that they will cost about 10 per cent more than 'standard' obsolete buildings, although an ingenious acoustical invention could conceivably reverse the cost picture." Arthur D. Morse, in his *Schools of Tomorrow—Today*, says that team teaching will raise the cost of operating a school, but not because of the building: "Although the new building will feature versatility, it will cost approximately the same as the traditional school. But team teaching with its upgraded salary scales is likely to add 10 or 15 per cent to the cost . . ."

TOO SOON FOR EVALUATION

The team-teaching idea has been in practice for so little time in so few communities that conclusive evidence of its effectiveness has not had time to accumulate. After all, the oldest project, in Franklin School, is only 4 years old.

And it is out of Franklin that most of the evaluation has come. Dr. Anderson's subjective summary indicates that team teaching is not "disadvantageous" to children, that its results warrant further experimentation and refinement of proceedings. As far as its effects on pupils go—in growth of personality, in adjustment and achievement—he thinks them "no less satisfactory" than the effects in more traditional setting. He has found no evidence that children suffer emotionally or academically or in any way feel "lost" in the process. The reactions of the teachers have been favorable. Parents of the children, according to Mr. Morse's report on Franklin School, seem more willing to express satisfaction than "the cautious officials of SUPRAD." Almost all say that their children enjoy their team-taught schooling and benefit from it.

The next logical step, obviously, is to put team teaching to the test. Plans for investigative studies and research projects are already being discussed in a number of quarters, and some proposals have been submitted to the Office of Education for inclusion in its cooperative research program. In due time, no doubt, more objective bases for judging the worth of team teaching will be at hand; but present evaluation is almost entirely in the realm of personal opinion and speculation.

Opinions and speculations, however, despite their short-comings as a body of evidence, are highly worth reviewing: many of them come from men and women renowned for their sound judgment; many have been formed against a background of long professional experience. That some of them are diametrically opposed should not disturb anyone: this is healthy evidence of the questioning and weighing that must go on until such time as research puts an end to uncertainties.

CLAIMS AND QUESTIONS

Opinions about team teaching are not sharply divided into two camps. Some of the proponents are as ready as the critics to point out practical problems and raise provocative questions; and many of the critics concede that team teaching promises much, at least in theory.

Among the advantages being claimed for team teaching are these:

It is good organization.   As a plan of organizing for instruction, it preserves the virtue and avoids the weakness of both the self-contained classroom and its opposite number, departmentalized instruction; it makes it possible to have every subject taught by a specialist, yet it preserves the interrelatedness of subjects and learning. It makes the most strategic use of each teacher's knowledge and skill, accommodates different levels of teacher responsibility and competence.

The pupil profits.   The pupil, having the academic advantage of being taught each subject by a teacher strong in it, is more likely to find scholarship attractive, to be challenged to work to capacity. His interests, abilities, and needs are more likely to be discovered when he is taught by two or more teachers working closely together than when he is taught by one teacher working more or less alone; and the flexible grouping and regrouping that characterizes many team-teaching programs provides more realistically for pupil differences than straight "ability" grouping. The quality of instruction that a pupil receives during any one term or school year does not depend on the competence of a single teacher.

The staff profits.   The teacher gets more professional and personal stimulation when he works on a team than when he works in isolation. There is better communication among staff members, more motivation for continuous curriculum improvement, more cooperative planning. Because the team places a premium on unusual ability and skill and on exceptional qualities of leadership, it encourages teachers to grow professionally.

The school profits.   There is more opportunity for flexible schedules and efficient use of space, materials, and equipment; in other words, the administration is encouraged to respond to changing needs rather than to be restrictive. Well-qualified teachers are more likely to be attracted to the school. Because the team has room for different levels of teaching ability, it makes it easier for the school to peg teachers' salaries to professional skill and leadership; easier, too, to provide in-service training for inexperienced teachers.

Among the many questions being raised in connection with team teaching are these:

What are we talking about?   Does not the present loose application of labels and terms lead to a possibility that the basic concepts of team teaching will be misused and abused? If, before we have precise definition and full understanding of team teaching, we leap aboard the bandwagon, do we not run the risk of missing entirely its idealistic purposes?

Are the assumptions sound?   On what basis have we judged inadequate the present methods of school organization and instruction? Can we safely assume that all teachers are qualified by temperament and training to work effectively as members of a team? Is the theory valid that some things can be taught more efficiently to large groups? Are we certain that children learn more from a subject-matter specialist than from a generalist?

How do we surmount the practical difficulties?   How can we get enough teachers specially trained in subject matter and team relationships? Enough skilled and gifted team leaders? How will we meet the increased salary and operating costs? How serious are the limitations of our present school buildings for housing this sort of program?

Could team teaching become form without substance?   Does not history suggest that our schools have a tendency to become so preoccupied with innovations that they make them the ends rather than the means they were conceived to be? Should not team teaching be evaluated on the basis of its contributions to classroom practice and not judged on the basis of administrative efficiency, popular expediency, or the glamor given by publicity? Is there not an ever-present danger that we will overemphasize organization and, in so doing, distort our sense of the educational values of the elementary school?

Some Types of Cooperative Teaching
in Current Use

Robert H. Anderson

Under the general heading of "cooperative teaching" may be found dozens of different patterns of school and staff organization. Some of these derive from, or are associated with, attempts to achieve greater flexibility in pupil grouping. Others are associated with efforts to eliminate the administrative and instructional characteristics of rigid, lock-step graded school structure. Still others involve the use of nonprofessional or paraprofessional assistants in the schools, and a few are the result of experimentation with mechanical devices, programed materials, and other technological resources. Most, however, have stemmed from a growing interdependence among teachers in the face of the increasing complexity of teaching responsibilities and the need for greater specialization in the professional ranks.

Woodring notes that team teaching might be more appropriately "called 'team organization and planning' because the teaching, at any given moment, usually is done by an individual rather than by a team."[1] Certainly this is often the case: a group of teachers may be joined together in a partnership concerned with instructional planning, coordination of schedules and resources, and general evaluation, but each teacher retains his essential sovereignty and performs teaching functions in privacy. If each teacher also deals primarily with "his own class" of pupils throughout the school week, and has a minimum of contact with the pupils of his teaching colleagues, then the label of "team teaching" would indeed be somewhat erroneous. Sometimes, however, the aforementioned teachers do in fact have a shared teaching responsibility for a good many children, so that many teaching decisions and outcomes are constantly examined by the total staff. It would seem that in such situations a more definite merg-

Reprinted from *National Elementary Principal* 44:22–26, January 1965, by permission of the publisher and the author. Copyright, 1965, Department of Elementary School Principals, National Education Association. All rights reserved. Dr. Robert H. Anderson is Professor of Education, Graduate School of Education, Harvard University, Cambridge, Massachusetts.

[1] Woodring, Paul. "Reform Movements from the Point of View of Psychological Theory." *Theories of Learning and Instruction.* Sixty-Third Yearbook, Part I, National Society for the Study of Education. Chicago: University of Chicago Press, 1964. Chapter 12, p. 292.

ing of sovereignties and an increase of side-by-side teaching activities may be expected to develop.

THE THEORETICAL IDEAL

One model of cooperative teaching, then, requires an extensive co-involvement of a number of teachers (let us say between three and six) in the entire range of instructive-related functions: planning, actual work with the same children, and evaluation. In this model, which some regard as the ultimate or ideal, all team members (including the children when appropriate) share jointly in the formulation of broad, overall instructional objectives and in the weekly or daily determination of the more immediate teaching goals. The model requires all team members to be at least minimally conversant with each other's specific daily plans and to be given at least periodic (e.g., weekly) opportunity to contribute to and criticize the plans of colleagues. Each team member, at least several times weekly, should carry on teaching functions in the actual presence of a colleague, whose own role at the moment might involve co-teaching, or assisting, or observing—it being the colleague's subsequent obligation to offer constructive advice or criticism in an evaluation session. This model, therefore, implies that arrangements can be made for extensive intra-team communication, and it obviously makes heavy demands upon the time, energies, and emotions of the teachers involved.

At this stage of development, this idealized model does not exist full-blown in any project known to the author. In all probability, hierarchically structured teams such as those in Lexington, Massachusetts, and Norwalk, Connecticut, come the closest to fulfilling the ideal model, yet even these have not yet solved all of the various problems that are involved.

Hierarchical structure, in which leadership is formally assigned and in which the leader enjoys a salary supplement or equivalent recognition, has not yet become very widespread. However, it now seems that there is a trend toward the formal assignment of leadership to the best qualified person in the team. The relatively superior teacher, who also has a significant professional specialty and the talent and appetite for carrying leadership responsibility, can expect in a growing number of communities to be assigned as "team leader" with a salary supplement up to $1,000 or more. In the minds of some proponents, this feature of team teaching organization promises to attract and retain a greater number of outstanding persons in the teaching profession.

Formal hierarchical organization in some instances calls for more than one level of responsibility and competence above the regular role of teacher. The title of "senior teacher" or "specialist teacher" may be used, for example, to denote a professional with above average qualifications and an assigned leadership role under the team leader. This arrangement tends to be found chiefly where there are fairly large teams (e.g., five to eight members) or where an effort is being made to provide leadership experience for future team leaders.

LESS FORMAL PATTERNS

Perhaps the most typical teaching teams pattern in current use is the semi-hierarchical structured team. Here, the members of the team are officially joined together in a close working relationship, the administration having designated various roles for the members (e.g., each member providing leadership in a given curriculum area) but all members having an essentially equal status. The person designated as "leader" is seen primarily as a parliamentary chairman or coordinator, without any unusual authority and without salary supplement or other tangible recognition of responsibilities carried. The leadership may actually rotate from member to member over a period of time, or the school principal may in effect be the team leader. An example of the latter is an outstanding project underway in the Hamilton School, a small elementary school in Newton, Massachusetts. Sometimes, the semi-hierarchical team is a good pattern to use in a school where there is apparent resistance to full-fledged hierarchy and/or where the administration is unsure as to which of the teachers have the talents and the temperament for leadership. In such situations, a gradual move can be made toward hierarchical structure as the staff becomes more accepting of the idea.

Many so-called team operations represent at best what might be called a voluntary federation of sovereign teachers. Membership in the team is not a formal obligation of the teacher, and his involvement in the professional planning and activities of his colleagues tends to be relatively minor. Nevertheless, this arrangement can be fruitful if the federated teachers take sufficient advantage of the flexibility and sharing that is possible. Leadership tends to be very informal, each teacher being in effect a freelance participant.

In both the semi-structured and the federated patterns, examples can be found that are "departmental" in flavor. Although such arrangements are far more common in secondary schools, some elementary schools have lately turned to the use of subject matter specialists as one way of providing more competent instruction across the curriculum. Some schools have, in effect, discarded the self-contained classroom organization, wherein each teacher as a generalist taught in all curriculum areas, and rearranged teaching assignments along departmental or subject matter lines. Since departmentalization has for some time been in general disfavor in elementary education, it is therefore a source of concern in some circles that such a trend is discernible.

DEPARTMENTALIZATION

It may be helpful to point out that conventional departmentalization, with which the so-called "self-contained" classroom has long been contrasted, is itself a form of self-contained organization. That is to say, the teachers in conventional departmentalization are almost literally autonomous in their various roles, each as independent of the other as are "self-contained" classroom teachers. The chief difference between the two conventional patterns, then, is explained less by the meaning of the phrase "self-contained" than by the distinction between generalist and specialist. Most authorities would probably concede that more competent instruction *area by area* is characteristic of the departmentalized pattern, but it is generally believed that this advantage is countervailed by the uncoordinated, fragmentary experiences the child receives at the hands of independent teachers, each unaware of his colleagues' work and each seeing only a certain aspect of the child's growth and performance.

With the emergence of team teaching, a fresh impetus has been given to the idea of specialist teaching. A significant difference, however, may be found in some of the current plans involving the use of subject matter specialists in the elementary school: the team-oriented concept of communication, coordination, and cooperation. "Cooperative departmentalization," then, is a term we may use in cases where separate specialists join together in a federation under conditions somewhat resembling team organization.

NONGRADING AND MULTI-AGE PATTERNS

By now the reader is aware of numerous variants of team organization and staff cooperation that may be found across the country at the present time. Some of these are primarily modifications of the old pattern of literal self-containment (generalist or specialist), while others are more valid examples of cooperative teaching ranging from loose federations all the way to formal, hierarchical team structure.

Two other trends in school organization may be identified, both having to do with the types of group memberships arranged in the school for children. The first of these is multi-age or inter-age grouping: the assignment of children to teams, classes, or instructional groups in which they associate with children of two or more age levels. One example is the multi-grade, multi-age grouping plan such as that developed about eight years ago in Torrance, California, where a primary class might include six-year-old, seven-year-old, and eight-year-old children, and an intermediate class might include nine-, ten-, and eleven-year-old youngsters. A second trend, closely related to the use of multi-age classes, is the abandonment of graded structure in favor of more flexible patterns of arranging and defining the vertical progress of pupils through the elementary school. It is not the purpose of this article to elaborate on multi-age and nongraded patterns, although this author is convinced of their merit and sees their acceptance and development as one of the important goals of American public schools in the years ahead.

One of the principal advantages of team teaching, and variants thereof, appears to be that it stimulates and fosters the further development of flexible grouping patterns and of the nongraded school itself. In many places where cooperative teaching has flourished, attitudes and practices associated with nongraded organization have tended also to flourish. Probably this is due to the more careful analysis that team teachers tend to make of their responsibilities and also to the increased flexibility they enjoy in responding to pupils' needs. We are tempted to argue, therefore, that experience with cooperative teaching is a useful strategic preparation for the adoption of a nongraded plan. Team teaching and nongradedness in combination, especially where multi-age groupings are also employed, appears to represent an ideal or ultimate form of elementary school organization.

TWELVE PATTERNS

In actual practice, at least twelve combinations of these organizational features and their opposites may be found at present in the United States.

In our chart, boxes 1, 2, 7, and 8 refer to self-contained classes in which there is either graded or nongraded vertical organization and in which the children are either of the same age or of different ages. In boxes 3, 4, 9, and 10, the same factors exist except that there is some form of multiple-adult cooperative staff organization in effect. In boxes 5, 6, 11, and 12, the same variables are now combined with full-fledged team teaching organization.

Our previous argument in effect supports box 6 (nongrading combined with team teaching and interage grouping) as representing the theoretical ideal. By implication, box 7 represents the theoretically least desirable combination. Probably boxes 5 and 8 are, in turn, the next best and next worst, respectively, although both strategic and value considerations make this a very difficult judgment. As an interesting exercise, the reader might ask himself which boxes represent in fact the next best and the next worst arrangements.

Possible Patterns of School/Class Organization

1	2	3	4	5	6
NG SC UA	NG SC MA	NG MSC UA	NG MSC MA	NG TT UA	NG TT MA
7	**8**	**9**	**10**	**11**	**12**
G SC UA	G SC MA	G MSC UA	G MSC MA	G TT UA	G TT MA

(Key)

G	Graded vertical organization (promotion/failure)
NG	Nongraded vertical organization (continuous progress)
UA	Unit age grouping (6-year-olds, 7-year-olds, etc.)
MA	Multi-age or inter-age groupings (6-7, 6-7-8, etc.)
SC	Self-contained horizontal organization (1 autonomous teacher)
MSC	Modified self-contained: cooperative departmentalization, semi-departmentalization, informal cooperation (several autonomous teachers)
TT	Team teaching horizontal organization

If one believes with this author that nongradedness is the most precious and desirable of the organization forms we may consider, then boxes 12, 11, 10, and 9 seem to be useful avenues in the direction of box 6. Experience to date does not offer much advice as to how best to proceed from box 7 to the Utopia of box 6, although it may be that one or another form of cooperative teaching is easier to understand and to implement than is the more ambiguous and complicated concept of nongrading. If this is the case, perhaps a concerted effort to develop team teaching will be a useful step toward the eventual achievement of a workable nongraded structure.

NONPROFESSIONAL AIDES

Some team teaching projects involve the extensive use of teacher aides and clerical aides. The Norwalk model reserves a fairly major role for the aide, and the Lexington model calls for two full-time aides supplementing a full complement of six or seven teachers. Many projects call for a more limited use of aides, e.g., a half-time aide serving six teachers. In the new Granada Elementary School in Belvedere-Tiburon, California, the staff positions for a team serving 100 pupils include one team leader, one senior teacher (five or more years of experience), one junior teacher (little or no teaching experience), one full-time intern, two student teachers, a half-time teacher aide, and several volunteer instructional aides (parents who help with health, library, and various aide functions).

Perhaps the most prevalent pattern, for financial reasons, is the one involving *no* aides, or at most a small allotment of a school secretary's time. In fact, team teaching is not dependent upon the availability of non-professional assistants; but it is rather disappointing that American schools have been so slow to recognize the crying need for supporting services, and those teams fortunate enough to have aides seem to be making more rapid progress in improving instruction.

PUPIL GROUPINGS

Team teaching is frequently associated with the use of varying sized instructional groupings, including large groups of 40, 75, 100 or more children on the one hand and smaller seminar groups (12–15 pupils) and working groups (5–8 pupils) on the other. Some critics have deplored large group instruction, especially for young children, and protested that teams seem not to arrange for seminar and working groups as often as would be desirable. This may well be a valid complaint, since most teams have been slow to develop small group instruction patterns. Regarding large groups, the critics have probably exaggerated both the extent to which large group instruction is actually carried on and the educational hazards of such instruction. Large group lessons, in part because they are usually prepared more carefully, are often superior in quality to lessons under conventional circumstances. It seems unlikely that teams will overindulge in this form of teaching, however, and in many existing team projects such lessons play only a minor role in the scheme of things. The great preponderance of team teaching is still done in class groupings of 20–30, although this may be due more to the habits of teachers and the influence of the architectural environment than to valid theories of educational grouping.[2]

Team teaching is not totally dependent upon flexibility in school design, although it is extremely helpful to have school spaces that lend themselves to various types of groupings. Existing school buildings usually have at least some flexibility, and sometimes they can be modified at reasonable cost. Especially urgent, it would seem, is alerting school boards and administrators to the need for flexibility in all *future* school construction.

Subgroupings within the total team may be based upon some pre-

[2] Anderson, Robert H. "The Organization and Administration of Team Teaching." *Team Teaching.* (Edited by Judson T. Shaplin and Henry F. Olds, Jr.) New York: Harper & Row, 1964. pp. 208–09.

sumed similarity among the youngsters, so that the students tend to reinforce each other in the learning process, or upon some presumed dissimilarities as in the case of deliberate heterogeneous grouping. Academic history and potential, social or personal factors, age, interests, learning styles and personalities, and many other factors may serve to explain the various subgroups that are formed. Increasingly, the varying talents and teaching styles of the adults in the team are also being taken into account.

MUCH YET TO LEARN

Cooperative teaching in the 1965 setting finds its origins in century-old trends, yet it has a special currency in this time of fundamental ferment and change. That so many patterns exist is a reflection of the American system of decentralized schools, each community having the freedom to shape its educational program (within broad limits) along its own lines.

At the same time, certain team teaching models in particular have tended to influence the general trend to date because they were among the first to be widely described in the literature, both professional and popular. Whether the influence of these early pilot programs will diminish as research and theory become more highly developed is a matter for speculation. Suffice here to say that cooperative teaching is still in a formative, even primitive, stage. Yet despite its newness, most observers are agreed that cooperative teaching represents an extremely promising and challenging field for further exploration.

OTHER REFERENCES

Bair, Medill, and Woodward, Richard G. *Team Teaching in Action.* Boston: Houghton Mifflin Co., 1964. 229 pp.

National Education Association, Project on the Instructional Program of the Public Schools. *Planning and Organizing for Teaching.* Washington, D.C.: the Association, 1963. 190 pp.

Herbert, John. *Team Teaching. A Working Bibliography.* (Mimeographed.) Horace Mann-Lincoln Institute of School Experimentation, Interim Reports. New York: Teachers College, Columbia University, August 1964. 39 pp.

Planning for Team Teaching:
The Human Considerations

Arthur R. King, Jr.

One of the liveliest of the several contemporary experimental designs in elementary and secondary education is that of "team teaching." The term "team teaching" is used quite loosely to indicate a wide number of designs for instructional organization, the common element being some type of planned sharing of responsibility by two or more teachers for the instruction of a group of students.[1]

The writer has maintained a close relationship with a number of team teaching experiments conducted during the past five years by schools cooperating with the Claremont Graduate School and supported by a grant from the Ford Foundation. It should be noted that all of these teams were composed of from two to seven teachers, the most typical being three or four. Gleaned from this field experience, prior to the full collection, analysis and interpretation of the data, are a number of suggestions which may be helpful to school men and women who are considering this type of innovation.

We are concerned here with a number of considerations affecting the *people* involved in the team teaching schools (teachers, pupils, administrators, counselors, and parents), not with the important considerations of curriculum design, staffing, and the several problems of educational logistics. Experience teaches us that a number of important results of a change in structure can be anticipated, while a number of others cannot. This fact augurs for flexibility of design, humility in proposing change, and willingness to modify initial assumptions and structure during the field trial.

Before discussing the several parts of the team teaching operations where human elements are critical, it seems important to talk generally about the nature of the school where the intended modifications will occur.

First, the secondary school is not a rationally derived, orderly, and

Reprinted from *The Journal of Secondary Education* 37:362–367, October 1962, by permission of the publisher and the author. Arthur R. King, Jr., is Professor of Education and Researcher, Education Research and Development Center, University of Hawaii, and Director, Hawaii Curriculum Center; and was formerly with Claremont Graduate School, Claremont, California.

[1] See Harris A. Taylor and John A. Brownell, "Theoretical Perspectives for Teaching Teams," *Phi Delta Kappan*, January 1962.

systematic social institution. The present form of the school was forged by long generations of experience, belief, assumption, experimentation, and is continually being bombarded by new knowledge, changing economic and social conditions, currents of thought, and systematic philosophy. In addition, it is being continually tempered by its close associations with general governments, families, cultural groups, and higher and lower institutions of formal education.

In spite of the school's ambiguities in purpose and program and its imperfections, school people—teachers and administrators—as well as students, parents, and state legislators, among others, have reasonably well defined roles within or in relationship to this complex institution. Each individual has some working assumptions, guidelines, sources of satisfaction in teaching, ways of working with pupils and colleagues which satisfy his professional and personal goals. School personnel are also tied to the existing organization for their salaries, their promotions, their professional futures, and their loyalties to present educational means.

In considering the human situation within which change is expected to occur, it is essential to recognize that many teachers and administrators are not innovators. Some are vigorous opponents of any change, others have a vision of the appropriate education which does not coincide with the modification of educational means being proposed (and time may prove them right). School personnel are most typically motivated by selflessness, insight, good will, and a vision of the highest professional behavior; they are also capable, during times of stress, of less commendable behavior—narrowness, fear, jealousy, willingness to be intimidated, and lack of reserve energy required for change and experimentation. In other words, all that we know about human beings and human groups applies to educational experimentation with teaching teams.

Team teaching breaks down, rather drastically in some of its models, the accustomed format for instruction. Flexible uses of time, space, and personnel are permitted. The teacher-pupil relationship is modified. The format for curriculum development is changed, responsibility for change being more strongly delegated to "energy centers" of teacher groups or teams. Unusual sizes of instructional groups, the large and the very small, are required. A hierarchy of teachers is usually included.

Each of these changes, as promising as it may be for the advance of secondary education, makes a number of assumptions about the fitness of this new format for persons involved in the educational process. Since team teaching is an attempt to change these traditional and understood ways of teaching, it is reasonable to expect an immediate or delayed reaction, both rational and emotional, to the proposal.

The following will be an attempt to discuss pertinent factors in this changing relationship.

THE IMPACT OF TEAMING ON TEACHER MEMBERS

One of the necessary assumptions behind team organization, as well as for all other educational means, is that the established relationships will be healthy ones for teachers. The organization should foster (1) in-service growth; (2) effective use of energy; (3) a good start for the beginning teacher; (4) curriculum development; and (5) teacher creativity. Preliminary data would suggest that teaming does tend to accomplish these ends. It has proved to be a successful format for the beginning teacher. The close working relationship with experienced persons has been almost universally an asset. The few exceptions occurred when the team leader was unable to fulfill his role effectively, or when there was antagonism within the team.

Experienced teachers have also proved to be effective team members. Most found the new relationship and instructional format stimulating and contributive to change. The only recognizable group of teachers who appeared to consistently disrupt teaching teams were those who can be classified as "weak teachers." Contrary to the expectation that the team relationship would support the less effective teacher, experience suggests that team members find the weaker teacher a barrier in the achievement of team goals. On the other hand, the "individualist" teachers, whom we had assumed might rebel against teaming, typically failed to do so and were often outstanding members.

The Claremont experiments found that teachers were willing to accept the differences in "status" associated with the creation of team leaders, senior teachers, or aides, as long as full participation was welcomed from all and the status leaders did not assume the right to set team standards and determine procedures.

The relationship between supplementary personnel, including clerical aides and part-time "auxiliary" teachers, was almost universally satisfactory, although great variations of the use of these personnel were observed.

Experience would suggest that the status of teachers on a faculty should be considered in forming teaching teams, with at least one member of established respect within the faculty being on each team.

The method of assignment to teams has created some concern among teachers. Teachers like to make the decision to partake in team teaching themselves; arbitrary assignment without consultation is resented, even by teachers who enjoy the team situation.

TEAM LEADERS AND TEACHING TEAMS

The presence of persons on a faculty with higher status and role definition than that of the typical secondary teacher, with the exception of
the traditional department head or coordinator, is an innovation in most
team teaching schools. Some attention to this new leadership structure
within the faculty should be given in planning. Is the teacher leader to
be appointed by administration or elected by team members? Experience
would indicate that quality leadership is usually chosen by either method.
A notable fact is that we do have in our schools teachers quite capable of
leading a group of their peers, persons with executive ability and the
capacity to weld a group of teachers together in common purpose.

It seems important to define the leadership role early in the planning.
Is leadership to be "formal" or "informal"? Does the leader have specified
responsibilities and authority? Is he to serve as the normal channel of communication between team teacher and administrator? Is he to share in
formal or informal appraisal of teacher members, to discipline, to require
reports, to screen for membership, to recommend for retention on the
team? These relationships should be clearly understood by all.

Although none of our cooperating schools has awarded a higher
salary for team leaders, this possibility has been continually discussed.
Opinionnaire data supplied by both team members and other teachers suggest that this innovation would gain considerable resistance from teachers.

STUDENTS AND TEACHING TEAMS

While perhaps less critical than the relationships between teachers
and the team teaching idea, the student's relationship to the team presents
a number of important aspects. A big question with students, and a bigger
one with parents, is, "Will participation with a teaching team remove me
(my child) from normal educational and social relationships with other
students in the school?"

The Claremont experience, even with teams covering half or more of
the students' day, has shown this not to be a significant source of permanent concern. However, there have been a few exceptions. Students and
their parents will need to be assured on this point and efforts made to
schedule students part of the day in classes with membership drawn from
the larger student population of the school.

Pupils seem almost universally pleased to be part of a newer, different,
and "better" way of learning. Team membership tends to satisfy the highly
aspirant secondary student who sees in the team a better form of education

and college preparation. Since the team at the high school level is composed most typically of students with like abilities, the anxiety over grading practices in honors or advanced sections of the subject is ever-present. Students must be assured that they will not be penalized for being in a special section.

For the minority of pupils who have an unfavorable view of the team, the problem universally centers in the relationship with a teacher. The multi-subject team is a unit, and reassignment is most difficult. This can be an advantage in that pupils tend to stay with their initial curricular choice and "slug it out" in spite of personal or academic difficulties.

While students in grades seven through ten in the secondary school almost always enjoy the acceleration and intensity of team organization, college preparatory pupils in junior and senior years display signs of a revolt against the firm organization of the team structure. These students appear to desire the adult role of making more of their own choices and of being dependent upon their own resources. The intensity of teacher and student effort in the team situation seems oppressive to many, though appreciated when completed and when the student has had time for retrospection about his school experience.

TEACHING TEAMS AND NON-TEAM TEACHERS

Schools planning to introduce team teaching organization should consider the entire faculty and staff as an important supporting and contributing element. Successful teams have been weakened or discontinued because of lack of acceptance by peers in the school.

It would seem essential to (1) gain wide participation by faculty, especially the opinion setters, in the initial plans for the change and (2) keep the teachers informed of developments—successes, problems, and failures. The entire faculty should adopt the experiment as a school project, with the assumption that any teacher may be a participant in a later year. In practice, most non-team teachers in an experimental school have been favorably disposed toward the team idea and have indicated interest in taking part in a later year.

THE SCHOOL ADMINISTRATION AND THE TEACHING TEAM

The Claremont experiments have demonstrated that the operating of teaching teams makes a significant change in the job of the principal and other school leaders. In the typical school organization each teacher is directly responsible to the principal, with less well defined relationships to counselors, curriculum workers, and to department heads. The teaching team creates a new type of human group within the school, the "teaching unit" (team) with its own membership, power structure, capacity to innovate. Its relationship with the principal tends to be as a unit, with the team leader or senior member acting as spokesman. Experience demonstrates that these instructional units present many more proposals for change of all types than do the equivalent number of teachers in a conventional organization. In a sense, the principal becomes a leader of teams, providing logistic support (books, materials, space, buses, money), encouragement, consultant help, and quality control. The problem of the changed relationship between the principal and team members (other than the leader) has already been mentioned. These lines of authority and communication need to be established and kept clear.

Multi-subject teams which work with students for a significant part of the day definitely take over much of the typical work of the guidance counselor—program advisement, personal and educational counseling, parent consultation, and diagnosis. The counselor can adopt a new role as consultant to the team, which seems highly desirable, or he can be concerned about his own position in the school.

The teaching team is promising means for in-service curriculum development but as yet we do not perceive how teams might best work with general and special subject consultants. Many examples of excellent curriculum development have been found in the majority of schools, but neither the apparent organizational patterns of the school nor the leadership personnel provided are transparently related to this success.

TEACHING TEAMS AND PARENTS

Experience with dozens of teams and hundreds of students in approximately 15 schools has demonstrated conclusively that parents are quite favorable toward team teaching. It would appear that in the early 1960's parents desire change and progress in their schools. The most common parent report has been that the child is progressing better in his subjects, is more enthusiastic about school, and is working harder. The parental concern about the possible segregation of the team child from the balance of the school has been noted earlier.

Some form of parent orientation/preparation seems warranted. Successful means of accomplishing this orientation have taken the form of memoranda, meetings prior to the team experience, and joint student/ parent assemblies in the evening, among others.

CONCLUSION

Although the team teaching experimental units in the Claremont Program have shown considerable education potential, it would appear to be far too early to freeze our designs. Each hypothetical structure carries within itself the characteristics which may lead to its own destruction. Experience in the field over a period of years will be necessary to decide whether or not team teaching is to be a firm part of the "new education."

The degree to which teachers, students, administrators, and parents find an understandable and profitable relationship to team teaching will have much to do with whatever success it may achieve.

We Call It "Team Teaching"—But Is It Really That?

Carl O. Olson, Jr.

Team teaching has been getting a good deal of publicity. It would seem that a great many schools already are involved in team teaching and the rest are bucking an irresistible tide.

Is the tide as strong as it appears? Did all the schools being talked about in connection with team teaching actually undergo the significant organizational changes required to convert to team teaching?

I recently completed a study of school organization that included an extensive examination of the literature on team teaching, visits to schools engaged in team teaching, and interviews with teachers participating in team teaching. I found that there is much less team teaching going on than current publicity indicates. In fact, in my opinion, there is very little *real* team teaching in the United States today.

The label "team teaching" is being improperly and indiscriminately applied to a wide variety of practices, few of which actually are team teaching. This mislabeling, if allowed to continue, could ultimately undermine the team teaching movement and deprive society of its potential benefits.

Most educators define team teaching something like this: A situation in which two or more teachers with complementary skills cooperatively plan and implement instruction for a group selected on the basis of particular needs. The commonly agreed on essentials are:

1. Cooperative planning and evaluation of content and instruction by the entire team for a group of pupils.

2. Flexible scheduling and grouping for special purposes.

3. Maximum use of individual teacher strengths, skills, and interests.

These essentials can be used as criteria for determining if what is going on in the schools is really team teaching.

IS EVERYONE IN THE ACT?

Every member of a teaching team should have a voice in determining what the content of *all* subjects will be. In this way, the experience, skill,

Reprinted from *Grade Teacher* 83:8, 12, October 1965, by permission of the publishers and the author. Copyright 1965 by Teachers Publishing Corp. Carl O. Olson, Jr., is Curriculum Coordinator, Fredonia Central School District, Fredonia, New York.

and insight of all the teachers go into determining the curriculum. This is one of the main advantages of team teaching.

Unfortunately, in actual practice, the entire responsibility for a particular subject often gravitates to one teacher. One teacher, for example, may become identified as the math teacher; he eventually assumes complete responsibility for math instruction and seldom involves other members of the team in basic decisions regarding the math program.

When carried to the extreme, this approach may lead to a kind of departmentalization. The more teachers on a team, the greater the chance of departmentalization. There is nothing inherently wrong with departmentalization, but it is *not* team teaching.

IS THE PROGRAM FLEXIBLE?

Truly flexible grouping is not often found. Groups frequently are set up on some across-the-board basis, such as general achievement or ability level, and pupils find themselves in just about the same group for all instruction. This is not fulfilling the promise of team teaching.

The typical team-teaching schedule of today provides only for large-group instruction. Seminar groups—12 to 15 pupils—are rare and so is the use of independent study.

Large-group activities usually are scheduled far in advance and take place at the same time week after week. When this happens, the schedule—not the needs of pupils—is determining the nature of the program. Long-range planning is impossible in a truly flexible program.

Team teaching calls for working with different kinds of groups—large groups and seminars—to meet different needs. A teacher who performs brilliantly in the large group may be a dud in the seminar. Yet most teams assume that every member is equally capable of performing all tasks—a supposition that results in failure to capitalize on individual strengths.

IS THERE COMMUNAL PLANNING?

Because of schedule conflicts and outside demands, many teams do not have sufficient opportunity for communal planning and evaluating. The planning of a general program involves time and effort. In order to assure the success of a teaching team, the teachers should be employed during the summer, at least when the team operation is first being organized. In addition, a period should be set aside each week during the school term for teachers to plan the day-to-day program and to evaluate instruction together.

Many activities that take place under the "team teaching" label may be desirable. But they are not team teaching. Two teachers sharing work loads may demonstrate fine "cooperative" teaching, but *not* team teaching. A teacher who occasionally addresses two or more classes at the same time may give some stimulating lectures, but he is *not* team teaching.

"So what?" you may ask. "If the practices are good, why does it matter that we call them team teaching?"

WHY THE TERM MUST BE PRECISE

Here are a number of reasons for precision in the use of the term "team teaching":

1. The public expects the results promised by team teaching if the school program is billed as team teaching.

2. If the term loses precise meaning, educators will lose the ability to communicate about it.

3. Failure to achieve the goals set for true team teaching may have adverse effects on staff morale.

4. Without precise labeling, it becomes difficult to evaluate team teaching on its merits alone.

Team teaching has not been successful everywhere it has been tried. When it has failed, it usually has been because the term was loosely applied to poor or undesirable practices. The history of American education furnishes many examples of excellent ideas that have been misinterpreted, abused, or even destroyed by zealous but unknowing advocates. Team teaching should be spared this fate—it should have a chance to rise or fall on its own merits.

Chapter 9

Team Teaching:
The Elementary School

Team Teaching: Practical Programs

William P. Colbert

What might a total school program be like if it were organized in the framework of team teaching? What type of equipment and facilities are needed? How do the pupils who are involved in this organizational plan feel about it? What are some current needs as viewed by people who have observed or worked with a teaching team? These questions and many other practical considerations are given attention in this section.

The reader will probably find the article by Robert Anderson, Ellis Hagstrom and Wade Robinson singularly comprehensive. This selection describes the team-teaching plan in the Franklin School at Lexington, Massachusetts, as it was five years ago. As pointed out by Stuart Dean in an article in the previous section, this project was begun in 1957 and was sponsored by Harvard University's School and University Program for Research and Development. At the Franklin School team teaching is *the* organizational pattern. Sometimes a form of team teaching coexists with another organizational pattern in a school setting. Such was obviously the case in the report by W. W. Farrar, of team teaching at the Saenz Elementary School in Alice, Texas, when three teachers working at different grade levels teamed to help pupils gain a better understanding of the sequence of events in reading.

Answers to questions regarding equipment and facilities will be found

Written especially for this book. Dr. William P. Colbert is an Assistant Professor of Education, University of North Carolina, Greensboro.

in almost every selection. Sometimes totally new buildings are proposed and erected to accommodate team teaching. Sometimes very little by way of facilities and equipment is added. Gladys Eakin and Eugene Spence tell us of a team-teaching endeavor in reading within the framework of their existing school facilities.

How do students feel about team teaching after they have worked with it for a period of time? This is another question that is often asked. Galen Jarvis and Roy Fleming answer this question in terms of the feelings and perceptions of a group of sixth-grade children. Teachers' feelings were also assessed on a less systematic basis in many of the programs.

If team teaching is to have a fair chance to prove itself worthy, a number of elements are identified as crucial. Arthur Haas, in evaluating the first year's experience at Elmcrest Elementary School, Liverpool, New York, with a nongraded team-teaching program calls our attention to the need for careful selection of staff, a continuous program of in-service education for teachers working on the team, and the importance of keeping members of the community informed about the program. Philip Lambert, William Goodwin and William Wiersma cite the need for research, using controlled techniques, to assess the value of team teaching and other innovations to pupils.

Even the most severe critics of team teaching will have to admit that the kind of study and thinking individuals and groups of teachers and administrators do, before adopting this organizational model, is at least healthy. This is perhaps more implicit than explicit in the case reports in this section. Therefore, the reader is urged to read the following selections with this in mind.

Team Teaching in an Elementary School

Robert H. Anderson, Ellis A. Hagstrom and Wade M. Robinson

In 1957–58 the personnel of Franklin School in Lexington, Massachusetts, were re-organized into four teams. Two of the teams were large, composed of five or six teachers. Two were small, composed of three teachers. The titles *team leader* and *senior teacher* were used to designate teachers who had responsibility for leadership in the teams. Classwork in each team was planned jointly by all team members, and through various redeployment procedures the children were taught in groups that ranged in size from six to more than a hundred. Members of the staff of Harvard University shared with the administrators and the teachers in Lexington in the formulation of program plans and in the analysis of the effectiveness of the program.

The Franklin School Project is a major activity within the School and University Program for Research and Development, hereafter identified by its initials *SUPRAD*. This program involves the school systems of Lexington, Concord, and Newton, Massachusetts, and Harvard University, and is supported in large measure by a ten-year grant from the Ford Foundation. The Administrative Board of *SUPRAD* approved the broad outlines of the teaching teams proposal in May, 1957, and the planning and recruitment proceeded with considerable speed. The planning provided for the following teams of teachers during 1957–58:

Alpha: three first-grade teachers (senior teacher in charge)
Beta: six second- and third-grade teachers (team leader in charge assisted by two senior teachers)
Gamma: three fourth-grade teachers (senior teacher in charge)
Delta: five fifth- and sixth-grade teachers (team leader in charge assisted by a senior teacher)

Each team was assigned a part-time clerical aide, and the two larger teams were each assigned a quarter-time teaching assistant. Preparations were completed for the principal and seven teachers to engage in pre-

Reprinted from *School Review* 68:71–84, Spring 1960, by permission of the publisher and the authors. Robert H. Anderson is Professor of Education, Graduate School of Education, Harvard University, Cambridge, Mass.; Ellis A. Hagstrom is Assistant Professor of Education, Emory University, Atlanta, Georgia; and Wade M. Robinson is Associate Professor of Education, Washington University, St. Louis, Missouri.

liminary planning in a six-week summer program under the supervision of Harvard instructors. The program was launched less than two months from the time it was first described on paper.

Among the reasons for establishment of the School and University Program for Research and Development was the belief that public school systems might more easily close the gap between educational ideals and educational realities if they joined with private universities in programs of research and demonstration. Relations analogous to those between medical schools and hospitals were seen as a way toward tough-minded research and unbiased evaluation of new ideas. Among these ideas was the contention that the existing organizational pattern of American schools and classrooms may be inadequate and unsuitable in view of the vast population increase and the severe shortage of professional workers as needs are now defined.

Related to this contention was the belief that too few first-rate people are attracted to teaching, possibly because of the low economic incentives, the low social position of the classroom teacher, and the general inadequacy of supervisory practices and lack of opportunities for professional growth in the typical school. The question was asked: "Would not more first-rate people be attracted to teaching if the economic and social factors were made more attractive and if there were more ready opportunity for professional growth?" Believing the affirmative to be true, *SUPRAD* set out in the Franklin School to test the feasibility and the effect of a team-teaching organization plan.

Implicit in all efforts to create more attractive conditions (economic, social, and professional) for teachers was the belief that these would lead to better instruction for children, through more effective performance of the teachers. It was hoped that the team organization would permit more flexible and appropriate grouping arrangements to meet individual interests. It was believed that children would be stimulated by association with larger numbers of children and with more than one teacher. It was expected that teachers would find more efficient and interesting ways of presenting lessons through having larger blocks of planning time and through doing more group planning. It was thought that the pooling of teachers' ideas and observations would lead not only to stronger teaching but to better pupil adjustment and more adequate pupil guidance. These and other benefits were seen as attainable if various administrative problems posed by radical changes in personnel organization could be solved.

The first year of the project was seen as an exploratory year, during which the participants hoped to discover whether a hierarchical pattern of team organization was feasible. The traditional pattern of self-contained classrooms, coupled with a system of uniform and undifferentiated salary and prestige for all teachers, was set aside, and a system was initiated wherein prestige roles and responsibilities were assigned to certain teachers and salaries were adjusted accordingly. The teachers in each team were asked to regard all the children in their team as the mutual responsibility of all. They were asked to plan the educational program jointly under the leadership of team leaders and senior teachers. They were invited to experiment with many kinds of class grouping and instructional techniques, using the physical facilities and the instructional resources of the building in whatever ways seemed appropriate and without regard to conventional definitions of the best class size.

One major objective of *SUPRAD*, and the Franklin School Project in particular, is to discover and to demonstrate new and more promising ways of utilizing teacher competencies. The roles of team leader and senior teacher were set up in an effort to accomplish two purposes: first, to provide rewarding and prestigeful roles to which persons of outstanding competence can aspire, roles which (unlike most supervisory and administrative roles in education) allow teachers to remain in direct association with pupils; and second, to create a collaborative relationship between teachers that offers promise of accelerating and enlarging the development of professional skills and insights. Implied in the latter purpose is that teachers in continuous and intimate association will more readily share their knowledge and express their needs, with the result that each has greater opportunity to learn from and contribute to the others. Hopefully, those persons with the greatest talents and a career dedication to teaching would work toward the prestige roles and through these roles constitute a significant source of strength for teachers of less experience, competence, or dedication.

Another objective of the project is to find more effective means of using the services of non-professional persons in the community and professionally trained persons who are unable or unwilling to devote full time to service in the schools. In the belief that classroom teachers now devote too much time to clerical and minor administrative duties, it was arranged that each team would have about half-time clerical assistance. Partly to compensate the team members for the extra demands that research activities would make on their time and partly in the hope of demonstrating that good use can be made of the part-time professional worker under team conditions, the two large teams were each assigned a quarter-time assistant teacher.

One hypothesis to be tested in the project is that certain kinds of instructional experiences can be at least as beneficial to children when they are taught in large groups (that is, groups that combine two or more standard size classes) as when they are taught under conventional conditions. It was believed that one prerequisite to testing this hypothesis was the development of instructional techniques appropriate to large groups. It was also believed that various content and skill areas probably lend themselves better than others to presentation in large groups. The teachers were therefore asked to develop such techniques and to identify such content, through various exploratory lessons.

The deployment of children in conventional elementary school situations is usually a static arrangement, each classroom group remaining intact and usually in the same homeroom throughout the day. In departmentalized situations, which are quite unusual below seventh grade, children may move from place to place but the class grouping is usually an unchanging one. Under team-teaching conditions, a number of more dynamic patterns of deployment and redeployment become possible. For example, children can be left in homeroom groups, homeroom groups (or portions thereof) can be combined in large groups, or children can be exchanged between homeroom groups. It is obvious that teachers, too, can exchange locations and instructional assignments. It remained to be tested, in the Franklin School Project, whether these kinds of redeployment under team-teaching conditions would be both manageable and desirable.

That education is an extremely conservative profession is well attested by the slow rate of its progress and by the meager financial and other support for the research on which intelligent change depends. Teachers themselves hold rather doggedly to traditional beliefs and practices, some of which may no longer stand the test of objective examination. The research worker has an almost inexhaustible mine to probe in education, yet his work is frequently blocked or slowed by the diehard forces of tradition and conservatism.

The Franklin School Project is especially notable because of the many beliefs and practices it has chosen to challenge. Among these are such widely held views as the following: individual professional autonomy, as exemplified in the self-contained classroom, is conducive to professional growth and satisfaction; the assignment of differential rewards, status, and responsibility to teachers will lead to poor morale and low productivity; an intimate and continuing one-to-one teacher-pupil relationship is more conducive to pupil security than the more varied relationships necessitated by a three- or five-to-one teacher-pupil relationship; there are advantages in having a single teacher manage all the subject-matter instruction for a given class; the ideal size of classroom groups for all kinds of instructional purposes is somewhere between twenty and thirty; and the lecture technique of teaching and its variants are essentially unsuitable as instructional approaches to young children.

Team organization may be understood best, perhaps, against the background of the more common organizational pattern of self-contained classrooms. In the typical self-contained organization, some twenty to thirty pupils are assigned to each teacher, and each group is placed in a classroom where most of the instruction takes place at the hands of that one teacher. She is expected to have the skills and the knowledge for competent instruction in virtually all the subject-matter areas. She must provide as best she can for the range of individual needs and abilities in her group. In addition, she must ordinarily perform a variety of clerical duties and supervisory tasks of a non-instructional nature. Under typical conditions, she has little contact with other teachers in the building, and she receives little supervision.

In contrast, under the team-teaching pattern, groups of teachers take joint responsibility for the instruction of a segment of the school population. Typically, from three to seven or eight certificated teachers take responsibility for the instruction of from seventy-five to 240 pupils of similar age and grade. The clerical and secretarial needs of these teachers are cared for by a clerical aide. The size of the team may be limited by the number of adults with whom a leader can relate effectively and by the number of pupils about whom the leader may reasonably be expected to have fairly specific information.

The teaching team is a formally organized hierarchy whose basic unit is the teacher. Generally, the teacher's experience or training or both have been of a general nature, or he does not wish to assume the responsibilities of a higher position. The position of teacher in the teaching team carries with it the status and prestige commonly accorded the position of teacher in the self-contained pattern today.

Above the position of teacher is that of senior teacher. Depending on the size of the team and the age of the pupils, the team may have one or more senior teachers. A small team may have none. The senior teacher is an experienced teacher who has special competence in a particular subject-matter area or in a particular skill or method. The senior teacher assumes responsibility for instructional leadership—both in his team and, if needed, across teams within the building—in the area of his special competence. Although the positions of senior teacher and team leader are regarded as terminal for many, a possible career line from this position might lead toward the position of team leader or toward such positions as system-wide staff specialist or supervisor or methods instructor at a teacher-training institution.

At the apex of the team hierarchy is the position of team leader. The team leader, a specialist in a content area that complements the areas of his senior teacher assistants, also exercises certain general administrative and coordinating functions. The team leader also has primary responsibility in his team for the identification of pupil needs and readiness and for the assignment of pupils to groups; for directing the continual re-examination and development of the curriculum; and for the training and supervision of junior and less experienced personnel on his team. To discharge his responsibilities effectively, the team leader is released from classroom teaching responsibilities for about a third of the school day. The career line from this position would probably lead to a principalship and perhaps to the superintendency.

In consideration of their additional training and increased responsibilities, senior teachers receive a salary increment beyond the teachers' schedule, and team leaders receive an increment beyond senior teachers'.

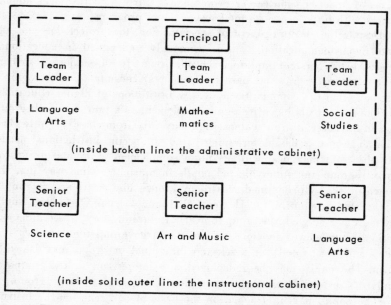

Figure 1. Pattern of Organization for Team Teaching

The role of the principal under the teaching teams organization will probably become one of enhanced prestige and responsibility, somewhat akin to the present role of director of instruction. Since team leaders and their subordinates are able to attend to many routine administrative and management details, the principal has more time and opportunity for leadership in curriculum development, instructional supervision, and guidance. Although the principal continues to have direct supervisory relations with regular classroom teachers, it is likely that he serves quite often as adviser to the team leaders as they carry out their leadership functions and curriculum-building.

A chief advantage of the school organization sketched here lies in the strength of leadership resources that reside in the school whose staff satisfies the specifications for each role. As shown in Figure 1, the principal and the team leaders, for example, may be viewed as an administrative cabinet. These staff members, augmented by the senior teachers, constitute an instructional cabinet. In effect they would together possess the range and depth of competencies of the curriculum-and-methods instructors in a teacher-training institution and hence would be well qualified to appraise and upgrade the school's program.

Thus, a school might expect to operate on the basis of a fairly stable nucleus of upper-echelon career people and a fairly high turn-over among teachers with little loss to its total instructional program.

Despite the encouragement of specialization, the project does not advocate departmentalization as it is commonly understood in educational circles. All teachers continue to teach all, or nearly all, subjects. Furthermore, teams may draw on part-time teachers, consultants, and resource personnel from the community or nearby institutions of higher education.

The team treats its entire pupil complement as a unit. But both group size and the bases of group composition may vary from class period to class period. The goal is flexible grouping based on specific instructional needs. Thus the team may deal with its pupil complement as a total group, or it may regroup and subdivide the pupils in much the same way that the teacher of the self-contained classroom groups and regroups the pupils who are her responsibility. The entire group of from 75 to 250 pupils may meet as a single large group to hear a lecture or story, to see a demonstration, or to view a movie. Or from the large group the extremes (retarded and accelerated) or a selected individual or group may be withdrawn. The pupils may be redeployed into interest or ability groups of standard size for follow-up activities after a lesson for a large group.

The pupils may be grouped on the basis of one criterion for instruction in arithmetic and on the basis of another criterion for instruction in the language arts or any other subject. Some pupils will have the same teacher for much of their instruction. Other pupils may meet a different teacher for nearly every subject. In the latter arrangement, a presumed advantage to the pupil is that he will come in contact with several adult models and personality types.

Special abilities and disabilities, such as talent in music, proficiency in French, or the need for remedial treatment in reading or speech, can also be accommodated in the schemes for grouping. Furthermore, the number of groups composed on any occasion may be fewer than the number of teachers on the team, thus releasing some teachers from instructional responsibility and enabling them to engage in other professional activities.

Some phases of learning—listening, reading, watching—can be engaged in as well by a large group of pupils as by a small group. Just what the maximum size of these groups may be under different conditions has not yet been determined. However, groups of 75 pupils have met routinely in the Franklin School, and groups of 140 or 215 are not uncommon.

Redeployment of pupils has taken place for instruction in reading and arithmetic at all levels—from first through sixth grade. Pupils in all grades have likewise had instruction in large groups. Data from 1958–59 indicate that about a third of all the instructional sessions involved groups of forty or more pupils and that there was considerable pupil movement and transfer in all grades.

Though groups of twenty to thirty are smaller than they need be for efficient and effective pupil participation in many kinds of learning activities, these same groups are too large for more nearly individual activities. Reciting, discussing, those activities that seem to require a high rate of interaction between pupils or between pupils and teacher can perhaps best take place in small groups ranging in size from ten or twelve down to a few. The flexibility of pupil grouping and redeployment facilitated by the team organization seems to offer a realistic solution to this problem.

Theoretically, then, the team provides the structure within which team leadership personnel engage in some supervisory and curriculum development activities. The team leaders take responsibility for assigning pupils to groups within the team. They coordinate the instructional efforts of junior personnel and also may have more time available for talking with parents. The team structure makes it possible for all teaching personnel to spend more time on planning and on the preparation of materials and less time on clerical and non-instructional supervisory duties. By taking advantage of the opportunities provided through the presence of specialists and clerical aides, and by taking advantage of the released time provided through the scheduling of large group lessons and through the creation of fewer groups than teachers, much more effective use of professional personnel can be realized under team organization than under the self-contained pattern. Furthermore, by holding team meetings before and after school, there is opportunity for discussion of instructional problems. In many respects, the team structure provides an extension of the training period with its emphasis on planning, observation, and evaluation.

The project does not claim that all the components of its program or model are unique. Many elements have been used in best educational practice for some time. The project is also aware of the existence of several versions and variants of teaching teams organization that are now being

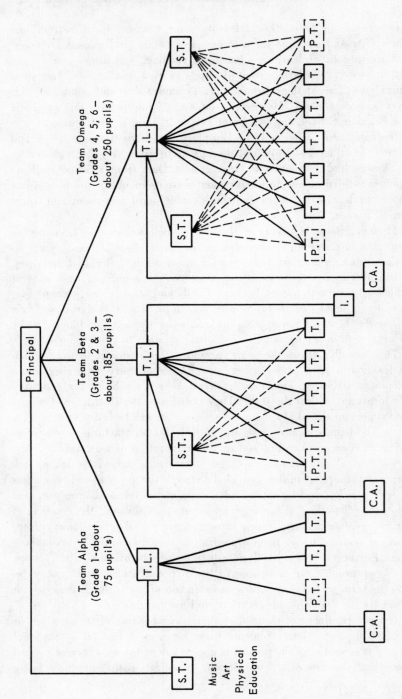

Figure 2. Organization for Team Teaching in Franklin School for 1959-60

developed throughout the country. What is unique about the Teaching Teams Project at Franklin School is the number and the particular combination of elements in its model.

At the beginning of the 1958–59 school year, several changes were made in the organization of the teams, resulting in the following arrangement:

Alpha: four first-grade teachers (team leader in charge)
Beta: six second- and third-grade teachers (team leader in charge assisted by a senior teacher)
Omega: eight fourth-, fifth-, and sixth-grade teachers (team leader in charge assisted by two senior teachers)

Again clerical assistance was provided, and part-time teacher service was made available to each team for research purposes.

The organizational pattern of Franklin School for 1959–60 is essentially the same as that for the preceding year. The organization may be presented most vividly, perhaps, by a diagram (see Figure 2).

There are at least two major differences between the organization for 1958–59 and for 1959–60. One is a difference in structure. For 1959–60, a new senior teacher position was created outside any team organization. This position of senior teacher specialist in art, music, and physical education gives the teaching teams more freedom in program planning and in use of space than they enjoyed under a former arrangement of special visiting teachers who, of necessity, worked on a fixed schedule involving system-wide considerations.

The other change is one of emphasis. Whereas before 1959–60, senior teachers were looked on essentially as grade-level chairmen or as assistant or substitute team leaders, in 1959–60 team leaders and senior teachers alike are becoming specialists in a particular instructional area. The team leader, in addition, assumes administrative responsibility for his team.

In the structure outlined in Figure 2, precise specification of qualifications and functions is still to be written. However, the hierarchy is seen as including a team leader, a senior teacher, a teacher, a part-time teacher, an intern, and a clerical aide.

The team leader (T.L.) is an experienced, mature master teacher of unusual talent who has had considerable experience, who has training well beyond the master's degree and who has had extensive training in curriculum and instruction, in supervision, human relations, and/or educational sociology. This person would have demonstrated an ability to work with teachers in a leadership role. About a third of his school day might be released for observation and training of subordinates, planning, curriculum development, research and evaluation, and parent conferences.

The senior teacher (S.T.) is an experienced, mature person with above-average talent and considerable advanced training, comparable to the well-regarded career teacher today, and with some specialized competence in a particular curriculum area.

The teacher (T.) category is seen as composed of two types of personnel: first, competent, experienced teachers of broad general training, and second, those of relatively little experience. The status of this position is seen as equal to that enjoyed by the typical teacher today.

The part-time teacher (P.T.) is a fully trained teacher, usually experienced, who is unable to teach full time. A combination of two or three part-time teachers might fill a billet which would otherwise require one full-time teacher.

The intern (I.) is a trainee in a program of teacher education doing full-time supervised teaching in a school for one semester. The work of the intern is customarily directed by a senior teacher or team leader working with the training school supervisor.

The clerical aide (C.A.) requires no professional preparation. This person will help with the routine, non-technical aspects of team operation: typing, rexographing, filing. It is possible that other sub-professional roles can be developed in this category, for example, technicians capable of producing instructional and demonstration materials.

The absence of precise specifications for the qualifications and functions of the several positions has resulted in some frustration and tension as individuals at all levels have tried to work together in ill-defined roles for which adequate criteria for selection were not available at the time personnel were appointed and in which the emphasis, in some cases, has changed markedly during the two years of the project. Personnel have been concerned about the absence of stated expectations for some areas.

The project staff has found that conventionally constructed school buildings with their rows of self-contained cells all the same size, divided by immovable partitions, do not meet the needs of most effective team operation. It is of more than passing interest to note that a new elementary school in Lexington, now on the architect's drafting boards, is being designed with the special requirements of team teaching in high priority.

In grouping, attention has already been directed to the possibilities and flexibility of the situation. But the flexibility and the freedom present problems that can be frustrating. They raise questions about criteria for grouping, about the availability and validity of instruments to evaluate pupils in terms of the criteria, about the transfer of youngsters from one group to another, about the merits of horizontal enrichment and longitudinal progression, and about the justification for large group instruction. These are examples of a host of questions that could be raised about pupil redeployment. It is toward the clarification and understanding of questions such as these that some of the efforts of both the school and university staff are now directed.[1]

In curriculum development, also, the opportunities the team structure offers for reflective and creative work and the challenges provided by the flexibility of the grouping arrangements have dictated a reexamination of the curriculum. Questions are immediately raised as to the objectives of the school, of a particular subject, or of a unit. Issues are raised on the criteria by which content is to be selected and how it is to be organized. Questions of the appropriateness of content, materials, and technique—with perhaps special interest in the use of technological devices—for groups of different composition and different sizes also demand attention. To these and similar questions, the attention of the project is also directed. Efforts are being made to define and clarify the problems involved and to develop and test various sequences of the curriculum.

The opportunity to come to grips with some of these issues in an atmosphere of collaboration and constructive criticism is one source of the attraction and the holding power inherent in the teaching-teams concept.

[1] Further, more definitive analyses of problems and implications are being written and will appear in the literature in the near future.

Sequence of Events

W. W. Farrar

In Alice, Texas, the six third- and fourth-grade teachers of the Saenz Elementary School are organized into a teaching team. It is their collective responsibility to structure a two-hour block of time in which their 197 students, divided into six groups according to their ability, study the language arts. Emphasis is placed on contributing to the students' understanding of sequence of events through carefully planned large- and small-group presentations and instruction.

Five rooms are occupied by the pupils with their teachers. One of the rooms, a large, 50'×30' area, serves as the homeroom for two classes. Used for lectures or demonstrations, it can accommodate three of the class groups at one time for the activities described in this article.

The experiment in team teaching of sequence of events began late in 1964. A unit or series of demonstrations on alphabetical order preceded the unit on sequence of events, which began on Wednesday, December 9, and ended on Tuesday, December 15, 1964. One of the reasons for the selection of these areas for emphasis was the low scores made by the pupils on a standardized achievement test.

Thirty minutes were allotted for each presentation or demonstration. On each of the scheduled days, after a brief homeroom period, Mrs. Mattie Bell Martin made a presentation to the less advanced pupils in Groups 1, 2, and 3. Mrs. Winifred Moore followed her with material for the more advanced pupils in Groups 4, 5, and 6.

Prior to beginning the schedule, the team met to exchange ideas and share materials with one or two teachers who were responsible for the planning and presentation. After the unit was under way, there were evaluation sessions.

GOALS

Seven goals were established for the language arts program:

1. To teach the arrangement of the events of a story in logical order.

2. To expand the concepts of proper sequence of ideas through audiovisual and written work.

Reprinted from *Audiovisual Instruction* 10:299–302, April 1965, by permission of the publisher and the author. W. W. Farrar is Curriculm Director of Alice Independent School District, Alice, Texas.

3. To train pupils to recall related experiences.
4. To train children to anticipate the sequence of ideas.
5. To teach children to associate ideas accurately.
6. To teach reading for information.
7. To give practice in making inferences based on logical sequence.

PREPARATION

In preparing the five-day demonstration, the team considered the necessity of closely relating the material to the experiences of the children. The vocabulary used was carefully screened at all times, and a check of the word lists accompanying the stories in the basic readers of the various levels was made.

An examination was made of the listings under "Sequence of Events" in the Teachers' Guides for the Scott Foresman texts, preprimer and grades one through four, and various other state-adopted series of teachers' editions along with the practice books accompanying the texts.

PROCEDURE

In beginning her presentation on Wednesday, Mrs. Martin introduced the idea of sequence of events by calling attention to the fact that the previous demonstration on alphabetical order was based on placing letters as they appear in the English alphabet. She then told the group that they would start putting sentences in correct order in describing things that happened in stories.

As an activity related to the experiences of the children, the subject "Our School" was chosen. Mounted pictures pertaining to each event were displayed in sequential order. In an effort to guide and strengthen the children's ability to think in a sequential manner, questions were asked, and the answers to the questions, previously written out, were placed in the card holder. The questions and answers were as follows:

1. How do you come to school?   (We walk to school.)

2. What do you do when you get here?   (We play in the yard.)

3. When do you come into the building?   (We come in when the bell rings.)

4. Where do you go then?   (We go to our rooms.)

5. What do you do when you get to your rooms?   (We read, tell stories, etc.)

The story, "The Three Bears," was told, and a transparency based on the story was flashed on the screen.

Next, scrambled sentence strips telling the story of "The Three Bears" were placed on the back of a large portable chalkboard and children chosen for this activity indicated the correct order by putting numbered cards in front of each. All sentence strips were printed in large manuscript letters.

Last, a transparency based on a four-sentence story, "The Picture," was shown along with the sentences. To see how much the children had grasped, a set of duplicated work sheets was given to each teacher for a follow-up activity when classes returned to their individual classroom groups. It was understood that each teacher would check and evaluate the sheet.

Mrs. Martin began the second day's demonstration by explaining the sequence in terms of 1, 2, 3, 4, and last.

She told the story of "The Gingerbread Boy" while showing a transparency pertaining to the story. Simple sentences on the story, printed on Manila tag board sentence strips, were shown to the pupils in mixed order. They then were arranged in sequential order by individual students with numbered cards. The pupils arranged the sequence of events by placing the large number card before the correct sentence.

In conjunction with the demonstration, the story, "The Ball," was used as the practice exercise for the day in the various classrooms.

The sound film, *The Little Red Hen*, was shown on Friday, the third day of the demonstration. Because this film was shown twice during the half-hour demonstration periods, Mrs. Martin was unable to carry out other activities as planned. In the few minutes of the period remaining after the film was shown, four colorful pictures illustrating "Tom's Birdhouse" were shown. An exercise based on these pictures had been prepared in advance, and was used in duplicated form as a follow-up activity in the individual classrooms. The sentence portion of the exercise was as follows:

_____ He put it on a tree.
_____ Tom made a house.
_____ Birds liked the house.
_____ He painted it red.

On Monday, Mrs. Martin retold the story of *The Little Red Hen* in order to refresh the children's memory regarding the sequence of events in the story. Then the same activity that had been carried out with "The Gingerbread Boy" was presented. The students then worked on a prepared, duplicated exercise on the story of the day. They disbanded at the period's end.

Cinderella, a filmstrip, was given two showings on the final day of demonstration. It was projected on the overhead projector screen, and the sentences accompanying each picture were read aloud by the teacher. Sentence strips mixed in sequence on the story were again arranged in sequential order by the students, using the same method as in other periods. The sentence strips were as follows:

_____ Cinderella went to the dance in the beautiful dress that the fairy gave her.

_____ At twelve o'clock she ran out, but she dropped one little glass slipper.

_____ The prince said he would marry any girl the slipper would fit.

_____ The slipper fitted Cinderella just right.

_____ She and the prince were married.

As a practice exercise, a four-sentence sequence on *Cinderella* was given to the teachers for use with their pupils after they returned to their classroom.

Following the demonstrations on Wednesday, Thursday, and Friday, a continuation of the work on sequential order was carried out in the individual classrooms, either from duplicated work sheets or exercises written on the chalkboard.

In her introduction Wednesday morning to the unit on sequence of events with Groups 4, 5, and 6, Mrs. Moore began with *time sequence.* She showed a chart entitled "Days of the Week." These sentences, with blanks to fill in, formed the body of the chart:

Yesterday was _____.

Today is _____.

Tomorrow will be _____.

She called on individuals to read aloud the sentences with the correct answers for that day of the week.

Place sequence was presented by means of a Texas Highway Map on which the route from Alice to Brownsville was traced. The students answered with the names of the various towns one would travel through on a trip to the border.

The idea of the combination of time and place in our lives was next introduced. Such sentences as the following were used:

1. We went to Corpus Christi on Saturday.
2. We went to church in Alice on Sunday morning.
3. We spent Sunday afternoon in Kingsville.

Pictures on the subject "Daily Activities at School" were then matched with sentence strips relating to the pictures; and, one at a time, students placed numbered cards to the left of the sentences, thus arranging them in a sequence.

Immediately afterward, the story of "The Three Bears" was told by the teacher with the changes of voice usually employed for good characterization. Three transparencies (two pictures on each frame) were shown, using an overhead projector. The exercise of matching sentence strips with numbered cards followed.

A duplicated series of stories with a mixed order of events was passed to the groups on their return to the classroom. They were "The Sleeping Beauty," "A Tall Story," "Washing the Dog," etc.

During the team meeting in the afternoon, the members agreed that a team "briefing" meeting on this follow-up exercise, prior to the morning session with the children, would have contributed to a more successful completion by the pupils.

On Thursday, a short review of the meaning of sequence began the lesson. The chart used in Wednesday's lesson was reintroduced and attention was called to the fact that the answers to the fill-in-the-blank questions were different on that day because of the sequence of dates.

"The Gingerbread Boy" was the feature of the demonstration. A related transparency was presented and the familiar story was told by Mrs. Moore. She asked questions based on the transparency, pointing to specific objects shown in the picture on the screen overhead. These questions brought out the story sequence and were asked in order to prepare the children for making a logical arrangement of events when called on to do so individually.

The matching of a correct number with proper sequence of the sentence strip was the next activity. The sentence strips used for "The Gingerbread Boy" are given here in correct order:

1. The little old man and the little old woman ran after the gingerbread boy.
2. As he ran down the road a second man ran after him.
3. A cow was eating grass near the road. She ran after him too.
4. Then a pig saw him and ran after him.
5. He tells the fox, "No one can catch me!"
6. At the last, we see the fox eat the gingerbread boy.

A variation of the procedure motivated the children's interest. Mrs. Moore allowed the child choosing the correct sentence to read the sentence to the class through the microphone. A forest of hands of children wanting to volunteer for the task of reading the correct sentence went up when this method was used.

The stories "The Picture" and "Indian Bread" were given to the teachers to be used as follow-up exercises when they returned to their classrooms.

Number sequence was stressed in the opening procedure of Friday's demonstration lesson by Mrs. Moore. A number line was affixed to the chalkboard with masking tape. Attention was called to the sequence found in the number system. Various students were asked to point out or name examples of number sequence encountered or used daily.

The Little Red Hen, a 10-minute sound film, was shown twice on Friday so that the sequence could be checked carefully. The rear-view projector was used for running this film. A group of sentences was placed on the portable bulletin board and then arranged in sequential order by the method used before. Ten sentences were used in this exercise. This number of sentences proved to be too many for a large number of the children to handle with reasonable confidence. The sentence strips for *The Little Red Hen* were as follows:

_____ One day the little red hen found some wheat.

_____ She asked the duck, the cat, and the pig, "Who will plant the wheat?"

_____ She asked them, "Who will cut the wheat?"

_____ "Now," she said, "Who will thresh the wheat?"

_____ Next she asked all three: "Who will take the wheat to the mill to have it ground into flour?"

_____ Then she wanted to know who would make the flour into bread.

_____ She baked some nice bread.

_____ Finally she asked: "Who will eat the bread?" They all said: "Oh, I will!"

_____ But they went hungry. The little red hen and her chicks ate the bread.

Monday's lesson began with an introductory period on sequence. Mrs. Moore called for the recitation of a familiar sequence, the days of the week, by one of the students. Next, the days of the school week were recited, and it was pointed out that this is another type of sequence.

The teacher then copied on the board a list of words often used to indicate sequence of events. She counselled the children to watch for these words when attempting to choose the correct order of sentences in a story.

She then showed large pictures illustrating the story, "Tom's Birdhouse," which had been prepared by the principal for use in an opaque projector. Discussion of the pictures followed.

Duplicated sheets with four sentences in mixed-up order were distributed. The students rearranged the sentences by numbers. These were taken up and given to the various teachers for checking.

More practice exercises, consisting of three duplicated stories, were taken back to the individual reading groups for follow-up exercises.

On Tuesday, the filmstrip *Three Billy Goats Gruff* was shown. A team member operated the filmstrip projector while Mrs. Moore read the subtitles to the class, modulating her voice to fit the various characters. The children followed this presentation with great interest.

Just before the filmstrip was shown, three members of the teaching team hastily cooperated in fastening sentence strips with masking tape loops to the portable chalkboard. It was then purposely turned to the wall so that students would have no opportunity to read them in advance. These sentence strips told the events of the story but not in sequence.

After the filmstrip was shown, the board was turned around and number cards were passed out. Mrs. Moore asked the children holding the cards to come to the front. Each attached a number to the left of a sentence, and if his selection was correct, he read it aloud to the group over the microphone. The sentence strips for *Three Billy Goats Gruff* were as follows:

_____ Once upon a time three Billy Goats lived on a hill.

_____ They did not find enough grass, so they decided to cross a bridge to a pasture with green grass.

_____ Now a big bad troll lived under the bridge.

_____ Little Billy Goat started out first.

_____ The troll wanted to eat him, but he said *Big* Billy Goat Gruff would be better to eat.

_____ Big Billy Goat also passed the big bad troll by telling him *Great Big* Billy Goat was even bigger than he.

_____ Great Big Billy Goat Gruff butted the big bad troll off into the water.

_____ He was never seen again.

A four-sentence sequence on *Three Billy Goats Gruff* was given for the children to arrange in order in the individual reading groups. The sentences were as follows:

_____ Great Big Billy Goat butted the troll off the bridge.

_____ Now a big bad troll lived under the bridge.

_____ Three Billy Goats lived on a hill.

_____ The troll waited to eat him but he said his brother was bigger.

Two other exercises, "The Ghost" (Halloween story) and "Babies," were given to the teachers for use in their classrooms.

CONCLUSION

Many hours of careful planning and preparation of materials were devoted to the organization of these demonstrations by Mrs. Moore and

Mrs. Martin. After the presentations were under way, constructive comments, a necessary part of team action, were invited. The following observation was made by a team member in reference to the story entitled "The Picture," one of the follow-up activities:

Very few made a perfect paper. Maybe the events could be in a definite order of sequence; for example, the children couldn't tell whether Sue made the dog first or Sue and Tom played first.

Another team member, referring to a follow-up activity, stated:

Since the sentence strip activity is the same as the duplicated one, some children are tending to list numbers by memorization or using their own copies taken during the demonstration.

This was easily corrected by changing either the order of the sentence strips or by having a different story for the follow-up activity.

Examples of typical class responses may be found in the following chart of three stories:

Stories	Correct Sentences							Pupils
	0	1	2	3	4	5	6	
The Billy Goats Gruff	1	–	6	3	15	–	–	25
Going to School	3	1	4	1	13	–	3	25
Cinderella	3	–	4	2	17	–	–	26

The demonstrating teachers made a special effort to select stories within the realm of the pupils' experiences. That they were most successful was agreed to by all members of the team.

As the teaching of other concepts continues at Saenz, so does that of sequence of events.

What is being attempted at Saenz? Perhaps the answer may be found in the words of Florence M. Diesman:

Team teaching? Just when the term takes on a specific meaning for me, I visit another school where the system is not what I had defined as *team teaching*. Visits to 21 schools, plus much reading, have given me varying concepts of the term "team teaching." But in all these schools, the chief value of team work lies in the fact that teachers are planning together, formulating specific goals, sharing achievements, and then evaluating their failures or successes. All are attempting to improve their instruction. All are enthusiastic about new ideas. And the many students I have observed are more interested in English language and literature than ever before.[1]

[1] Diesman, Florence M. "Team Teaching Has Many Forms." *The English Journal* 53:617, November 1964.

Team Teaching and Independent Reading

Gladys A. Eakin and Eugene S. Spence

Combining the efforts of a group of teachers into a team to teach an independent reading program has not only simplified the work for the classroom teacher, but it has also improved the total effectiveness of the reading program. The primary aims of the Bethel Park independent reading program are the teaching and maintenance of reading skills and providing children the opportunity to read as rapidly and efficiently as possible on a level commensurate with their ability. To do all this for thirty different boys and girls, to provide a complete program of phonics instruction, workbooks, oral and silent reading evaluation, discussion, and literature for all levels of achievement and interest, is a complex and very demanding assignment for even the best experienced teachers. However, the organization of the intermediate grade teachers into a team with teachers being responsible for particular parts of the program for all children has also resulted in favorable acceptance of the promises for team teaching. One of the teachers involved in the team serves as chairman or team leader and accepts part of the responsibility for assisting with the smooth operation of the program.

SCHEDULING IS IMPORTANT

In the Bethel Park program, children in grades four through six in each building have reading scheduled at the same time. Although the program is very carefully planned and organized, much flexibility is possible for both student and teacher. The pupils in these six rooms, there are two classrooms for each grade, are divided into groups regardless of grade placement but are assigned to groups with other children of similar reading levels. These groups then meet the teaching team according to the schedule developed for that particular building. Following the routine of the four day schedule of a group of children, which for these purposes we

Reprinted from *Elementary English* 39:266–288, March 1962, with the permission of the National Council of Teachers of English and Dr. Spence and Miss Eakin. Dr. Eugene S. Spence is Assistant to the Supervising Principal and Miss Gladys A. Eakin is Supervisor of Reading, Bethel Park School District, Bethel Park, Pennsylvania.

shall label Group A, will illustrate how the complete program functions.

On the first day of the four day cycle, Group A meets with one of the teacher team for a half period of workbook activities. Each pupil works independently in a workbook which is a level easier than his grade equivalent score on a standardized reading test. He progresses through a sequence of workbooks selected from many series for the variety of experience with work study materials they offer him. He may move to the next level at any time he can attain on the reading test a grade equivalent score one year higher than the level to which he is aspiring. The teacher gives help where needed, always with the aim of helping each pupil become as independent and accurate in his work as possible. He supervises pupil checking of workbooks, keeps records of materials completed by each pupil, and administers tests individually or in small groups as pupils progress. During the latter half of the period another teacher supervises Group A in partner oral reading while the first teacher supervises workbook activities with another group. These two teachers work as a team in two rooms with four groups of children. In partner oral reading, children are paired according to oral reading ability and share a reader or trade book which they have selected. The reading must be done so quietly that only the partner can hear it. The book is one level easier than the pupil's grade equivalent score on the reading test.

The second day, Group A, with three other groups, meets with a third member of the teaching team in a large multiple purpose room for literature and sharing activities. Children become familiar with the best of children's literature. Frequently the teacher reads to the pupils. They react to the teacher's reading and share their own reading with each other through dramatization, panels, illustrating, skits, oral reading of exciting or humorous selections, or any other type of reaction reporting.

The third day, Group A returns to the classroom where they were the first day for another half period of workbook activities with the first member of the teaching team. This day the second team teacher supervises work with self-help phonics and vocabulary materials. Phonics cards which include study cards and test cards were developed in our schools for this program. Word wheels and vocabulary cards are also used for self-help materials.

The final day of the cycle, Group A with the three other groups returns to the multiple purpose room, again under the supervision of the third member of the teaching team. Half of the large group work with test lessons during the first part of the period. During the latter part they read silently from a reader or trade book which they have selected from the classroom or building library.

PROVISION FOR SLOW READERS

Children who score below 5.0 on the standardized reading test do not participate in the independent reading program described above but meet each day with the same teacher. They are divided into three sub-groups according to their reading ability and needs. The teacher works with these children as in a formal primary grade reading program, using a basic reader with accompanying workbook and following the teacher's guide. Children who haven't completed the primary materials continue with them. Others use materials from a different basic series so that repetition is avoided. Any child who has completed the basic materials may, upon attaining a score of 5.0 on the reading test, move out of this group into one of the other eight groups which work independently.

Four of the six teachers form two teams, each of which works with four different groups. The teacher who works with the large groups in the multiple purpose room meets all eight groups, four at a time. One teacher meets each day with the formal groups. The pattern of the reading program may vary from building to building and from year to year depending upon the number of classrooms in the intermediate grades in that building and upon the number of pupils in the formal groups. At the beginning of the term there will frequently be more than one classroom of children in the formal groups.

Our philosophy of reading calls for each group to move through the primary grades in a continuous program beginning each year where they left off the preceding year. Emphasis is placed upon working at a level where they can be very successful in reading rather than on completing a given amount of material. Children are not tested for admission to the independent program until they have completed third grade materials. So, if there are more pupils in the formal groups at the beginning of the year than can be cared for adequately by one teacher, a temporary change is made in the organization: two teachers may be assigned to work with these children. Instead of four teachers working as two teams, three may form a team, one responsible for supervising the partner oral reading for all groups, one responsible for the work with self-help phonics and vocabulary materials and part of the workbook supervision, and the third responsible for most of the workbook supervision. When a building has seven classrooms of intermediate grades, the assignment for the teacher in the multiple purpose room is divided between two teachers so that one is responsible for literature and sharing activities, the other for test lessons and silent reading.

The Bethel Park elementary schools have had an independent reading program for approximately ten years, but it had been organized on a self-contained classroom basis. The utilization of the team-teaching idea in the reading program has met with enthusiastic approval from the faculty, and future standardized test results should show increased pupil benefits derived from the type of organization previously described. Careful study with approved statistical methods will be made of the standardized test results before and after the introduction of the team teaching technique.

Team Teaching as Sixth-Graders See It

Galen M. Jarvis and Roy C. Fleming

Team teaching is challenging the self-contained classroom organization. Educators as well as laymen feel the need for a more efficient deployment of personnel, instructional materials, and physical facilities.

Before embarking on a program of team teaching, boards of education, administrators, and teachers usually raise a number of practical questions: What are pupils' initial reactions to team teaching? What do children like about team teaching? What do they dislike about it? Are children overwhelmed by large instructional groups? Can they adjust to having five or six teachers? After experiencing a team-teaching program, do the pupils prefer to continue in a team-teaching situation or in a regular classroom?

The purpose of this paper is to report the reactions of children who took part in a team-teaching project at the Devonshire Elementary School in Skokie, Illinois, a suburb of Chicago.

Most studies of team teaching minimize pupils' opinions or give incomplete evidence on pupils' feelings. A review of articles on team teaching in the elementary school, listed in the *Education Index* from 1958 to 1964, shows only an occasional reference to interviews of pupils and no transcript of their responses (1).

The literature indicates that elementary-school children adjust to having more than one teacher and benefit academically from a flexible program of studies. Lambert found that children "seem to adjust quickly to the idea of having several teachers instead of one. They make more friends and join more activities; most of all, they find school more interesting than they had previously" (2).

Anderson reported that a few children expressed or manifested feelings of being lost or insecure in a team-teaching situation; however, the proportion was much smaller than he had expected. Anderson concluded that "the overwhelming weight of opinion as expressed by both children and their parents is enthusiastic for team teaching" (3).

The Devonshire team-teaching experiment emphasized large- and small-group instruction. Large groups had seventy-five pupils, and small groups ranged from four to fifteen. Children were grouped according to

Reprinted from *Elementary School Journal* 66:35–39, October 1965, by permission of the publisher and the authors. Galen M. Jarvis and Roy C. Fleming are both with Devonshire School, Skokie, Illinois.

achievement and ability as measured by standardized tests and teachers' judgments.

The instructional team consisted of a team leader, two regular teachers, and four certified teachers who worked part time. Two part-time teachers worked six hours a day, and two worked three and a half hours a day. The team also had the services of a full-time clerk. Flexible physical facilities were available.

The regular teachers and the team leader had responsibility for curriculum-planning, for instructing class groups, for evaluating children's academic and social growth, and for reporting to parents. The part-time teachers had responsibility for some small-group instruction, for general supervision, and for marking papers. The team clerk did general office work and occasionally supervised children.

ORGANIZATION AND SCHEDULING

Although the daily schedule for the 150 pupils was complex and varied, one basic organizational scheme was used during the semester. Under the scheme, the individual pupil's instructional group might, during any one day, vary from four to seventy-five pupils.

Each regular teacher assumed responsibility for planning and for large-group instruction in one major academic area (language arts, social studies, mathematics, or science). The associate teachers (or part-time teachers) supervised and instructed small groups in these areas. The regular teachers also taught small groups in subject areas in which they were not doing large-group instruction.

Mathematics instruction was organized into classes of various sizes. Children were assigned to the classes on the basis of ability. Each regular teacher and each associate teacher were assigned to one class. Mathematics was taught in small groups for pupils of low ability. There was independent study for pupils of high ability.

The grouping plan for literature-reading was similar to that for mathematics. Ability groups were assigned to a specific teacher on a regular basis.

For each homeroom group of seventy-five pupils, the schedule called for four periods of an hour each for social studies and language arts, and for three hour-long periods a week for science. For each homeroom unit, social studies and language arts were back to back on Monday, Wednesday, and Friday. On Tuesday and Thursday, language arts and social studies alternated back to back with science in the mornings. The afternoon science period was scheduled for one homeroom at a time. While one homeroom had science, the other homeroom had a free reading period and spelling.

All children had mathematics four mornings a week for fifty minutes. The art period occupied the fifth day of the week. The literature groups met twice a week for two hours in the afternoon.

Three times each week for half an hour, all children worked on research. The research period offered opportunities for a number of activities including special help for individuals and small groups, use of the library, work on special projects individually and in groups, conferences with teachers, homework, group and individual guidance by the teacher.

Monday, Wednesday, and Friday afternoons included a cycle of an hour and a half. The 150 pupils were scheduled for this block of time in groups of fifty. Thus, each pupil had three half-hour periods in music, physical education, reading or library. The schedule included:

Monday
  Music
  Physical Education
  Programmed Reading
Wednesday
  Music
  Physical Education
  Programmed Reading
Friday
  Library
  Physical Education
  Programmed Reading Material

During the periods in this cycle the regular teachers were free to participate in planning and evaluating.

On any one day a pupil might:

Work in a group of twenty in a writing laboratory.

Take a spelling test with seventy-five pupils.

Work for forty minutes on a science assignment in a group of seventy-five pupils.

Spend ten minutes, along with four other pupils, conferring with the science teacher about an experiment they were going to demonstrate soon.

Spend the mathematics period with as few as ten or as many as forty-five pupils.

Be in a reading group with from twenty to thirty-five children.

Take a current-events test with seventy-five of his peers and then go into a room with eighteen pupils to continue work on a construction project.

Be in a physical education class or a vocal-music class with fifty pupils.

EVALUATION

After five months an evaluation was made. Ten sixth-graders were interviewed—six girls and four boys, randomly selected from 155 pupils who took part in the team-teaching experiment.

Before selecting pupils for the interviews, the reasons for evaluating the project and the method used to select pupils to be interviewed were carefully discussed with all pupils. The pupils were told that the school needed their evaluations to learn the strengths and the weaknesses of the team-teaching project.

Each interview lasted about twenty minutes. Selected questions, which the team teachers thought important to the evaluation of the project, were read one at a time to each pupil and, as the pupil reacted, the interviewer recorded the comments. The team leader interviewed five pupils, and the principal interviewed five.

The randomly selected pupils were asked ten questions in the interview. Four of the questions are not included in this report because they deal with specific instructional procedures used in various subject areas and are not peculiar to team teaching.

The interview questions and a summary of the children's responses follow.

What was your initial reaction to team teaching? How did you feel during the first few weeks of school?

Most pupils interviewed reported that their first reaction to team teaching was one of surprise to the newness of the situation. Evaluation of the experience seemed to vary according to the pupil's willingness to accept the novelty. Some pupils did not like team teaching at first because it was new. One child said he was "confused, didn't know what classes to go to." Others liked team teaching for the same reason. One pupil said he "knew it would be different—fun."

How do you feel about team teaching now that you have been involved with it for a semester?

Pupils' reactions to this question were uniformly positive, though some were not enthusiastic. Pupils singled out specific activities or conditions they liked or disliked about the team-teaching situation. Two responses capture the general flavor: "Well, now I am getting used to it I like it better." "Better instruction. You stay on the subject." Other children said: "Like it better than in the beginning. Now it's much more organized." "It is different and good experience." "It is pretty nice except in home-room it gets noisy." "It is really better. Can get more individual attention."

Can you explain in detail some of the things you liked about team teaching?

Pupils' responses to this inquiry seemed to center on the frequently changing schedule of activities, on having more than one teacher (in all cases at least five), on changing from room to room for different subjects, and on homogeneous grouping. Pupils said: "I like changing classes." "I like having different teachers rather than just one." "It is like the junior high—getting to meet more children." One child summed up his evaluation by saying, "I like to switch classes and stuff like that. I like the homeroom with a lot of kids."

Can you explain in detail some of the things you do not like about team teaching?

The children made many detailed comments when they were asked to tell what they liked about team teaching, but they had few comments about things they disliked. Yet, negative evaluations were solicited so that team members could make whatever adjustments were necessary.

Most of the negative responses were prompted by general aspects of the program. The following comments are typical: "In homeroom, you don't get a chance to talk." "Don't like gym with girls because it's hard to do some of the things." "Not good to work with seventy-five [children] —too noisy." "Missed some assignments because of being in many classes and different teachers."

How do you feel about being in a homeroom with seventy-five pupils and being taught in a large group?

All the children had reservations about large instructional groups. Their dislike for these groups was based on the lack of opportunity to communicate with the teacher.

Children said: "Don't get a chance to talk to the teacher. You are really quiet." "I don't feel you have as good instruction, but then you break up in smaller groups." "Large groups get confusing at times, but it's okay. You get to meet a lot of kids this way." "I don't talk too much in large group. I like small groups. You get more attention." "I like breaking down in small groups from large groups." But pupils saw a difference between large groups for homerooms and large groups for instruction. Pupils said: "I like seventy-five in a homeroom." "Doesn't bother me to be in a homeroom with seventy-five pupils." In general, pupils did not like large groups because they made it difficult to get a chance to say something or to get help. As one pupil put it, "When you're stuck with something, you can't ask about it because there is a long line around the teacher's desk." Some children had another problem: "Tall kids block the view sometimes."

Keeping in mind what you now know about team teaching, if you were given a choice between a regular classroom with one teacher and being in a team-teaching group, which would you choose?

"Team teaching," was the reply of every pupil interviewed. The children went on to explain: "I would take the team teaching. You can do more." "I've learned a lot, and it is boring in one classroom with one teacher. I've had that experience." One child said: "I like team teaching. Regular classroom I did not like. I like changing classes and having different teachers."

The findings of our study indicate that:

In the beginning, the pupils were overwhelmed by the team-teaching situation, but they adjusted quickly.

The pupils felt that the main advantage of team teaching was the opportunity to be in small instructional groups and to have different teachers.

The pupils felt the main disadvantage of team teaching was the "overcrowding" of seventy-five pupils in homerooms.

The pupils would choose team teaching over a self-contained classroom.

This report supports other studies, which found that elementary-school children have a high positive feeling about team teaching.

REFERENCES

1. *Education Index*, Vols. XXIX–XXXV (June, 1958—June, 1964).

2. P. Lambert. "Team Teaching for the Elementary Schools," *Educational Leadership*, XVIII (November, 1960), 85–88.

3. Robert H. Anderson. "Team Teaching in the Elementary School," *Greenwich Public School Bulletin*, III (June, 1959), 1–3.

First-Year Organization of Elmcrest Elementary School: A Nongraded Team-Teaching School

Arthur Haas

In July, 1963 ·the SCHOOL BOARD JOURNAL published an article entitled "Liverpool Elementary School." This school was designed to encourage a nongraded elementary program, large-group instruction, flexibility, and adaptability for the future. Basically, Elmcrest Elementary School, as it is now called, consists of a central rectangular area housing administrative areas and four hexagonal clusters containing six classrooms and a central instructional space. Separation of the clusters into teaching areas is accomplished by use of folding partitions and, with the exception of the teacher's wardrobe, all classroom furniture is on wheels and can be moved.

The library is centrally located and contains 10 study carrels plus two project rooms. The purpose of this type of construction is to afford individual pupils and groups of pupils of all sizes an opportunity to work in the library.

ORGANIZING THE SCHOOL

During the spring and summer of 1964, the staff for Elmcrest was recruited. A nucleus of experienced teachers from within the district were transferred to the building. However, most staff members were either in their first year of teaching or had one or two years' experience in other districts. Routinely, in interviewing candidates for staff positions a "mock-up" of the building and one cluster was shown to the applicants. The purpose of this procedure was to have candidates tell the interviewer what could be done in a building of this design. In essence, we were seeking staff members who viewed the building as an opportunity to provide an excellent program for pupils rather than an intolerable threat to all that they knew about how schools should be designed.

The staff consisting of 33 teaching members was organized into seven teams: Leadership Team—principal, pupil personnel consultant, and instructional consultant; Resource Team—teachers of art, library, music, physical education, reading, dental hygienist, and nurse; Kindergarten

Reprinted from the *American School Board Journal* 151:22, 70, October 1965, by permission of the publisher and the author. Arthur Haas is Principal, Elmcrest Elementary School, Liverpool, New York.

Team; Team I and II for six- and seven-year-olds; Team III for eight- and nine-year-olds; and Team IV for 10- and 11-year-olds. A secretary, two half-time teacher aides, a library aide, and a custodial staff of three were on the nonteaching staff. During 1964–65, approximately 760 pupils attended Elmcrest Elementary School. This figure included approximately 250 kindergarten pupils who attended school half time.

A 7½-day workshop was held in August, 1964, to orient the staff. During this workshop teachers, under the guidance of the Leadership Team, established coordinated nongraded reading, mathematics, and spelling groups. This meant that reading groups were established within teams so that there would be a minimum of overlapping of groups working at the same level. For example, in Team IV there were 18 reading groups for what would be considered the fifth- and sixth-grade pupils. These 18 groups were coordinated so that they extended from the usual third grade to the usual seventh grade level. Thus, during the reading period, each pupil was able to function at his instructional level. The same type of organization was established in mathematics and spelling. In practice we shifted pupils according to their needs when they were ready to be shifted.

In the areas of language arts, science, and social studies, teachers cooperatively established units which outlined goals, procedures, materials to be used, and evaluative and grouping procedures.

Three methods have been developed for grouping pupils in these areas:

1. Diagnostic Grouping

In this procedure an end of the unit test reflecting achievement of the goals outlined in the cooperatively developed unit was administered early in the unit, generally after the introductory large-group session. Those pupils who achieved a high score assumed responsibility, under the direction of a staff member, for independent study which enlarged their skills, knowledge, and abilities in the unit being studied. In addition, the results of this diagnostic test were used to group children for instruction within the unit.

2. Interest-Activity Grouping

In this procedure pupils were given small- and large-group instruction and then grouped on the basis of interests within a particular unit; for example—on Team II a unit on animals provided opportunities for pupils to do individual library research, make dioramas, murals, read storybooks illustrating what they were learning, listen individually or in small groups to teacher-prepared magnetic tapes, and view individually or in small groups appropriate filmstrips.

3. Heterogeneous Homeroom Grouping

In this procedure teachers taught their homerooms. Homerooms were established to provide a broad spectrum of abilities within a given age range plus a balance of boys and girls.

Throughout the program at Elmcrest, staff members put heavy emphasis on the progress of the individual pupil. Team meetings are held four times a week on school time.

At these meetings the progress of the individual pupil is carefully reviewed to determine whether pupils should work individually or in small or large groups. The principle of flexibility to meet the needs of individual pupils is of paramount importance as teams plan the program for pupils. The resources of study carrels and small- and large-group instructional areas are viewed as methods of promoting individual pupil growth.

DIAGNOSTIC READING PROGRAM

In harmony with implementing the concept of meeting individual pupil needs through flexibility, a diagnostic reading program was also instituted in the first year at Elmcrest. Under this program necessary reading skills were identified and a procedure established for finding those pupils who needed remedial instruction in these skills. This was then followed with the necessary remedial procedures to help individual pupils.

The program has been carried on in this fashion:

1. Needed basic reading skills were identified.

2. A diagnostic test was recorded on magnetic tape to identify pupils who were weak in particular reading skills.

3. The test was so constructed that pupils were able to respond to questions on special data-processing cards.

4. The taped test was broadcast through the public address system to a full team of 130 or 140 pupils.

5. The data-processing cards used by pupils to respond to the taped test were forwarded to the district office data-processing center, and an item analysis for each pupil was received within four hours.

6. On the basis of the item analysis, pupils were identified who needed help in particular reading skills.

7. Pupils were grouped according to the remedial instruction they needed. For example, as a result of one test there was a group who needed help with initial "th," another group who needed help with initial "ch," and still another group who needed help in initial "sh."

8. Each group received remedial instruction through the use of magnetic tapes and coordinated worksheets. By this procedure a pupil

could receive the lesson several times if needed; in addition, makeup lessons for absentees could also be administered.

9. A retest to determine the effectiveness of the remedial instruction was then administered. Further remedial action is continued where necessary.

PINS AND CLINS PROGRAM

A Pupil Interest and Needs Program (PINS) and Class Interest and Needs Program (CLINS) was instituted to augment the regularly scheduled opportunities for children to go to art, music, library, and physical education resource areas.

The Pupil Interest and Needs Program provided an opportunity for the resource teachers to have children come to resource areas on the basis of their needs regardless of age level.

For example, the physical education instructor cooperated with the nurse in giving annual height and weight examinations. This information, coupled with the professional observation of the nurse and the physical education instructor, was used to identify a group of pupils who needed remedial help in physical coordination. These pupils were from all age levels and were brought to the gymnasium during the PINS program for remedial instruction to help develop better physical coordination. Another interage group who needed help in strengthening their arm and chest muscles was also identified and given special exercises.

In the library six- and seven-year-old pupils who were ready to learn research skills were taught during the PINS period. The art and music teachers also utilized the PINS period for instruction across age lines.

The Class Interest and Needs Program (CLINS) was devoted to working with classroom size groups of pupils who:

1. Needed further specialized experience at resource stations or

2. Needed to augment their classroom program with an experience at a resource station.

For example, if a music class showed particular interest in creative writing of music to poetry and the music teacher wanted an additional opportunity to work with this group, he could ask the class to return during the CLINS period. In addition, if a unit was being carried on in science and there was a need to call on a resource teacher to participate in the program, the CLINS program provided the avenue for this type of activity.

Two examples illustrate this: the music teacher demonstrated musical instruments as part of a unit on sound and the physical education teacher, who had a strong science background, dissected a calf's heart for pupils studying the circulatory system.

PUBLIC RELATIONS PROGRAM

In order to keep the community informed about the Elmcrest program, a great deal of information was given to the community prior to the opening of Elmcrest. However, this program was not stopped. The elements of the public relations program consisted of an active Parent Teachers Association, a regularly issued Elmcrest newsletter, regularly scheduled parent conferences, and periodic releases in the newspapers. In addition, *kaffee klatches* were instituted for parents to come to school in groups no larger than 15 to discuss the Elmcrest program with the Leadership Team. These meetings were held during school hours and in the evening. In addition, parents were invited to visit classrooms and watch our program in action in the usual "Open School Week." Television programs were also used to keep parents aware of Elmcrest. And, most important of all, we provide a program which is dedicated to meeting the needs of pupils.

EVALUATION OF FIRST YEAR

The design of Elmcrest Elementary School is particularly suited to developing a nongraded team-teaching program which promotes continuous progress for each pupil. Although considerable progress has been made this first year, there is still room for improvement. In evaluating the first year's experience, the following three points are appropriate for Elmcrest and any other school contemplating a departure from a "bells and cells" school:

1. There is a need for careful selection of staff members.

2. There is a need for a continuous in-service program to assist staff members in implementing a nongraded team-teaching program that promotes continuous progress for each pupil.

3. There is a need to keep members of the community informed about the educational program.

A Study of the Elementary-School Teaching Team

Philip Lambert, William L. Goodwin and William Wiersma

Team teaching has become increasingly common over the past five years. The purpose of this article is to update earlier articles (1). Most of the new information comes from a two-year controlled study conducted under the auspices of the University of Wisconsin.

No attempt will be made here to review the results on pupil interaction, adjustment, and achievement. Readers interested in these areas are directed to the report prepared for the Office of Education, U.S. Department of Health, Education, and Welfare (2). This article reviews the organizational design of the study, describes the hierarchical arrangement in the team, considers a controlled study of pupil discipline (relating it to the nature of the team structure), and briefly discusses suggestions to improve team-teaching organizations.

DESIGN

Two elementary schools in Madison, Wisconsin, provided the pupils for this study. The schools served primarily the lower socioeconomic families in the city. About 25 per cent of the families were receiving funds under the public assistance program; 60 to 70 per cent of the fathers were employed in unskilled or semiskilled occupations.

Three organizations that together enrolled about 350 pupils were involved in the study. Two of these organizations were the team and the self-contained organizations in Washington School, which housed about 60 per cent of the pupils in the study. The third organization was the self-contained organization in Longfellow School, which enrolled the remaining 40 per cent of the subjects. Since the project ran for two years, the exact number of pupils in any particular class changed from time to time.

Before the experiment, there were two classes of about twenty pupils each for every grade from first through sixth in the Washington School. Under the experimental design the pupils at Washington were separated,

Reprinted from *Elementary School Journal* 66:28–34, October 1965, by permission of the publisher and the authors. Dr. Philip Lambert is at the University of Wisconsin, Madison; Dr. William L. Goodwin is at Bucknell University, Lewisburg, Pennsylvania; and Dr. William Wiersma is at the University of Toledo, Toledo, Ohio.

grade by grade, into two sections: experimental and control. A table of random numbers was used to assign pupils to these sections.

The self-contained organization at Washington School continued to use a modified self-contained approach, that is, the traditional self-contained approach with assistance from specialists in art, music, and physical education (3). This organization was used in one class of each grade (1–6). The classes under this arrangement were housed in one section of the school.

The experimental team organization was housed in another section of the school. Two multigrade teaching teams were formed. The primary teaching team served the pupils who would have been in Grades 1 through 3. The intermediate teaching team taught pupils who would have been in Grades 4 through 6. Flexible scheduling was an important feature of the team approach. Groups were formed on the basis of the demands of the subject and each child's interests and potentialities. In social studies and science, for example, there was much large-group instruction, with pupil panels, debates, movies, and resource speakers. There were also smaller follow-up, special interest, discussion and work groups. These groups varied in composition according to the material that had been presented.

Longfellow School, which served as a second control organization, had only one class for each of the first six grades. Had funds been available to add instructional staff at the school, the design of the study could have been strengthened. An experimental and a control group would have been formed in Longfellow School to provide a replication of the Washington design. However, Longfellow School was included as a second self-contained organization to measure possible contamination of variables at Washington School and to add power to the statistical analyses.

The three organizations—the classes taught by the teaching teams at Washington School, the classes taught by teachers using the self-contained approach at Washington School, and pupils in self-contained classes at Longfellow—proved to be essentially equivalent in mean intelligence quotient as measured by the California Short-Form Test of Mental Maturity. The mean intelligence quotients were 107.8, 105.4, and 107.5, respectively.

THE HIERARCHICAL ARRANGEMENT

There has been much discussion of the wisdom of a hierarchical arrangement of teachers in the team framework. It is fully realized that team leadership should be assigned only to individuals who have credentials that warrant such an appointment (4). The senior author of this paper was an early advocate of the hierarchical structure (5). The position has been approved by some and severely criticized by others.

Many educators favor the hierarchy, with commensurate pay increases for the higher positions (6–14). Mahoney opposes the hierarchy and calls for co-ordinate teachers of equal rank (15). Drummond (16), Howe (17), and Weiss and Morris (18) are openly critical of the structural model. King (19) advises no higher salaries for team leaders, for he has sensed considerable teacher resistance to this arrangement (but certainly not from the leaders themselves). Another writer states:

> If there is enough additional work and responsibility for the chairman of the teaching team, perhaps that member should be paid for the additional work, but not for so-called superiority of teaching [20:120].

His remarks are extended by Ploghoft, the most outspoken critic of the hierarchical approach. Ploghoft charges that the hierarchical model "borders on professional chicanery" and continues:

> First since the Lambert plan requires a team leader and teaching members who are less competent (that is why they are paid less) than the leader, the administrator must intentionally recruit some inadequate teachers or arbitrarily classify some as less competent than the leader [21:220].

Rather than counterattack such a vulnerable statement, let us cite Stoddard, who quite deftly states the basic assumption underlying the hierarchical structure:

> Let us face it. The classroom teacher is the last practitioner in the western world to respond to the industrial revolution. In the classroom there is practically no division of labor; apart from the textbook there is small utilization of equipment. . . .
> Below the college level, all teachers are supposed to be equally replaceable parts. . . . A teacher is supposed to make progress in the profession not through promotions in rank with corresponding salary differentials, but simply by staying on the job. . . . Monetary incentives are not the full answer to any personnel problem, but to reject them as irrelevant is to doubt the basic appeal of a capitalistic society [22:156–57].

The hierarchical structure was used in setting up the primary and the intermediate teams in Washington School. The two teams were organized along the lines of the basic model used in the Wisconsin Improvement Program (23:201–2). Two experienced teachers, one of them designated team leader, were joined by two teacher interns to make up the primary team. The same pattern was used in the intermediate team. One instructional secretary was hired. She divided her time between the two teams. Experienced teachers did not teach all subjects. Rather, each taught those subjects in which he or she had special competencies or interests.

Most of the interns had a degree in a field other than education and were working for a Master's degree in elementary education. Normally they had had no school-teaching experience except for the previous summer session during which they had taught in the University Laboratory School. Each semester two new interns were integrated into the instructional program of each team. The time and the activities of the interns were divided between the two experienced teachers and involved all teaching duties and responsibilities.

The instructional cost for the experimental team was almost equal to the cost for the three corresponding teachers of self-contained classrooms. Since the team employed only two experienced teachers, the regular salary of one teacher was available for distribution. Each intern was given about a thousand dollars a semester (the total yearly cost for interns was four thousand dollars); the half-time instructional secretary received fifteen hundred dollars a year; and the team leader received a thousand dollars more than his regular salary.

Faculty members at Washington School were given the choice of staying to help try out new teaching methods or of transferring to another school in Madison. No teacher was forced to teach on a team; only strong advocates of the team or the self-contained organization were retained or employed. To counteract possible Hawthorne effects, all organizations were stimulated by university consultants and new teaching aids (teaching machines, overhead projectors, and tape recorders).

The hierarchical model seemed to work well. The fixing of responsibility seemed well received and was certainly desirable from both the administrative and the instructional points of view.

DISCIPLINE

Students preparing to be teachers have been characterized as actively concerned about whether they will be able to maintain discipline in the classroom. Although few controlled studies of discipline under team teaching have been made, several sources report subjective impressions that discipline problems were minimized under the team approach (24–34). Only one writer reported increased discipline problems; these problems appeared in the second grade, but not in the fourth and the sixth grades of that project (35).

Discipline was studied in our project. Two former public school teachers were trained to observe discipline. They were given a list of discipline infractions. The infractions were separated into five mutually exclusive categories from least serious to most serious. Inter-observer reliability was established at .74 after ten training periods.

Observations were balanced by subject area and teacher. Each team teacher was observed for three thirty-minute periods, while each teacher in a self-contained classroom was observed for four thirty-minute periods; in all, there were twelve observations for each of the teaching teams and twelve each for the lower three grades and the upper three grades of both self-contained organizations.

The results were tabulated and analyzed using the Kruskal-Wallis one-way analysis of variance by ranks (36:184–93). The results demonstrated that the particular school, with its pupils and its general attitude toward discipline, has more influence on discipline than the organizational framework. Only one difference was statistically significant: interns had significantly more disciplinary infractions than experienced teachers on the team. This finding partially verified a concurrent finding based on the Flanders interaction analysis (37), namely, that the team had a significantly larger number of discipline problems mainly because of the large incidence of such infractions when interns were teaching.

RECOMMENDATIONS

It would appear that the intern program is providing teachers from a source that is otherwise difficult to tap. On a teaching team the interns are afforded more than one teacher-model to consider selectively and to imitate. Differences between the inexperienced interns and the experienced certified teachers suggest that a team made up of four experienced teachers might be more desirable. The instructional secretary would be kept on in her present status. This arrangement might mean a prohibitive increase in the cost of instruction, however.

A reasonable compromise might be to replace one intern with an experienced teacher, to form a team composed of three experienced teachers, one intern, and a half-time instructional secretary. Under this arrangement the increase in cost would be appreciably less than under an arrangement that called for a team of four experienced teachers.

A second recommendation for school systems that have team projects: Train a pool of teachers of self-contained classrooms in team techniques, possibly as an in-service function, so that replacements for teams would be available as the need arose. Collegiate institutions are not yet teaching team-teaching techniques to students in training.

During the two years of the experiment, certain difficulties arose in preserving stability in the intermediate team (38). One of the experienced teachers left the team during the first year because of pregnancy. After she left, communication problems arose among the remaining teachers. The second year found an entirely new team at the intermediate level. The team leader and the experienced teacher came on the team while their ideas of team teaching were still being developed.

The resulting unstable team organization differed in many respects from the stable primary team with its continuing teachers. While the primary team outachieved its self-contained counterparts, the intermediate team lagged in achievement. In classroom interaction, silence or confusion was particularly evident in the classes of the intermediate team. The result was that appreciably less time was spent on subject matter.

The obvious difference between the two teams in time spent, or emphasis, on content can be interpreted either negatively or positively from the standpoint of the unstable intermediate team. Negatively, it could be said that the lack of team stability, coordination, and organization drastically reduced class time that should have been spent on course content. Positively, it could be said that the unstable teaching team was able to achieve about as much as the teachers of the self-contained grades, even though the team spent less than two-thirds as much time on content.

It is possible, however, that a stable intermediate team would have had less confusion and could have devoted more time to content, with the result that pupil achievement would have been greater. Had a pool of teachers familiar with team techniques and concepts been available, replacements from the pool might have prevented the discontinuity that resulted.

A final recommendation: Research on organizational structure is needed: schools introducing team teaching, nongrading, or other innovations have an obligation to use controlled techniques to assess the value of the innovation to the pupils. Failure to evaluate carefully may result in the adoption of procedures that are ineffective or detrimental.

REFERENCES

1. The research reported here was supported by the Cooperative Research Program of the Office of Education, U.S. Department of Health, Education, and Welfare.

2. P. Lambert, W. Wiersma, W. L. Goodwin, and R. F. Roberts. *Classroom Interaction, Pupil Achievement and Adjustment in Team Teaching as Compared with the Self-contained Classroom.* Cooperative Research Project No. 1391. Madison, Wisconsin: University of Wisconsin, 1964.

3. L. J. Stiles. "Individual and Team Teaching," *Wisconsin Journal of Education*, XCII (June, 1960), 7–10+.

4. V. M. Cashen. "Using Specialists as a Team," *Educational Leadership*, XIX (November, 1961), 115–17.

5. P. Lambert. "Team Teaching for the Elementary School," *Educational Leadership*, XVIII (November, 1960), 85–88+.

6. R. H. Anderson, E. A. Hagstrom, and W. A. Robinson, "Team Teaching in an Elementary School," *School Review*, LXVIII (Spring, 1960), 71–84.

7. H. A. Becker. "Team Teaching," *Instructor*, LXXI (June, 1962), 43–45.

8. R. N. Bush. "The Team Teaching Bandwagon," *California Journal of Secondary Education*, XXXV (March, 1960), 207–8.

9. A. S. Fischler. "The Use of Team Teaching in the Elementary School," *School Science and Mathematics*, LXII (April, 1962), 281–88.

10. R. E. Gross. "Emerging Horizons for the Social Studies," *Social Education*, XXIV (January, 1960), 21–24.

11. P. Lambert and N. J. Boyan. "Team Teaching—Is Your School Ready for It?" *Michigan Journal of Secondary Education*, II (Spring, 1961), 3.

12. F. C. Mayer and J. H. Wooldridge. "Preparing for Team Teaching at West Clermont," *American School Board Journal*, CXLV (July, 1962), 10.

13. N. C. Polos. "The Teaching Team in Action," *Journal of Secondary Education*, XXXVI (November, 1961), 415–19.

14. J. L. Trump. "A Look Ahead in Secondary Education," *Bulletin of the National Association of Secondary-School Principals*, XLII (January, 1958), 5–15.

15. W. M. Mahoney. "Try Co-ordinate Teaching," *American School Board Journal*, CXXXIX (November, 1959), 13–14.

16. H. D. Drummond. "Team Teaching: An Assessment," *Educational Leadership*, XIX (December, 1961), 160–65.

17. H. Howe. "The Curriculum, the Team, and the School: An Examination of Relationships," *Journal of Secondary Education*, XXXVII (October, 1962), 353–61.

18. T. M. Weiss and M. S. Morris. "A Critique of the 'Team Approach,' " *Educational Forum*, XXIV (January, 1960), 207–8.

19. A. R. King, Jr. "Planning for Team Teaching: The Human Considerations," *Journal of Secondary Education*, XXXVII (October, 1962), 363–67.

20. A. K. Tink. A summary of the presentation made by A. K. Tink at the Forty-fifth Annual Convention of the National Association of Secondary-School Principals at Cobo Hall, Detroit, Michigan, February, 1961, as reported in the *Bulletin of the National Association of Secondary-School Principals*, XLV (April, 1961), 119–20.

21. M. E. Ploghoft. "Another Look at Team Teaching," *Clearing House*, XXXVI (December, 1961), 219–21.

22. G. D. Stoddard. *Education 2000 A.D.*, pp. 141–64. Edited by C. W. Hunnicutt. Syracuse, New York: Syracuse University Press, 1956.

23. R. H. Anderson. "The Organization and Administration of Team Teaching." In J. T. Shaplin and H. F. Olds, Jr. (editors), *Team Teaching*. New York: Harper and Row, 1964.

24. L. L. Bloomenshine. "Team Teaching in San Diego—the First Year," *Bulletin of the National Association of Secondary-School Principals*, XLIV (January, 1960), 181–96.

25. G. G. Bruntz. "The Team Approach to Social Science Teaching," *High School Journal*, XLIII (April, 1960), 370–74.

26. B. Giltinian. "We Solved the Problem of Size," *English Journal*, LII (February, 1963), 89–93.

27. S. R. Jonsson. "Team Teaching? Enthusiasm Is High," *New York State Education*, L (November, 1962), 14–16.

28. J. O. Loretan. "Team Teaching: Plus and Minus in New York City's Junior High Schools," *Bulletin of the National Association of Secondary-School Principals*, XLVI (January, 1962), 135–40.

29. R. Marsh. "Team Teaching—New Concept?" *Clearing House*, XXXV (April, 1961), 496–99.

30. D. O. Montague. "Team Teaching in Berkeley's Burbank Junior High School," *Journal of Secondary Education*, XXXVI (November, 1961), 420–22.

31. M. F. Noall and L. Jensen. "Team Teaching at Roosevelt Junior High School, Duchesne County, Utah," *Bulletin of the National Association of Secondary-School Principals*, XLIV (January, 1960), 156–63.

32. R. Sweet and P. Dunn-Rankin. "An Experiment in Team Teaching Seventh-Grade Arithmetic," *School Science and Mathematics*, LXII (May, 1962), 341–44.

33. H. A. Taylor. "Claremont Graduate School Program for Team Teaching," *High School Journal*, XLIII (February, 1960), 277–82.

34. J. O. Ward. "Another Plan for Co-ordinate Teaching," *American School Board Journal*, CXL (February, 1960), 10.

35. A. S. Adams. "Operation Co-teaching, Dateline: Oceano, California," *Elementary School Journal*, LXII (January, 1962), 203–12.

36. S. Siegel. *Nonparametric Statistics for the Behavioral Sciences*. New York: McGraw-Hill, 1956.

37. N. A. Flanders. *Interaction Analysis in the Classroom*. Minneapolis, Minnesota: College of Education, University of Minnesota, 1960.

38. P. Lambert and W. L. Goodwin. "Interaction Variations in an Unstable Team Organization." Paper read at the meeting of the American Educational Research Association, Chicago, February, 1964.

Selected Bibliography

Team Teaching: The Elementary School

Adams, Andrew S. "Operation Co-Teaching: Dateline: Oceano, California." *Elementary School Journal* 62:203–212, January 1962.
Reports team teaching with fourth and sixth grades. Began as an alternative to double sessions and ended as a permanent practice. Found greater achievement, personality adjustment, and teacher response than in self-contained classroom.

Anderson, Robert H. "School-University Cooperation and the Lexington Project." *Journal of Educational Sociology* 34:882–86, April 1961.
Describes elementary school team teaching project in Lexington, Mass. The public school and Harvard University joined forces and author describes opportunities and problems that arose.

Anderson, Robert H. "Team Teaching." *NEA Journal* 50:52–54, March 1961. Also in *Education Digest* 26:5–7, May 1961. Reply by Anne Hoppock in *NEA Journal* 50:47–48, April 1961. Also see *Nation's Schools* 65:62–65, May 1960.
Defines team teaching and describes five programs: Franklin School in Lexington, Massachusetts; Norwalk Plan in Norwalk, Connecticut; University of Wisconsin Plan in Madison, Wisconsin; Jefferson County Plan in Colorado; and Evanston Plan in Illinois. Cites results, problems, and theoretical advantages of team teaching.

Bach, Frank and Murphy, Donald. *Team Teaching on the Elementary Level.* 16mm color film, Hollywood, California, Bailey Films, Inc., 6509 De Longpre Avenue. Also see *Library Journal* 89:320, January 15, 1964.
Explains purpose and methodology of elementary school team teaching. Traces motivations and plans for beginning it in Cashmere, Washington.

Bahner, John M. "Team Teaching in the Elementary School." *Education* 85:337–341, February 1965.
Advocates team teaching. Says the pattern combines all the advantages of the self-contained classroom and departmentalization.

Bair, Medill and Woodward, Richard. *Team Teaching in Action.* Boston: Houghton Mifflin, 1964.
Gives team teaching principles, characteristics, facilities, methods, and evaluation. Describes details of Lexington (Massachusetts) Project for third and fourth year pupils in Franklin and Estabrook Schools. Stresses teachers must exhibit a firm commitment to team teaching in order to have a successful program.

Beggs, David W. *Team Teaching: Bold New Adventure* (Edited by David W. Beggs, III) Indianapolis, Indiana: Unified College Press, Inc., 3600 Washington Blvd., 1964.
Collected essays on aspects of team teaching by twelve advocates from team supervisory, administrative, and teaching roles. Attempts to show how it fits into elementary, junior, and senior high schools.

Beggs, David W. and Buffie, Edward G. (Editors). *Independent Study.* Indiana University Press, 1965. pp. 51–82.
Describes independent study, team teaching facilities, and instructional materials for the elementary school.

Boutwell, W. D. "What's Happening in Education? What Is Team Teaching?" *PTA Magazine* 57:16–25, May 1963.
Gives the rationale behind team teaching as a new approach in elementary education. Gives illustrations from several school systems.

Bradley, P. A. "Individualized Instruction Through Cooperative Teaching and a Programmed Text." *National Elementary Principal* 43:46–49, May 1964.
Found team teaching in a large class, combined with individual study with a programmed text, did not result in significant differences.

Buechner, Alan C. "Team Teaching in Elementary Music Education." *Music Educators Journal* 50:31–55, November-December, 1963.
States team teaching offers tremendous possibilities for relating music to other fields of knowledge in a meaningful way.

Cunningham, Luvern L. "Keys to Team Teaching." *Overview* 2:54–55, October 1960. Also see *Elementary School Journal* 62:119, December 1961.
Analyzes some of the considerations in effective team teaching. Emphasizes the importance of team members.

Cunningham, Luvern L. "Team Teaching: Where Do We Stand?" *Administrator's Notebook* 8:1–4, April 1960.
Discusses reorganization of staff into teams. Describes four types: Team Leader; Associate; Master-Teacher–Beginning-Teacher; and Coordinate Team.

Cunningham, Luvern L. "Viewing Change in School Organizations." *Administrator's Notebook II:* September 1962. Also see *Administrator's Notebook II:* April 1960.
Entire issue is devoted to change in traditional school organization.

Darling, W. "Team Teaching: Wisconsin Improvement Program." *NEA Journal* 54:24–25, May 1965.
Points out difference between team teaching and practices that are mistaken for it. Gives four criteria and illustrates how each of these is met in the Wisconsin Improvement Program.

Dean, Ray B. "Team Teaching in the Elementary Schools." *American School Board Journal* 145:5–6, December 1962.
Opposes self-contained classroom. Describes team teaching plan in effect for 32 years in Sacramento, California.

Drummond, Harold. "Team Teaching: An Assessment." *Educational Leadership* 19:160–165, December 1961. Also in *Education Digest* 27:5–8, February 1962.
Gives examples of five meanings of the term "team teaching." Notes that the cost of team teaching personnel need not be higher than costs of a self-contained classroom even if differential salary scales are used for team members.

Fink, D. R., Jr. "Selection and Training of Teachers for Teams." *National Elementary Principal* 44:54–59, January 1965.
Urges careful analysis of requirements for selecting various members of teaching teams. Recommends training for team teaching.

Fierster, L. *A Study of Organizational Forms of Team Teaching in the Public Elementary Schools in the United States.* Doctoral Dissertation, Teachers College, Columbia University, 1964. Also in *Dissertation Abstracts* 25:225.

Located 49 schools in U.S. emphasizing some form of team teaching. Defines term and points out two categories: hierarchical and peer cooperative.

Fischler, Abraham S. "The Use of Team Teaching in the Elementary School." *School Science and Mathematics* 62:281–288, April 1962. Also see *Science Education* 46:406–415, December 1962.

Describes team teaching as a way of organizing for change. Gives rationale for team planning. Cites curriculum development involved, problems to be resolved, and staffing considerations.

Ford Foundation. *Time, Talent, and Teachers.* New York: the Foundations, 1960.

Briefly describes flexible school organization, team teaching, electronics, and staff utilization projects in elementary and secondary schools. Included are schools in Lexington and Newton, Massachusetts and in Evanston, Illinois.

"Four in One." *Newsweek* 62:100, November 25, 1963.

Gives an account of large classroom accommodating four teachers and students at Dilworth Elementary School in San Jose, California.

Gilbert, Edward H. "A Design for School Improvement." *Administrator's Notebook* 7:1–4, May 1959.

Describes various patterns of school organization being tried out under the School Improvement Program in the Midwest. Includes brief description of team teaching at fifth and sixth grade level at Price Elementary School, Fort Wayne, Indiana.

Gilberts, Robert D. *The Interpersonal Characteristics of Teaching Teams.* Doctoral Dissertation, University of Wisconsin, 1961. Also in *Dissertation Abstracts* 22:1882.

Found compatibility among members of teaching teams did not affect the professional quality of work in the classroom but did relate to informal relationship outside class. Expressions of teacher-satisfaction did not relate to compatibility.

Goodlad, John I. and Anderson, Robert H. *The Nongraded Elementary.* (Revised Edition). New York: Harcourt, Brace and World, Inc., 1963. pp. 67–68, 97–99, 129–130, 211, 223.

Describes development of the nongraded elementary school. Includes material on team teaching.

Gross, Calvin. "Team Teaching in Pittsburgh." *Education Digest* 28:12–14, November 1963.

Gives an account of a 1960 team teaching experiment in ten Pittsburgh schools in kindergarten through high school. Describes role of team members.

Hamilton, Andrew. "Is Team Teaching for Your Child?" *PTA Magazine* 58:4–6, May 1964. Also in *Reader's Digest*, June 1964.

Discusses ways of organizing staff, curriculum, space, and equipment. Describes team teaching in Lexington, Massachusetts; Evanston, Illinois; Claremont, California; etc.

Hayes, Charles. "Team Teaching in Culturally Deprived Areas." *National Elementary Principal* 44:60–65, January 1965.
A team mother aide and male teachers are features of a project in Pittsburgh. A mental health team and an adult evening school help bring the home and school closer together and closer to the students' needs.

Heathers, Glen. "Field Research on Elementary School Organization and Instruction." *Journal of Educational Sociology* 34:338–343, April 1961.
Discusses projects established to test new plans for organizing and conducting instruction in the elementary school. Includes specialist teaching, teaching teams, departmentalization, ability grouping, cross-graded grouping, etc.

Heathers, Glen. "Research on Implementing and Evaluating Cooperative Teaching." *National Elementary Principal* 44:27–33, January 1965.
Gives procedures for researching cooperative teaching and evaluating results. Describes methods of introducing the program into a school. Cites typical weaknesses of studies. Specific and helpful article.

Hoffa, H., and Fawcett, T. "Team Teaching and Art Teaching." *School Arts* 62:18–20, February 1963.
Recommends art educators view team teaching as something to be undertaken cautiously. Includes description of Lexington's team plan.

Jackson, Joseph. "Analysis of a Team Teaching and of a Self-Contained Homeroom Experiment in Grades Five and Six." *Journal of Experimental Education* 32:317–322, Summer 1964.
Found a team of teachers can adjust the work much more to the needs of a student than an individual teacher can. Experiment carried on in Dearborn, Michigan.

Jaffa, N. Newbert and Brandt, Richard. "An Approach to the Problems of a Downtown School." *National Elementary School Principal* 44:25–28, November 1964.
Account of attempts of a Baltimore elementary school faculty to increase the achievement of all the pupils through nongraded organization, team teaching, and in-service education.

Keliher, Alice V. "Team Teaching." *High Points* 44:65–68, May 1962.
Gives reasons for viewing large classes taught by a team skeptically at the elementary school level.

Keppel, Francis and Perry, Paul A. "School and University: Partners in Progress." *Phi Delta Kappan* 42:174–180, January 1961.
Description of the Franklin Elementary School Project in Lexington, Massachusetts.

Lalaime, Arthur. "Elementary Schools Designed for Team Teaching." *Audio-Visual Instruction* 7:540–541, October 1962.
Briefly describes team teaching facilities at Naramahe Elementary School at Norwalk, Connecticut and Flowing Wells Elementary School at Tucson, Arizona.

McMahon, Eleanor. "Principals' View on Team Teaching." *National Elementary Principal* 44:34–43, January 1965.
On basis of interviews with ten elementary principals, author determined their experiences with team teaching were beneficial to student learning, teacher development, and administrative efficiency.

Morlan, John. "Think Twice About Team Teaching." *Instructor* 73:65, 72, September 1963.
Gives six factors that should be examined prior to adopting a team teaching program.

Morlan, John. "The Team Approach to Large-Group Instruction." *Audiovisual Instruction* 9:520–523, October 1964.
Gives guidelines for team-teaching and new approaches which are effective in implementing it.

Morse, Arthur D. (producer). "The Influential American." *CBS News.* New York: 485 Madison Avenue. Transcript available.
TV program presented November 13, 1960 describes team teaching at Franklin School in Lexington, Massachusetts.

National Education Association, Department of Elementary School Principals. "Team Teaching." *Elementary School Organization: Purposes, Patterns, Perspectives.* Yearbook. Washington, D.C.: the Department, 1961. pp. 78–92, 115–125.
Discussion of school organization including team teaching. Gives a historical description of graded and nongraded schools.

National Education Association. Project on Instruction Report. *Planning and Organizing for Teaching.* Washington, D.C.: the Association, 1963. p. 190.
Analyzes vertical school organization (graded, nongraded, and multigraded school organization) and horizontal organization (team teaching, self-contained classroom, departmentalization, etc.).

National Education Association. *Project on Instruction: Schools for the Sixties.* New York: McGraw-Hill Book Co., 1963. pp. 71–98.
Overview volume of publications of Project on Instruction. Describes grading, nongrading, team teaching, etc.

"Planning and Operating the Middle School." *Overview* 4:52–55, March 1963.
Combined upper elementary grades (5–6) with lower secondary grades (7–9) at Bedford School in Mount Kisco, N.Y. Subject matter ungraded as rapidly as possible. Organized around teaching teams.

"Plan Takes Lockstep and Buries It in Space." *Nation's Schools* 72:86–89, October 1963.
Reports ungrading and team teaching in the Josiah Haynes Elementary School, Sudbury, Massachusetts. School was planned and built for ungrading and team teaching.

Profiles of Significant Schools: Heathcote Elementary School, Scarsdale, N. Y. New York: Educational Facilities Laboratories, Inc., 1960.
Describes physical plant. Plan implements nongrading and team teaching.

Reasoner, Robert W., and Wall, Harvey R. "Developing Staff Interaction in Team Teaching." *National Elementary Principal* 44:84–86, January 1965.
Points out the principal is vital to team teaching success through a careful selection of teachers, assistance in planning and evaluating, and leadership in stimulating creative flexibility.

Roberts, G. M. *Case Studies of Two Nongraded Elementary School Programs.* Doctoral Dissertation, University of Tennessee, 1964. Also in *Dissertation Abstracts* 25:2830.
Recommends nongrading and team teaching on the basis of a study of reading performance.

Ross, Charles Lee. *An Experiment in the Reorganization of Instruction in the First Grade*. Doctoral Dissertation, University of Tennessee, 1964. Also in *Dissertation Abstracts* 24:651.
Evaluated Morristown team teaching plan. Two groups compared: a traditional group which attended first grade on a full-day basis with one teacher and an experimental group which attended on a half-day basis with two teachers. Both groups generally achieved equally well except in arithmetic computation.

Shaplin, Judson T. "Team Teaching." *Saturday Review* 44:54–55, 70, May 20, 1961.
Recommends team teaching as one way to improve the quality of instruction in the self-contained classroom. Gives the direction of team teaching.

Shaplin, Judson T. and Olds, Henry F., Jr. (editors). *Team Teaching*. New York: Harper and Row, 1964.
Advocates of team teaching discuss organization, administration, research, and public relations.

Slobodian, J. J. "Team Teaching Experiment Proves to Be Effective." *Ohio Schools* 42:27, February 1964.
Describes first grade team teaching experiment in three classrooms in North Lima Elementary School. Teachers are enthusiastic about the arrangement and they report the students responded well in reading, and were above the median on standardized tests.

Taylor, H. and Olson, K. "Team Teaching with Trainable Mentally Retarded Children." *Exceptional Children* 30:304–309, March 1964.
Reports inaugurating a team teaching program at Slover Special School in Fontana, California. Adapted recommendations for organizing team teaching in an elementary school to this special school.

"Toward Improved School Organization: Further Look at Horizontal Structure." *National Elementary Principal* 41:93–115, December 1961.
Gives rationale, organization, administration, and professional reactions to team teaching, departmentalization, self-contained classroom, etc.

Chapter 10

Team Teaching: Junior and Senior High School

Team Teaching in the Secondary School: A Step in the Right Direction?

William P. Colbert

It seems only natural for educators in our society, that is often credited with having the best of everything for so many of its citizens, to want the best educational program for all children. And although there are a number of differing views as to what is the best educational program, there are a number of ingredients or elements that enjoy wide acceptance. We are happy to note, for example, that the development of responsible citizenship is still considered to be at the heart of the matter. We are pleased, also, to see that the individual—his learning difficulties and potential—is a major interest of educators, and this emphasis is more on the action level than ever before. Then, too, there is considerable interest in putting learning more in the hands of the learner. Or, as Harold Davis puts it in a selection in this chapter describing the team teaching efforts of 27 school districts in the Greater Cleveland Area, "helping students develop responsibility for their own learning." "This," says Davis, "is the ultimate educational objective of every teaching team."

Many other educators who are excited about team teaching as an organizational scheme for American schools feel that this plan has tremendous potential for helping us provide the best possible education for our children. Is this really so? The answer of course depends on many

Written especially for this book. Dr. William P. Colbert is an Assistant Professor of Education, University of North Carolina, Greensboro.

things—a number of which curriculum workers cannot even anticipate in the planning stages of a program. Perhaps the best we can do in this case is to learn by sharing the experiences others have had.

The purpose of this chapter, then, is to offer the reader some glimpses of the hopes and problems others have experienced and some means they have used for effecting an organizational change. And although the reports deal entirely with the secondary school most of the objectives, problems and questions these writers treat are basic to any level. Melvin Heller and Elizabeth Belford, for example, consider the kinds of relationships teachers must develop to work successfully in a team-type organization and discuss some basic kinds of teaching techniques in large and small group instruction.

Facilities are treated, in detail, by Carl Peterson who provides considerable factual data on the Easton Area High School in Easton, Pennsylvania. Many readers will no doubt be surprised to learn that this school was built at a cost somewhat below the average for the year 1965. The problems of flexible scheduling and the larger purposes of scheduling are dealt with by J. Lloyd Trump who has devoted considerable thought and study to this area in recent years. His contribution in this chapter is comprehensive and singularly outstanding. Herbert Klausmeier and William Wiersma report on a study dealing with team teaching and achievement carried out in five junior high schools at Racine, Wisconsin. These researchers conclude in favor of team teaching and suggest some conditions which they see as musts for the team arrangement.

Planning for Team Teaching

Harold S. Davis

A successful team teaching program depends more on people than upon the purse, more on faculties than upon facilities. One may find dormant programs in schools "designed for team teaching" and dynamic programs in archaic buildings.

Once the mental walls that separate teachers have been crumbled, the physical barriers are easily removed. Administrative leadership and careful planning are the keys to success.

LOOKING FORWARD

In Greater Cleveland, 27 forward-looking school systems, affiliated with the Educational Research Council, are proving that sound educational ideas may be rapidly implemented through a program of in-service education. In 1962, nine superintendents volunteered to study innovations in the field of staff utilization. This work-study group met monthly with consultants provided by the E.R.C.

As a result of their recommendation to the other 18 superintendents, in September, 1963, the "Greater Cleveland Staff Utilization Project" was launched. The first assignment given the project director was to familiarize principals and teachers with team teaching techniques. Recognizing that effective change in curriculum and methodology comes about through growth in understanding not through duress, it was decided that all teams would be formed on a voluntary basis. Teachers would be encouraged to work together as equals. Rigid, hierarchical structures were to be avoided.

IN-SERVICE EDUCATION

A series of individual conferences were held with all superintendents to obtain suggestions for a plan of action. These conferences were then followed by workshops for principals and curriculum directors. Questions were answered about team teaching, flexible scheduling, pupil-teacher

Reprinted from *Education* 85:333–336, February 1965, by permission of the publisher and the author. Copyright, 1965, by The Bobbs-Merrill Company, Inc., Indianapolis, Indiana. Dr. Harold S. Davis is Director, Educational Research Council of Greater Cleveland, Cleveland, Ohio.

ratio, facilities for large-group instruction, small-group discussion and independent study. In follow-up meetings, principals had the opportunity to talk with Dr. J. Lloyd Trump about how team teaching had been implemented in other parts of the United States.

Several principals, recognizing the value of introducing team teaching in their buildings, arranged faculty meetings designed to study objectively the school's educational program. When teachers became aware of weaknesses in traditional methods, they were ready to consider innovation. Many faculty groups expressed a desire to read about staff utilization experiments, to discuss methodology, and to visit teaching teams.

Pamphlets developed at the Educational Research Council were distributed to hundreds of schools. One pamphlet, entitled "Why Team Teach?" provided a rationale for the method. Another, "Planning a Team Teaching Program," gave practical suggestions for conducting large-group instruction, small-group discussion and independent study. A comprehensive "Team Teaching Bibliography" was compiled and hundreds of books, pamphlets, and articles pertaining to team teaching were made available to those wishing more information.

As team projects were developed in various schools, they were described in a pamphlet entitled "A Survey of Team Teaching in Educational Research Council Schools" and in "A Supplement" to the original survey. These contained names, locations, and telephone numbers of administrators and participants. Teachers were encouraged to visit, to observe, to question and, of course, to make notes of things that they liked.

DEVELOPING THE PROGRAM

When teachers in a building voluntarily decide to develop a team approach, administrators should join them in cooperative, democratic planning. Through active participation, administrators help to build harmonious interpersonal relationships so essential to the operation of a successful school.

The principal must be careful, however, to avoid dominating planning sessions. When the social climate is characterized by tension or submission, teachers are unlikely to have sufficient motivation to contribute constructively. Where administrators and teachers operate in partnership, the level of instruction and morale is usually high.

CURRICULUM IMPLICATIONS

A basic way to plan a unit of work for team teaching is to study the curriculum content and answer three questions:

(1) What can students learn best from explanations by others?

(2) What can students learn by interaction between themselves and their teachers?

(3) What can students learn by themselves?

The answer to the first question suggests large-group instruction; to the second, small-group discussion; and to the third, independent study.

Large-group instruction should be used to provide students with the best possible teaching the school can muster for the given phase of the subject. Guest speakers, films, tape recordings and television should be utilized when those resources can supplement the teacher's presentation or when they can do the job better than the teacher. Grouping 50 or more students for appropriate instructional purposes conserves the time and energy of teachers, fosters more efficient use of building space, and makes the introduction of technical aids economically feasible.

Small-group discussion is essential if students are to be closely involved in the free exchange of ideas. Evidence in the field of group dynamics has shown such interaction cannot effectively take place within the standard class of 25–30 students. In fact, experience in hundreds of schools has indicated the maximum size for small-group discussion is 15.

Discussion in small groups improves interpersonal relations among students, promotes problem solving and develops more effective communication skills. When teachers listen to such groups, they are able to analyze students' reactions to course content and assess their knowledge of it. They can observe the ability of each individual to handle data and to solve problems.

Independent study should place an emphasis on creative, meaningful research that will stretch and strengthen the minds of students. It should mean study in a learning center where reference books are readily available, a place where the teacher can provide direction when needed. Students are expected to gradually grow in self-correction, self-analysis, and self-direction. In fact, the ultimate educational objective of every teaching team is to help students develop responsibility for their own learning.

ADMINISTRATIVE IMPLICATIONS

After the inception of a team teaching program, administrators should provide participants with substantial and continuing assistance. Excessive responsibility thrust suddenly upon the team members could lead to frustration or antagonism. The administrator should help team members with problems of scheduling, room arrangement, provision of needed equipment, and intrastaff relations. Non-participants are sometimes prone to be jealous or resentful if they are not kept fully informed. On the other hand, close cooperation between all members of the faculty may lead to rapid dissemination of new techniques and to a comprehensive school improvement program.

Although team teaching ultimately conserves time and energy, extra effort must be expended in planning and preparation. The development of a team teaching program should not be rushed. After inception, a common planning period for team members must be provided. As initial problems are resolved and new procedures developed, pressures gradually diminish. To alleviate the press of time, clerical assistance should be provided to free teachers from non-professional tasks.

BUILDING FACILITIES AND EQUIPMENT

Although some buildings severely handicap the development of teams, new uses for old facilities may often be found. For large-group instruction, many teams in Greater Cleveland use an auditorium, a little theater, a multipurpose room, a cafeteria, band room, choral room, study hall, or school lobby. Some, finding no suitable space, have removed walls between rooms. A few fortunate teams are in flexible buildings which contain either modern lecture halls or classrooms separated by folding walls.

Each building contemplating a team approach should be equipped with at least one overhead projector and a thermographic or diazo copier for making transparencies. This modern teaching tool has become indispensable for large-group instruction. It is further recommended that the projector be placed in the large-group area and left there, rather than checking it in and out of an audiovisual room. When it is easily accessible, it is more likely to be used.

Because the overhead projector was relatively new to many teachers, a pamphlet entitled "Illuminate Your Lecture" was prepared and distributed to over 300 Educational Research Council schools. This pamphlet explains how to make transparencies and how to use them effectively in large-group instruction.

Space and equipment for small-group discussion poses no problem. Classrooms, library conference rooms, and cafeterias have all proven excellent. The only requirement is that students be able to engage in face-to-face discussion. Although it is advantageous to work with only one small group at a time, many teachers have found they can easily supervise two groups within the same or adjoining rooms. This, of course, depends upon the rapport established between teacher and pupils.

Space for independent study is usually difficult to locate. Libraries in secondary schools are often inadequate and in elementary schools are frequently non-existent. In such schools, teams have improvised by using some classrooms part time for independent study while others are used for small-group discussion. The addition of reference shelves, book trucks, tapes and records, earphones, filmstrip viewers, and other media make such a plan feasible.

Hopefully, educators look forward to the day when the instructional materials center will be the educational hub of every school plant.

CONCLUSION

Operational problems may be minimized through careful and continuous planning but, as in any new program, smooth operation cannot be expected from the beginning. The only way to avoid errors is through experience, and no one has ever found a way to gain experience without making errors.

In Greater Cleveland, progress in using efficient staff utilization techniques has not been uniform nor would we expect it to be. However, step by step, modern methods of instruction are being introduced and an exchange of ideas is taking place between those planning new programs and those who already have obtained practical experience.

Designing Your New Building to Incorporate Team Teaching

Carl H. Peterson

In almost all the numerous school districts now planning a newer, larger, and more up-to-date high school, there runs the thread of a common problem: how to incorporate all the facilities needed to inaugurate an effective team teaching program, one that will allow alert local administrators and teachers to fully implement the exciting educational concepts this program makes possible, without risking taxpayer ire by including items which the local economy league can classify as unnecessary expenditures.

This article, written on the basis of three years' successful experience with team teaching in a new high school designed with this concept in mind, is presented with a view toward clarifying the problem of just what are and what are not the building facilities needed for team teaching.

ELABORATE FACILITIES NOT REQUIRED

The effectiveness of a team teaching program is in no way directly proportional to the elaborateness of the facilities. This should come as good news to necessarily cost-conscious school board members, since nothing could be closer to the truth.

Granted, a few school systems have built edifices to team teaching which would not appear overly unassuming were they to be judged on standards of Pentagonal space requirements. This is not to say that these systems do not have functional team teaching programs. The point, however, is that *sometimes* team teaching programs don't work out just the way they were planned. Too many fixed team teaching facilities such as elaborately tiered lecture rooms can become sources of acute embarrassment in later years to school planners who find that these expensive arrangements lie unused most of the day due to reasons ranging from scheduling difficulties to administrative turnover to plain teacher resistance.

Reprinted from *American School Board Journal* 148:61–64, November 1965, by permission of the publisher and the author. Carl H. Peterson is Director of Secondary Education, Norwalk, Connecticut, and was formerly Principal of Easton Area High School, Easton, Pennsylvania.

EMPLOY FLEXIBLE RATHER THAN FIXED
FACILITIES WHEN POSSIBLE

Secondary education today remains fixed in the grip of rapid change, and it seems to those who bother to look ahead that this "pattern of flux" will remain constant in the years immediately ahead. It appears logical that what is particularly desirable now are as many *flexible* rather than fixed building facilities as possible, installed with the idea of incorporating future change. Of a certainty these include those having to do with the team teaching.

The Easton Area High School team teaching program has been described in two prior articles in [the *American School Board Journal*]. Judging from the requests we receive for our brochure on team teaching, the program is well-known throughout the nation. Yet, if we wanted to dispense with our team program tomorrow and return to completely traditional teaching, we could easily do so. This is because members of the Easton Area Joint School Board; our Superintendent of Schools, Edward Tracy; and our Architects-Engineers, Buchart Associates of Lancaster, Pa., had the foresight to provide *built-in-flexibility* when they designed our 2,000 pupil senior high school.

MOVABLE CLASSROOM WALLS

For example, [the walls of] one half of our regular classrooms are [soundproof, wooden partitions] which can be removed entirely or moved in modular units of 460 sq. ft. Thus, by moving two classroom walls over the required number of feet, we are able, for example, to construct a large group lecture room capable of holding 100 students, and two seminar rooms which we can use in a variety of ways: for small-group and individualized instruction, teacher workrooms, resource materials, etc.

The advantages of being able to take down a wall without the accompanying sound of falling plaster cannot, we feel, be overemphasized. As our school system continues to grow in enrollment, it will be necessary at some future date to construct additions to our present high school plant. Thus, we may wish to alter the present interior structure of our main building, as so often happens in any building addition or remodeling.

We anticipate no difficulty in doing this as our building is so constructed that although the paneled walls dividing each classroom combine solidity with the look of permanence, we will be able to create extra large "lecture-laboratories," a series of intimate small group instruction or teacher workrooms, and other modular space units, at will.

We recommend that school planners regard interior walls as part of a building's *equipment*, dividers that can be moved at will, rather than as fixed, immovable parts of the structure itself.

AVAILABILITY OF TEAM TEACHING INSTRUCTIONAL FACILITIES

There are numerous variations of effective team teaching programs in operation, and each board and its architect will have to determine the building layout optimally suited to *their* program.

At Easton, our high school operates on the school-within-a-school plan. Three grade level principals supervise their own "schools" of approximately 700 each in grades 10, 11, and 12, in separate wings of the building. Although the entire program is coordinated by a head principal, each of these "schools" is as autonomous as it can possibly be made.

Thus, we have provided team teaching instructional facilities in each of our three grade level wings. Each wing contains a large group instruction room available to the teachers of that grade, plus two small group or seminar rooms used for individual and small-group instruction and teacher workrooms. Each grade level wing also has its own audio-visual aids and resources materials room.

The pertinent factors involved here are that these rooms are instantly available to our teachers when they need to use them and that they are conveniently located for *maximum use*.

A number of team teaching programs are organized on a departmental basis. In these arrangements, team teaching instructional and resource areas should be grouped near a "departmental area," although a large group lecture room or "hall" will in all likelihood be shared by members of several departments.

USE OF THE AUDITORIUM

Candid administrators will admit that one of the most expensive and little-used areas in most schools is the auditorium. This is perhaps the primary rationale behind Easton's avoidance of tiered lecture rooms designed specifically for team teaching. We already have one in our 850-capacity auditorium.

If we wish to present a large group lecture combining several of our teams, which number 100 students each, we hold it in our auditorium. This enables our team teachers to avail themselves of facilities superior to any we could afford to put into a separate lecture hall: a 50 by 30-ft. stage; built-in large screen; ample and comfortable seating; projection room; and outstanding acoustics. These facilities and more are, of course, standard features of most auditoriums. Thus, we are employing the principle of *multiple use*, a simple expedient that can make eminently practical what sometimes appear to be financially questionable building facilities.

PORTABILITY OF FURNITURE AND EQUIPMENT

We are often questioned as to the type of furniture we use in our large group lecture rooms and the extensiveness of the equipment.

Here again simplicity is the keynote. Our large group lecture rooms feature movable tablet armchairs, typical of those utilized in many colleges, with a rack beneath for students' books.

Our small-group or seminar rooms contain an oval table surrounded by 14 folding metal chairs. Each of these rooms can be utilized to greater capacity by moving in additional folding metal or tablet armchairs.

Each large group room contains a portable tripod screen or a detachable wall-mounted screen, an opaque, overhead, and 16 mm. projector, a slide projector, and, when the teachers wish to use them, a tape recorder and record player.

Some of our teacher-lecturers prefer to utilize a portable public address system, some do not. These "portable lecterns" are extremely practical and consist of a light case about the size of a tape recorder. When opened, the top becomes the remote speaker, which can be conveniently placed halfway down the room, and the bottom, the lectern which contains the main speaker and microphone. An added advantage is a 15-ft. extension cord which permits the mike to be detached from the lectern and used as a lavaliere microphone, allowing complete freedom of movement.

With this equipment and furniture, our staff is able to deliver effective lectures to groups of approximately 100 students. Note that none of the equipment or furniture considered essential to our large group lecture program is "fixed," in the sense that it cannot be removed and used in other parts of the building by other teachers, if we so desire. In effect, we have felt it necessary to purchase no particularly specialized pieces of equipment for large group lecturing beyond that found in the typical moderately well-equipped secondary school.

OTHER FEATURES DESIRABLE, PROVIDED—

This article has emphasized that buildings can be designed to house team teaching programs with relatively little, if any, extra costs involved. However, we wish to stress the point that each district must build its plant *with its own program and basic architectural features in mind.* Those schools wishing to eliminate a separate auditorium and combine it with the gymnasium or cafeteria may well find that one or two strategically located, smaller lecture halls, containing such features as a raised stage and built-in sound equipment, may serve as extremely functional and by no means economically unsound adaptations.

With closed circuit television becoming a reality in more and more school districts, some school boards consider it entirely reasonable to install fixed television receivers in each room. While admittedly this may be an impossibility at present for all school districts, certainly provisions for present or future installation of television equipment should be made for all lecture rooms in which it is planned to offer instruction to large numbers of students.

There are numerous other items of equipment particularly adaptable to team teaching programs, and many are available to school systems at reduced cost under certain provisions of the National Defense Education Act. An excellent example is a commercially-made "Teaching Center," which is simply a teacher's desk with an overhead projector mounted on one side. The teacher can project transparencies on the wall behind her while seated at the desk facing her audience. The desk also contains provisions for storing transparencies.

School board members and administrators may find it advantageous to consider installation of single units such as this, which combine the features of two or more normally separate pieces of equipment, from the point of view of both cost and convenience. It seems advisable to recognize at the outset in any school planning enterprise that it is entirely possible to purchase so many pieces of excellent mechanical equipment designed for instructional purposes as to leave little space for the student!

FACTUAL DATA ON THE EASTON PLANT

The Easton Area High School, despite the fact that it is large, extremely comprehensive, and offers facilities and services to students beyond those found in the typical secondary school, was constructed at a per pupil cost below the state average for high schools at the time it was built. Although it contains three schools within one school with four separate administrative suites staffed by a principal for each grade and a head principal, and has a separate nine-shop vocational building and swimming pool, the total per pupil cost was $2,336 and the square foot cost $17.59.

For districts interested in construction of a smaller, less complicated building incorporating team teaching, the per pupil cost would be correspondingly less.

The Easton team teaching program itself operates with a minimum of built-in aids to instruction and with no permanent rooms designed exclusively for team teaching. The advantage to us, in addition to low initial cost, is that we can install whatever additional fixed facilities and extra equipment we deem necessary, *after* our working program has proved to us that we need and should incorporate additional features.

Our school board, superintendent, and architect were sufficiently foresighted to provide the school with the two basics necessary to all team teaching programs: *adequate space and ample flexibility*. All else is superfluous until experience proves the need for change.

Schools Within A School: A Teaching Team Organization for Junior High Schools

Harris A. Taylor and Raymond F. Cook

California, because of its large number of four-year high schools, has the greatest concentration of seventh and eighth grade intermediate schools in the United States. Most of the approximately 1,200 elementary school districts in California use the two year, seventh-eighth grade form of organization. Where newly unified school districts have a reasonable choice between a seventh-eighth-ninth grade junior high school and a seventh-eighth grade intermediate school, the latter is most often chosen and is labeled "junior high school" by the school district.

The seventh-eighth grade form of organization for junior high schools is justified in the same manner as is the conventional seventh-eighth-ninth grade organization. At its earliest stage of development, the junior high school was intended to be like a lower level high school and upper elementary grades were modified accordingly. Later, the "link" concept was introduced in which the junior high school was conceived as providing a transition from elementary school to senior high school. In other words, the purpose was to get pre-adolescent and early adolescent students ready for the high school. Later, the idea that the junior high school should be viewed as a distinct and separate organization geared specifically to the special needs of junior high school students was introduced. A few school districts maintained the view that the junior high school, particularly the seventh-eighth grade school, should be an extension of the elementary school, housing pupils from kindergarten through grade eight.

Frequently, the decision to adopt an organizational scheme for schools is dictated by housing problems and later justified educationally by the district. Aside from this fact, the educational justification for junior high schools is generally made according to the amount of teacher control and guidance the planners envisage for students and, conversely, the amount of student self-direction and independent action they desire. Many times this choice is presented in terms of a continuum with pupil guidance and control at one end and content instruction in depth at the other. The

Reprinted from *High School Journal* 48:289-295, January 1965, by permission of the University of North Carolina Press, Chapel Hill, North Carolina, and the authors. Harris A. Taylor and Raymond F. Cook are both with the Rowland Elementary School District, Pomona, California.

amount of departmentalization seems to be a reflection of the district's choice.

In 1962, the Rowland Elementary School District, located near Pomona, California, was in the process of planning a number of new schools to meet rapid growth. A study was undertaken to ascertain whether the seventh-eighth grade program based on the self-contained classroom was really the most desirable form of organization. At this stage of development the district had the option of selecting any one of several organizational schemes; this would not be possible a few years hence.

ROWLAND SPECIFICATIONS

The Rowland Elementary School District, at the present time, comprises a region of moderately priced housing tracts, sub-standard housing, small farms and orchards, large land holdings, and heavy industrial installations. Land zoning has not been in effect very long, and these various types of land use are intermingled without any recognizable pattern. A sizeable percentage of the junior high school students come from homes where the incentive to do well academically is not stressed. Many of these students also come from homes where another language is used extensively. This, along with other factors, causes the school to stress language development and pupil guidance. However, the essential character of the district is changing and will continue to change. More middle and upper middle class families will inhabit the area as the value of the open land increases and as the land available in surrounding areas decreases.

After a detailed study of the nature of the district in the past, present, and predictable future, the professional staff concluded that the junior high school program should have a strong guidance orientation as well as a strong emphasis on subject matter. In essence, what was required was the "best of two worlds." The task was to devise an organizational scheme in which most teachers would be teaching in their academic majors (or academic minors in a few instances) as well as being deeply involved in the counseling of students with the assistance of a highly trained counselor. It was also desired to evolve a system where small groups of teachers would be responsible for knowing definite groups of students very well.

Planning Group

With these specifications in mind, a planning organization was developed through which the teachers and administrators of the district, a consultant from the Claremont Graduate School, and the school architect could communicate. The heavy involvement of teachers and school principals insured that the organizational pattern would be both understandable and workable. The involvement of the architect in the early stages was a great asset making possible his genuine understanding of the district's educational plans before setting down one line on paper. In other words, it was thought desirable that the new design follow function.

The Plan

Designing a new school presented a challenge to develop an improved program for the intermediate grades. The strong teacher-pupil relationships developed in the existing guidance oriented, self-contained classroom program were regarded as desirable assets to be maintained. The increasing demands for a greater stress on academic achievement seemed, however, to demand some sort of departmentalized school. It was felt that such a school should possess the following characteristics: (1) Maximum utilization of teacher potential, (2) Opportunities for pupil exploration of curriculum areas which might become centers of concentrated study later on, (3) Opportunities for pupils to develop to their greatest potential.

A School-Within-A-School

The plan developed contemplates housing 720 pupils in a cluster-type school of three units, each unit to accommodate 240 students. Each unit has been designed to provide the educational experiences for a group of students enrolled for a two year period. Each year, the new group of seventh graders will be assigned to units and will remain members of their respective units for two years. A team of seven teachers will be assigned to each unit to plan and develop the educational program. The team will be assisted in evolving this plan by a group of specialists who will serve the entire three-team school. The physical education, homemaking, practical arts, and foreign language programs required facilities that could not be developed in each unit.

The Development of the Teams

The curriculum requirements in relation to the structure of the staff and the design of the educational environment indicated many lines of inquiry and decision. Agreement was reached on time allotment in terms of student-subject minutes a week; this distribution, which served as a base for further planning, was set as follows:

Social Studies	250 minutes
Language Arts	400 minutes
Mathematics	250 minutes
Science	100 minutes
Foreign Language	100 minutes
Music	100 minutes

Art	100 minutes
Practical Arts	100 minutes
Physical Education and Health	250 minutes
	1,650 minutes

A study of the relationship of student personnel, teachers, and the time allotment schedule dictated the number of classes required a week:

Within the Unit	*Classes per Week*
Social Studies	40
Language Arts	64
Mathematics	40
Science	16
Music	8
Art	8

By Specialists	*Classes per Week per Child*
Physical Education	5
General Shop	2
Home Economics	2
Foreign Language	2

The allotment of time is a mechanical process. Insuring that the proposed design will, in fact, produce the desirable educational consequences is another matter. The selection of individual teachers qualified to lead inquiring minds toward greater understanding and accomplishments and willing to accept the challenge of developing a new philosophy toward teaching, was recognized as the crucial factor in the success of the design.

Staffing each unit with team teachers presented many possibilities of combination. For purposes of illustration, one possible combination is shown below:

Teacher I	Music	8 periods
	Art	8 periods
	Social Studies	8 periods
Teacher II	Social Studies	20 periods
	Science	6 periods
Teacher III	Social Studies	10 periods
	Language Arts	16 periods
Teacher IV	Language Arts	24 periods
Teacher V	Language Arts	24 periods
Teacher VI	Mathematics	25 periods
Teacher VII	Mathematics	15 periods
	Science	10 periods

With the exception of instruction in foreign language, the specialized programs not included in the team structure require special facilities in a separate building designed to serve the entire school. The academic program for each unit will be developed by the team of teachers therein; it is desired that they operate under conditions of complete flexibility within their unit. The utilization of various-sized groupings from large groups to individualized instruction is dictated by the nature of the activities undertaken.

Teacher freedom from non-teaching clerical tasks secured through the employment of teacher aides, is vital to the success of this type of program. The teacher's mastery of *time* must be encouraged; the use of teacher aides is but one useful technique in solving the time problem. Flexible scheduling of student time outside the unit, allowing team meetings, preparation and conference time, and other teacher activities, is within the control of the unit teachers.

The principal of the school will play a different role in the Rowland Junior High schools than in conventional organizational plans. The administration of the school will, of course, still remain his responsibility. However, curriculum, discipline, parent involvement, and utilization of teaching materials will no longer be his direct responsibility. The principal will exercise his influence through team leaders, who, in turn, will accept the responsibility of cooperative planning with team members. The principal, guidance counselor, librarian, and other specialists will be considered as resource persons assisting teams in the development of a sound educational experience for each student.

The Coordinating Council

A weekly meeting of a council consisting of team leaders, guidance personnel, the librarian, and a representative from the specialist group will be scheduled by the principal. The function of the council will be to consider such matters as coordination of total school facilities, concerns of the principal, problems of the librarian, inter-team activities, scheduling of time for each team to utilize specialists, scheduling of the use of equipment, evaluation of the total school program, and setting of events for the week.

The Team Meeting

The schedule will provide in-school time for team meetings. The functions of these meetings will include the development of a weekly schedule, curriculum planning, coordination of counseling, team study of individual student problems, the consideration of operational procedures, and free discussion of issues.

IN-SERVICE EDUCATION

During the winter and spring of 1963, after the organizational plan had been adopted and the building plans drawn to accommodate it, a series of minimum days were used by the staff to work out arrangements for gaining experience with various parts of the plan. As a result, teams of teachers were formed in order that instructional plans such as large and small groupings, individual study, etc. could be tried.

The newly formed teaching teams met with the district administrative staff and the consultant from Claremont Graduate School to explore ways of working together as teams. One of the major objectives of the consultant was to help the staff set realistic goals for themselves. Major pitfalls were identified and discussed; it was pointed out that it would take a team of teachers several years to approach maximum utilization of the new organizational plan. It was stressed that the teams would go through stages of development and that the "Hawthorne effect" would probably be operating at the beginning but would diminish with the passage of time.

The early trial runs of the new organizational plan demonstrated the need for greater sophistication in building a flexible schedule. Consequently, a planning board was developed which, along with a system of colored cardboard inserts for denoting subjects, teachers, and facilities, allowed the teams to deal efficiently with the large number of existing variables. Even then, the building of a weekly schedule demanded several hours of each teacher's time before a workable one could be developed. However, with additional experience and the development of several key schedules which could be modified slightly as needed, the time demanded for schedule construction dropped drastically.

A highly important strategy was that of not supplying cut and dried answers to the teachers but rather listing possible alternatives from which a course of action could be chosen. To add support to this strategy, the district gave the teachers assurance that it was respectable to abandon an ineffective course of action in favor of one holding greater promise.

During the late spring of 1963 the principals of the two existing junior high schools, Alvarado and Grandview, began working with the teachers and members of the central administration to develop specific plans for these two schools coinciding with the new organizational form. In the period from September, 1963, through January, 1964, these two schools have been completely organized under the new plan. The results thus far have far exceeded the expectations of the planning group.

Team Teaching and Achievement*

Herbert J. Klausmeier and William Wiersma

Team teaching is being tried in many subject fields in the schools of the nation. Proponents of team teaching report that the students enjoy the experience and benefit from it and that participating teachers, administrators, and other personnel express favorable opinions of instructional teams. No observable ill effects upon the social and personal being of the student are reported as resulting from team teaching. According to Stuart[1], these conclusions about instructional teams are based primarily upon speculation and personal opinion.

Student achievement is used infrequently to determine the effects of team teaching. A commonly used evaluative instrument is the attitude or opinion questionnaire, administered only to the participants. Satisfactory control groups are usually not secured.

Illustrative of the research on instructional teams thus far, Sweet and Dunn-Rankin[2] report, concerning an experiment with seventh-grade arithmetic, that eighty per cent of the students had a generally favorable feeling toward the instructional team program. Bloomenshine and Brown[3], using a standardized achievement test in English skills, found the median gain

Reprinted from *Education* 86:238–242, December 1965, by permission of the publisher and the authors. Copyright, 1965, by The Bobbs-Merrill Company, Inc., Indianapolis, Indiana. Dr. Herbert J. Klausmeier is at the Research and Development Center, University of Wisconsin, Madison; and Dr. William Wiersma is Assistant Professor of Education, University of Toledo, Toledo, Ohio.

* This study was supported financially by the Wisconsin Improvement Program—Local School Systems and Teacher Education, John Guy Fowlkes, Director, and by the Research Committee of the Graduate School of the University of Wisconsin with funds from the Brittingham Trust, which provided research leave for the senior author.

The Racine Public Schools are experimenting at all school levels with a variety of promising innovations. The administration of the schools, the instructional staff, and the supervisory staff gave a large amount of time to the current project. This article reports the work of many people. The opinions toward the end are those of the author.

[1] Stuart, D., "Team Teaching: A Review," *School Life,* Vol. 44 (September, 1961), pp. 5–8.

[2] Sweet, R. and Dunn-Rankin, P., "An Experiment in Team Teaching Seventh Grade Arithmetic," *School Science and Mathematics,* Vol. 62 (May, 1962), pp. 341–44.

[3] Bloomenshine, L. and Brown, T., "San Diego, California Conducts Two-Year Experiment with Team Teaching," *National Association of Secondary School Principals Bulletin,* Vol. 45 (January, 1961), pp. 146–66.

for students in an instructional team arrangement to be above the norm in all areas except spelling.

In the same study for American history, the gains in scaled scores on a standardized history achievement test were about the same for the team teaching group and a control group of regular classroom students. The authors reported that their comparisons were somewhat clouded because the groups did not score the same on a pre-test.

PARTICIPATING STUDENTS

The experiment reported in this article was carried out in five public junior high schools of Racine, Wisconsin. The subject fields were seventh-grade English and social studies. The students were of low or average ability. The criteria for identifying the students of each ability level were:

Low: Otis I.Q. of 70-95; Metropolitan Reading standard score 44 and lower.

Average: Otis I.Q. of 96–114; Metropolitan Reading standard score 45-54.

ACHIEVEMENT TESTING

The students were given the same form of pre- and post-achievement tests in English and social studies. The test in each subject field was comprised of multiple-choice items and was constructed by a committee of teachers in the respective subject fields in terms of clearly defined objectives. The students were allowed one hour for each test.

The pre-test was administered early in the school year and the post-test late in the spring of the same year. The tests were subjected to an item analysis, and the non-discriminating items were eliminated. Reliability coefficients for the post-tests, computed by the Kuder-Richardson Formula 20, were .94 for English and .95 for social studies. Thus, these tests were reliable and valid for the purposes of this experiment.

EXPERIMENTAL AND CONTROL GROUPS

The instructional team was made up of three fully certified teachers and was responsible for the instruction in English and social studies in a multiple-class period. This team was located in School A and the students of low and average abilities in School A were the two experimental groups.

Students of average abilities in the other four schools were used as four control groups for the average group of students in the instructional team. Of these four schools, B and C used heterogeneous grouping and

Schools D and E used homogeneous grouping, with all pupils being placed in low, middle, or high ability sections. To secure a control group of low ability students Schools D and E, which used homogeneous grouping, were combined. The reason for combining was because of the low number of low ability students. Schools B and C had even fewer low ability students, too few to treat as a control group. The accompanying diagram shows the groups.

> *Experimental groups*
>   School A:
>   One low I.Q. group
>   School A:
>   One average I.Q. group
> *Control groups*
>   Schools D and E:
>   One low I.Q. group
>   School B: Average I.Q.
>   students from heterogeneous classes
>   School C: Average I.Q.
>   students from heterogeneous classes
>   School D: Average I.Q.
>   students from homogeneous classes
>   School E: Average I.Q.
>   students from homogeneous classes

An equal number of boys and girls was selected for each experimental and control group. Random samples of 74 low and 224 average ability students were drawn from the total population. The low ability experimental and control groups were comprised of 37 students, and the experimental and four control groups of average ability had a total of 224 students, with unequal numbers in the five schools, approximately 45 from each of the five schools in the study.

RESULTS

Four analyses of covariance were computed on the achievement scores to determine the effects of the team instruction in comparison with the other arrangements. The results for English are presented first. For the low ability students the adjusted mean for School A, instructional team, was 53.00 while the adjusted combined mean for Schools D and E was 41.88. This difference was significant at the .05 level.

The adjusted mean scores in English of the average ability students in the five schools were: A, instructional team, 68.85; B, heterogeneous,

69.67; C, heterogeneous, 63.25; D, homogeneous, 67.87; and E, homo-geneous, 71.57. For the average ability students, School A, instructional team, was significantly higher (.05 level) than School C which used heterogeneous grouping. However, it was slightly lower (not significantly) than School B which also used heterogeneous grouping. School A fell between the two schools which used homogeneous grouping and was not significantly different from either.

The results for social studies showed no significant difference between the adjusted means of School A and Schools D and E combined for the low ability students. The actual difference between the two means was less than one point.

The adjusted mean scores in social studies for the average ability students in the five schools were: A, instructional team, 56.10; B, 53.81; C, 56.49; D, 58.28; and E, 53.94. For the average ability students the mean score in School A was significantly lower (level .10) than School D. However, it was significantly higher (level .10) than Schools B and E.

In summary, students of low ability did better in English under team teaching conditions than under homogeneous grouping but did not do better in social studies. However, they did as well in social studies under team teaching. In English, students of average ability gained significantly more than students in one heterogeneous arrangement. In social studies, students of average ability gained more than students in one homogeneous and one heterogeneous arrangement.

UTILIZING STRENGTHS OF TEAMS

With the few modest but significant advantages of instructional teams over other arrangements to students of low and average abilities, one rea-sonably questions whether the small advantages are worth the effort and expense of rearranging schedules, spaces, and instructional personnel. The writers believe that instructional teams are effective. They further hypothe-size that if instructional teams are to become the typical pattern of instruc-tion, or even a significant proportion of it, other conditions must be incorporated into the team arrangement.

Briefly, each instructional team should have a leader, and this leader should be given the responsibility and remuneration commensurate with leadership. Each team might well consist of the leader, an interne, another certified teacher, and a secretary or lay reader for a few hours per week.

If eighty per cent of the teaching is by instructional team in the junior high school, about twenty per cent of the total staff would be team leaders. With a graduate degree and three to ten years of experience, the team leader should be paid $9,000 to $14,000 per year, even when this gives the leader a salary equal to the building principal. The interne should earn about $2,500 and the other teachers from $4,800 to $8,000, whether they work in the team or individually.

Most of the other teachers will be beginning teachers, married women who are experienced teachers, and others who enjoy teaching but do not wish to assume the responsibilities of leadership or put in the fifty or more hours of work per week which is required of the team leader.

Team teaching is now popular; many school systems are trying out different types of teams. If educators could capitalize upon its real merit of giving teachers high responsibility and reasonably adequate pay, the instructional team concept might result in greatly improved pupil learning and pupil adjustment over a longer period of time.

No administrative arrangement or instructional device will probably have much effect upon improving the quality of education unless many more young men of high caliber can be attracted to classroom teaching as a lifetime career. The team leader concept as outlined could accomplish this. As inferred from the authors' conversations with prospective and experienced teachers, many beginning single female teachers, and many married female teachers endorse the idea of married male teachers and devoted mature single females becoming responsible team leaders and being paid accordingly. However, large numbers of able young men cannot be recruited into teaching unless their opportunities for higher pay and greater responsibility are increased substantially.

Flexible Scheduling—Fad or Fundamental?

J. Lloyd Trump

The one-room school is a feature of the American heritage praised in stories and defended emotionally by some great and ordinary men who studied there. I attended one for a year and a half. Moreover, the first school in Indiana wherein I taught and became principal was produced by closing eight one-room schools and recouping high school students transferred elsewhere. I know about one-room schools.

These one-room schools had several built-in advantages. Time was more at the disposal of the teachers and pupils in those schools. A teacher could, and the good ones did, spend more time with one group of students when they needed more time. He could reduce the time for other groups who did not need so much on a given day or week. The students in those schools had more time away from class groups and could plan to use their time for their own purposes because they had more of it at their disposal. Student groups could, and were, easily changed. Sometimes the teacher combined grades to teach certain concepts, even taught the whole school on occasion, and in fact ungraded the work from time to time. Although the space in the school was limited both in quantity and quality, it was readily at the disposal of teachers and pupils by moving chairs, tables, or portable partitions. A number of other advantages could be cited, as well as defects, but enough are provided to make the point. There was flexibility in the one-room school and good teachers and students made the most of it.

Unfortunately, we became so enamored with this one-room school structure that when we grew larger educationally, we continued it as the self-contained classroom, failing to recognize the limitations thus imposed on both teachers and students. A group of students was locked in with one teacher with whatever strengths and limitations that teacher possessed. It was difficult and expensive to introduce educational technology into these rooms. The graded system stratified pupils so that a room became a fourth grade room or a class became tenth grade English, forcing us to devise

Reprinted from *Phi Delta Kappan* 44:367–371, May 1963, and *Music Educators Journal* 52:51–53, 139–143, November-December 1965, by permission of both publishers and the author. Dr. J. Lloyd Trump is Associate Secretary, National Association of Secondary-School Principals.

many ways to fit students with diverse interests and talents into that rigid framework.

Small secondary schools possessed some of the same advantages of the one-room schools. But these advantages disappeared when schools became larger. Administrators and teachers confused equality of opportunity and democracy with uniformity. A smooth running school became the objective. We know the rigid patterns that developed. Classes were of standard size; optimum teacher-pupil ratio goals were established; class periods were uniform in length; curricular content was fitted into standard size Carnegie units. Administrators developed many kinds of quantitatively defined institutional arrangements for learning and for dealing with teachers.

Finally, however, we are recognizing and learning ways to cope with the problem: how to return the use of time, space, numbers, and content to those who need it—the teachers and their students—in even the larger schools that symbolize so well our concept of education for all youth. We are also learning how to cope with an equally important additional problem: how to treat a pupil as an individual even though he is one in a great mass of students. Moreover, we are beginning to realize that only basic changes can produce what may be regarded truly as professional status for teachers. Solving those problems constitutes the exciting challenge of our day. Let us look at what some schools are doing and what others need to do.

THE USE OF TIME

Flexible scheduling is now the subject of many articles and speeches and even some books. This is an educationally stylish topic. What causes this development? What are the techniques and some limitations?

A superficial reason for the current interest in flexible scheduling is the availability of new mechanical aids to the schedule maker. School administrators, like many other persons, enjoy working with gadgets. That there is real danger in confusing speed and flexible scheduling was pointed out by this writer some years ago: "Modern electronic data processing equipment can be a boon to the further development of quality in education. It can also be used to do faster what should not be done anyway and thus delay or forestall changes that could improve dramatically the services of schools to individual students. . . . The primary investigation of the schedule maker should *not* be to discover what data-processing equipment is available to help make the schedule . . ."[1]

The point is, that we must quickly disassociate speed from the concept

[1] J. Lloyd Trump, "Developing and Evaluating a Class Schedule to Help Each Pupil Learn Better," *Journal of Secondary Education*, Vol. 36 (October 1961), pp. 338–345.

of flexible scheduling. Doubtless electronic aids can facilitate better use of time by students and by teachers, but concentrating first on machines may well delay achieving the kind of flexibility that is needed.

Other traps may ensnare those who would engage in flexible scheduling. Certainly, one of the basic reasons for changing schedules is to provide different institutional arrangements for education. For example, principals and teachers, understandably dissatisfied with the rigidity of today's schedules, determine that some courses need more time than others or that some classes need to meet less often but for longer periods of time on certain days. Such considerations lead almost inevitably to the "modular concept" of flexible scheduling. Instead of the conventional 45- or 55-minute periods, these schools adopt a 15-, 20-, or 30-minute module which means in essence that instead of six periods a day, the school schedule includes 12, 16, or 24 periods in a day. School subjects then are scheduled for a different number of modules, sometimes the same number each day in the week, or sometimes for various numbers of modules on different days in the week. A degree of flexibility results, but once the change is made, the new schedule can become almost as rigid as the one it replaced (see Table I).

Another type of flexible schedule is represented by rotating periods, sometimes of varied lengths, or even by rotating special schedules on different days. A school following conventional curricular organization patterns wishes to make it possible for a student to take six or seven subjects instead of the conventional five or six. Subjects are scheduled to meet four times a week instead of five. Some periods may be longer than others. Subjects are scheduled on a floating basis to fill out the five-day week. Although this change is sometimes called flexible scheduling, the new program also can become quite rigid and actually contributes relatively little to the improved use of time by students and teachers (see Table II).

A more flexible arrangement is represented by schools engaging in a variety of team teaching approaches (see Table III). One form is to schedule six teachers and 180 students for a two-hour block of time. Teachers and students may divide their time among large group instruction, small seminar-size discussion groups, and independent study. All of the students may watch a film for 18 minutes, then separate into one group of 90 for a supplementary presentation by one of the teachers, and into four groups of 15 each for discussion with four other teachers, with the remaining 30 students scheduled into a library or workroom for independent study under the supervision of the other teacher. The changed arrangements can last for 36 minutes, or any other particular time, so long as the total two-hour block is maintained. Then the students are rearranged so all have small group work and independent study. Obviously, this approach represents a more flexible use of time, space, and student groupings than is possible in a conventionally organized school. But again, flexibility is limited, this time by the two-hour block.

A few schools organize instruction almost completely on the team

TABLE I
15-minute modules—
same schedule every day

8:00		. . . . . .
8:15	Mathematics	. . . . . .
8:30		. . . . . .
8:45		. . . . . .
9:00	Speech Correction	
9:15		. . . . . .
9:30		. . . . . .
9:45	Science	. . . . . .
10:00		. . . . . .
10:15		. . . . . .
10:30	Music	. . . . . .
10:45		. . . . . .
11:00		. . . . . .
11:15	Spanish	. . . . . .
11:30		. . . . . .
11:45	Music Practice	. . . . . .

An alternative example—two-hour classes,
Monday through Thursday, and one-hour classes on Friday

Time	Monday	Tuesday	Wednesday-Thursday	Friday
8:00	Biology	Geometry	Same as	Biology
9:00				English
10:00	English	French	Monday-Tuesday	French
11:00				Geometry
12:00	Lunch and Activities			
1:00	Physical Ed.	Study or Elective	Same as Monday-Tuesday	Phys. Ed.
2:00				Stu-Ele.

teaching basis, with large group, small group, and independent study arrangements. Such schools achieve still more flexibility in scheduling. Typically, these schools also use a modular approach. Large classes of 100 or more students in a given subject may be scheduled for two 20-minute modules (40 minutes) twice a week. Seminar-size groups of 15 or fewer students in the same subject area are scheduled for two modules, twice a week, at different times in the day from the large group and possibly on

TABLE II
Rotation of Classes—Standard Periods

Time	Monday	Tuesday	Wednesday	Thursday	Friday
8:00	1*	1	1	1	2
9:00	2	2	2	3	3
10:00	3	3	4	4	4
11:00	4	5	5	5	5
12:00	Lunch				
12:30	6	6	6	6	7
1:30	7	7	7	Special	Special

Rotation of Classes—Periods Vary in Length

Time	Monday	Tuesday	Wednesday	Thursday	Friday
8:55-10:26	1	2	4	5	6
10:30-11:26	2	4	5	6	1
11:30-12:26	3	3	3	3	3
12:26-1:04	Lunch				
1:04-2:30	4	5	6	1	2
2:34-3:30	5	6	1	2	4

(*Numbers indicate different subjects.)

TABLE III

Team Teaching
Block of Time

Time	Monday through Friday
8:00 9:00	3 U.S. History + 3 English teachers schedule 180 junior students as they deem desirable
10:00	Planning Period for Team
11:00	Conventional Classes
12:00	Lunch
12:30 1:30	Same as above but with different students, e.g., sophomores

different days in the week. Independent study in each subject is scheduled for each student, depending on his interests and talents, for three, four, or more consecutive modules on different days in the week.

These schools typically stand ready to change at will the independent study of their students, but hold fairly systematically to the scheduled time for large group instruction and small group discussion. Thus, even these flexible schedules can become rigid in part while remaining flexible in other aspects. For example, the conventional (and without research basis) idea that an English class must meet five days a week, 50 minutes per day, at the same hour of the day, with one teacher in charge, is replaced by the concept that English meets twice a week, 40 minutes per time, in classes of 120, with the best teaching available, plus one meeting in classes of 15, 40 minutes each time, with a teacher in charge. Thus, the new schedule says in effect that English requires 120 minutes per week of group instruction, plus whatever time (80 minutes or more) the staff determines, for independent study by students in English workrooms (see Table IV). The danger is that the staff may become so enamored with these arrangements that the "flexible schedule" becomes rigidly established. This may be true especially if the schedule is made with expensive data-processing equipment.

What is the ultimate in flexible scheduling? No one knows for sure, but the goal necessarily is to return to teachers and students as much freedom as is reasonable in the use of time, space, numbers, and content for instruction.

A relatively undisciplined answer to the question was represented more than three decades ago by the extremists in the Progressive Education Movement. For example, at the beginning of the day, the teacher was supposed to have asked her students, "What do you want to do today?"

TABLE IV

A Partial Student Schedule
Different Days, Varied Periods

	Monday	Tuesday	Wednesday
8:20 8:40	History LG*	English LG	History LG
9:00 9:20	French Sem*	French LG	French Lab
9:40 10:00	History Sem	Homemaking LG	English Sem
10:20 10:40	P E	Science Sem	P E
11:00 11:20		Homemaking Lab	
11:40 12:00	Math LG		Math LG
12:20	Lunch		
Etc.	Humanities RC*	Typing LG	Science RC

* LG—Large Group Instruction, Sem—Small Group Discussion, RC—Resource Center—Independent Study.

It was reported that if the students said that they wanted to go fishing, school was dismissed and the students learned about fish, water habitats, the economics of fishing, and what not. Whether that situation ever existed or not, the fact remains that this proposal represented a child-centered answer to the question. Actually, I suspect in most instances teachers influenced very much the decisions that students made. A major problem, however, in that situation was that it would work only with one teacher and one group of students—and education was back to the one-room school days.

The goal, then, in a larger school is to develop orderly procedures that permit teachers and students as much latitude as possible in developing various aspects of instruction and learning. The following appear to be necessary ingredients: the class schedule may be changed daily on the basis of teacher requests; each student, under competent direction and with appropriate controls, makes decisions regarding his part in the established schedule; conflicts for students and teachers are reduced to a minimum;

teacher loads and pupil loads are such to permit on the one hand maximum professionalization of teaching and on the other the maximum potential learning opportunities for students; the school knows what its students are doing and follows reasonably equitable personnel policies for teachers; the whole scheme is financially feasible and logistically operational.

The Brookhurst Junior High School, Anaheim, California, provides for daily schedule changes by teachers and students. Individual teacher members of teaching teams determine three days in advance what students they want to teach, in what size groups, for what length of time, in what places, and with what technological aids. Teacher job specification forms containing this information are turned in to their team leaders. The team leaders and a clerk then assemble to make a master schedule for the day, which includes what students "must" follow. The master schedule then is duplicated and made available to the students and their counselors. In a daily 20-minute meeting, with the advice and consent of his counselor, each student makes his own schedule, filling in his choices for the considerable amount of time open to him. He may spend his time in independent study in the art room or library or someplace else. The counselor either approves or rejects this decision. Then the student makes out his own schedule for the day in quadruplicate. One copy is for himself, one for the office, one for the counselor, and one for his parents. The schedule is developed mainly by hand. Doubtless mechanical aids could simplify the process and help to avoid conflicts and some other problems that arise. Time could be saved for both students and teachers. It should be noted, however, that the concepts of schedule-making come first and the machines that facilitate the process come second in their planning.

The John F. Kennedy High School, Silver Spring, Maryland, did not include a program clock or bell system in this new building. Teachers meet daily in grade level teams and can change the schedule at will. This program and others like it in a sense represent an advancement over the block-of-time schedule described earlier in this statement. The larger the number of teachers, the larger the number of students, and the greater the amount of time that are grouped together, the more flexible teachers and students can be in using time.

Table V, illustrating a partial schedule, shows how various groups might be scheduled during a given week. Three hundred sixty students are involved. All 360 are assembled in one place on Tuesday for a 35-minute mathematics test. Science teachers have scheduled 3-hour field trips on Monday, Wednesday, Thursday, and Friday, 90 students each day. Orchestra rehearsal for 90 students occupies 80 minutes Monday and Thursday. A 24-student vocal ensemble practices for 40 minutes on three days. The 360 students are divided in half for large-group presentations in his-

Table V Partial Schedule for One Week

Code

Width of Block = number of students   Length of Block = Time

Science Field Trip (90 Students – 3 Hours)

Remedial Reading (20 Students – 1 Hour)

Orchestra (90 Students – 80 Minutes)

Vocal Ensemble (24 Students – 40 Minutes)

Mathematics Test (360 Students – 35 Minutes)

History (180 Students – 40 Minutes)

English (15 Students – 40 Minutes)

Not shown: Many other groups and much time spent by pupils in independent study in all subject areas.

tory on Wednesday and Friday. Small-group discussion sessions and re-medial reading groups occur at other times. Independent study and other groups are similarly scheduled. This sample schedule is adapted from the author's booklet, *Focus on the Individual—A Leadership Responsibility*.[2]

The Meadowbrook Junior High School, Newton Centre, Massachusetts, has devised a "Priority Period" scheme to give teachers and pupils control over time. They have reduced the number of periods per week that classes meet in order to provide a number of free periods for students and teachers. Both groups then use these periods for high priority activities. A teacher wants a group of students for remedial work. A student wants more time in the music room, shop, or science laboratory. These and other priorities can be realized. Data processing cards avoid conflicts and provide class lists to check attendance during the priority periods.

Will these people and others following similar or even more imaginative practices fall back into a rigid schedule? Such a development is possible but certainly less probable than in the case of the approaches described earlier in this statement. Further use of automated instruction devices (teaching textbooks and machines) and the development of computer-operated instructional systems will encourage further individualization of instruction and consequently more individual scheduling. Today's self-contained classrooms and rigid schedules permit little more than gestures in recognizing individual differences among students and teachers. If the real purposes of flexible scheduling are kept constantly in mind, this con-cept will be a *fundamental* operation in quality education and not a *fad*. However, the use of time is inseparably related to other aspects of the edu-cational program. We must record and emphasize these relationships.

THE USE OF NUMBERS, SPACE, AND CONTENT

The significance of flexible use of numbers, space, and content has been explained by this writer in a number of publications, the most detailed of which is *Focus on Change—Guide to Better Schools*.[3] Essentially, this concept says that some teaching and learning can occur effectively with larger numbers of students than found in the conventional class group of 25 or 30, not only to save time and energy for teachers and money in the school budget, but also to make logistically possible contacts between all students and the best teaching that the school can muster aided by the use

---

[2] J. Lloyd Trump and Lois Karasik, *Focus on the Individual—A Leadership Responsibility*, filmstrip: 135 frames, color; booklet: 33 pp. (Washington, D.C.: National Association of Secondary-School Principals, National Education Association, 1965).

[3] J. Lloyd Trump and Dorsey Baynham, *Focus on Change—Guide to Better Schools* (Chicago: Rand McNally, 1961).

of modern technological aids to instruction. Small classes of 15 or fewer students, the number that can realistically be involved during a reasonable period of time in effective discussion, are essential for other purposes of instruction. And students need to spend much more time than now working as individuals, or in groups of two or three, in specially designed work-rooms for every subject area included in the school curriculum. Thus, the size and the nature of pupil groupings changes with the purposes of teaching and learning.

(Guidelines for developing these three phases of instruction are available without charge from the author of this article.)

Spaces in the school also vary with the purposes of learning. The multi-purpose classroom found so often in today's schools violates this principle. It is educationally wrong and financially wasteful to attempt to engage in large-group instruction, small-group discussion, and independent study in the same room even with flexibly operated walls. Specifically designed spaces for learning with specialized facilities are essential.[4]

Flexibility in curricular content is another essential ingredient in the flexibility concept. The present conflicts among subjects in competing for pupil time need to be resolved by programs of basic and depth education that provide for each student logical and sequential content in all areas of human knowledge, and, at the same time, with opportunities for study in depth in those areas where the student has special interests and talents. Flexibility further requires that each student be able to progress through the various phases of these subjects according to his own talents and interests.

FAD OR FUNDAMENTAL?

Whether flexible scheduling is a fad or fundamental depends entirely on how it is accomplished. If school leaders seek easy answers, some of which are described in this article, and change their schools accordingly, largely because it has become fashionable, flexible scheduling is, of course, only a fad and soon will vanish from the educational scene. However, if educational leadership engages in a never-ending search experimentally to seek soundly based answers to the question of how to return the enlightened use of time, space, numbers, and curriculum to the teachers and students, then flexible scheduling is absolutely fundamental in the search for better education.

One other thought must be injected before closing this statement. The author does not wish to criticize adversely many principals and teachers

[4] J. Lloyd Trump, "Places to Learn," *Audiovisual Instruction*, Vol. 7 (October 1962), pp. 516–517.

who are demonstrating minor deviations from conventional ways of organizing teaching and learning. Those who engage in even the smallest experiments and demonstrations are courageous. What they do is visible; therefore, their position becomes vulnerable to the attacks of the conservatives who enjoy criticizing those who dare to seek better answers. Since it is not easy to change educational procedures, small steps may well be the best way to start in many schools. The important matter is that those who take small steps need constantly to remind themselves, their colleagues, and the public they serve, that the small steps constitute only the beginning of the journey.

We salute those principals and teachers whose school environment permits big steps. We also say, please evaluate carefully what you are doing so we may all know what to avoid when we go down similar roads. Also, extend your evaluation horizons to include the goals we seek beyond mere acquisition of facts measured by conventional standardized and locally constructed tests. Let us all seek to determine whether students are developing more responsibility for their own learning, whether they are becoming more creative, whether they practice habits of intellectual inquiry, whether they communicate better and more effectively with other persons, whether they think more critically, whether they are better adjusted human beings, and whether they are achieving a number of other very important educational outcomes. These are fundamental goals. They are not educational fads.

Team Teaching and Staff Utilization in Ridgewood High School

Melvin P. Heller and Elizabeth Belford

The problems inherent in staff utilization and team teaching are complicated, especially in regard to teacher morale, personal and interpersonnel relationships, communications, and team planning; but the rewards for those who accept the concepts of team teaching are great. At Ridgewood High School, Norridge, Illinois, the entire school program is an implementation of these concepts. The problems faced and the decisions reached have led to insights which are expressed as answers to a number of subsequent questions. This article presents pertinent information relative to staff utilization for all school districts which are interested in these approaches.

WHAT ARE SOME BASIC CONSIDERATIONS IN TEAM TEACHING?

If team teaching is truly to be team teaching, it is obvious that a spirit of cooperation must be developed. Perhaps in no other teaching situation is the need for mutual understanding among the faculty members as important and vital to the success of the enterprise. It is not easy for teachers to share their ideas in a manner which is free from excessive ego involvement and professional jealousies and biases. Team teaching will not eliminate these psychological influences, but problems attendant to them can be minimized.

One not thoroughly familiar with the situation might fear that team teaching would stifle imagination and initiative on the part of the individual teacher. However, in practice, the reverse is true. In fact, team teaching challenges the creativity and individuality of each teacher to a great degree. Although the planning of the major learning experiences will involve some compromises, the specifics necessary to implement these generalities provide an excellent opportunity for the creative and imaginative teacher to utilize his abilities. In the follow-up sessions relative to the large group, the teacher is handicapped only by his ability and imagination and

Reprinted from the *Bulletin of the National Association of Secondary-School Principals* 46:105–122, January 1962, by permission of the publisher and the authors. Copyright, 1962, Washington, D.C. Melvin P. Heller is Associate Professor of Education, Loyola University, Chicago, Illinois, and was formerly Assistant Superintendent and Curriculum Director, Ridgewood High School. Miss Elizabeth Belford is Co-chairman of the Humanities Team, Ridgewood High School, Norridge, Illinois.

that of his pupils. Not only does he have the chance to put into practice his own ideas, but also he has the advantages of sharing in the thinking of the other members of his team.

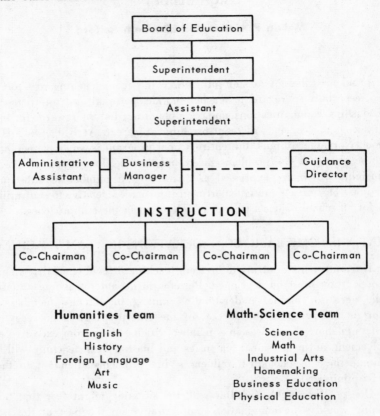

Organizational Chart

A team is not necessarily composed only of members of the same subject area as, for example, an English team or a history team. At Ridgewood High School, the teams are broader in scope and are classified as humanities and math-science teams. A humanities team consists of teachers of history, English, music, art, and teachers of various foreign languages. A math-science team includes teachers of biology, mathematics, industrial arts, home economics, business education, and physical education.

There are many advantages to this kind of organization. The team approach uses to best advantage not only the major teaching knowledge of each staff member, but also the special interest areas he may have pursued in conjunction with or in addition to his major teaching area. These combined knowledges, when encouraged, developed, and nurtured by team planning, should result in a well-organized, effective large-group offering.

The seminar situation which follows such a large-group presentation again gives free rein to the teacher. A knowledge of group dynamics is essential in the effective management of these pupil seminars, and the teacher must employ skill in suggesting topics for discussion and in guiding the resultant pupil discussion to sound conclusions. The opportunity to pursue a unit first in a large group and then in a small group can provide the teacher with a broadening, satisfying experience. This in turn should encourage and inspire him to develop even more effective units in the future.

In addition, the team teaching approach gives the teacher the time to develop his own ideas concerning the best way to teach a specific learning experience. When there are large blocks of unscheduled time during the school day, as must be the case, the teacher will be able to meet with the members of his team, daily if necessary. In spite of many protestations to the contrary, many teachers fail to plan their lessons adequately simply because such planning must be done on their own time due to the rigors of a schedule which prohibit the teacher from thinking leisurely in the company of his peers.

Another advantage of team teaching is that each teacher learns to criticize his fellow teachers as well as himself because the situation lends itself to the development of self-analysis. This attitude which encourages self-analysis is a boon to supervisors in that the teacher soon becomes accustomed to the presence of colleagues in his classes. Thus when the supervisor comes to the classroom to observe, the presence of one more educator is not especially significant.

Moreover, under the system of team teaching it is imperative that the supervisor keep abreast of the learning experiences to which the pupils are exposed because these learning experiences vary so much from the large-group situation to the small-group situation that a firsthand observation is essential for complete understanding of the sequence, continuity, and integration of the subject matter. Thus, it is almost a matter of professional necessity that the supervisor make frequent visits to the classrooms.

From what has gone before, it must be obvious that not all teachers are willing or able to participate in team teaching. Some teachers may prefer to work by themselves because they are not interested in the degree of professional intimacy so necessary to team teaching. In other words, not all teachers are temperamentally suited to share, to work together, to compromise, to develop group awareness. Thus, no indictment is intended when it is stated that team teaching requires a professional and personal attitude which not all teachers possess, perhaps cannot possess, and perhaps do not want to possess.

HOW SHOULD TEACHERS BE ORIENTED?

The orientation of teachers to the team approach includes two kinds of education—that involving experienced personnel and that involving beginners. In the case of experienced teachers accustomed to a conventional school system, it is necessary to revise their thinking regarding their roles as staff members. The position they held formerly in relationship to other teachers within the same system is far different from that in a school employing team teaching methods. They must be reminded that it will no longer be possible for them to plan, to conduct their classes, and to evaluate results separately and independently of the other members of the staff. On the contrary, their individualism must be channeled into special uses and situations. In most instances, they must think in terms of the team, plan with the team, and use the resources of the team. The teacher must learn to think of the over-all picture—of the whole program—and not of the approaches he employed, no matter how successfully, when working with a conventional type of class.

This is not to say that a teacher cannot be creative or individualistic. On the contrary, ample opportunity is afforded by seminar and individual study situations for using all of the originality, fresh approaches, and new ideas a teacher can summon. It is in the planning stages and in the large-group presentations that the teacher must adapt himself to thinking of the integrated program. The advantages and opportunities for better teaching, for more varied and effectual presentations, and for constantly renewed enthusiasm are far greater when a number of teachers work together than when one works alone.

Educating a teacher to think in this way and to give his whole-hearted support to this program is a time-consuming project. A lengthy planning session is necessary to allow time for the team members to meet and to establish the rapport which will permit them to express their ideas without hesitation or fear of rejection. Only by actually planning together do they become aware of the almost limitless possibilities of such an approach. The first sessions may progress slowly, but getting acquainted is the necessary beginning step toward the spirit of cooperation and acceptance which will result in effective exchange of ideas and successful planning.

The task of educating beginning teachers to the team approach is similar but perhaps somewhat less difficult, if one grants that beginners are willing to accept advice from more experienced teachers. However, because of the type of courses which these beginners have studied in conventional teacher-training institutions, they may have developed some of the same attitudes and expectations as the experienced teachers in regard to their relationship to other staff members, and so they profit from the same orientation program planned for the former group. The orientation program must help the beginners feel free to express ideas and to ask questions if the team is to reap full benefit of each member's talent.

The orientation or workshop period is also an ideal time for instruction in the technical aspects of the large-group presentation. Correct operation of such equipment as overhead projectors, slide and film projectors, and effective use of the microphone are essential if teachers are to offer a smooth-flowing, well-organized presentation free from distractions and unforeseen interruptions. The use of these mechanical aids must be mastered so that their operation is automatic while the teacher's full attention is devoted to the instructional material.

In a good orientation program much help can be derived from those who are skillful in the application of principles of group dynamics. Perhaps there is no other system which requires high morale and mutual acceptance of one's colleagues to the extent required by a staff utilization organization. If team teaching is truly team teaching, the truth of this postulate becomes apparent.

The importance of a well-planned orientation program cannot be over-emphasized. The feeling of confidence instilled in the teachers by extensive planning before the beginning of the school year insures a greater degree of smoothness of operation once the plans are put into action with the pupils. The confidence of the teaching staff, imparted to the pupils, is reflected in their rapid adjustment and increased effectiveness. Likewise, if a major portion of the curriculum planning has been done in advance, more time can be devoted to analyzing the degree of success or failure of the plans and revising them for better results.

WHAT TECHNIQUES ARE NEEDED IN LARGE-GROUP INSTRUCTION?

Effective large-group instruction, as in all learning situations, requires interaction between the teacher and the pupil. Because the group is larger than a conventional class, it is perhaps more difficult for the teacher to involve the individual pupil in the learning process. The job of the teacher is to motivate the pupil, to interest him, to help him abstract himself from the large group of from 100–150 persons in which he has physical presence so that the pupil will learn in a psychological group size of two, a group composed of the teacher and the pupil.

This interaction between the teacher and the pupil is dependent upon the activity of the learner. To many educators this activity is often interpreted as physical activity which is focused upon the completion of some project. Such an interpretation, however, is shortsighted. The crucial factor in the learning situation for the learner is his *mental* activity. A pupil may be overtly very passive and docile, but his mind may be racing. Because of the great importance of mental activity, the teacher may use several techniques or approaches to keep the learner interested. The use of visuals, for example, in conjunction with lectures can be of immense aid and effectiveness; however, they can be just as much of a detriment if improperly handled. Careful thought must be given to what type of visual best suits the instructional purpose, what number is best for change of pace, and what number merely constitutes superfluous distraction from the point. In addition, humor, gimmicks, changes of pace, rhetorical and real questions may be used. All have some value in involving the pupils actively in the learning situation. However, one cannot overemphasize the importance of mental activity, the *sine qua non* of learning on the ideational level.

One of the best ways to insure this desired intellectual interaction is to provide the pupil with a structural approach to the presentation, setting a framework within which the teacher and the pupil can interact. Although a structure overtly imposes limitations, the boundary lines are flexible in that they will not impede or prevent depth perception. Even the simplest of truths becomes profound when it is perceived and interpreted by an able thinker.

The means of providing this necessary structure are varied and familiar. The teacher may utilize an outline, a set of study questions, a topical reference to salient points singled out for emphasis, or a brief summary of the lecture for discussion purposes. Certainly, the type of structure as well as the degree depends upon many factors involved in the teaching-learning situation. It is sufficient to say, therefore, that adequate planning on the part of the teacher and his team members will determine the structure which is most suitable for the ability level of the pupils.

WHAT IS THE FUNCTION OF A SEMINAR?

Following the large group, pupils divide into classes of fifteen or fewer to pursue the subject of the presentation. These groups are referred to as seminars and emulate their college-level counterparts in that they usually center upon discussion. The seminar organization is not limited, however, to "discussion" subjects such as history and literature. The approach is employed with good effect in foreign languages, physical education, mathematics, science, and other subjects.

In the field of mathematics, large-group instruction covers unfamiliar concepts and methods of solving new types of mathematical problems, while the seminars concern themselves with assuring the understanding of principles, checking the errors in homework, and ascertaining the reasons for these errors. The small size of the group enables each person to question as often as necessary for thorough understanding. The seminars can be conducted effectively by pupil chairmen, as they are in other areas, with the teacher serving in his capacity as a consultant, guide, and resource person. Even in physical education and science, the large-group presentation, combined with small groups for laboratory work or activity periods, has proved effective.

Foreign language large groups may be devoted to cultural aspects of the subject, geography of the country, and customs of the people; or, if the teacher chooses, to some new phase of grammar. The seminar-sized groups give each pupil more opportunity to participate and to ask questions, and allow instruction, obviously, to be more individualized than in a conventional system. The primary aim of the seminar, to develop pupil responsibility for his own learning, is served in the languages by means of pupil chairmen just as in seminars in other fields. Under the direction of these chairmen, pupils can check homework, take turns translating, carry on question-and-answer sessions, and converse in the foreign language. The teacher is present to correct errors which the pupils fail to observe and to explain new ideas, but the responsibility for the smooth and efficient conducting of the class belongs chiefly to the pupils. Being alert to the errors of others and trying to avoid errors on their own, the pupils are more aware and interested in the progress of the class than when they rely upon the teacher to initiate each exercise and to offer all the necessary corrections to their work.

It is sometimes practical and desirable for specialized seminars to be formed whenever pupils need to work at a rate of speed noticeably faster or slower than the majority. In general, pupils learn from the individual differences of the members of their group, but in the case of accelerated or remedial levels, separation is sometimes more helpful. Such a separation naturally results in differentiated assignments, an integral feature of this system. Under the staff utilization plan, the exceptional groups may work at their own rate, receive more or less homework according to their ability, and have the difficulty of the assignments adjusted to their level.

The additional time so often desired for dealing effectively with these pupils can be provided, also. While one teacher handles the large-group presentation, team members are freed to remove the accelerated and/or remedial children from the lecture and spend the time more profitably on material pertinent to their needs.

In the opinion of some, the strength of this program lies in the area of individual study rather than in seminar. Curiosity and desire for further investigation of a topic or whole field of topics stem from the discussion and probing which take place in the seminar. It is there that the student gains his first knowledge of a subject; it is there that he glimpses vast unexplored fields beyond this limited knowledge; it is there that the desire is born to investigate further, to find out for himself about the facets of the subject which are too many and too deep to pursue with the entire group.

The two types of study, then, are interdependent. If one wishes to move toward a strong program in individual study, he must first expend enthusiastic and arduous effort toward the development of effective seminars.

WHAT IS THE SIGNIFICANCE OF INDIVIDUAL STUDY?

Perhaps the most important phase of the learning situation is the time provided by the schedule for individual study opportunities. During this time the pupil can pursue with depth those ideas and concepts presented in the large group and explored in the seminar. Examples of individual study areas are the language lab, the math lab, science and humanities, resource centers, and project areas. It is essential that the teacher in charge of the individual study area have academic competence in that area if the learning situation is to be meaningful at the optimum level for the pupil. The availability of expert professional assistance encourages the pupil to probe deeply in his pursuit of knowledge. This never-ending search will be successful to the degree that the pupil is able to accept and to develop a sense of self-responsibility for learning.

In spite of the difficulties in evaluating this sense of self-responsibility, self-directed depth perception is a worthy objective for all students. In addition to the large-group lectures and the seminar discussions, the individual study opportunities are designed to play an important role in the realization of this goal.

WHAT CONSIDERATIONS ARE VITAL TO CURRICULUM?

Planning the curriculum is a difficult task in a school utilizing the team teaching approach as it is in all schools. If the planning is difficult, however, the implementation is even more challenging. If the school purports to be a comprehensive high school in that it has curriculum offerings designed to provide for the needs of a heterogeneous student body, the problem is compounded further. Why are these problems so imposing?

1. One major difficulty is the scheduling. If the schedule does not provide for flexibility to the extent that team members may shift easily to "manage" pupil groups of various sizes, the alternative may lead to a conventional schedule of "tying" a teacher to five or six sections of a subject offering. It is clear that a conventional teacher load is not conducive to efficient team teaching, and it obviates the possibility of intelligent staff utilization.

2. Another major problem is the utilization of the staff, qualitatively and quantitatively. One of the financial advantages of the staff utilization concept is that fewer teachers can do more professional work with more children than is the case in conventional schools. If the team-teaching approach, however, is to be a *team* approach and if large-group, small-group, and individual study opportunities for pupils are scheduled, the

greater the variety of courses the greater the number of teachers needed. Obviously, the inconsistency pointed out must be avoided.

3. Still another curriculum problem is that of providing enough "tracks" to meet the heterogeneous needs of the student body. If a staff is spread out too much, the concept of team teaching is defeated. Yet, the provisions for individual differences of the pupils must be made possible. One solution to this problem is to utilize effectively the individual study opportunities. This solution does not involve more teacher time if the student is sufficiently self-motivated. With emphasis on the individual, the individual study opportunities can best serve the heterogeneous student body of the high school.

As must be true in all curriculum development, there must be provisions for continuity of offerings, sequential development, and integration of knowledge. All these elements are essential, but it is the latter element which is of paramount importance in a team teaching approach. The compartmentalization of knowledge becomes almost ludicrous when a team of teachers pool their intellectual resources and each staff member begins to use his talents. The crossing of subject matter lines is an inevitable result of the team approach; and this blending of ideas, this relating of concepts, this intertwining of thought represent integration of knowledge.

To go a step further, this integration will make enrichment an essential phase of the learning situation. This enrichment may take various forms. For example, it may relate history to art, music to science, math to physical education; but whatever the form, it is an attempt to delve more deeply into at least one academic area so that deeper, wiser, and more profound perceptions, analyses, syntheses, and judgments may be formulated by the learner.

WHAT IS THE ROLE OF A TEAM CHAIRMAN?

The designation of "department chairman" has been superseded in the Ridgewood plan by the office of team chairman, which combines the duties of planner, coordinator, consultant, organizer, liaison officer, master teacher, and supervisor. His chief functions are those of supervisor, coordinator, and intermediary in the communication between team members and the administration. Although not actually members of the administration, team chairmen have certain administrative responsibilities such as assigning team members to supervise study areas, and shifting personnel to use their teaching talents to the best advantage. Therefore, team chairmen must have administrative competence in addition to the professional attributes listed above.

Under the team teaching system, one finds divergent views as to course content, approach to presentation, and teaching techniques. It is the problem of the team chairman to sift these differing views and guide the team to the choice of the ones best suited to furthering the ultimate aims of the program. This requires experience, good judgment, skill in group dynamics, and tact. It requires, as well, a mind open to the suggestions of team members. The chairman must be willing to try new ideas or ones differing from his own personal preferences. Since he is in a position to exert influence, he is obligated to examine carefully all suggested methods in relation to the desired end. Great care should be taken, to permit the development of an organizational climate which will encourage new ideas from all staff members.

A department chairman in a conventional school system is frequently a specialist in one subject only, but the chairman of a team of teachers must have a broad background in his general area in addition to specializing in his own teaching field. In order to plan intelligently and to coordinate the efforts of teachers in a number of fields, such as history, English, foreign languages, art, and music, a chairman must at least be well enough acquainted with these areas to avoid imbalance in the instructional program and to provide for presentation of all the essential facts with special emphasis on certain fields at the necessary time.

Once plans are formed for a unit of study, the attention of the team chairman turns to coordinating and supervising the execution of the plans. The amount of coordination possible varies, of course, from one unit to another, but even in instances where there seems to be limited, superficial carry-over from one subject to another, an imaginative teacher can weave together the threads of a theme, an underlying principle, a contrast or a basic purpose to show pupils how interrelated all knowledge is. Great care must be taken, however, so that the pupils feel stimulated by such an all-inclusive program rather than merely saturated.

It is a long-established principle that transfer of training does not take place automatically. It must be guided purposely and purposefully by the teacher. In his supervisory role, the team chairman must see that all team members are aware of the material from other fields which can be tied in with their special areas. Many of these items can be pointed out in the planning sessions; however, if one teacher overlooks or neglects to elaborate upon these to pupils, he can seriously weaken the entire unit. It depends for its strength upon the cooperation and the mutual effort of the whole team.

The chairman cannot, because of his own teaching schedule, be aware of all instruction being given in his field; however, there are many avenues of communication other than firsthand observation by which he can keep informed, rather accurately, of the quality of instruction in any given area. He can be influenced by planning sessions, comments of team members, questions asked at team meetings, and the type of tests used by the teachers. A chairman can become aware, by these means, of signs of excellence or weakness among his team members. He must be alert to these signs and be as quick with his praise as with his criticism. If any teacher, beginner or experienced, does not seem to be adapting well to the team approach, the chairman must make himself available for consultation—to analyze the problem or problems of the teacher and offer suggestions for the correction of it.

A position of leadership in a team can be greatly enhanced and strengthened by the good example of superior teaching on the part of the chairman himself. The master teacher must follow suggestions even more imaginatively and directions more exactly than he would in a traditional teaching situation because of the number of teachers looking to him for direction and example. This is particularly true in the case of those new to the team teaching organization. It might be wise for a chairman to keep records of the units which seemed most interesting and thought-provoking, and the methods which seemed to bring about the best results. Analysis of these would produce helpful guides to future planning.

One relatively unexplored area to tax the imaginative and supervisory powers of a team chairman is that of the individualized study program which goes along with this type of teaching. The Trump plan calls for approximately one third of a pupil's time to be spent in various study areas, the largest and most general of which are referred to as "resource centers." These centers fall under the direct or indirect supervision of the chairman of the appropriate areas—the Humanities Resource Center under the direction of the humanities team chairmen and the Science Resource Center under that of the math-science chairmen. These rooms, ideally, should be equipped with books, instruments, displays, realia, and whatever other materials would be necessary for or conducive to promoting interest in that area of study. The pupils should be encouraged to embark upon individual projects resulting from this stimulation of interest. Before this ideal can be realized, however, pupils must become adapted to thinking for themselves and awakened to a feeling of responsibility for their own enrichment and education. Accustomed as pupils are to direct assignments, limited freedom—mental as well as physical—and textbook-centered learning, they are slow to respond to such an opportunity. They must be educated to the limitless possibilities of such a study program and inspired with enthusiasm for working on their own.

HOW CAN PUPIL RESPONSIBILITY BE DEVELOPED?

One of the most suitable opportunities for pupil responsibility to be developed is the seminar where a student chairman has leadership functions. The chairman, as a result of planning sessions with the teacher, begins the class discussion and is responsible for its continuity and smooth progression. Such pupil chairmanship may bring about a deeper feeling of involvement than that felt in a traditional learning situation. If a question arises which pupils cannot answer, the teacher, of course, is present to solve the problem and to provide additional information beyond the knowledge or conclusions of the group.

Careful analysis is required to determine whether or not the catering to a select few pupils is a superior technique to the revolving chairmanship where each pupil has a turn. Regardless of the chairmanship assignment, it is expected that each one may feel increasingly responsible not only for the progress of the class, but also for his own contributions to it.

A pupil is much less likely to remain inconspicuous and to avoid recitation in a group of fifteen than in a conventional class of thirty. He becomes conspicuous in this small group if he does *not* participate. As the student becomes increasingly aware that contributions are expected of him, and as he becomes increasingly less hesitant about expressing his opinions, he develops increased intellectual curiosity, which leads him to gather more informative, worthwhile contributions for future discussions.

In the development of the attitude of pupil responsibility for learning, an apparently paradoxical situation may result. The more able the pupil, the less he will rely upon the teacher for knowledge; but the more he will require the intelligent guidance of the teacher so that his knowledge may be used wisely and effectively. If this danger is to be minimized and if the factual contributions are to be woven into a meaningful pattern, the influence of the teacher is necessary no matter how much self-responsibility the pupil develops. If the teacher is really a teacher, there can be no exception to this conclusion.

WHAT IS THE ROLE OF AN INSTRUCTION ASSISTANT?

The role of the instruction assistant is to perform any non-professional task which will free the teacher to perform professional tasks. The duties involved range from attendance taking to supervising seminars under the direction of the teacher. Since the concept of what is professional is controversial, the role of the instruction assistant is variable, but in every instance the responsibility for what he does falls upon the teacher and the team chairmen. The teacher may delegate tasks to the instruction assistants, but he may not abrogate his responsibility. Since the value resulting from what the instruction assistant does is derived by the teacher in that his work of teaching may be more effective, the untenability of abrogating authority by the teacher is very clear.

The professional staff must work closely with the instruction assistant so that, by example and through theory and professional meetings, the assistant may learn more about the art and skill of teaching. At the end of the school year, the assistants who are most capable will stand an excellent chance of becoming regular staff members, or else they will be assisted in finding suitable professional positions in another system, assuming they obtain the necessary training.

Among the tasks which the instruction assistant may perform, the following are typical: take attendance, supervise study areas, work in language lab, work in reading lab, grade papers, assist in management of seminars, assist during large-group presentations, set up labs, do plantings for botany, and supervise some extracurricular activities.

If the teacher and the instruction assistant are to work well together, they must understand each other's role and they must be relatively free from interpersonal friction. The greater the knowledge and applicability of group dynamics and psychological principles, the smoother the functioning of the team.

WHAT ARE THE ADMINISTRATIVE CONSIDERATIONS IN STAFF UTILIZATION?

The administrative considerations involved in operating a school system under the staff utilization concept are sufficient to challenge the ingenuity of any administrator. Even such details as attendance reports and other factors relative to pupil accounting are difficult to routinize due to the intricacies of the type of schedule necessary to put this system into practice.

In general, the schedule must provide for instruction for all pupils in large groups, seminar (or small) groups, and in individual study. The percentage of pupil time recommended by Dr. Trump in each of these phases is 40%, 30%, and 30%, respectively.

With homogeneous groupings of a workable size to provide for individual differences and with teams of teachers assigned to teach the pupils, the problems of scheduling are multiplied. To complicate matters further, it is necessary to give each teacher large blocks of unscheduled time during the day so that he can meet and plan with other teachers on his team. And to add to the complexity even more, if integration of subject areas is to be achieved effectively, it is necessary to schedule the humanities teachers at a time (morning or afternoon) when the science-math teachers are unscheduled. If all teachers were scheduled at the same time, they could not call upon each other's talents to enrich their presentations. It is also necessary to schedule the instruction assistants so that the team to which they are assigned may be able to utilize their services most effectively. Certainly, absenteeism among the teachers can play havoc with their assignments and, since the intricacies of the staff utilization plan may minimize the value of a substitute teacher, it is essential that the schedule be sufficiently flexible so that the staff may "cover" for the absent teacher. As a precautionary measure, it is wise to employ a full-time unassigned person, perhaps an instruction assistant, who can be pressed into service in an emergency. If financial factors prohibit this employment and/or if several teachers are absent on any given school day, expediency must rule and the administrator may find himself as a substitute in a teaching role until the full staff is available.

Because of these factors attendant to the schedule, each school interested in staff utilization must make the specific modifications peculiar to its own situation. After an efficient, well-developed schedule is in operation, the possibilities for flexibility and effectiveness become clearer and clearer so that the arduous task of building the schedule is more than compensated by the advantages derived.

It was mentioned above that the schedule must provide for homogeneous groupings of a "workable" size. What is workable depends upon one's interpretation, but it is obvious that a large group must be greater in number than a conventional class size and that a seminar group must be small enough so that pupil participation is enhanced. The maximum size of a large group, of course, will be determined by pupil enrollment and the physical facilities of the school building. Perhaps an acceptable minimum enrollment in a large group is 75 pupils, although this number is not sacred. When there are too few pupils in a large group, the staff utilization concept is destroyed because the teacher's time is not used most effectively if his presentations are delivered to small groups of pupils.

For effective seminar discussions, experience has shown that 12–16 pupils is best. If there are too few pupils, the student chairman may not have enough status and the dynamics of the small unit may not be sufficiently strong to evoke effective discussion; on the other hand, if there are approximately 20 or more pupils in a seminar, the unity of the group is difficult to maintain and pupil participation may be no less frequent than in a conventional class.

Relative to individual study, it is necessary that small groups of pupils be assigned to a study area supervised by a teacher and/or instruction assistant who has the educational background to assist the pupils in their work. This assignment of staff must be weighed in terms of teacher load as well as degree of pupil responsibility.

The physical facilities of the school are very important, also. They must be concrete examples of the abstract concepts of *staff utilization*. Large-group rooms must be provided and equipped with the audio-visual equipment necessary to illustrate the presentation. Seminar rooms must be provided so that there is a physical setting conducive to the intimacy of small-group dynamics. The individual study areas must be equipped with the materials and the resources which are designed to motivate and to assist the pupil in his studies. A school which is built to implement the concepts of *team teaching* is a positive and integral ingredient in the success of the program.

Selected Bibliography

Team Teaching: Junior and Senior High School

And No Bells Ring. 16 mm. film. Commission for the Experimental Study of the Utilization of the Staff in the Secondary School, National Association of Secondary School Principals. Washington, D.C.: 1201 Sixteenth Street, N. W.; 2 reels.

Film in two parts presents recommendations of the "Trump Commission." Encourages secondary school experimentation. Gives basic ideas of team teaching, independent study, etc.

Anderson, Edward J. "Crackling Excitement in the School Corridors; Team Teaching at Wayland, Massachusetts." *Life* 54:78–84, March 22, 1963.

Advocate of team teaching describes high school program in Wayland, Massachusetts.

Also see Journal of Secondary Education 36:354–356, October 1961; Nation's Schools 65:83–91, April 1960; Time 78:42, October 20, 1961; and Bulletin of NASSP 46:123–126, January 1962; and 47:118–127, March 1963.

Anderson, Robert H. "Organizational Character of Education: Staff Utilization and Deployment." *Review of Educational Research* 34:455–469, October 1964.

Points out a school experiment usually simultaneously involves other changes. Nongrading, for example, stimulates interest in team teaching and other regrouping plans. Discusses team teaching, sub-professional personnel, the flexible school, nongrading and technology.

Anrig, Gregory R. "Promising and Perplexing Aspects of Large Group Teaching Experiments." *Bulletin of NASSP* 46:253–260, January 1962.

Gives pros and cons. Says team teaching allows the modern teacher to reach more students, receive more pay, and train nonprofessionals and aides by example and by precept. Hierarchies, however, might create tensions. Also says achievement levels are often disappointing in large groups.

Arnold, William. "Is Team Teaching the Answer?" *School and Society* 91:407–409, December 14, 1963. Also in *Education Digest* 29:20–21, March 1964.

Warns against jumping on the bandwagon. Indicates team teaching offers promising possibilities if there is a thorough preparation, planning, and coordination.

Baynham, Dorsey. "A School of the Future in Operation." *Phi Delta Kappan* 42:350–354, May 1961.

An account of Ridgewood High at Norridge, Illinois. This school has put all of the recommendations of the "Trump Commission" into operation including large and small group instruction, independent study, and team teaching.

Also see School Management 8:113, October 1964; North Central Associa-

tion Quarterly 40:208–213, February 1965; *Bulletin of NASSP* 45:273–274, January 1961; 46:105–122, January 1962; and 46:59–64, December 1962.

Baynham, Dorsey. "Selected Staff Utilization Projects in California, Georgia, Colorado, Illinois, Michigan, and New York." *Bulletin of NASSP* 46:15–98, January 1962.

Gives a sampling of projects being conducted in junior and senior high schools in six states as a part of the NASSP Committee on Staff Utilization. Describes experimentation with team teaching, preparation of teacher-specialists, use of technology, large and small group instruction, etc.

Beggs, David W. "Decatur-Lakeview Plan." *Overview* 3:42–43, 47–48, December 1962. Also see *Bulletin of NASSP* 44:254–256, January 1960; 45:85–92, January 1961; 46:193–202, January 1962; and *American School Board Journal* 148:21–22, May 1964.

Principal Beggs describes some of the major tasks in reorganizing the Decatur (Illinois) High School to meet recommendations of the "Trump Commission." Discusses adapting the system to traditional buildings, restructuring faculty duties, restructuring classes into large and small groups, obtaining community cooperation, and solving specific operational problems. Team teaching, large and small group instruction, independent study, multimedia teaching aids, flexible scheduling, and programmed instruction are some of the changes introduced.

Beggs, David W. *Team Teaching: Bold New Adventure.* (Edited by David W. Beggs, III). Indianapolis, Indiana: Unified College Press, Inc., 3600 Washington Blvd., 1964.

Collection of essays on aspects of team teaching by twelve people from team supervisory, administrative, and teaching roles. Attempts to show how team teaching fits into elementary, junior, and senior high schools. Writers are advocates of the team approach.

Beggs, David W. and Buffie, Edward G. (Editors). *Independent Study.* Bloomington, Indiana: Indiana University Press, 1965. pp. 1–67, 83–219.

Describes school programs, facilities, instructional materials, team teaching, and flexible scheduling.

Brown, B. Frank. *Appropriate Placement School: A Sophisticated Nongraded Curriculum.* West Nyack, N.Y.: Parker Publishing Co., Inc., 1965.

Gives details of the multiphased curriculum for primary, intermediate, junior, and senior high schools. Includes chapters on school buildings, the library, dropouts, and the disadvantaged student. Describes team teaching, nongrading, large and small groups, independent study, etc.

Brown, B. Frank. *Nongraded High School.* Englewood Cliffs, N.J.: Prentice-Hall, 1963.

Describes nongraded Melbourne High School organized in 1958. Includes discussion of team teaching.

Bush, Robert N. and Allen, Dwight W. *A New Design for High School Education.* New York: McGraw-Hill, 1964.

Presents theoretical framework of team teaching built on practice. Plan calls for teachers who diagnose what is to be learned and how and when it is attacked.

Corrigan, D. and Hynes, R. "Team Teaching: Proceed with Caution." *Clearing House* 39:312, January 1965. Also see *Social Education* 38:205–208, April 1964.

Discusses provisions and arrangements which should be made before beginning a team teaching program.

Costin, R., *et al.* "Six Years of Organization and Staff Utilization." *Bulletin of NASSP* 46:122–131, October 1962.

Reports practices at O'Farrell Junior High in San Diego, California. Uses flexible scheduling and utilizes teacher proficiencies, community resources, and technological devices.

Hanson, L. F. "School Using Programmed Materials." *Audiovisual Instruction* 8:101–103, February 1963. Also see *PTA Magazine* 56:16–17, March 1962.

Grade level listing of school systems using programmed materials. Useful for planning independent study activities.

Howe, Harold. "Needed: A Radical Change." *Saturday Review* 43:73–74, September 17, 1960. Also see *Journal of Secondary Education* 37:353–361, October 1962.

Advocates changes along the line of the Trump Plan.

Howe, Harold. "Experimentation at Newton." *California Journal of Secondary Education* 35:117–118, February 1960. Also see *Bulletin of NASSP* 44:122–138, January 1960; 44:201–205, April 1960; and *Saturday Review* 48:48–50, January 16, 1965.

Describes large-group instruction at Newton High in Newton, Massachusetts.

King, Jonathan. "In Which the Bell Tolls." *Saturday Review* 43:84–85, 99–100, October 15, 1960.

An Educational Facilities Laboratories official describes changes in form and structure of education and its buildings which contribute to transformation in schools. Gives three approaches to school design and gives examples of facilities found in several school systems. Discusses grouping, team teaching, and TV teaching.

"Locus of Change: Staff Utilization Studies." *Bulletin of NASSP* 46:1–323, January 1962.

Entire issue devoted to experiments including team teaching, independent study, nongrading, etc.

Lovetere, J. P. "Instructional Team: An Approach to a More Effective Junior High School Organization." *Clearing House* 41:301–303, January 1967.

Describes plan devised to reduce the number of exposures that junior high students and teachers have without losing the advantages of departmentalization. Organization is based on instructional teams.

Manlove, Donald C. and Beggs, David W. *Flexible Scheduling.* Bloomington, Indiana: Indiana University Press, 1965.

Shows how to use large-group, small-group, and independent study to achieve more flexible scheduling.

Peterson, C. H. "Team Teaching in the High School." *Education* 85:342–347, February 1965. Also in *Education Digest* 30:22–24, May 1965. Also see *American School Board Journal* 145:11–13, October 1962; and 149:15–17, November 1964.

Says team teaching helps solve certain instructional and curricular problems such as scheduling, individualized instruction, class size, effective use of time and talent, independent study, and chances for recognition.

Profiles of Significant Schools: Schools for Team Teaching. New York: Educational Facilities Laboratories, Inc., 1960.
Describes team teaching, schools being built for it and schools planned for the future.

Profiles of Significant Schools: High Schools, 1962. New York: Educational Facilities Laboratories, Inc., 1961.
Gives examples of high schools designed to facilitate team teaching.

Sand, Ole, *et al.* "Report on Some National Studies in Education." *Bulletin of NASSP* 47:163–181, April 1963. Also see *Bulletin of NASSP* 47:120–123, May 1963.
Director of NEA Project on Instruction discusses instructional issues and gives recommendations. Includes practices and trends in team teaching.

Shaplin, Judson T. "Team Teaching." *Saturday Review* 44:54–55, 70, May 20, 1961.
Gives three alternatives to the self-contained classroom. Discusses difficulties of the team teaching approach and many advantages including specialization in teaching, grouping of students, etc.

Shaplin, Judson T. and Olds, Henry F., Jr., *et al. Team Teaching.* New York: Harper and Row, 1964. Excerpt: "Antecedents of Team Teaching." *School and Society* 91:393–407, December 14, 1963.
Says criticism of schools reached a high point in 1953, and continues, but that out of this has emerged a climate favorable to change. Discusses five areas of change in relationship to team teaching: recruitment, training and career prospects of teachers; organization of schools into larger units; revisions of the curriculum; grouping for instruction, and development of technological aids.

Sharkan, W. W. *An Evaluation of the Team Organization Plan of Staff Utilization in Relationship to the Educational Development of Students in the Junior High Schools of Allentown, Pennsylvania.* Doctoral Dissertation, Pennsylvania State University, 1962. Also in *Dissertation Abstracts* 23:3742.
Eighty students (two groups) were compared in each of four junior high schools; forty taught by the team plan, and forty by the departmentalized plan. Better academic work in language arts, mathematics, science and social studies found in both high and low ability students taught by the team approach.

Taylor, D. N. *A Study of Opinions of Educators Concerning Proposals to Reorganize Secondary Schools to Accommodate Large- and Small-Group Instruction, Independent Study, and Team Teaching.* Doctoral Dissertation, Columbia University, 1962. Also in *Dissertation Abstracts* 23:4270.
Studied reactions to proposals of Trump Plan. Compared expected and actual results.

Thompson, S. D. *An Analysis of Achievement Outcomes: Team Teaching and Traditional Classes.* Doctoral Dissertation, Stanford University, 1963. Also in *Dissertation Abstracts* 24:3240.
Studied 209 high school seniors. Found achievement outcomes significantly favor traditionally-taught group over team teaching group when examined immediately after a unit, and favor team classes twenty days thereafter.

Thomson, Scott D. "Can Team Teaching Aid Learning?" *Journal of Secondary Education* 36:423–429, November 1961. Also in *Dissertation Abstracts* 24:3240.
  Discusses four additional elements usually used with team teaching: varied class size, modified period length, teacher aides, and technological devices. Gives analysis of research, factors of learning aided by team teaching, and endorses team teaching.

Trump, J. Lloyd. "Places to Learn." *Audiovisual Instruction* 7:516–517, October 1962. Also see *Phi Delta Kappan* 47:37–39, September 1965; *Bulletin of NASSP* 46:299–304, January 1962; 47:11–20, May 1963; and *Education* 85:327–332, February 1965.
  Points out provisions must be made for small group, large group, and independent study in an adequate school. Shows their relationship to curricula, methods of teaching, instructional material, etc.

Horizontal Organization—
Ability Grouping

Chapter 11

Homogeneous vs. Heterogeneous Grouping

Ability Grouping: The Research Is Inconclusive

Marian Pope Franklin

How should we group students for classes? This is a horizontal organizational question that must be faced by each school staff. It can be decided to form classes on the basis of some likeness, or homogeneity. The characteristic used could be the students' ages, ability, achievement, learning style, or study habits. An alternative to grouping on the basis of a likeness is to form classes on the basis of differences, or heterogeneity. In such an arrangement, students are grouped with others who are quite different. If achievement is used, for example, the students would be at many levels of achievement in a heterogeneous class.

One basis for forming so-called homogeneous groups has been the ability of the students. This practice was introduced as early as 1920 in some of the Detroit, Michigan schools. Intelligence test scores were used for forming classes and students of similar abilities were placed in the same class. During the next decade the practice spread to other schools, reaching a peak in the thirties. Some school systems abandoned the practice in the forties and fifties. During the past decade, ability grouping has again been revived and has been flourishing. The NEA Research Division found in 1957–1958 that 77.5 per cent of the school districts of 2,500 and over in population were making some use of ability grouping in the elementary grades and 90.5 per cent in the secondary. The reported percentage is

Written especially for this book. Dr. Marian Pope Franklin is Professor, School of Education, at The University of North Carolina in Greensboro.

probably inaccurate. Some schools that reported the use of ability as a basis for forming classes actually used achievement. Nevertheless, despite known mistakes in labeling, it is fair to say the practice of ability grouping is again spreading.

Some advocates of the practice do not seem to realize it is impossible to form a truly homogeneous group because there is much variation among students and within individuals. Ability, for example, is made up of a number of factors including memory, induction, deduction, verbal comprehension, number factor, space factor, and creativity. These abilities appear in various combinations in people. Two IQ scores of 120, therefore, do not indicate identical intelligence. One person might be high in word fluency while the other might be high in number factor. Each would have different skills, talents, and abilities. To group students on the basis of a total IQ score, then, does very little to really restrict the range of ability.

WHAT DOES RESEARCH SAY?

The research on the subject is conflicting. About half of the studies report students do better when they are grouped homogeneously on ability and the other half report they do better when grouped heterogeneously. The results, then, are inconclusive. Furthermore, the design of many of the studies is often weak.

The readings in Chapter 11 are from both proponents and opponents of the issue. Hansen and Heffernan oppose ability grouping and report research studies that support their position. Goldberg and Passow cast serious doubts on the practice. Hart reports research which supports homogeneous grouping. Woodring recommends homogeneous achievement grouping in high school. Olson maintains no one plan of grouping can be considered superior for inducing growth in achievement. Strevell and Oliver identify grouping plans they found in the literature and favor flexible grouping within a classroom rather than across-the-board ability grouping. The bibliography leads to further readings on the subject.

What Does Ability Grouping Do to the Self-Concept?

Maxine Mann Hansen

"I am in the low fift Grade I am to dom."

"I happened to be a little smarter than the rest."

These quotations are from answers given by two fifth-grade pupils when asked, "How do you happen to be in this fifth-grade group?"

Do these self-reports give any indication of ways in which these children see themselves? Does the fact that these children have spent most of their five school years under ability grouping have anything to do with the self-concepts—"myself as I see me"[1]—that they are reflecting?

RECURRING INTEREST IN ABILITY GROUPING

During the twenties and thirties the literature contained many references to homogeneous or ability grouping. In the following years interest in the subject seemed to decrease. Perhaps it was felt that the problem had been satisfactorily solved. In the two years since the first Sputnik, with the subsequent re-evaluation of American education, the grouping question has been raised again. It is repeatedly suggested that perhaps ability grouping might be the answer to the problem of improving our educational program. The philosophy involved in ability grouping is not without some merit. It *is* one attempt to meet the problem of individual differences. However, the emphasis seems to be primarily on differences in potential for academic achievement. Seldom is the question raised as to possible emotional impact on the child in this type of school organization. One finds such comments as, "Teachers observed that the . . . groups were exceedingly happy." This might indicate some subjective evaluation, but there is no evidence of objective data to support such observations.

Is ability grouping good in the way children look at themselves? Is it good in the way teachers look at children? Combs refers to Raimy's original definition of the self-concept in 1943 as, "the more or less organ-

Reprinted from *Childhood Education*, April, 1960, Vol. 36, pp. 357–360, by permission of the Association for Childhood Education International, 3615 Wisconsin Avenue, N.W., Washington, D.C. 20016. Dr. Maxine Mann Hansen is at Wisconsin State University, Whitewater, Wisconsin.

[1] J. Murray Lee and Dorris M. Lee, *The Child and His Development* (New York: Appleton-Century-Crofts, Inc., 1958), p. 26.

ized perceptual object resulting from present and past self observation . . . (it is) what a person believes about himself."[2] Combs then goes on to say,

> . . . the individual himself infers from his experiences who he is and what he is. He perceives of himself as . . . liked or unliked, acceptable or unacceptable, able or unable, depending upon his experiences with the world about him, but most particularly from how people who inhabit that world treat him. All these perceptions contribute to his perception of himself, to his phenomenal self.[3]

Combs and Soper point out the confusion in terminology that has arisen around this comparatively new theory, the self-concept. One such case is the error of using "self-concept" and "self-report" synonymously. The term, "self-report"—what the individual *says* he is—is not a synonym for "self-concept" but may be valuable as a means of exploring the self-concept.[4]

DESCRIPTION OF GROUP

In a limited study among a group of 102 fifth-grade children, this writer attempted to obtain some self-reports which might offer clues to self-concepts. These children were classified into four ability groups upon entrance to first grade. Grouping at that time was based upon results of group intelligence tests and reading readiness tests. Labeled only by the teachers' names, groups are referred to in informal teacher conversations as "the highest group," "the lowest group," "second high," "second low." For the purposes of this study they will be referred to as Sections One, Two, Three and Four in descending order of estimated ability. Thirty children responded in Section One, twenty-nine in Section Two, twenty-five in Section Three, and eighteen in Section Four.

METHOD OF THIS STUDY

A group questionnaire adapted from a study made by Keliher was used to obtain information as to how children see themselves in ability grouping.[5] The children were told that the writer was making a study to find out what children were thinking and that their teacher had said she

---

[2] Arthur W. Combs and Donald Snygg, *Individual Behavior* (New York: Harper & Bros., 1959), p. 127.

[3] *Ibid.*, p. 128.

[4] Arthur W. Combs and Daniel Soper, "The Self, Its Derivative Terms, and Research," *Journal of Individual Psychology*, XII (November, 1957), pp. 137–8.

[5] Alice V. Keliher, *A Critical Study of Homogeneous Grouping* (New York: Teachers College, Columbia University, 1931), p. 109.

believed they would be willing to help. They readily agreed. Blank sheets of paper were then distributed. When children asked whether they should write their names on the papers, they were told that it would not be necessary. It was suggested that perhaps it would be easier to write exactly what they thought if they did not. Some children expressed relief while others insisted upon identifying their papers.

The following directions were given with sufficient time between questions for the children to think and write as fully as they wished.

Please write a number One at the top of your paper. After the number One write the grade you are in. Now write a number Two under the number One and tell me *which* fifth grade you are in. Now write a number Three and tell me how you happen to be in *this* particular fifth-grade group rather than some other group. Now put a number Four on your paper and answer this question with just a "yes" or "no." Is your very, very best friend in this room? Now write a number Five on your paper and answer this question with just a number. How many years have you gone to this school?

The first, fourth and fifth questions were blinds to allay any suspicion on the part of the children, while the second and third were designed to obtain the information.

DISCUSSION OF DATA

Since the groups are officially labeled by teachers' names, one might expect the children to identify them in this manner. About one-third of Section One did make this identification, but almost two-thirds of this group used such terms as "high fifth," "high," "best," "top fifth." Only three children in Section Two and six in Section Three used such identifications as "second highest," "second high," "second to the highest," "C room," "third fifth grade." In Section Four, as in Section One, two-thirds of the group used terms such as "low fifth grade," "low," "lower," rather than the teacher's name. Ways in which children identified their groups are presented in Table 1.

TABLE 1

Ways In Which Children Identified Their Groups

Identification of Group	Section				Total
	1	2	3	4	
By ability placement	19	3	6	12	40
By teacher's name	11	26	17	5	59
By other means	0	0	2	1	3

While only forty of the entire sample identified their groups in terms of ability placement, over two-thirds of Sections One and Four responded in this manner. What experiences have brought about such clear identification in *these* sections? Since they are not with other groups for comparison, could this be a reflection of teacher attitudes which have been ingrained in children?

The reasons these children gave for their placement help to bring their self pictures into even clearer focus. Such responses as "I'm smart,"

TABLE 2

Children Reflect "Smartness" and "Dumbness" As Reasons For Placement

Reasons Given by Children	Section				Total
	1	2	3	4	
1. "I do not know."	...	14	12	...	26
2. "My name was on the list." "They put me here." "I passed."	5	6	6	...	17
3. *In positive terms of ability or achievement*: "I" responses: "I'm smart." "I was good in something." "I worked hard." "I made good grades."......................	21	1	2	...	24
"We" responses: "We're smarter." "We all know about the same things." "We can work a little faster."................	3	3	...	...	6
"This is the best fifth grade."	1	...	...	...	1
"This room works as fast as I can."	...	3	...	...	3
4. *In negative terms of ability or achievement*: "I" responses: "I am too dumb." "I am not so smart." "I can't think good." "I was not doing very good last year."..............	...	...	2	6	8
"We" responses: "We aren't smart." "We don't know very much." "Most of us are lazy."	...	...	1	7	8
"Low book."	...	...	...	1	1
5. *In somewhat neutral terms of ability or achievement*: "I was in this level for fifth grade."	...	1	...	...	1
"I work the best I can."	...	...	1	...	1
"As well as we work we get in this grade." ...	...	...	1	...	1
"What kind of grades you made."	...	1	...	...	1
6. Other reasons	...	...	...	4	4
Total	30	29	25	18	102

"We're smarter," "I'm too dumb," "We don't know very much," account for half the answers to the third question. The reasons the children gave for their placement are presented in Table 2.

In Section One twenty-five children gave positive responses in terms of ability or achievement—twenty-one of them in positive "I" terms. There were no negative responses from this group. In the next lower section, Section Two, there were only seven responses in terms of ability or achievement and in Section Three only five. In Section Four, the lowest, the fourteen responding in terms of ability or achievement gave negative responses —six in "I" terms, seven in "we" terms. It is interesting to note that there are no negative responses in Sections One and Two, few in Section Three, and *only* negative responses in Section Four.

Again one may ask, "What are the experiences which have contributed to the way the children in the 'top' and 'bottom' groups see themselves? Could teacher rejection of the low group and acceptance of the high group help to account for it?" There is administrative recognition of these attitudes in the practice of giving a teacher a high group after she has had a low group for a year.

Before we grasp the straw of ability grouping as the answer to instructional problems brought about by individual differences in academic potentiality, we need to re-examine what has already been done with ability grouping. Because of the negative attitudes such as those revealed by the "low" group in this study, ability grouping was abandoned in the thirties. Are we going to repeat the same mistakes in the sixties?

RECOMMENDED READING

J. Wayne Wrightstone, *What Research Says to the Teacher About Class Organization for Instruction* (Washington, D.C.: NEA, 1957).

ACEI, *More About Reading* (Washington, D.C.: The Association, 3615 Wisconsin Avenue, N.W., 1959).

Questions Parents Ask

Helen Heffernan

Homogeneous Grouping! Yes? No?

A parent asks:

When schools opened last fall, parents were notified in a letter that children would be grouped on the basis of their scores on intelligence and achievement tests. My son was placed in an average group. During the year he seems to have lost interest in school. He used to play with all the children in the neighborhood; now he avoids the children who are in the superior group. He doesn't seem to get along with his playmates as well as he used to do. He seems to have lost confidence in himself. We have encouraged him to work harder to get into the superior group.

What about ability grouping—is it desirable or undesirable?

One of the outstanding national authorities on child development, Dr. Willard C. Olson, Dean, School of Education, University of Michigan, says:[1]

> There appears to be a very persistent belief that many instructional problems would be solved if one could only put together the children who are alike with respect to the subject of instruction. Thus, it is often proposed that children be put into ability groups for reading, for arithmetic, etc.

About 30 years ago, extensive experimentation with ability grouping was carried on in school systems throughout the United States. Olson[2] reviews two studies of significance. Hartill[3] carried on a study with fifth and sixth-grade pupils in New York City. He found no significant differences between gains made by those grouped homogeneously and those grouped heterogeneously. Russell[4] studied children in grades four, five and six in San Francisco grouped into high, average and low sections according to reading ability. Tests showed no reliable differences in the achievement of these children as compared with children instructed in heterogeneous groups.

The classical study on this issue continues to be that of Dr. Walter W. Cook, Dean, School of Education, University of Minnesota, who presents

Reprinted from *Grade Teacher* 81:8, 122, 123, April 1964, by permission of the publisher and the author. Dr. Helen Heffernan is Chief, Bureau of Elementary Education, California State Department of Education.

evidence to show that regardless of efforts to reduce the heterogeneity of a group, considerable heterogeneity still remains. While classes may be relatively homogeneous in one phase of a subject such as arithmetic reasoning, they may be heterogeneous in some others such as arithmetic computation.[5] Later in the same study Dr. Cook warns:

> . . . it is very important to know the limitations of such grouping. The harm resulting from homogeneous grouping is inherent in the assumption that the group *is* homogeneous and that instructional materials and procedures can be adjusted to the needs of the group as a whole . . .[6]

From these and many comparable studies we have objective evidence which should convince us of the futility of attempting to improve teaching by mechanical grouping processes which de-emphasize the importance of creating instructional situations in which each child can develop his personal resources.

During the past century, many school people have devoted their energy to trying to discover ways of coping with the wide range of individual differences among children by some means of organization. Dr. Harold G. Shane[7] identifies some 35 different plans. The idea of organization to make education more effective is so intriguing that it will probably continue through educational history.

In January 1963, however, a group of twenty leaders in elementary education, meeting in Washington under the auspices of the Department of Elementary-Kindergarten-Nursery Education of the National Education Association, said:[8] ". . . no existing evidence demonstrates that any one pattern of organization results in a higher degree of academic achievement for all children . . ."

On the basis of this statement which is supported by sound research, schools need to give particularly serious attention to some of the effects ability grouping may have on children.

Here we are confronted with the specter of "common sense"—that full partner of "unproved beliefs." Says the unsophisticated, "It's just *common sense* to put children who are alike together. It makes teaching easier."

But both of these common sense conclusions are utterly fallacious and completely unproved. Research on individual differences has completely disproved the notion that all children are alike. Even if two children achieve identical scores on a standardized reading test, they are not identical in reading ability because the score in each case will represent the summation of a different set of score items which constitute the test.

Such grouping may make teaching easier for certain teachers but not for all. When teaching assignments are made, teachers with seniority usually demand the bright or average groups. This means that children with many personality or learning problems are assigned to the newcomers to the staff and therefore frequently to the least experienced teachers. The teaching may become easier but for whom? School morale usually suffers.

Learning becomes more difficult for many children. Children learn much from the discussion of ideas by their peers that they could never get for themselves from the printed page. By working with other children with a wide range of capacities, a child secures a realistic self-image. He can see his own strengths and limitations. He can evaluate himself and need not be forced to accept the low expectancy imposed upon him by a mechanical system of classification.

When children are placed in groups recognized by them and their peers as incompetent, they suffer loss of status and are frequently shunned by their age mates who have adult-imposed standards of social acceptability.

Dr. Olson[9] concludes his analysis of the "unsuccessful attempts to stimulate the growth of children in school subjects by various schemes for grouping" with this statement:

> There is a strong present trend in the United States for a child to remain with a group in which he is a good physical and social fit and to adjust the work within the grade to his needs. At the same time there is a vocal minority that asks for a grouping by ability on the basis of belief rather than data.

Dr. Julia W. Gordon, Director, Child and Youth Study, State Department of Education, New Jersey, says:[10]

> The way we put children together in groups reveals how we regard human beings. Do we believe that human welfare and the welfare of our democratic society are best served by developing to the maximum the potential within each individual? Or do we believe that individuals are expendable?

Dr. Gordon sets up a rationale based on the question: "What human processes do we need to understand?" She analyzes these processes in terms of (1) the human being as an energy system, (2) perception and learning, (3) emotions, and (4) socialization. In terms of the agreements among the behavioral scientists, she then concludes that grouping should be characterized by these factors:

1. Grouping should be flexible.

2. Grouping should be in terms of the purposes of the individual child.

3. The basic group with which the child spends most of his day should be as heterogeneous as possible.

4. The number in basic classroom groups should be small enough for face-to-face encounters.

5. The same group of children should remain together for a long-enough time to develop a stake in each other's welfare and growth.

6. Each child should have time alone to strengthen his trust in himself.

7. Each child should have opportunity to share what he has with his peers and be challenged by them.

8. The position of adults concerned with grouping should be such that the other aspects of grouping may be advanced.

Dr. Gordon is telling us throughout this penetrating analysis of the problem that our decisions with regard to children are a true measure of how much we value human beings. Communities and school systems looking toward achieving excellence in education must always seek first what has already been found out about any proposed innovations in grouping. Many new attention-attracting proposals are only new names for devices which have been tested, found wanting and discarded decades ago but not without tragic injury to the development and personality of children involved.

Let us seek, rather, such unspectacular solutions to the problem of greater achievement in education as careful selection and proper education of teachers, more effective curriculum content and patterns, smaller enrollments to provide a higher degree of individualization, properly staffed and equipped libraries and instructional materials centers in every elementary school, and available expert consultation service in child growth and development, curriculum subject matter fields and special problems.

Let us look with concern at easy answers and panaceas that may prove to be ways to divert our attention from the real problems that are confronting education today.

REFERENCES

1. *Child Development,* by Willard C. Olson, 2nd edition (p. 48), D. C. Heath & Company, 285 Columbus Ave., Boston 16, Mass.

2. *Ibid.,* p. 429.

3. *Homogeneous Grouping as a Policy of the Elementary Schools in New York City,* by R. M. Hartill, Bureau of Publications, Teachers College, Columbia University; out-of-print but probably available in libraries.

4. "Interclass Grouping for Reading Instruction in the Intermediate Grades," by D. H. Russell, *Journal of Educational Research* (39: pp. 462–470, 1946), Dembar Publications, 303 E. Wilson St., Madison, Wisconsin.

5. *Grouping and Promotion in the Elementary School,* by Walter W. Cook. Series on Individualization of Instruction, No. 2 (1946, p. 29), University of Minnesota Press, 2037 University Ave. S.E., Minneapolis 14, Minn.

6. *Ibid.,* p. 33.

7. "Chapter III. The School and Individual Differences," in *Individualizing Instruction,* by Harold G. Shane (1962, p. 49), The 61st Yearbook, National Society for the Study of Education; University of Chicago Press, 5750 Ellis Ave., Chicago 37, Ill.

8. *Agreements in Elementary Education*, Department of Elementary-Kindergarten-Nursery Education (March 1963), National Education Association, 1201 16th St. N.W., Washington 6, D.C.

9. Olson, *op. cit.*, p. 429.

10. "Grouping and Human Values," by Julia W. Gordon, *School Life*, Vol. 45, No. 9 (July, 1963), pp. 10–15; School Life, U.S. Dept. of Health, Education and Welfare, Office of Education, Washington 25, D.C.

The Effects of Ability Grouping

Miriam L. Goldberg and A. Harry Passow

The Talented Youth Project was organized in 1953 to carry on research into the nature of talent and the academic behavior of pupils classified as gifted. The project is supported by the Horace Mann-Lincoln Institute of School Experimentation of Teachers College, Columbia University, New York City.

Since its inception, TYP has been involved in several major research efforts dealing with problems of gifted high school underachievers; appropriate mathematics programs for high ability junior high school students; provisions for outstanding students in small, rural secondary schools; the effects of special guidance programs on academic performance and aspirations; the relationship between "creativity" and academic performance; and the effects of ability grouping on the academic, social and personal growth of intermediate grade children.[1]

Some of the findings from the grouping study will be described here. Further information on the work of the Talented Youth Project can be secured on request from the Director of the Institute.

THE EFFECTS OF ABILITY GROUPING

The major concern of recent studies of ability grouping has been with the effects of the gifted themselves. Attention to the effects of ability grouping procedures on the total school population is limited to the flurry of studies which appeared in the early 1930's under the rubric of "homogeneous vs. heterogeneous" grouping.

With a few notable exceptions, the findings from these investigations were restricted in scope due to small sample size, short duration, and limited areas of assessment. The total body of research gives inadequate

Reprinted from *Education* 82:482–487, April 1962, by permission of the publisher and the authors. Copyright, 1962, by The Bobbs-Merrill Company, Inc., Indianapolis, Indiana. (Footnote has been renumbered.) Dr. Miriam L. Goldberg is an Associate Professor, Teachers College, Columbia University; and Dr. A. Harry Passow is Professor of Education, Teachers College, Columbia University, New York City.

[1] For a recent report on these activities, see A. Harry Passow and Miriam L. Goldberg, "Talented Youth Project: Progress Report 1962," *Exceptional Children* 28:223–231, January 1962.

attention to the effects of special classes for the gifted on the school behavior of the rest of the population.

To seek at least partial answers to questions about the effects and the
effectiveness of narrow- and broad-range ability-grouped classes, the Talented Youth Project in cooperation with the Board of Education of the
City of New York, undertook a two-year study. The specific purpose of the
study was to explore differences in achievement, social and personal relations, interests and attitudes toward self and toward school of intermediate
grade children when grouped in classes with various ranges of intellectual
ability.

The general hypothesis tested was as follows: *Neither the presence nor
absence of gifted pupils, nor the range of abilities in any given classroom,
nor the relative position of a particular ability level within the range will
affect the attainment of elementary school pupils.*

THE RESEARCH DESIGN

To assess the effects of ability grouping on the academic and personal-social learning of elementary school pupils, a population had to
be identified which covered a sizeable portion of the total intellectual
continuum and which could be divided into classes of varying breadth of
ability range.

Five ability levels were designated, as follows: gifted, IQ 130 and
above; very bright, IQ 120–129; bright, IQ 110–119; high average, IQ
100–109; and low and below average, IQ 99 and lower. In order to assess
each ability level either alone or in combination with one, two, three or
four of the other levels, 15 grouping patterns were organized.

In the spring of 1956, New York City elementary schools in four of
the five boroughs were asked to submit the distribution of the Otis Alpha
IQ scores of their fourth-grade pupils. All schools which listed at least four
pupils with IQ's above 130 were invited to participate. As a result of this
requirement, many schools were excluded. Most of the schools excluded
were located in the culturally disadvantaged areas of the city.

Forty-five elementary schools cooperated in organizing some 3,000
pupils into 86 fifth-grade classes for September, 1956. These classes were
to remain intact, barring normal mobility, for two school years. Each class
fitted one or another of the fifteen patterns. Only those pupils (about
2,200) who were in their original classes at the end of the sixth grade and
on whom complete pre- and post-test data were available were included in
the final population that was studied.

Teachers were assigned to the experimental classes in the usual
manner for the particular school. No attempt was made to control or even
investigate class differences in content or teaching method since the purpose

of the study was to discover the effects of ability grouping, *per se,* and not of predetermined special provisions.

To derive as complete a picture as possible, a variety of commercial and specially developed testing instruments was used. The assessment included pre- and post-tests in each of the following areas: academic achievement, interest, attitudes toward self, attitudes toward more and less able pupils, attitudes toward school, teacher appraisal, social acceptance, leadership status.

The findings reported here, however, relate only to the effects on academic achievement of the presence or absence of gifted pupils, of ability range and of relative position in that range.

ACHIEVEMENT INSTRUMENTS

To assess growth in achievement, the subjects were pre- and post-tested on alternate forms of the *Science Research Associates (SRA) Achievement Series* (Grades 4–6). The test consists of four areas: (1) Work Study Skills, (2) Reading, (3) Language Arts, and (4) Arithmetic. Each of these major areas is divided into two or more sub-sections. The grade level range for each of the nine tests is from 2.0 to 10.0. In addition, *Stanford Achievement Tests* in Science and Social Studies (Intermediate level, range from grade 1.1 to 12.0) were administered at the same time. The only tests which provided an adequate ceiling for the gifted pupils were the *Stanford Achievement* Science and Social Studies tests (12th grade top) and the *SRA* Arithmetic Computation test where the pre-test scores of the gifted group were sufficiently low to allow for substantial increments from the beginning of the fifth to the end of the sixth grades.

EFFECT OF GIFTED STUDENTS

A comparison of the achievement gains of the four lower ability levels in classes where they were with gifted pupils and in those in which there were no gifted, found the following results:

1. In science, the presence of gifted pupils had a consistently upgrading effect. In every instance where gifted pupils were present, all the other pupils made greater gains than in classes where the gifted were absent. Although the differences were often small, the pattern of differences was significantly consistent.

2. In social studies the presence of the gifted had an upgrading effect only on the achievement of very bright and bright pupils, and this only when there were less able pupils present. When these latter pupils were absent, the very bright and bright did better in social studies without the gifted than with them.

3. In all other subjects, the presence of the gifted was not consistently upgrading nor downgrading. In reading, language and work study skills, the differences where the gifted were present were minimal. Only for the bright group was there a significant effect in favor of the absence of the gifted. In arithmetic, the presence of the gifted tended to lower achievement increments for some of the groups; and only for the low and below-average did their presence have a significantly positive effect.

THE EFFECTS OF ABILITY RANGE

Analyses were made of the various narrow and broad range patterns with the following results:

1. A comparison was made between the broadest pattern in which all ability levels were represented with the five narrowest range patterns, in which each of the ability levels was alone. Except for the gifted, for whom average increment in the narrowest range pattern was slightly higher than in the broadest, each of the other ability levels showed slightly greater increments in the broadest range situation than in the narrowest range classes. However, few of these differences were large enough to be considered educationally important.

2. The fifteen patterns were collapsed into three range categories— Narrow (one or two ability levels), Medium (three ability levels) and Broad (four or five ability levels), and achievement increments for each ability level. When the three ranges were compared, the Broad-range pattern was consistently superior to the Narrow in all subjects except reading. In social studies, arithmetic reasoning, arithmetic computation, and total average, the Broad-range classes were also superior to the Medium-range classes.

When the five ability levels were considered together, the Broad-range grouping seemed to be consistently related to greater increments than either of the two other situations in most of the subject areas in which range had an effect on achievement. However, for any one ability level the differences were generally too small to be of significant educational importance.

RELATIVE POSITION

Each of the three intermediate groups was varied in five positions: (a) alone; (b) upgraded, with one or two levels above and none below; (c) downgraded, with one or two levels below and none above; (d) equilibrium—in the middle of a three- or five-tier group; and (e) broad—in some position other than equilibrium in a four- or five-level group.

Comparisons between achievement gains in the various positions for any one ability level revealed the following:

1. Only in social studies and arithmetic computation were there significant differences due to position. In both of these subjects the "alone" and the "broad" positions were related to greater gains for all ability levels than were the "upgraded," "downgraded," or "equilibrium" patterns combined.

2. For no subject was there a significant difference between being "upgraded" or "downgraded." These two positional arrangements resulted in essentially comparable gains.

3. In general, no one position was consistently superior to any other for all ability levels in all subjects.

DIFFERENCES AMONG CLASSES

Even when achievement differences due to ability, range, and relative position had been accounted for, a considerable portion of the differences in individual achievement growth still remained unexplained.

Further analyses were made of the extent to which classroom variation within patterns could account for some of the variations. For every ability level in every pattern and for each subject there was great variability from class to class. In some instances, within a given pattern the difference in achievement increments between two groups of pupils of comparable ability was as much as four and a half years. On the average, the difference between highest and lowest class in any subject was more than a full year.

The gifted group showed the greatest variability across all subjects, with an average difference between greatest and least gains of more than two full years. The low and below-average pupils showed the least variability from class to class, with a mean difference of only one year and two months.

So great were the differences from class to class that they often exceeded the achievement differences due to ability. In social studies, science and arithmetic computation, in which all pupils had sufficient test space, there were instances where the gains made by a single ability level in one class differed more from the gains made by comparably able pupils in another class (in the same pattern) than they did from gains made by more or less able pupils in their own classes.

TEACHER EFFECTIVENESS

Using pupil achievement as a measure of teacher effectiveness it was possible (a) to determine the extent to which "strong" teachers of one subject were also "strong" teachers of all other subjects and (b) the extent to which teachers who were successful with one ability level were also successful with other ability levels. The findings suggested that:

1. Some teachers were more successful than others in the general attainment of all pupils across several subjects and across several ability levels.

2. Most teachers were more successful in handling several ability levels in one or two subjects than they were in handling all subjects for a particular ability level.

3. It was more difficult to achieve comparable results in several subjects for the brightest, least difficult for the slowest pupils.

4. Some subjects, such as arithmetic and social studies, were more readily taught with comparable results to several ability levels simultaneously than was a subject such as science.

ASSESSMENT OF GROUPING

Many administrators, teachers and parents have long believed that ability grouping represents a solution to the problems of educating children of varied levels of intellectual ability. The objections that have been raised to the practice of grouping rarely deal with the academic outcomes of narrowing the ability range, but rather with the social and emotional effects that might result.

Despite the apparent logic of the contention that a teacher can achieve better results when confronted with a group which is relatively similar in learning ability, the available research on grouping practices does not provide consistent support for this contention.

This study set out to assess the effects of ability grouping *per se*, without any attempt to predetermine, control, or examine the content or methods used in the various patterns. If, as is so often believed, narrowing the ability range in a classroom facilitates the provisions of more appropriate learning tasks, makes more teacher time available to pupils of a given ability level, and stimulates the teacher to gear his teaching up or down, depending upon the level of the group, then pupils of each ability level should do better just as a result of being in classes where the ability range is limited.

The evidence from this study suggests that such is not necessarily the case. Not all teachers took advantage of the narrower range to do the very things which such grouping should have made possible. Some teachers were more effective in handling several ability levels together than other teachers were in handling a single ability group. The variation among classrooms was far greater than the variation among patterns when pupil intelligence was held constant.

The findings of this study cast serious doubt on the effects of ability grouping *per se* in raising the academic attainment of pupils. The pattern representing the broadest ability spread appeared to be most consistently associated with greatest academic gains for all pupils. However, the actual achievement differences between patterns tended to be small and no one pattern or combination of patterns was best.

In the absence of specific plans for changing the content and methods of teaching so as deliberately to provide the most needed and challenging learning situation for each group of pupils, ability grouping does not seem to make any appreciable difference.

The fact that teacher emphases in some subjects as against others varied from classroom to classroom within any one pattern, suggests that such stresses are more a function of teaching interest or competency than a result of carefully planned learning activities appropriate for pupils of differing intellectual capacity. Analysis of increments relative to grade level at the beginning of fifth grade indicated that the gains made in the two school years was not a function of high or low status at the beginning. Teachers' choice of emphasis seemed to be related to factors other than pupil status in a particular subject.

The ability level of the group did not always determine the amount of academic growth. Except for science, which was emphasized more when there were low and below-average pupils, the other subjects were or were not stressed at the discretion of the teachers regardless of starting point or pupil ability.

No conclusions can be drawn from this study as to the effectiveness of ability grouping where specific, consistent curricular adaptations are made. The only conclusion that may be drawn is that *narrowing the ability range per se, without specifically designing varied academic programs for the various ability levels, does not result in consistently greater academic achievement.*

ASSESSING TEACHER EFFECTIVENESS

The examination of teacher effectiveness in handling several subjects or several ability levels, though not related to the basic hypotheses of the study, revealed some provocative findings. The low concordance among the achievement gains in the various subjects raises some questions as to the ability of one teacher to handle the entire elementary school curriculum, especially for the gifted pupils. Although there were some teachers who did well in all subjects, and others who did poorly, most teachers achieved far better results in one or two subjects than they did in others.

Despite the fact that elementary school teachers believe that it is easier to teach all subjects to a narrow ability range than to teach one subject to a class with a broad spread of ability, this study found the reverse to be true. Although it did appear to be easier to attain comparable results with fewer ability levels than with the broad range, especially in science, most teachers were more successful in teaching a given subject to several ability groups simultaneously than in teaching all subjects to narrow range classes.

On the basis of this study, ability grouping *per se* did not have any positive effect on the academic attainment of fifth- and sixth-grade pupils. The variations in achievement were influenced more strongly by teacher and group differences in individual classrooms than they were by ability range, position, or even the intellectual ability of the pupils.

The Effectiveness of an Approach to the Problem of Varying Abilities in Teaching Reading

Richard H. Hart

THE PROBLEM

The problem of providing for the needs of pupils of varying ability has long challenged the resourceful and conscientious teacher. In the field of language arts in the elementary school, the grouping of children within a classroom as the means of adjusting the instructional program to the needs of the pupils has been utilized with success.[1]

Such a developmental program had been in effect at Peter Boscow School for a number of years. Each teacher had at least three groups in reading. Each group was reading in a developmental basal text on their own level regardless of grade placement. If a fourth grade group was reading on an easy third grade level, difficult fourth grade level, etc., they were given reading materials at that particular level. Similar groupings were effected in other areas of the language arts—such as spelling.

The faculty at Peter Boscow School believed that such grouping was necessary in a heterogeneous, self-contained classroom, if a developmental program in reading was the objective. However, experience with standardized achievement tests and actual classroom performance of pupils had revealed that in the average classroom there is a very wide range in the reading achievement and ability of pupils. An Informal Reading Survey[2] given by each teacher in the intermediate grades revealed this range in ability to be greater than desirable in every 4th, 5th and 6th grade class.

A range in ability typical of the variation found in every class is outlined in Table I. The teachers readily perceived that to divide such a class into three groups for reading instruction would be far from adequate. The Table reveals the need for nine such groups. To settle for less would result in some pupils being asked to study skills already mastered while other pupils would be required to perform at a level beyond their capacity. And to have nine instructional groups in one classroom would be most unreasonable.

Reprinted from the *Journal of Educational Research* 52:228–231, February 1959, by permission of the publisher and the author. Richard H. Hart is at the Peter Boscow School, Hillsboro, Oregon.

[1] William H. Burton, *Reading in Child Development* (New York: Bobbs-Merrill Company, Inc., 1956), pp. 505–519.

[2] Albert Emmett Betts, *Foundations of Reading Instruction* (New York: American Book Company, 1946), pp. 438–87.

TABLE I

Results of Informal Reading Inventory
(Grade 5-B)

Reading Grade Placement	Number of Pupils
8 plus	2
7	4
6_2*	4
6_1*	3
5_2	5
5_1	4
4_2	3
4_1	4
3_2	2

* 6_2 indicates that the pupil is performing at the sixth grade, second semester level; 6_1 indicates that the pupil is performing at the sixth grade, first semester level, etc.

TABLE II

Composite Results of Informal Reading Inventory
(Nine Intermediate Grade Classrooms)

Reading Grade Placement	Number of Pupils
7 plus	27
6_2*	30
6_1*	33
5_2	33
5_1	32
4_2	28
4_1	19
3_2	12
3_1	19
2_2	11
2_1	5
1 basic	6
Primer	2

* 6_2 indicates that the pupil is performing at the sixth grade, second semester level; 6_1 indicates that the pupil is performing at the sixth grade, first semester level, etc.

THE PLAN

Table II is a composite of the results of the Informal Reading Inventory for the 4th, 5th, and 6th grades at Peter Boscow School. Whereas each teacher in his own heterogeneous, self-contained classroom had seven to nine distinct groups, collectively the teachers had thirteen groups dis-

TABLE III

Teacher	Pupils	Reading Level
A	27	Grade 7 plus
B	30	" 6_2*
C	33	" 6_1
D	33	" 5_2
E	32	" 5_1
F	28	" 4_2
G	28	" 4_1
H	10	" 3_2
	14	" 3_1
I	6	" 2_2
	6	" 2_1
	6	" 1 basic
	2	" Primer

* See Table I or II for explanation of grade placement designations.

tributed among the nine teachers. If the children were grouped according to ability, each teacher would have one or two instructional groups in reading. The teachers concerned had believed that some form of ability grouping would help solve the problem. It was decided to experiment with a program similar to one reported in the February 1956 issue of *Elementary English*.[3]

DESCRIPTION OF PROGRAM

Each pupil was given the Reading Battery of the California Achievement Tests, the Durrell-Sullivan Intermediate Reading Survey, and the 1950 S-Form California Short-Form Test of Mental Maturity. On the basis of the results of these tests, the pupils were divided into ability groups as shown [in Table III].

A block of time 85 minutes in length was set aside daily for the teaching of the language arts—reading, spelling, writing, and English. During this time grade level designations were dissolved. Pupils of similar ability from the 4th, 5th, and 6th grades met with a particular teacher for language arts instruction. Each teacher used a developmental approach in the teaching of reading.

HYPOTHESIS

It was thought desirable to test, as part of an evaluation of the above program, the following hypothesis: Children's achievement in reading will be significantly greater in a reading instructional program where pupils

[3] Walter B. Barbe, and Tina S. Waterhouse, "An Experimental Program in Reading," *Elementary English*, XXXIII (February 1956), pp. 102–104.

are grouped homogeneously according to ability than in a heterogeneous situation, all other factors being equal.

PROCEDURES FOR EXPERIMENTATION

The decision was made to compare the pupil achievement in reading under the experimental program (ability grouping) for a period of one year (Sept. to Sept.) with the pupil achievement for a similar period of time under the regular program (heterogeneously grouped, self-contained class).

It is most difficult to control all the factors in an experiment in the area of curriculum. However, it is the writer's opinion that the following factors were controlled to a significant degree in this experiment:

1. Teachers.   This often is the most variable of all factors in experiments involving curriculum. However, five teachers taught reading to five fourth and fifth grade classes under the regular program, and the same five teachers taught reading to five fourth and fifth grade classes under the experimental program, with one exception. At the fourth grade level there was a turnover of one teacher. The principal of the building, the intermediate grade teachers, and the parents believed both teachers to be equally competent in the teaching of reading.

2. Instructional Methods.   As was mentioned previously in this paper, a developmental approach was used in teaching reading to both groups. Since the same teachers were involved in teaching both groups, it is the writer's opinion that this factor was controlled.

3. Pupils.   The pupils were comparable in every way—equal natural ability, equal home influence, etc., since they were drawn from the same identical community within a two year period.

4. Teaching time.   Equal emphasis was given to the language arts in both the regular and the experimental program. An equal amount of time was given to the teaching of reading in the regular program as compared to the experimental program.

5. Class loads.   Class loads were very comparable under the two programs.

6. Instructional materials.   Instructional materials were not identical in every case, but were very similar in every case.

TABLE IV

Fourth to the Fifth Grade

	Regular Reading Program Sept. 1955 to Sept. 1956 Group A	Experimental Reading Program Sept. 1956 to Sept. 1957 Group B
Number of cases	47	49
Median IQ	111	102
Mean gain	10.2 mos.	20.5 mos.
Standard Deviation	6.90	7.67
S. E. of the Mean	.982	.903

T Ratio[4] equals 7.72. The difference is very significant and the null hypothesis can be rejected with confidence.

Fifth to the Sixth Grade

	Regular Reading Program Sept. 1955 to Sept. 1956 Group C	Experimental Reading Program Sept. 1956 to Sept. 1957 Group B
Number of cases	49	45
Median IQ	111	111
Mean gain	8.67 mos.	18.0 mos.
Standard Deviation	7.10	6.41
S. E. of the Mean	.982	.966

T Ratio equals 6.81. Again the difference is very significant.

[4] J. P. Guilford, *Fundamental Statistics in Psychology and Education* (New York: McGraw-Hill Book Company, Inc., 1950), pp. 208–210.

RESULTS

The achievement of the pupils from the fourth to the fifth grade (Sept. to Sept.) and from the fifth to the sixth grade (Sept. to Sept.) under the regular reading program and under the experimental program were compared as measured by the Reading Battery of the California Achievement Test. The comparison was analyzed statistically and produced the results shown [in Table IV].

CONCLUSION

The results of this experiment indicate that reading achievement under the experimental program was significantly greater than the reading achievement under the regular program. All other factors being equal, it is this writer's opinion that this study gives strong support to those teachers and administrators who believe that ability grouping has merit and deserves serious consideration.

Ability Grouping: Pros and Cons

Willard C. Olson

How children are to be grouped for instruction has been—and continues to be—a subject of much debate and research. Children can be grouped on the basis of chronological age, sex, mental test scores, interests, behavior, achievement levels in one subject or across the board, or any combination of these and other characteristics. I know of one school where pupils are grouped on the basis of height (not so absurd as it sounds), but I'll return to that later.

In the graded elementary school the common bases for grouping continue to be chronological age, length of school attendance, and success in the previous grade. Within a grade, children may be divided into slow, average, and fast learners and put into groups labeled X, Y, and Z, or Orange, Blue, and Green, or something else. Or they may be grouped into two sections—one made up of high achievers, the other of all the rest. The division may be made on the basis of reading or mental tests or other criteria. At any rate, it is this kind of division that most people have in mind when they think of ability grouping.

Sometimes the highly gifted are segregated in special classes or even special schools. Sometimes it is the very slow or handicapped or very troublesome children who are grouped apart from the others.

Any innovation in school organization is likely to receive much publicity. It may be acclaimed by some and attacked by others. Widely publicized at the present time is the nongraded, or ungraded, school, in which several grades are combined into a unit or program and individual progress is stressed. For example, the first three grades may be combined into an ungraded primary program. In it a child may spend two years or three or four, depending on his progress.

WHICH TO CHOOSE?

Many types of ability grouping are possible. Claims and counterclaims have been made for the various plans, but no large claims are justi-

Reprinted from *PTA Magazine* 60:24–26, April 1966, by permission of the publisher and the author. Dr. Willard C. Olson is Dean of the School of Education at the University of Michigan in Ann Arbor. Dean Olson's article was modified from an article he wrote for *Grouping in Education: A Report Sponsored by the UNESCO Institute of Education*, edited by Alfred Yates, published by John Wiley and Sons, Inc., New York, 1966.

fied for any particular one. Yet parents—and teachers and school administrators, too—want to know whether one plan is better than another. Before making a judgment there are questions to ask and answer: Better for whom? For children, teachers, school administrators, taxpayers? For some children or all children? Better for what? The individual child's learning, his all-around development, his self-concept? By studying children's growth and development we can get some of the background we need for judicious consideration of any particular proposal for grouping. Let's start with what we know.

We know that nurture is essential to growth. Deprivation regularly has an effect on both plants and animals. More nurture than can be assimilated (what we call "forcing") is ineffective or has only fleeting results. Right now we are hearing a good deal about the effects of deprivation, both economic and cultural, on the health and development of children from poverty-stricken families. There is a good deal of talk about enrichment also.

If a number of deprived children were to be divided into two groups, and if a low level of nurture continued for one group while the other received extra health care, more sensory experiences, and more mental stimulation, we could expect the different nurtures to produce differences in the children. But the differences would be due to the differing nurture, not to the grouping.

In studies that evaluate grouping, however, the contrasted groups typically have very similar experiences. Even if the experiences provided in school were markedly different, the children's experiences outside school would normally continue to be the same. This would work against positive results from the grouping. The stimulation or lack of stimulation at home and from parents would continue as before. The children would be subject to the same influences from community institutions and the mass media, and their self-initiated learning would continue as before. Thus the continuance of the same experiences outside school would tend to offset whatever effects the different experiences in school, due to the grouping, might have.

Under all grouping plans, influences outside school continue to affect the child. That is why, in the Head Start program, efforts are made to involve the parents and change the nurture at home at the same time that the pre-school center provides children with extra nurture.

We know, of course, that children are not alike. Individual differences show up in their varying degrees of readiness for certain experiences and instructional materials. For example, in a classroom a standard book will be too difficult for some youngsters and too easy for others. Critics have often complained about the practice of having only one set of readers or arithmetic books for the whole class. Some have proposed ability grouping as a way out—usually without success.

Individual differences persist. Children's growth curves for specific characteristics are continuous over long periods of time. They do not bob up and down in an unpredictable fashion. Except when there has been previous deprivation, as in the case of children in the Head Start program, special measures designed to alter growth curves are seldom successful. All this indicates that the way a group is formed cannot be expected to have a significant influence.

There is much evidence to show that any change made through a brief period is not likely to persist. This is why psychologists wonder whether the gains made by Head Start children will be lost if the extra nurture they are receiving stops when they enter school. Also, minor effects of extra nurture quickly disappear as the individual's potential is reached, and they cannot be sustained much beyond that point. We would expect that grouping would give temporary extra "dosage," but with only temporary effects, if any.

Hence every study of the effects of grouping should contain a built-in "durability" test over time. One such study indicates that single grades have no demonstrable superiority over double grades or within-grade differentiation in elementary school for success in high school. Another shows that ability grouping in high school does not make for academic success in college. In short, studies of grouping show a monotonous series of negative results.

THE PATTERN PERSISTS

Longitudinal studies of children (that is, studies of the same children over a long period of time) demonstrate not only highly continuous growth in a single characteristic but also stability in the progress of one characteristic compared with another. Children in a given group do not all achieve at the same level in their school subjects. Moreover, each child's achievement level varies from subject to subject. This variability among children and in individual children continues over time. Remedial teaching does not change the picture of differential achievement that emerges as we study children at a given time and over an extended period.

Whether we believe that resemblances among children of the same family stem from inheritance, common experiences, or both, the fact is that similarities of about 30 to 40 per cent of paired differences in school subjects are accounted for by membership in a family. Thus only a limited amount remains for manipulation through grouping. The achievement of a boy in reading can be predicted about as well from the reading score of an older brother at the same age as by giving the child an intelligence test. Superficial differences in grouping are unlikely to alter basic potentials.

Over the years there has been a slow and persistent trend toward paying more attention to age in grade groupings. Fewer children are held back to repeat a grade. The lowered retention rate has resulted in a decrease in "overageness" and hence a narrowing of the age range in a grade. Grade groups also have a younger average age because of the higher promotion rates.

This trend has resulted in more overageness in boys than in girls. Sex differences in ability to read are so regular and predictable that simply splitting a group by sex brings about a greater contrast than does any other grouping plan for reading instruction.

Even when children are grouped for instruction in some other way the significance of age and sex remains. For example, additional time spent on instruction doesn't compensate for the age deficit of children admitted to school early. Such children achieve less than do children of equal ability who are without the age deficit. In learning there is an advantage in simply being older (up to a point).

When there are varied goals, it may be an advantage to have several criteria for grouping. If we measure a group of children of a given chronological age on any one factor, there is great variety. But if we include several factors, there are fewer differences; that is, there will be greater homogeneity.

This fact has been illustrated by studies of what is called "organismic age." This is a computed age, composed of such diverse things as mental age, reading age, height age, weight age, dental age, carpal (wrist bone) age, and grip age. The range in organismic age for a group is commonly less than for any of the parts of which it is composed. The most important parts, according to many advocates of grouping, are those most closely related to achievement goals.

THE CASE FOR AGE

Grouping by age has been attacked for maintaining the "lockstep" in education—the same pace for everybody. It can be argued, however, that grouping by age produces greater homogeneity on more things for a group as a whole than does any other single factor. For individual achievements, results are the same as for other methods of grouping. The chronological-age method is a simple, defensible, and explainable technique for bringing manageable numbers of children into contact with instructional materials and with an appropriate number of teachers. Thus the traditional method—grouping children by age—not only is convenient but also has a good deal of statistical justification.

When narrower age ranges have been used, the results have been less than spectacular. This is why midyear entrance and promotions have been abandoned in many big-city schools. As we said earlier, the long-term trend in grouping and promotion practices produces grade groups with greater homogeneity in chronological age.

I mentioned a school in which pupils are grouped on the basis of height. It is a junior high school. The groups thus formed differ substantially in weight, because of the high correlation between height and weight. Height is related to other signs of physical maturing, such as secondary sex characteristics. It is also related to such things as interests, ability to compete in games, and natural groupings by free choice. Grouping by height has little effect on homogeneity in achievement. Yet so far as can be determined, the results in growth in achievement are as good when grouping by height as when grouping on an intellectual basis. The children appear satisfied with the method. The plan deserves wider study if only to dramatize how little real difference there is in the results of competing grouping plans and therefore the wide choice that is available.

Often a study of the individual child—his status in many growth factors, his relationships with his family, his teacher, and the group—will result in making a change that produces a comfortable fit or at least an improvement. This consideration of the individual acknowledges that in the Age of the Computer there is still a place for the human correlator.

There are, of course, things other than information about human development that influence decisions on grouping. Various values and goals enter into a choice.

For instance, other things being equal, the cost of one plan as compared with that of another may determine the decision. Some people see a long-range technical and financial advantage in the new technology, such as programed instruction and scheduling by computer. Others oppose such devices on the ground that they will increase costs, with no better results.

People often advocate nongraded classes, departmentalization, or team teaching for reasons other than their superiority in helping children to learn. Team teaching, for example, may offer teachers greater opportunities for specialized instruction, increased use of technology, or the possibility of higher pay and more recognition for a master teacher.

If a person puts a high premium on saving time in preparing for a life career (time that may or may not be translated into achievements and earnings), he is likely to favor grouping plans that involve acceleration. Some persons may be opposed in principle to any plan that produces a social or racial imbalance in a class, whatever it promises in the way of higher achievement. Some argue for or against a plan according to whether or not it preserves democratic values.

Another consideration is the possible effect of one or another plan on a child's self-concept. Will placing him in a slow group lower his self-estimate and self-confidence, his acceptance of himself, feelings of belongingness, sustained motivation, or productivity?

The fact is that the results of research on grouping tend to be small, inconsistent, complicated, and difficult to interpret. On the basis of what we know now, no one plan can be considered superior for inducing growth in achievement. The major explanations for differences in achievement appear to be in the rate of children's growth and the nurture that supports it.

It is possible that almost any plan of grouping, administered with understanding, can preserve many important goals and values. There is much latitude, then, in choice of plans. Ease and simplicity of administration, economy, satisfaction of children, teachers, and parents—these and other values all enter into the decision-making process.

Grouping Can Be Flexible Within the Classroom

Wallace H. Strevell and Pauline Oliver

Several considerations prompted the Gulf School Research Development Association to restudy the question of classroom grouping in the Houston area of Texas. The findings of earlier research had led to the conclusion that simply separating children into classes according to intelligence test quotients has not resulted in increased achievement for individual children. The slow learners still get low scores on achievement tests while the rapid learners do not score higher as a result of ability grouping, although teachers claim certain social advantages from ability grouping. The teachers assigned rapid learner classes are the most satisfied, since these groups are inclined to show superior results in any case.

A study of professional literature disclosed 24 varieties of grouping practices. Promotion and grade levels represent traditional forms of grouping. The current trend is to maintain a fairly tight correlation of age to grade on the age-grade chart and to look askance on any marked deviation therefrom. The majority of school systems favor annual promotions. Departmentalization usually starts at about the seventh grade level, but promotion by subject areas seldom takes place before the tenth grade. Within this framework it is conceivable that some sort of homogeneous grouping of classes at any age-grade level could be organized, provided there are enough pupils to sectionalize, either for all subjects or for particular subjects.

The complications arising from such an attempt at homogeneous grouping are commonly understood: As soon as children are sectioned on the basis of one characteristic or trait they are found to be entirely heterogeneous in any number of other factors; the range of scores in such classes on the measurable criterion trait violates normal distribution, and, while the logical sequel should be to gear the instructional materials to the class level on the criterion trait, in practice a complexity of learning factors makes this almost impracticable.

Reprinted, with permission, from *The Nation's Schools* 59:88–91, February 1957, by permission of the publisher and the authors. Copyright 1957, The Modern Hospital Publishing Company, Inc., Chicago. All rights reserved. Wallace H. Strevell is Professor of Education and Chairman, Department of Administration and Supervision, and Pauline Oliver is a Research Fellow; both in the College of Education, University of Houston, Houston, Texas.

GROUPING WITHIN CLASSES

Consequently, no matter what the administration may have done about assigning children to classes initially, almost all teachers at all levels are found to engage in various types of grouping within their classes. This makes it possible to identify several types of within-class groupings: ability level grouping, talent grouping, differentiated curriculum grouping, tutorial grouping, opportunity grouping, and competitive grouping; or common interest grouping, motivation grouping, committee grouping, and discussion grouping; also social grouping, teamwork grouping, grouping for leadership, grouping for recognition, and socio-dynamics grouping. These informal groupings are frequently organized and reorganized; they arise from necessary purposes and fade when their usefulness passes.

Without going in great detail into administrative problems that evolve from the exigencies of grouping, such as the necessity of assigning transferred pupils, keeping records, giving tests, reporting marks to parents, providing suitably qualified teachers, scheduling and others, we must examine closely what relationship exists between grouping and the learning process and its purposes.

Obviously there are learning experiences which a child can have only in group situations, and these are universally held to be essential to building character, teamwork, leadership, effective and correct human relations, and participation in complex and purposeful group activities. Knowledge and skill are not enough; it takes wide and diverse experience in the application of knowledge to produce the mature and educated individual. Both purpose and value derive from social ends.

The experienced teacher is especially sensitive to a great power that rests in what is termed "motivation." When Thorndike demonstrated the laws of learning he made it clear that these laws are of unequal force. The drive to learn is of supreme importance, and the teacher knows that of several available ways of motivation the most effective usually is "group purposing." So the teacher is vitally concerned on this score with his grouping arrangements, whether it be a group of the whole or groups within the whole. Incidentally, the parents are also concerned, because they sense that the ideals of their children are influenced by the company they keep. Thus a teacher recognizes that application of knowledge is a function of grouping.

PRESENT TRENDS IN PROFESSIONAL THINKING

By whatever plan of grouping then, whether homogeneous or heterogeneous, structural or operational, formal or informal, there are these present trends of professional thought that are worthy of note:

1. Lest the gifted child be neglected, he should face the challenge of competition with his intellectual peers, and, despite the fact that childishly trying this or that only to cast it aside may be quite essential to growing up to adult individualism, he should have the opportunity at least of advancing consistently deeper into the field of his special talent.

2. All children require the growth experience of playing various rôles in many kinds of group situations.

3. In group action the teacher can impart the principles of Americanism and democratic living and provide ever so many opportunities for children to plan, organize, administer, mature in responsibility, and find efficient ways to coordinate their activity.

4. Grouping is at its very best when it bears directly toward a timely teaching goal, and for many teaching situations group learning is more efficient.

5. The mixture of abilities, skills, backgrounds, traits and interests of an ordinary class is a great challenge to the teacher. With a mixed class the teacher cannot rely on last year's lesson plans or expect stereotyped responses; he must design many strategies to bring about natural evolution of group learning and have complete satisfaction in the results.

SCORE CARD DEVELOPED

A study commission of the research association on provisions for individual differences and basis for grouping, under direction of Evelyn Thompson, professor of education at the University of Houston, sought (1) to clarify the educational basis for grouping and (2) to determine the characteristics in pupils to be considered as a basis for grouping. The outcome of their study was a "Grouping Practices Score Card" which has been tested and proved a sensitive criterion instrument.

The instrument [starting on page 458] is experimental and its results have not yet been correlated with class size, grade levels, teacher's experience, curriculum policies, time allotments, or school policies, but it is thought that an item analysis of the score card could be a useful resource for in-service improvement. When applied in five school systems to 65 individual classroom teachers at several grade levels, it was found that the incidence of grouping practices among teachers ranged from 23 to 3 of the practices, with a median of 16. In other words the median teacher had employed 16 different types of grouping in her classroom during the previous three months. All but four of the 24 grouping practices had been used by more than half the teachers.

When the score card is administered, a separate rating is prepared for each classroom by the teacher or by an interviewer. Full credit is allowed if an equivalent or better practice is recorded in any of the 24 categories for which model grouping practices are described. A cumulative score is obtained for each classroom, and it is possible to take the average of these classroom scores as a school's average score. In the pilot study it was found that the average scores of the schools ranged from an incidence of 20 to 10 practices, with a median school average score of 14.

The philosophy of the instrument is not based on a theory of homogeneous grouping or of heterogeneous grouping but on flexibility in grouping. The intrinsic values of each child experiencing in school each day several different rôles in various types of group work is the essential motif. Thoughtfully studied, the instrument composes for the school a picture of its group processes, showing areas of strength and weakness.

Twenty-Four Types of Classroom Grouping Practices: An Experimental Score Card Developed for Teachers' Use

1. Ability Grouping Within a Class

For the development of a certain skill, the classroom is divided into two or more groups on the basis of inadequacies in that skill. There is no group naming and the class time is given to individual work, small group work, and class discussion. Ability grouping in reading differs slightly in that the groups use basal readers of different levels, and each group is dealt with as a class within itself.

2. Adequate Group Records

Records are kept of the progress and growth of each child. Records are of these types: (1) Official records, which are objective. (2) Individual records, which are more personal. (3) Current anecdotal records. (4) Progress charts, which are kept by teacher and children together. These serve as guides to future grouping.

3. Committees for Study Projects

For acquisition of knowledge in a lifelike situation, the class outlines the area to be studied, setting up topics to be investigated, projects to be done, and problems to be solved. The class then divides into groups on the basis of desire to engage in a phase of the work or a project. Each individual is responsible to the group, and each group fulfills a particular function for the class, thus introducing social responsibility and teamwork.

4. Grouping for Leadership

In cooperative group planning, leadership is not considered the exclusive privilege of the teacher or of a few gifted children. The child acts as leader who can contribute most to the group as a whole in a particular project.

5. Grouping for Basic Citizenship

Autocratic classroom control tends to produce authoritarian personalities; therefore the teacher's aim is a democratic group situation where all problems of policy are discussed with the children, conditioned to their maturity. The leader (teacher) as fully as possible acts as a regular member of the group. Decisions on what to do, when to do it, and how to do it are made cooperatively.

6. Interest Grouping

For the development and extension of interests, children select their own groups by joining the one working on the project that interests them most or contains persons with whom they want to work. The emotional climate of a classroom has been found to be an important factor in educational behavior.

7. Grouping Gifted Children

(The gifted child is defined as the child with a high level of general intelligence—generally above 120 IQ—as measured by traditional tests.) Gifted students work together on special projects but are not permanently separated from the class. They are able to do more intensive research and much wider reading and therefore make valuable contributions to the class goal.

8. Individual Success Through Grouping

In order that every child in the class may attain success through grouping, the democratic teacher makes extensive provision for group activities in which each individual contributes his part and can succeed. The teacher helps students define a problem and then sees that each one works on that part of the problem which he can handle most successfully. To do this a teacher must know his students' abilities, handicaps, strengths and weaknesses, both social and academic.

9. Grouping for Motivation

Under the guidance of the teacher, the children set up a common goal and all activities lead to the achievement of that goal. Since the children see the purpose of what they are doing, motivation is strong, and they are anxious to acquire understandings and skills necessary to achieve their goal.

10. Regrouping for Development

Many times during the year it is necessary to rethink the grouping of children, which is done not so much on the basis of standard scholastic achievement but on the basis of a child's ability to live and work successfully with the group.

11. Grouping for Social Guidance

For guidance in social relationships, studying a child's status and participation as a group member by use of sociogram and anecdotal records has been found helpful. For the older child, self-evaluation of action with a group, such as may be recorded by wire, tape and disk recording machines, plus good guidance instruction, has brought about more desirable social behavior.

12. Sociometric Grouping

To fulfill social needs and discover children who are unhappy, rejected and ignored, a teacher uses a sociogram. A follow-up is made every two or three months to detect changes that have come about. The sociogram often reveals group structure, subgroups, leaders and isolates.

13. Grouping for Special Talents

(Talent here is taken to mean special abilities which are not necessarily associated with a high intelligence quotient.) Children with special talents are made to feel they belong to a group and that they have something to contribute if they do art work, music work, dramatization, creative writing, handicraft, administrative planning, or whatever the field of their special talent. Their product is brought before the class for enjoyment and enrichment.

14. Team Grouping

Two children of similar ability in a particular field work as a team and check each other's work, either written or oral. This is not a substitute for direct teacher observance, which is vital if a teacher is to know the causes of the weaknesses and differences of the children.

15. Reporting to Parents

The elementary school teacher, after careful preparation is made, sits down with parents of each child once or twice a year (oftener if the need arises) and discusses his achievements and needs, growth and status, using a record folder. The conference type of reporting is a mutual exchange of information between teacher and parent, and enables a teacher to know a child better. In the secondary school, provision is made to bring parent and teacher together by use of "Open House" and "Parents' Night."

16. Promotion as a Type of Grouping

Since research has proved failure and retardation do not stimulate effort but on the contrary discourage it, a child is not promoted at arbitrary intervals on arbitrary standards. He makes continuous progress, rapid or slow, depending on the whole child. This implies a planned learning situation into which he is promoted.

17. Termination of Grouping

Time allotment for group activity depends on the purpose of grouping. It should cease when interest wanes, need is fulfilled, or skill is mastered. Each child daily works with several different groups; they are flexible and temporary.

18. Differentiated Curriculum in Grouping

The subject matter related to a given unit of work will differ for children at various stages of individual development, as will the skills used and the understandings expected, but the work of the class is correlated in the unit. In the secondary schools, however, individual differences are provided for by use of elective classes either in different areas or in a subject.

19. Assigning Transfer Pupils

The transfer pupil without sufficient records is placed in the smallest class of his chronological age available where the teacher and pupils can make him feel welcome and at ease. With this emotional climate established, the teacher observes the pupil and groups him experimentally until she comes to know him. On the basis of objective evidence, he may be re-assigned to the class where he will be successful and well adjusted.

20. "Buzz" Grouping

"Buzz" groups are short-run groups which encourage full participation of everyone in a classroom. This is particularly suited to high school age students. It is informal and easy to conduct. Membership is determined by numbering off or designating corners of the room; only a few minutes of time are allotted (approximately 20 minutes) unless agenda have been drawn up; a chairman and a reporter, often a volunteer, are chosen quickly and informally. Class opinion or feeling is thus obtained whereas only a few students may express themselves in full class discussion.

21. Tutorial Grouping

A rapid learner is paired off with a slow learner for practice in the skill of a particular field (often arithmetic or spelling in lower grades). It can be done with a rapid learner and several slow learners if the children are mature enough to take responsibility.

22. Measuring Progress Within Groups

In the basic reading (other skills may be substituted) program, the grouping is according to reading abilities. Each group will use reading tests suitable for its level of work or development. Testing is done for the goals of that particular group.

23. Discussion Groups

Informal face-to-face grouping, with much conversation, encourages children to be alert, inquiring and able to express themselves effectively.

24. Opportunity Class Groups

In larger schools, the administration forms classes for special needs such as arithmetic weaknesses or language handicaps. As these problems are taken care of, the children are placed in other classes where they have an opportunity to be successful. In smaller schools, a special teacher works with children having such problems for about an hour a day until they gain skill and confidence.

Ability Grouping, Segregation, and the Intellectual Elite

Paul Woodring

The general facts about individual differences in learning capacity are well known. We disagree as to just how much of these differences result from inherited limitations and how much are the result of variations in early experiences and opportunities in and out of school; but no one seriously doubts that the differences do exist or that they must be faced by educators.

They can be faced in any one of six ways: separate schools for the gifted and other separate schools for the retarded; grade skipping for some and retardation for others; universal promotion, but with attempted individualization of instruction within the classroom; so-called "homogeneous grouping" which actually is not homogeneous at all, but rather grouping by mental age or IQ within an age group; an ungraded system in which each child moves along at his own best pace without annual promotions; and grouping (within the comprehensive school) on the basis of demonstrated achievement and capacity in each separate subject, so that a child may be in a fast section in one subject, a slower group in another, and with other children of similar social maturity for recreational activities.

It is easy to find objections to any of these proposals; yet, we must choose, unless we can find something better. The ungraded system may be best in the lower grades. But at the secondary level, the last procedure listed seems most sensible, most consistent with the stubborn facts of individual differences, and least likely to do harm to any individual adolescent. It makes possible an easy and free association of all kinds of students during periods of social and recreational activity. It offers some difficult scheduling problems, but these are not insurmountable except in very small schools.

Ability grouping by separate subjects is now the practice in many schools, and the practice is growing. Something of the sort was suggested in the report of the NEA conference on the Academically Talented Pupil in High School. I have been one of the many who have urged its wider adoption.

Reprinted from *School and Society* 87:164–165, April 11, 1959, by permission of the publisher and the author. Paul Woodring is at Western Washington State College, Bellingham, Washington.

Somewhat to my surprise, the counterattack has been heavy and, at times, abusive. A fighting rear guard of educators has chosen to obscure the real issues by hurling charges containing the emotionally toned words, "segregation" and "intellectual elite." The argument runs something like this: "Segregation is bad. Ability grouping is a form of segregation; *ergo*, segregation on the basis of ability, even for a few hours a day, is just as bad as segregation in Little Rock."

The fallacy lies in the major premise. The word, "segregation," has taken on a bad odor, but let us not forget its true meaning. Segregation, according to the dictionary, means merely separation or selection. It becomes an evil only when the separation is of extended duration, leads to social distinctions, or handicaps an individual in his legitimate pursuit of his natural or constitutional rights.

The Supreme Court has ruled that segregation by race is such an evil. It does impose social barriers and handicaps individuals in their legitimate pursuit of rights guaranteed under the Constitution. Segregation by race within the public schools is neither morally sound nor educationally justified, because a white child, a Negro, and an Oriental, if of roughly the same capacity for learning a subject, can effectively study side by side and can learn from each other.

But it does not at all follow that separation on an ability basis for periods of instruction will deprive anyone of his natural rights. Nor does it follow that a mathematical genius can learn effectively in a class of students who are backward or average in mathematical ability. He will be ready for calculus when others are still working on arithmetic, and the two can not be taught easily in the same classroom, by the same teacher, and at the same time.

All schools practice some sort of separation or selection. Harvard, by selecting its students rigorously, segregates them for a time from the boys not admitted; Princeton segregates by not admitting women. All elementary schools, except one-room country schools, separate children during periods of instruction. In most schools, the separation is on the basis of chronological age: six-year-olds do not study with 12-year-olds. In the high school, all athletic teams, debate teams, and bands separate students on the basis of ability. There are numerous logical and necessary bases for separation or selection, and changing the word to segregation does not change the logic, even though it may inflame the emotions. We may legitimately disagree as to whether it is best to group children by chronological age, mental age, social maturity, or readiness for each separate subject, but nothing is gained by using emotionally toned words.

The notion that ability grouping in each separate subject will lead to the development of an "intellectual elite" is another logical fallacy that needs to be laid to rest. If there were any real danger of such a development in America, it would come far more from separate schools for the gifted, including colleges and private schools with high entrance standards, than from the kind of ability grouping within the comprehensive high school that Dr. Conant and I and many others have proposed.

An elite is a group of people who are given special recognition, special privileges, and special rewards. The purpose of ability grouping—and its probable result—is not to develop such a group, but rather to provide better learning situations for fast and slow learners alike.

The fear that ability grouping, or any other change in the schools, could lead to the development of an intellectual elite in America shows, at best, a limited understanding of our culture. We simply aren't that kind of a people. If we ever have an elite in the United States, it will not be an intellectual one. It is much more likely to be an elite of movie stars, rock-and-roll artists, and football players. In a very real sense, we already have such an elite, while the intellectuals go unheralded and unsung. It might not be a bad idea to try to bring the prestige, income, and recognition of some of our academically talented people—teachers, for example—up to at least that of salesmen and truck drivers. But the danger that intellectuals will ever become a true elite in our country is remote, indeed.

Selected Bibliography

Homogeneous vs. Heterogeneous Grouping

GENERAL REFERENCES

Balcom, Lois. "San Angelo Builds Three Rails for the Three R's." *Reporter* 19:28–31, October 30, 1958.
Report of ability grouping in San Angelo, Texas, for grades 1–12.

Bettelheim, Bruno. "Grouping the Gifted: Opinions Differ." *NEA Journal* 54:8–11, March 1965.
Gives pros and cons on ability grouping.

Borg, Walter R. *Ability Grouping in the Public Schools.* Madison, Wisconsin: Dunbar Educational Research Services, 1966.
Analyzes differences in the effect of ability grouping upon elementary, junior high, and senior high students. Surveys the literature and also reports results of his own study which compared achievement, study habits, peer status, attitudes, personality, and self-concept of 4,000 pupils in ability and in random grouped classes over a four-year period.

Carpenter, Finley. "Can the Argument About Pupil Grouping Be Resolved?" *School of Education Bulletin* (University of Michigan), 30:106–109, April 1959.
Examines assumptions underlying homogeneous and heterogeneous grouping. States conditions make each position plausible.

Eash, Maurice J. "Grouping: What Have We Learned?" *Educational Leadership* 18:429–434, April 1961.
Claims ability grouping is undemocratic and damaging to the self-concept.

Ekstrom, Ruth B. *Experimental Studies of Homogeneous Grouping: A Review of the Literature.* Princeton: Educational Testing Service, 1959. pp. 1–26.
Found thirteen studies favored homogeneous grouping, fifteen reported no advantage, and five reported no results.

Essex, Martin. "How Good Is Ability Grouping?" *PTA Magazine* 54:14–16, 35, September 1959.
Points out the need for better tools for identifying pupils' abilities.

Lawson, D. E. "An Analysis of Historic and Philosophic Considerations for Homogeneous Grouping." *Educational Administration and Supervision* 43:257–270, May 1957.
Says homogeneous grouping in one subject may extend the heterogeneity in another.

Luchins, Abraham S. and Edith. "Children's Attitudes Toward Homogeneous Grouping." *Journal of Genetic Psychology* 72:3–9, March 1948.
Concludes homogeneous grouping develops a caste system with negative effects on values and social and emotional health.

MacLean, Malcolm S. "Should the Gifted Be Segregated?" *Educational Leadership* 13:214–220, January 1956. Also in *Education Digest* 21:5–7, April 1956.

Advocates homogeneous grouping on the basis of ability. Says it does not violate democratic principles because today's society needs varied leadership skills.

Miller, W. S. and Otto, Henry J. "Analysis of Experimental Studies in Homogeneous Grouping." *Journal of Educational Research* 21:95–102, February 1930.
Says there is no clear-cut evidence that homogeneous grouping is either advantageous or disadvantageous. A comprehensive table summarizes important homogeneous studies up to 1930.

National Education Association. *Project on Instruction: Schools for the Sixties.* New York: McGraw-Hill Book Co., 1963. pp. 88–92, 96, 132.
Says efforts to set up groups in terms of ability and/or achievement do little to reduce the over-all range of pupil variability with which teachers must deal. Recommends, however, sometimes using selective grouping and regrouping by achievement, particularly at the secondary school level.

Passow, A. Harry. "The Maze of the Research on Ability Grouping." *The Educational Forum* 26:281–88, March 1962.
Cites research on ability grouping. Summarizes reasons the studies reported make it difficult to generalize. Gives need for further evidence.

Stonecipher, B. L. "Grouping in the Classroom." *Education* 83:77–79, October 1962.
Cites characteristics and merits of different types of homogeneous grouping such as ability, chronological age, interests, social age, and handicaps.

Torrey, Robert D. "Citizenship Education for the 'Gifted Adolescent.'" *Progressive Education* 33:78–84, May 1956.
Opposes grouping gifted students homogeneously on the basis of IQ. Says it tends to be drawn along social class lines. Believes tests have a middle- and upper-class bias.

ELEMENTARY SCHOOL

Austin, Mary and Morrison, Coleman. *The First R: Report on Reading in Elementary Schools.* New York: Macmillan Co., 1963. pp. 75–80.
Points out homogeneous grouping often gives a teacher the false impression she has thirty readers with identical abilities and leads to ignoring individual differences. When grouping is heterogeneous, the conditions are similar. Recommends flexible small grouping. Favors the ungraded approach, at least in reading, with children free to progress according to their achievement.

Balow, Irving H. "Does Homogeneous Grouping Give Homogeneous Groups?" *Elementary School Journal* 63:28–32, October 1962.
Says procedures more sophisticated than achievement tests will have to be used to form a truly homogeneous group.

Barbe, Walter B. and Waterhouse, Tina S. "An Experimental Program in Reading." *Elementary English* 33:102–104, February 1956. Also see articles by Barbe in *Education* 82:465–467, April 1962; and 85:137, November 1964.
Tried to determine if students in grades 4–6 could be better provided for in homogeneous reading groups. Reports a great deal of progress can be

made when students are grouped according to their reading level. No control group used for comparison.

Barthelmess, Harriet and Boyer, P. A. "An Evaluation of Ability Grouping." *Journal of Educational Research* 26:284–294, December 1932.

Describes Philadelphia experiment in ability grouping in grades 4–5. Heterogeneously grouped classes used as control. Results of achievement test given one school year later showed statistically significant achievement in arithmetic, in technical English skills, and in reading skills for the homogeneously grouped classes. Improvement was found in each of the groups (high, low, and medium).

Bremer, Neville. "First Grade Achievement Under Different Plans of Grouping." *Elementary English* 35:324–326, May 1958.

Compared reading achievement of low-, average-, and high-readiness students in grade one in the regular classroom with similar homogeneously grouped students in Amarillo, Texas. Found factors in addition to method of grouping accounted for reading achievement differences. Scores for high-readiness children in heterogeneous class were higher than scores of comparable students in homogeneous classes.

Brite, L. R. *Effect of Ability Grouping on Personality Variables of Slow-Learning Fifth Grade Pupils.* Doctoral Dissertation, Utah State University, 1963. Also in *Dissertation Abstracts* 24:4080.

Projective tests were used to determine effects of grouping slow learners together as compared to random grouping. No significant differences were found in aggression, inferiority feelings, or depression in samples of the same sex from the two groups but there were significant differences in performances on an achievement battery between boys and girls.

Cluff, James. *The Effect of Experimentation and Class Reorganization on the Scholastic Achievement of Selected Gifted Sixth Grade Pupils in Wichita, Kansas.* Doctoral Dissertation, University of Arkansas, 1964. Also in *Dissertation Abstracts* 25:1676.

Found academic achievement of 6th grade gifted pupils was not significantly affected by ability grouping after a two-year period. Participants felt, however, there was increased motivation, better social adjustment, and better work and study habits.

Cushenbery, D. C. *The Intergrade Plan of Grouping for Reading Instruction as Used in the Public Schools of Joplin, Missouri.* Doctoral Dissertation, University of Missouri, 1964. Also in *Dissertation Abstracts* 25:1780.

Found the use of the Joplin (departmental) Plan in grades 4–6 resulted in reading achievement above the national grade norms and in excess of mental-age grade expectancy. Principals, teachers, and parents widely accepted the plan.

Other readings favoring and opposing use of the Joplin Plan in reading found in *Elementary School Journal* 55:99–103, October 1954; 64:280–286, February 1964; 64:387–392, April 1964; and in 65:38–43, October 1964; in *Journal of Educational Psychology* 51:69–73, April 1960; in *Journal of Educational Research* 55:567–572, August 1962; and 56:317–321, February 1963; in *Journal of Experimental Education* 31:273–278, March 1963; in *Saturday Evening Post*, October 1957; and condensed in *Reader's Digest* 122:41–44, January 1958.

Degrow, G. S. *A Study of the Effects of the Use of Vertical Reading Ability Groupings for Reading Classes as Comparison with Heterogeneous Groupings in Grades Four, Five, and Six in the Port Huron Area Public Schools of Michigan over a Three-Year Period.* Doctoral Dissertation, University of Michigan, 1963. Also in *Dissertation Abstracts* 24:3166. *Found vertical ability grouping in reading in grades 4–6 did not contribute to reading achievement gains in Port Huron area schools. Found parents, teachers, and principals favored the plan.*

Deitrich, F. R. "Comparison of Sociometric Patterns of Sixth-Grade Pupils in Two School Systems: Ability Grouping Compared with Heterogeneous Grouping." *Journal of Educational Research* 57:507–513, July 1964. *Attempted to determine effects of ability grouping on school adjustment of sixth-grade pupils. Concluded ability grouping (either homogeneous or heterogeneous) neither added nor detracted.*

Dewar, John A. *An Experiment in Intra-Class Grouping for Arithmetic Instruction in the Sixth Grade.* Doctoral Dissertation, University of Kansas, 1961. Also in *Dissertation Abstracts* 22:2247. Also see *Elementary School Journal* 63:266–269, February 1963. *Eight 6th grade classes were selected in Johnson County, Kansas to determine effectiveness of ability grouping for arithmetic. Teachers' thought ability grouping with differentiated material was valuable. Majority of the students liked it.*

Echternacht, C. and Gordon V. "Breaking the Lock Step in Arithmetic." *Arithmetic Teacher* 9:86–89, February 1962. Other readings favoring and opposing the Joplin Plan in arithmetic found in *Arithmetic Teacher* 10:12–17, January 1963. *Describes changing arithmetic instruction from a self-contained to a Joplin Plan achievement arrangement in grades 4–6 at Park School, San Mateo, California.*

Ernatt, R. *A Survey of Pupils Attitudes Toward Inter-Grade Ability Grouping for Reading Instruction.* Doctoral Dissertation, Wayne State University, 1963. Also in *Dissertation Abstracts* 25:2651. *Concluded sufficient statistically significant negative reaction was recorded to warrant serious consideration concerning the advisability of instituting or continuing an intergrade ability grouping plan for reading instruction.*

Franseth, Jane. "Does Grouping Make a Difference in Pupil Learning? Research Offers Leads." *Toward Effective Grouping.* Washington: ACEI, 1962. pp. 25–36. Condensed in *Education Digest* 28:15–18, January 1963. *Gives assumptions of ability grouping and cites research evidence that challenges them.*

Goldberg, Miriam, *et al. The Effects of Ability Grouping.* New York, N.Y.: Teachers College Press, 1966. *Assessed the effects of ability grouping on the academic and personal-social learning of elementary school students. Findings raise some serious questions about the adequacy of the one-teacher classroom, especially for the able pupils. Found ability grouping is inherently neither good nor bad. Its value or harm depends upon the way it is used. It may be used effectively when it grows out of the needs of the curriculum and when it is varied and flexible. Study found no support for contention that ability grouping causes negative effects on self-concept, aspirations, interests, attitudes toward school, and other nonintellectual factors.*

Goldworth, Mary. "Effects of an Elementary School Fast-Learner Program on Children's Social Relationships." *Exceptional Children* 26:59–63, October 1959.
Found ability grouping of gifted in grades 4–6 did not have an effect on friendship patterns and group cohesion.

Groff, Patrick. "Comparisons on Individualized (IR) and Ability Grouping (AG) Approaches as to Reading Achievement." *Elementary English* 40:258–64, March 1963.
Annotation of thirty-nine studies and reports of comparisons of individualized reading programs with ability programs.

Holmes, Darrell, and Harvey, Lois. "An Evaluation of Two Methods of Grouping." *Educational Research Bulletin* 35:212–222, 1956.
Analyzed two methods of grouping for arithmetic and concluded that the method of grouping was not crucial. Found the results were not related to grouping procedures.

Hull, J. H. "Is Ability Grouping Taking Schools in the Wrong Direction?" *Nation's Schools* 73:71, 129, April 1964.
Favors ability grouping. Says those who attack it do not understand the need for refining the graded system. Opposite view by Rodney Tillman in same issue.

Jacobi, F. H. "Changing Pupils in a Changing School." *Educational Leadership* 17:283–287, February 1960.
Staff of desegregated school developed a plan called "overlapping ability grouping" to help with wide range of ability. Evidence revealed students achieved.

Johnson, L. G. *A Description of Organization, Methods of Instruction, Achievement, and Attitudes Toward Reading in Selected Elementary Schools.* Doctoral Dissertation, University of Oregon, 1964. Also in *Dissertation Abstracts* 25:6433.
Report of a study of reading instruction in four Eugene, Oregon schools with: (1) an individualized reading plan; (2) heterogeneous grouping with basal reader; (3) homogeneous grouping with basal reader in a self-contained room; and (4) homogeneous grouping with basal reader in a Joplin Plan. Concluded reading programs were similar in all four schools regardless of organization. There were no significant differences in attitude toward reading.

Karnes, Merle, et al. "Efficacy of Two Organizational Plans for Underachieving Intellectually Gifted Children." *Exceptional Child* 29:438–446, May 1963.
Assessed the efficacy of placing underachieving gifted students from grades 2–5 in homogeneous classes with gifted students who were achieving at a level commensurate with their abilities as compared with placing them in heterogeneous classes with a wide range of intellectual ability. Found homogeneous grouping had merit because it appeared to foster increased achievement, improved perceptions of parent-child relationships, and improved creativity.

Kincaid, Donald and Epley, Thelma. "Cluster Grouping." *Education* 81:136–139, November 1960.

Describes an ability grouping practice in Los Angeles City Elementary Schools. By definition in Los Angeles a cluster group is a small group of 2–10 pupils. Clustering a group of gifted pupils in a classroom with pupils from average to superior ability has been found beneficial.

Koontz, William F. "A Study of Achievement as a Function of Homogeneous Grouping." *Journal of Experimental Education* 30:249–253, December 1961.

Compared achievement of 4th grade pupils in homogeneous and heterogeneous classes. Found no difference in achievement. Concluded many variables that need to be controlled evaded control in the study. Recommended further investigation.

Kyte, George C. "Maintaining Ability Grouping in Spelling." *Phi Delta Kappan* 30:301–306, 1949.

Study in grades 3–6 demonstrated the need for regrouping. Observed the tendency of homogeneous groups to become heterogeneous. No control group or statistical measures were used.

Manolakes, George. "Oral Language and Learning." *Instructor* 74:9, 16, November 1964.

Recommends reassessing some instructional practices such as readiness programs, grouping, and the teacher's role to find ways to encourage oral language development. Questions isolation of less proficient children into homogeneous groups.

McCracken, R. A. "Using Reading As a Basis for Grouping." *Education* 84:357–359, February 1964.

Describes results of an investigation with 971 students in grades 2–6 to determine whether informal reading inventories could be used advantageously as a basis of grouping students for reading instruction. Found the inventory successful in determining instructional levels.

McCall, William A. "A Comparison of the Educational Progress of Bright Pupils in Accelerated and in Regular Classes." *Twenty-Seventh Yearbook of the National Society for the Study of Education, Part II,* 1928.

Sixty-seven pairs of students, matched for MA and CA, were compared for achievement in reading, spelling, and mathematics over a two-year period. The pupils ranged over grades 3 to 7. Those grouped homogeneously gained about 7 months in the two-year period over the mixed-class students. Concludes one can be 62 per cent certain that growth in these abilities is more favorable in segregated classes.

Morgenstern, A. *A Comparison of the Effects of Heterogeneous and Homogeneous (Ability) Grouping on the Academic Achievement and Personal-Social Adjustment of Selected Sixth-Grade Children.* Doctoral Dissertation, New York University, 1963. Also in *Dissertation Abstracts* 24:1054.

Found significant differences in favor of homogeneous grouping in specific subject areas such as language and word meaning.

Parker, J. Cecil, and Russel, David H. "Ways of Providing for Individual Differences." *Educational Leadership* 11:168–74, December 1953.

Recommends ways of meeting needs within an elementary heterogeneously grouped class such as sub-grouping, use of a variety and a range of instructional materials, use of a variety and range of methods and experiences, and flexibility in assignments, responsibilities, and activities.

Pinney, G. C. "Grouping by Arithmetic Ability: An Experiment in Teaching Arithmetic." *Arithmetic Teacher* 8:120–123, March 1961.
Study of sixth-grade achievement grouping. Control group not used. Concludes program is a success.

Provus, Malcolm M. "Ability Grouping in Arithmetic." *Elementary School Journal* 60:391–398, April 1960.
Report of study designed to study the effect of ability grouping in grades 4–6. Results favorable to plan.

Raymond, Margaret. *An Investigation of Homogeneous Grouping for Reading Versus Grouping Within the Classroom.* Master's Thesis, San Diego State College, 1956.
Study compares achievement of fourth graders grouped homogeneously by ability with that of those grouped within the classroom. Found no significant difference. Concluded, however, brighter children achieve better under homogeneous grouping.

Robinson, Glen. "Principals' Opinions About School Organization." *National Elementary Principal* 41:39–42, November 1961.
1961 NEA survey of 721 elementary school principals reveals they favor a school with 400–500 pupils, in grades K–6 with self-contained classes of 20–25 pupils. Principals were equally divided on ability grouping.

Rothrock, D. G. "Heterogeneous, Homogeneous or Individualized Approach to Reading?" *Elementary English* 38:233–235, April 1961.
Writer compares the effectiveness of three approaches of organizing a reading class at McPherson, Kansas. Concludes that great improvement in reading achievement can result under each of the three methods from good teaching with appropriate materials and stimulation.

Shane, Harold G. "Grouping in the Elementary School." *Phi Delta Kappan* 41:313–318, April 1960.
Identifies thirty-two different grouping plans.

"Some Tentative Conclusions About Grouping." *Education Briefs* 40:1–5, 28–29, May 1964. Also in *Education Digest* 30:47–49, November 1, 1964.
Lists conclusions generalized from research on grouping and concludes that factors other than grouping procedures must be responsible for the differences in progress of children grouped heterogeneously or homogeneously according to ability.

Torrance, E. Paul. "Peer Pressures in Homogeneous and Heterogeneous Groups." *Rewarding Creative Behavior.* Englewood Cliffs, New Jersey: Prentice Hall, Inc., 1965. pp. 187–220, 260. Also see *Elementary School Journal* 62:139–147, December 1961.
Reports study with 4–6th grade students in Minneapolis. Students were grouped homogeneously and heterogeneously. Data revealed greater disruptive social stress in heterogeneous classes than in homogeneous classes when they were thus divided for creative activities. Researcher says these results should not be interpreted to mean teachers should always form homogeneous groups for creative tasks. There are times when it is advantageous to increase social stress. Says the decision concerning grouping must be influenced by the type of development which is of concern.

JUNIOR AND SENIOR HIGH SCHOOL

Abrahamson, David. "The Effectiveness of Grouping for Students of High Ability." *Education Research Bulletin* 38:169–182, October 14, 1959.
Findings of study indicate no superiority of preparation for college can be claimed for either the special high school or the honor-class programs as contrasted with the comprehensive high school which grouped students heterogeneously. Found achievement in college depended upon general ability rather than the high school from which they came.

Adams, Philip C., Jr. "Ability Grouping in Junior High School." *Journal of Health, Physical Education, Recreation* 35:83, May 1964.
Describes ability grouping in physical education in a junior high school in Montgomery County, Maryland. Recommends it and says the school plans to continue it.

Balow, Irving H. "Effects of Homogeneous Grouping in Seventh Grade Arithmetic." *Arithmetic Teacher* 11:186–191, March 1964.
On the basis of a study in southern California author concluded sectioning on the basis of arithmetic tests given at the end of sixth grade and teacher judgment does not result in homogeneous sections. Study suggested teachers were teaching to the least capable in each section.

Barton, D. P. *An Evaluation of Ability Grouping in Ninth Grade English.* Doctoral Dissertation, Brigham Young University, 1964. Also in *Dissertation Abstracts* 25:1731.
Found random grouping as effective as ability grouping for ninth-grade English students when effectiveness is measured by English achievement, marks, number of underachievers, and lessening of pressures to cheat. Teachers believe, however, that they do a more effective job of teaching when range of ability is reduced.

Baumgartner, R. A. "A Differentiated Curriculum for Homogeneous Groups." *Emerging Practices in Mathematics Education.* Twenty-Second Yearbook. Washington, D.C.: National Council of Teachers of Mathematics, a department of the NEA, 1954. Chapter 2.
Advocates a two-track program for 9th and 10th grade mathematics with course objectives outlined for all four high school years.

Bicak, L. J. "Achievement in Eighth Grade Science by Heterogeneous and Homogeneous Classes." *Science Education* 48:13–22, February 1964. Also see *Science Teacher* 31:50, October 1964.
Gives the design and statistical analysis of data of a homogeneous and heterogeneous grouped eighth grade.

Billett, R. O. "A Controlled Experiment to Determine the Advantages of Homogeneous Grouping." *Educational Research Bulletin* 7:133–140, May 2, 1928.
Advocates ability grouping after a three-year study with experimental and control groups in ninth-grade English.

Brown, B. Frank. "An Answer to Dropouts: The Nongraded High School." *The Atlantic* 214:36–89, November 1964. See further references in Chapter 4 bibliography.
Describes the nongraded Melbourne High School. Provision is made for bright, average, and slow students.

Cawelti, Gordon. *The Status of Administrative and Instructional Provisions in Ability Grouped Classes of Mathematics and English in Selected Midwestern High Schools.* Doctoral Dissertation, State University of Iowa, 1962. Also in *Dissertation Abstracts* 23:2749. Also see *Bulletin of NASSP* 47:34–39, March 1963; and *Education Digest* 29:23–25, September 1963.
Describes administrative and instructional procedures followed in providing ability grouping in 9th and 10th grade English and mathematics classes.

Clark, Gwyn R. and Noall, Matthew F. "Better Staff Utilization in Hurricane High School Through Language Arts Reorganization." *Bulletin of NASSP* 45:223–227, January 1961.
Homogeneously grouped nongraded English classes resulted in gradual student improvement. Teachers rotated among various sections and taught as a team.

Clark, Leonard. "Ability Grouping—A Third Look." *Bulletin of NASSP* 47:69–71, December 1963.
Reminds the reader that ability grouping and curriculum tracks are not the only devices for providing for individual differences. Recommends grouping within the secondary school class, differentiated assignments, individualized instruction, flexible promotion system, nongraded school, etc.

Conant, James B. *The American High School Today.* New York: McGraw-Hill, 1959. pp. 49, 55, 57.
Recommends achievement grouping in required subjects with special programs for slow readers, for academically talented, and for highly gifted pupils.

Cromble, Mona G. "Dr. Conant Looks at Grades 7, 8, 9." *California Journal of Secondary Education* 35:452–459, November, 1960.
Says Dr. Conant recommends grade 8 be fully departmentalized with ability grouping on the basis of achievement in each subject.

Drews, Elizabeth. *The Effectiveness of Homogeneous and Heterogeneous Ability Grouping in Ninth Grade English Classes with Slow, Average, and Superior Students.* U.S. Dept. of Health, Education, and Welfare, Office of Education, Co-operative Research Grant, Project No. 608. Washington, D.C.: Superintendent of Documents, Government Printing Office, 1959.
Reports students and teachers prefer homogeneous grouping. Found low-ability pupils participated more actively in classroom activities and reported more interest in school and more confidence in their own ability.

Fick, W. W. *The Effectiveness of Ability Grouping in Seventh Grade Core Classes.* Doctoral Dissertation, University of Kansas, 1962. Also in *Dissertation Abstracts* 23:2753.
Found ability grouping did not produce significant changes in pupils' attitudes toward themselves.

Glancy, Philip B. "Brookside Junior High, Sarasota, Florida, Strives for Quality Education." *Bulletin of NASSP* 46:157–160, January 1962.
Describes large-group instruction and team teaching. Grouping was on basis of similar abilities in most instances.

Hansen, Carl F. "Ability Grouping in the High Schools." *Atlantic* 206:123–127, November 1960.
Recommends four-track ability grouped high school system.

Hay, Morris E. "Effective Learning Through Grouping in Junior High School." *California Journal of Secondary Education* 32:11–13, January 1957.
Discovered homogeneous ability grouping revealed few significant differences between groups but wide differences within each.

Hood, C. E. "Do We Expect Too Much from Ability Grouping?" *Clearing House* 38:467–470, April 1964.
Describes Custer Plan used effectively in Miles City, Montana. Gives pros and cons.

Howell, W. J. "Grouping of Talented Students Leads to Better Achievement in the Secondary School." *Bulletin of NASSP* 46:67–73, March 1962.
Reports a study of grouping talented students in Penfield, New York, lends support to ability grouping.

Humphrey, J. W. "Dexter Plan for Ability Grouping." *Clearing House* 35:423–426, March 1961.
Explains 7th and 8th grade achievement grouping in arithmetic and English. Despite some disadvantages, plan found to be workable and desirable.

Kolson, Clifford J. "A Workable Approach to Grouping." *Clearing House* 36:539–544, May 1962.
Discusses pros and cons of homogeneous and heterogeneous grouping. Recommends the use of the quadrant of expectancy as a tool for determining grouping. Says effective grouping involves: narrow range, non-stigmatized students, recognition of different rates of learning, ease of administration, and no extra financial commitment.

Kvaraceus, William C. "The Behavioral Deviates in the Culture of the Secondary School." *Frontiers of Secondary Education.* Proceedings and Conferences on Secondary Education. Syracuse: Syracuse University Press, 1958. pp. 18–27.
Points out age-grade grouping: (1) implies to teachers and pupils an equality and homogeneity that does not exist and leads to undifferentiated instruction through use of the single text and identical assignment; (2) reinforces the already overly strong youth culture. Recommends broader grouping by overlapping age membership in some classes and ability achievement grouping in others.

Lauchner, A. H. and Horner, H. F. "What Are Current Trends In Grouping Students for Effective Instruction?" *Bulletin of NASSP* 43:6–7, April 1959.
Advocates junior high ability grouping.

Lovell, J. T. "Bay High School Experiment." *Educational Leadership* 17:383, March 1960.
Homogeneous experimental group made greater gains in 10th grade English than heterogeneous control group. Same thing did not occur in algebra and history.

Manchester, Clyde R., and Silberberg, Norman. "Staff Attitudes Toward a Special School Program for the Talented." *Bulletin of the NASSP* 47:58–68, March 1963.
Staff reports ability grouping in mathematics and science in St. Paul, Minnesota public secondary schools had a positive effect on morale of teachers and a negative effect on counselors. Staff felt plan should be continued and recommended it be extended into other subject areas.

Martin, W. B. *Effects of Ability Grouping on Junior High Achievement*. Doctoral Dissertation, George Peabody College for Teachers, Nashville, Tennessee, 1958. Also in *Dissertation Abstracts* 19:2810.
Found little evidence ability group benefited any of the segregated groups.

McCown, George W. *A Critical Evaluation of the Four Track Curriculum Program of the District of Columbia Senior High School with Recommendations for Improvements.* Doctoral Dissertation, University of Maryland, 1960. Also in *Dissertation Abstracts* 21:2558.
Evaluated achievement of honors track and basic track students with that of heterogeneously grouped students. Differences on all measures favored honors track students.

McDaniel, M. C., and Faunce, R. C. "Ability Grouping: An Issue at the Junior High School Level." *Teachers College Journal* 34:64–69, November 1962.
Points out pros and cons.

National Education Association, Project on Improving English Composition. *Improving English Composition.* (Edited by Charles Bish and Arno Jewett). Washington, D.C.: the Association, 1965.
Report on a five year project for improving English composition begun by NEA in 1962. Recommends, among other things, multi-track program for English students.

Otto, Henry J. "Grouping Pupils for Maximum Achievement." *School Review* 67:387–395, Winter 1959.
Discusses the basic educational issues and practical problems associated with grouping. Advises use of homogeneous grouping in the required content and skill subjects and heterogeneous grouping in all others beginning in the seventh grade.

Phillips, J. A. *Ability Grouping and Teacher Attitudes: An Exploratory Study of Junior High School Teachers and Their Commitment to Ability Grouping.* Doctoral Dissertation, Michigan State University, 1961. Also in *Dissertation Abstracts* 22:172.
In a study of 440 Maryland junior high teachers, researcher found most teachers preferred ability grouping. Found some inverse relationship between teacher's commitment to ability grouping and his ability to create good rapport with students.

Ramey, A. R. "New Look at Ability Grouping in the Junior High Schools." *California Journal of Secondary Education* 31:289–291, May 1956.
Study revealed teachers tend to teach to the average child in any group and to neglect individual differences. Ability grouping resulted in classes where achievement differed little.

"Sectioning in High School." *School and Society* 87:518, December 19, 1959.
A short report on Herbert J. Klausmeier's study in three Wisconsin high schools to determine how sectioning affected social relationships. Concluded sectioning required subjects did not adversely affect social relationships.

Torgelson, John W. *A Comparison of Homogeneous and Heterogeneous Grouping for Below-Average Junior High School Students.* Doctoral Dissertation, University of Minnesota, 1963. Also in *Dissertation Abstracts* 25:2300.
Concluded homogeneous grouping for below-average junior high students was not superior to heterogeneous grouping.

Turnbough, Roy C. "Curriculum Design—Strength and Weaknesses of the Track System." *Bulletin of NASSP* 45:72–74, April 1961.
Assistant Superintendent of J. Sterling Morton High School and Junior College, in Berwyn, Illinois, describes its ability grouping plan. Lists eight difficulties inherent in any grouping system.
Usilaner, Hiram. "The Four-Track System in Physical Education." *Bulletin of NASSP* 44:132–135, October 1960.
Recommends grouping pupils as homogeneously as possible according to their physical skills.
Vergason, G. A. "Critical Review of Grouping." *High School Journal* 48:427–433, April 1965.
Presents findings of studies. Shows results conflict. Calls for adequate research.
Wilcox, John. *A Search for the Multiple Effects of Grouping Upon the Growth and Behavior of Junior High School Pupils.* Doctoral Dissertation, Cornell University, 1963. Also in *Dissertation Abstracts* 24:205.
Tested four hypotheses and found: a more positive self-concept among pupils below IQ 90 as they were more homogeneously grouped; attitude toward school of pupils grouped homogeneously was more positive below IQ 104, and more negative above IQ 105; no significant relationship between homogeneity of grouping and achievement in critical thinking; and mean level of achievement improved as schools grouped more homogeneously. Recommends rigorous curriculum differentiation and establishment of group standards.

Index